# THE
# EASTERN
# EUROPE
# COLLECTION

# A
# HISTORY
## OF
# HUNGARY

## Dominic G. Kosáry

*Domokos G. Kosáry*

ARNO PRESS & THE NEW YORK TIMES
New York · 1971

Reprint Edition 1971 by Arno Press Inc.

Reprinted from a copy in
The Newark Public Library

LC# 77-135813

ISBN 0-405-02755-9

The Eastern Europe Collection
ISBN for complete set: 0-405-02730-3

Manufactured in the United States of America

PUBLICATIONS OF THE
BENJAMIN FRANKLIN BIBLIOPHILE SOCIETY, VOLUME II

# *A History of*
# HUNGARY

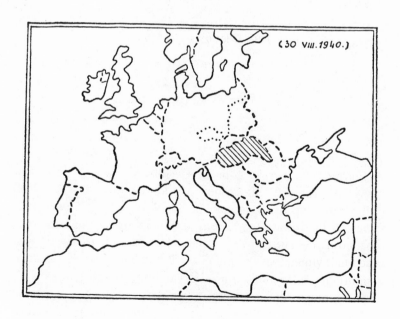

(30 VIII. 1940.)

# A HISTORY OF
# HUNGARY

DOMINIC G. KOSÁRY, Ph.D.

PROFESSOR OF HISTORY
EÖTVÖS COLLEGE, BUDAPEST

*With a Foreword by*
PROFESSOR JULIUS SZEKFÜ

EIGHT MAPS AND FOUR HALFTONES

THE BENJAMIN FRANKLIN
BIBLIOPHILE SOCIETY
Cleveland    1941    New York

PRINTED AT THE *Country Life Press,* GARDEN CITY, N. Y., U.S.A.

The purpose of the Benjamin Franklin Bibliophile Society, founded in 1935, is to promote the understanding of the cultural endeavors of the peoples of East-Central Europe. Opinions expressed by the authors of its publications do not necessarily correspond with those of the Society.

*To the Memory of*

## COUNT PAUL TELEKI

LATE PRIME MINISTER OF HUNGARY, PRO-
FESSOR OF GEOGRAPHY, PRESIDENT OF
EÖTVÖS COLLEGE, BUDAPEST, ETC., ETC.

# ERRATA

P. 34, LINE 10: for *1125*, read *1225*

P. 55, LINE 4: for *Kaltai*, read *Kalti*

P. 121, LINE 19: for *write*, read *unite*

P. 128, LINE 16: after the word *campaign*, insert *"against the Turks at that period"*

P. 303, LINE 8: for *1899*, read *1889*

P. 354, LINE 6: for *loose*, read *lose*

P. 371, LINE 3: for *even*, read *often*

P. 375, LINE 20: for *no one*, read *few*

P. 377, LINE 9: for *conducted*, read *concluded*

P. 377, LINE 25: for *October 21*, read *October 31*

P. 383, LINE 27: for *were*, read *was*

P. 391, LINE 7: for *pursuing*, read *pursuit*

P. 398, LINE 23: for *responsibility*, read *co-responsibility*

P. 399, LINE 21: for *destruction*, read *diminution*

P. 401, LINE 10: for *Bela*, read *Voytech*

P. 410, LINE 16: for *2.2.*, read *2.7*

P. 412, LINE 29: for *unitarian*, read *unitary*

P. 414, LINE 26: for *Julio*, read *Julius*

P. 415, LINE 18: for *the*, read *them*

# FOREWORD

Here by the River Danube it is hard to gauge the measure of interest that will be shown towards this work in far away America. I do not know how many will want to read about Hungary, a small country in the Eastern Hemisphere. Yet I shall endeavor to bring into relief a few of those trends in Hungary's history that may be of some interest even in the New World.

Hungary at present is the only state in Europe that was founded by one of the nomadic mounted peoples of the enormous Eurasian steppes. The Magyars do not belong to the Latin, the Teuton, or any of the Slavic family of races, their forebears being Ugrians, related to the Finnish and Turkic peoples. Some of these tribes began to migrate westward before the birth of Christ. They built several great empires, but all of these disappeared without a trace. Only the Magyars were able to strike roots in Europe by abandoning their nomadic life and adopting western civilization. For centuries, they were the only Turko-Ugrian people on earth that was Christian,—Catholic and Protestant.

The home of the Magyars, since the end of the 9th century, has been the Carpathian Basin, the boundaries of which, forming an oval shape, remained essentially unchanged. After the First World War, this territory was divided among other peoples. Today the country begins to resume its original shape again, outlined by its natural borders. There is nothing unusual about a people and its state surviving for a long period. Yet the survival of the Magyars is a phenomenon worth observing more closely since it has to do with an isolated people, without kin and without family.

For centuries, the Holy-Roman and the Byzantine Emperors, the Sultans of the Ottoman Empire and the Habsburg monarchs tried everything in their power to subjugate this lone tribe. The Magyars were few indeed, but they never surrendered. Century after century, they fought desperate struggles against superior forces. There was a time in Europe when Hungary was considered the bulwark of Christianity.

Since the number of the Magyars was decimated in these struggles, more and more non-Magyars were allowed to settle in Hungary. Political leadership was exercised by the Magyars but in such a manner that other racial minorities lived in peace and contentment together with their hosts. There was an innate element of traditional tolerance in the Magyars, based partly on

practical principles, according to which non-Magyar
elements were not abused but instead admitted to part-
nership. The relations between Magyars and their nationalities were essentially unchanged until the 19th
century, when the new nationalism began to threaten
the old moral unity of the Carpathian Basin.

I could refer also to other details: how, for example,
the Magyars refrained from murdering and burning
one another during the religious wars which devastated
so many countries in Europe. But I doubt whether this
could command interest in our times. Instead, I invite
the young historian whom I have known since the time
when he was an outstanding student at the Pázmány
University of Budapest, to review the history of his race.
He has written it with no blind bias but with respect
for other peoples and for humanity as a whole.

JULIUS SZEKFÜ

# CONTENTS

X THE ERA OF DUALISM I. Political and International
Issues, 1867–1905 . . . . . . . . . 282

XI THE ERA OF DUALISM II. Social, Economic and
Nationality Issues, 1905–1914 . . . . . . 312

XII HUNGARY IN THE WORLD WAR. Bolshevism and Its
Downfall, 1914–1919 . . . . . . . . 348

XIII THE LAST TWENTY YEARS, 1919–1940 . . . 397

CONCLUSIONS . . . . . . . . . . . 432

BIBLIOGRAPHY . . . . . . . . . . 439

KINGS OF HUNGARY . . . . . . . . 456

PRINCES OF TRANSYLVANIA . . . . . . 458

PREMIERS OF HUNGARY . . . . . . . 459

GENEALOGICAL TABLES . . . . . . . 461

STATISTICAL DATA . . . . . . . . 464

INDEX . . . . . . . . . . . . 469

# ILLUSTRATIONS AND MAPS

## ILLUSTRATIONS

## MAPS

xiii

# INTRODUCTION

*Quid autem magis in scribendo requiritur quam veri dicendi sincera fides, falsique vitandi studium? Non dubito igitur quin mihi verus et aequus censor veniam det, si rem, prout est, ingenua scriptione detexero.*

STEPHEN SZAMOSKÖZY (1570–1608)
*Rerum Transylvanarum Liber III. 37.*

The first Hungarian ever to set foot on the soil of the New World was a 16th century humanist and Protestant scholar, *Stephanus Parmenius Budaeus.* He accompanied Sir Humphrey Gilbert to Newfoundland in 1583 to acquire "any remote, barbarous and heathen lands" by the command of Queen Elizabeth of England. Parmenius was born in the fortified capital of Hungary, Buda, then in Turkish hands. Seeking education abroad, like many other Hungarian youths, he went to Oxford and to London, where the famous collector of autographs, Master Hakluyt, introduced him to Sir Humphrey. Upon his arrival in Newfoundland, Parmenius wrote to Hakluyt, but this was the last word heard from him, as he was shipwrecked on the return voyage.[1]

Among those who were lost, wrote Captain Haie,

[1] E. Pivány, Hungarian-American connections. Budapest 1927.

xv

"was drowned a learned man, an Hungarian, borne in the citie of Buda, called thereof Budaeus, who in pietie and zeale to good attempts, adventured in this action, minding to record in the Latine tongue, the gesta and things worthy of remembrance, happening in this discoverie, to the honour of our nation . . .". Parmenius Budaeus wished to report to the wealthy European nations an unknown, new world, about which contemporary Hungarians knew hardly more than that it had been discovered "for the great glory of Christianity".[1] After the passage of centuries, my task will be the very opposite to that of my early compatriot, for the situation has undergone a tremendous change. The United States have become a world power, embracing half of the American continent from coast to coast. Its dimensions and development were so unprecedented that, viewed from the New World, Europe in comparison appears as an impoverished, somewhat old-fashioned parent. And just because, among the variety of peculiar European traditions and conditions, the distant observer cannot easily find his way, some of the details of the picture are of the utmost importance.

This volume proposes to acquaint the reader with a remote, little known region of Europe, the historical evolution of which seems rather blurred at first glance. It does this, not solely "to the honour of our nation", as Captain Haie put it, but because of the conviction that, through the observation of certain facts, the historian may, though in modest measure, serve the cause

[1] Istvánffy (1583–1615), *Historia Regni Hungarici,* p. 16.

of human understanding, and even that of a rapprochement between peoples.

As those who live in East-Central Europe need time
and experience to think in American terms, so, pre-
sumably, the average American, when making a study
of Europe, must first become acquainted with the different viewpoints and characteristic conditions of the
Continent. For instance, the American may well ask
the following question: Why have not the peoples of
Europe, or at least those in some section of the continent, formed some more or less close federation
modelled after the example of the United States? The
study of European history makes clear to us that these
peoples often differ greatly, not only in language, but
also in history, inherited traditions and present desires.
Europe and its problems may better be understood
through a search into its history. With a clear compre-
hension of the main historic trends, one realizes that it
is far from being merely a maze of facts relating to
feuds, warfare, and dynastic connections.

Examining any chapter of Hungary's thousand-year-
old history, old or new, one comes across problems that
are correlated with specific conditions pertaining to the
whole of that region of Europe. Therefore it seems
advisable to draw the reader's attention to a few aspects
that lead to a better understanding not only of the
peculiarities of Hungary's development, but also of
those of East-Central Europe. It seems necessary, too,
to throw light on the conceptions employed by this
book, conceptions generally accepted by Hungarian re-

search. The new generation of Hungarian historians regards *East-Central Europe,* where Hungary also lies, as a special region within European civilization, with a character of its own the history of which has to be written by adopting a comparative method.

## EAST CENTRAL AND CARPATHIAN EUROPE

If we spread out the map and approach the European continent from America, we see first the western countries, Great Britain and France. Farther east, in the large middle part of the continent generally known as Central Europe, we find Germany, and on the eastern steppes, Russia.

In making a regional division of Europe, it is customary for geographers to slice off the large Scandinavian and Mediterranean peninsulas to the north and south respectively: then they examine separately the British Isles and the terraces of France on the west; and far to the east, the steppes of Russia. The remaining territory is usually termed Central Europe. Upon closer examination of this broad division, however, we find that between Central Europe proper and the endless Russian lowlands there is a distinct belt running vertically from the Baltic to the Balkans. This strip is subdivided into sharply defined sections. The northern, open portion, for instance, known as the Polish region, which connects the Russian plains with those of Germany, is of an entirely different character from the southern unit of the belt, the latter being clearly outlined by the arc of the Carpathians. As is often pointed

## DURABILITY OF FRONTIERS IN EAST CENTRAL EUROPE, 1000–1920

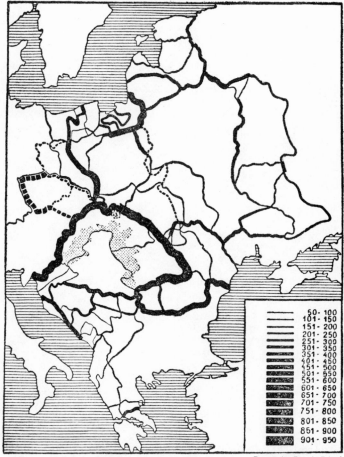

| | |
|---|---|
| | 50- 100 |
| | 101- 150 |
| | 151- 200 |
| | 201- 250 |
| | 251- 300 |
| | 301- 350 |
| | 351- 400 |
| | 401- 450 |
| | 451- 500 |
| | 501- 550 |
| | 551- 600 |
| | 601- 650 |
| | 651- 700 |
| | 701- 750 |
| | 751- 800 |
| | 801- 850 |
| | 851- 900 |
| | 901- 950 |

*Drawn by Dr. A. Rónai*

The thickness of frontier lines marks the respective length of their duration. The broken lines are the frontiers of the more important countries included by different empires. The shaded area within Hungary marks the ever-changing frontier-belt of the territory once occupied by the Turks.

out, the whole region lies between East and West. It is more or less landlocked, only its northern and southern tips reaching an inland sea. The westernmost spurs of the great East-Eurasian steppes, as well as the easternmost formations of the varied regions and mountain systems are to be found here, a decidedly western pattern. This meeting of East and West is most striking in the Carpathian Basin, where its central lowland, known as the Hungarian Plain, is edged by the chain of the Carpathians.

This particular territory of Europe has been made known to Americans chiefly through immigrants; in the 19th century through heroes of liberty, Kossuth for instance; and in more recent times, through writings and pamphlets relating to the political changes of the past quarter-century. A distant observer is seldom altogether clear as to the development this region has undergone, what the several small peoples there have achieved, and how they have solved their individual historic problems.

All this may appear quite complicated at first glance; for more than one people are concerned, each differing in origin and in tradition from the others. Each race, moreover, has had to solve *even analogous* problems in characteristically distinctive ways. In East-Central Europe, the more important historic rôles were played: (i) in the north, around the water system of the Vistula River, by the Poles; (ii) to the south of them, in the clearly defined Carpathian Basin, by the Hungarians, and, (iii) still farther south, by the Croats, who, for a long period, lived in close political association with the

Hungarians. Southwest of the Poles lived the Czechs. Their home, the Bohemian Basin, protruded deep into Germanic Central Europe and was closely defined also by regional interdependence with it. Down to the south and southeast, on the upper part of the Balkan peninsula, lived the Serbs and Rumanians, who, as against the westward orientation of the peoples mentioned already, joined the Orthodox, eastern world under the influence of Byzantium. Later, the Czars of Russia considered themselves as their head.

Europe is not merely a geographical conception; It also means the culture that spread during the Middle Ages, together with western Christianity, to an ever-widening territory. Its eastern border-belt, ever since the 10th century, when the Hungarians, and, to the north, the Poles, embraced Latin Christianity, was the region of East-Central Europe. This was the front line of defense facing the pagan onslaughts arriving in waves from the direction of the Eurasian plains.

The eastern frontier of the Catholic and Protestant religions in Europe coincides with the eastern boundary of Hungary. European conceptions in religion, art, statecraft and social problems all found genuine echoes there, century after century. The different peoples took their part in this according to their talents and historic rôles. To the Orthodox peoples of the south and the southeast, European ideas were transmissible only in relatively recent times, as these ideas ceased finally to be linked explicitly with the western forms of Christianity, and the peoples of the northern Balkans began to ex-

tricate themselves from the bonds of the Mohammedan
Turkish Empire.

Consequently, on this part of the Continent, between
Central Europe proper and the great eastern plains,
there lived several small peoples, differing from each
other in language, origin, and historic rôle, likewise
facing different tasks of different character and importance. Thus, as it were, this part was a diminutive model
of Europe to which, and especially to the Carpathian
region, one may aptly apply the definition of the French
historian Sorel used with reference to the old Austria:
*Une petite Europe dans la grande.*

Whatever divergent political rôles fell on the different peoples of this region from time to time, scholars
nevertheless have discovered certain analogous characteristics that may be inherent in the borderland position
between East and West or in certain more or less similar
social conditions, the result of a common habitat. This
part of the Continent, therefore, underwent a special
regional development; and its historical evolution represents a sub-type, one might say, of the larger complex
of Europe's history. The region to which this specifica-
tion may be applied we call *East-Central Europe*. If we
turn our attention to its most clearly defined and decidedly characteristic unit, the Carpathian system, we
may even speak of a *Carpathian Europe*.

COMPARATIVE METHOD

There is hardly a historian who could claim knowledge of the mother tongues and literatures of all these

peoples. On the other hand, their respective histories must not be examined separately in isolation from each other. If one writes the history of Hungary, for instance, it must be examined also from the broader point of view of the history of the whole of East-Central Europe, of which it has formed an organic part and in which it has been one of the most important factors. The historian must place it in the frame of the evolution of East-Central Europe and compare it with the history of other neighboring East-Central European peoples. One section of the region can hardly be torn away from the others, to be reviewed independently, or to be compared only with territories depending on different conditions, as, for instance, in Western Europe.

As to the record the Hungarian people can show in political, spiritual, economic and social development; how they solved their relations with their neighbors, with peoples small and great as well as with other nationalities: we can see this clearly and according to its merits only if we first know something of the respective conditions in the whole of East-Central Europe. We have to know the conditions in the other East-Central European countries, and the main outlines of their political, cultural, economic and social life; also the nationality problem and the relations between the different peoples. One has to know what it was possible to achieve, and what other peoples have achieved there.

During the past hundred and fifty years, Hungarian jurists and historians have frequently emphasized the evident existing similarity between English and Hungarian constitutional development, pointing out, *inter alia,* that Magna Charta (1215) and the Hungarian Golden Seal (1222) are almost contemporaneous. By now we know that while such distant parallels are interesting, the constitutional development of Hungary is much better understood if it is fitted into the framework of the whole of East-Central Europe, where it played a really important part. In this particular border region of Europe, where new institutions often lived together with old ones, and often had to withstand much outside pressure, life could not take a course identical with that of the West.

In examining the history of East-Central Europe, it is always advisable to use the comparative method. This method is necessary also when we examine the history of factors of state-building. This is a particularly interesting problem in the region concerned, called by the Swedish geographer Kjellén, a *critical zone,* one which, according to the rather far-fetched opinion of some writers, is characterized by political instability. It is beyond doubt that on a territory like this, always subjected to strong pressure, achievements of statecraft were threatened with premature extinction. Thus, in all probability, they had to be built on foundations laid with great care, and maintained with more effort than was necessary in the West. Indeed, here only solidly built, historically proven solutions are lasting, the political storms being too violent for poorly founded structures.

No matter what our opinion may be, we may con-

cede the stability of Hungary during long centuries. The
fact that the organization of the Hungarian state assured the natural economic and geographic unity of the
Carpathian Basin, was an important contribution in the
history of East-Central Europe. Through a more thorough examination of the region's history, it becomes evident that Hungary, from the time of its inception, was
the firmest and most steadfast political formation in
Carpathian Europe. Furthermore, owing to its central
position, the fate of other Carpathian peoples depended, to a certain extent, upon that of Hungary.

## THE PROBLEM OF SMALL PEOPLES

Related to all this, is the problem of small peoples, for
whom, in the form of prophecies, many have sounded
the death-knell. It has been stated that the time of small
states has passed, the future being set aside exclusively
for the great powers. Ellen Semple, American pupil of
the German geographer Ratzel,[1] conveyed this thought
previous to the First World War thus: "The day for the
national existence of small peoples is passing". And
added, as an example, "despite superior civilization and
national heroism", Greece of old "has fallen a victim to
almost every invader". Truly enough, human life and
creation are indeed mortal and transitory, yet this rule,
as proved by history, does not apply to the small nations
alone. Great empires, like ancient Persia, have likewise
vanished, without leaving behind to humanity any such
civilization as Greek antiquity.

[1]Ellen Semple "Influences of Geographic Environment", London, 1911.

It seems evident that in the question of small peoples two principles are to be brought into harmony. According to one, small peoples can furnish worthwhile achievements, they can lend fresh colors to the life-work of humanity, provided they are granted the possibility of developing their special individualities and talents. The other principle is rooted in the realization that it is suicidal for fragments of peoples, numbering but a million or two, to seclude themselves in warring isolation, refusing to search the means of unavoidable peaceful collaboration with neighbors with whom they are tightly knit together in the same region.

Therefore it may be deemed important that one or more East-Central European peoples created such political organizations in the past that cooperation became possible for several peoples inhabiting contiguous areas. Such was the example, among others, of Croatia, forming for eight hundred years an autonomous appanage of the Hungarian Crown, without endangering its own development.

## THE PROBLEM OF NATIONALITIES

The author, as well as the reader, inevitably finds himself confronted with the problem of nationalities, a delicate question even in our day. Complaints as well as self-defense in this respect may appear to be propaganda. Neither one should be our aim. Historians cannot count themselves among those who consider everything to do with their people correct for that reason alone. There can hardly be complete objectivity, owing

to the human element involved, but with honest and
serious historic examination many errors can be
avoided. This is the course one has to choose and follow, for it is generally those who emphasize their objectivity who use this term as a mere expression, without
much to back it up.

A distant observer may easily be confused with the
oft-repeated phrase that in the region under discussion
a number of different peoples are inseparably mixed up.
True, on some territories, notably where great masses
of different peoples meet, intermingling is considerable.
A perfect ethnic boundary cannot be drawn, yet this
should not mean that the whole question is hopeless and
be dealt with accordingly; for it cannot be proved
either that there are no evident ethnographical units
there at all. It is thought best to examine the problem
from the viewpoint of every aspect of its human elements. Similar recognition is thought due to the guarantee of a peaceful community of several peoples, and
the creation of such political institutions as do not im-
peril the existence of small nationalities. It seems certain that to write a history from a universal, human
viewpoint and simultaneously from a national one is a
more difficult task in this region than anywhere else.
Yet it has to be attempted.

OPINIONS ON SLAVISM AND GERMANISM

In order that we may see clearly, we shall have to
consider two theories—both erroneous in our estima-
tion, for they attempt to explain East-Central Europe's

historical evolution from a one-sided and distorted point of view. According to one theory, enjoying wide publicity, the principal factor of history in this region is Slavism. This explains the region's peculiar development as being basically determined by a conflict between Slavism and Germanism. This theory, whose political meaning is overly simplified, found credit during the last few decades chiefly among some French writers. Contrary to this conception, it is clear that in this region there are to be found not only Slavs, but Hungarians and Rumanians, who are in no way related to the Slavs. It is clear, too, that the largest Slavic power, Russia, is not in East-Central Europe, and that it underwent a different evolution from that of the people who live there. In fact, it exerted strong, often hostile pressure upon the peoples of East-Central Europe. There is no unified Slavic history. The best example of this is the Polish-Russian antagonism, and the differences emphasized by Polish historians between the histories of these two peoples. In the evolution of East-Central Europe, it is not Slavism, but the historical activities of the different peoples that is the decisive factor. The idea of a broad and united Slavism was closely associated, primarily, with the growing self-consciousness of nationalities in the early 19th century. In the first phase of this, composed chiefly of cultural and literary aspects, the smaller peoples referred, with due pride, either to their venerable past or to their extensive kinship. Poets and writers of the different smaller Slavic peoples were no exception to this, and invoking

the legendary common ancestry, dreamt of a great
Slavic unity, an ideal exploited by the expansionist designs of imperialist Russia.

As soon as nationalism, however, arrived at its second
phase, viz., that of political aspirations, it brought
about, instead of the unity of all Slavs, the special distinct self-consciousness and divergent desires of the individual peoples of each of them separately, amplifying
the natural differences between them. Just as there is
no unified Finno-Ugrian nation, so one can hardly speak
of a unified Slavic nation. They may differ as much
from each other as the Teutonic English do from the
Teutonic Germans. Kinship in language means nothing
as to any necessary political solidarity.

We arrive likewise at erroneous results if we view the
relation of this region to Germanic Central Europe with
stiff one-sidedness, either from one angle or another. According to a few writers, for example, the peoples living
in the territory east of Central Europe (*Ostraum*), were
inferior and backward, and could not possibly have participated on their own account in European civilization. Therefore the Germans must be credited with
transferring both Christianity and every other new
trend, as a matter of fact, all civilization, to these peoples. It is further stated that all advances in agriculture,
urbanism, and, generally, a more adequate economic
life, were established in the *Ostraum* by mediaeval German settlers who provided models for the inhabitants.
All these peoples have been brought up under German
tutelage, so to speak, and similar strains were derived

from common German influence. These views are counterbalanced by other one-sided ones, which either dis-
claimed any foreign influence whatsoever, or else credited them exclusively to remote non-German sources, or
attempted to find altogether independent national
specialties in everything.

The truth is, naturally, somewhere between the two.
It is evident that the German region, constituting a
large and central portion of Europe, always exerted a
very strong influence on the neighboring smaller countries situated to the east. But this influence was far from
being of the same intensity everywhere; neither was it
of identical character. Thus political relations between
the German Empire on the one hand and the different
greater units of East-Central Europe were not equi-
distant in operation or of the same nature. This becomes
clear if we take as an example the political relations of
Bohemia, Poland and Hungary on the one hand, with
the German Empire on the other, in the 11th and 13th
centuries. Bohemia, though a separate principality, was
an integral part of the Holy-Roman Empire. Poland
for a long time was in a state of feudal dependence on
the Emperor. On the other hand, the situation was
again different in the Carpathian Basin, where Hungary was able, comparatively early, to organize its national independence on solid lines. In the latter region,
mainly on account of the early stability of the Hungarian state, relations with the Empire, as well as the
ethnic frontier, were much clearer and better consolidated than in the north.

Hungary embraced Christianity, and with it a Western orientation, at the time of Christian universality. The civilization of Hungary, as it developed after the Middle Ages, was not built up under the influence of one-sided cultural trends, connections and traditions. Besides German influence, the great importance of which must not be underestimated, an early and powerful Italian influence made itself felt, and direct cultural ties with Western Europe were also evident. In the Middle Ages there was a lively intercourse with France especially, later also with the Protestant Netherlands, and to some extent, with England. Consequently, in addition to natural connections, spiritual and economic, with Central Europe proper, Hungarians traditionally maintained intellectual intercourse and direct contacts with all Europe. Hungarian civilization never developed under the influence of a single region or people, but always reflected an independent, yet broadly European character. Already in the 12th century, the anonymous notary of King Béla III, the first Hungarian historian whose work was left behind for posterity, studied in Paris. The connections with Central Europe faced a crisis in times when the country's independence was in danger. For instance, the foreign oppression of Emperor Leopold I at the end of the 17th century not only did not mean further extension of European culture, but inevitably aroused bitter resistance.

It would be an inferior method to explain history merely on the basis of arguments for and against certain foreign influences. The substantial question here is whether the ethnic individuality of a people, Hungarians for instance, contributed actively to Christian and European civilization, and whether it developed its own civilization by adopting general European ideas according to its independent and individual characters. To this one may give an affirmative answer. We do not overstep the bounds of obligatory modesty if we state that the real forces forming the history of Carpathian Europe were the inhabiting peoples themselves in proportion to their rôles in history.

The following chapters will attempt to relate the history of Hungary. They cannot give a detailed narrative, packed with dates of merely local importance. Instead, they will endeavor to point out, in a wider perspective, the rôle played by Hungary in the Carpathian region, and, through that, in the evolution of the whole of Europe.

The author is greatly indebted to Professor J. Szekfü of the Budapest University, for allowing him to see the manuscript of the last, still unpublished chapters of his History of Hungary. The results of the historical synthesis of Professor Szekfü and Dr. Bálint Hóman, Minister of Education, were used at many points in the present volume. The author also wishes to thank Professor Watson Kirkconnell of MacMaster University for the final checking of the English text.

# I

## THE CARPATHIAN BASIN

*Origin and Settlement of the Magyars*

The scene of Hungarian life for over ten centuries has been the fertile basin surrounded by the Carpathian Range. As has often been noted by geographers, this closed-in territory duly influenced the creation of a unified state.

A glance at a relief map makes clear the unity of the Carpathian Mountain System outlining the basin of the Tisza River in a semicircle, which the French geographer Himly called "the Magyar system." It splits the vertical belt of East-Central Europe into three zones. The one *north* of the Carpathians comprises the Polish terrain, defined by the Vistula and its tributaries. It is difficult to draw an exact line either to the east or the west of the Polish region, although it differs from both the German and the Russian plains, and has a central position of its own. Even the ethnic line has suffered changes, the Germans, for instance, having surged far eastward from their original boundary at the Elbe River.

*South* of the Carpathians the Balkan peninsula forms the lower zone of this East-Central European belt, its territory falling into two climatic divisions. The sea-shore, particularly Greece, is Mediterranean in character, akin to Italy and Spain. Behind this littoral, the landlocked part is known as the Continental Block, and is subdivided into three irregular mountain regions, the Montenegrin, the Pindus, and the Balkans proper. Some consider the lines of the Save and Danube Rivers as the northern boundary of the Balkan zone, but historic, rather than geographic, factors should be considered. The northern and southern zones of this East-Central European belt clearly define the boundaries of the central basin so strikingly outlined by the high ranges of the Carpathian system.

The great arc of the Carpathians, extending to a length of almost a thousand miles, circumvallates the Hungarian lowlands like a natural fortified wall. For those approaching from the east this is the first great obstacle rising out of the plains. Only twice were its mountain ramparts effectually pierced: in 1241 by the Mongols and in 1849 by the Czar's armies, but in the latter case the defending Hungarian forces were engaged elsewhere by the invasion of Austrian troops. The area of this mountain-walled basin is about 135,000 square miles forming a hydrographic unit. Its drainage system centers around the Danube into which all but two insignificant waters empty inside the Basin itself. Some call this region the Danube Basin, just as they

called the Austro-Hungarian dual state the Danubian
Monarchy. Actually there are several Danube basins,
since this mighty European river, considerably longer
than the Rhine, runs a course of no less than two
thousand miles, touching several basins of importance.
The first of these is the Swabian-Bavarian basin, down
as far as Passau. Next comes the Austrian basin, ending
at the "Hungarian Gate", *Porta Hungarica,* at Dévény.
In the succeeding, Carpathian or Hungarian Basin, the
Danube changes from a mountain stream into a lowland river that spreads out and slackens its current.
This is the largest of the Danube basins, and extends
from a few miles east of Vienna down to the Iron Gate.
Here, forcing itself through the southernmost peaks of
the Carpathians, it enters into its last, the Bulgaro-
Rumanian basin.

Within the Carpathian Basin itself, one may define
certain transitions, rather than separate regions of
different character. Only Transylvania may be treated
as a distinct entity within the larger one. On the other
hand, the narrow strip on the north, known today as
Slovakia, can hardly be termed such a closed territory,
especially as it is divided by several ranges, its valleys
running from north to south toward the center of the
Carpathian drainage system. Geographers, emphasizing
the unity of this system, point out that the products
of the different regions supplement one another, the
agricultural products of the lowlands and the mining
and timber of the surrounding mountains, for instance;
also that intensive agriculture on the plain cannot be

pursued without irrigation, which, in turn, would be
hardly possible without the storage possibilities of
Subcarpathian Ruthenia.

While the Balkan zone is characterized, geographically, by "the confusion of its mountain ranges,—the
great depression surrounded by the folds of the Carpathians forms the most perfectly closed basin of all
Europe. . . . There are two primeval facts, which the
two main geographical features have stamped here on
human history, viz., the tendency for all to unite around
the central point of gravity . . . and the protecting
action of the main mountain girdle."[1]

Previous to the Migration of Peoples, two great empires, the Chinese and the Roman, ruled on the extreme
edges of the enormous Eurasian continent. Separated
by immeasurable distances, roaming hordes of "bar-
barians" inhabited the infinite, unknown wastes between them. The Great Wall of China and the Roman
*Limes* were erected against them, the latter following
the course of the Rhine and Danube Rivers. The western portion of what is Hungary today, known as Transdanubia (*Pannonia* in Latin), was a well organized
province of the Roman Empire. Of its numerous towns
and cities the significance of *Aquincum,* on the northern
outskirts of Budapest, is proved by its excavated ruins.
Several Transdanubian cities are built on the site of
former Roman settlements, yet no real continuity can

[1]Count Paul Teleki, *Evolution of Hungary and Its Place in European
History,* Macmillan, New York, 1923; pp. 14-15.

be detected, though, as relics of Roman rule, graves, roads, and ruins abound.

In the east, around Transylvania, the Roman emperor Trajan annihilated the state of the Dacians in the early second century. There too, Roman rule was established; but Dacia could not match Pannonia, either in importance or in intensity of Roman influence. As a matter of record, Dacia protruded from the defence line and was connected with the Roman Empire only by a narrow corridor.

In 271 A.D. the emperor Aurelian evacuated all Roman subjects from the province, and thus all conditions of Roman life ceased to exist there.[1]

About the time of Julius Caesar's conquest of Gaul, the France of our time, the Chinese in the east defeated the powerful Asiatic empire of the Huns, who consequently were compelled to turn westward across the great plains toward Europe. At the end of the 4th century they reached the Volga River and forced the different Teutonic races against the Roman *Limes*. The latter soon gave way, and the migration of peoples, surging westward in ever stronger waves, definitely transformed the *status quo* of ethnic relations.

Three distinct waves of this great migration may be distinguished. First came the Germanic peoples, who adopted Christianity and founded a long line of new states. These were under pressure from the east by the so-called Turkic peoples: first came the tribes com-

[1]The widely discussed theory of the continuation of either Dacian or Roman survivors in Transylvania has been completely refuted by A. Alföldi in the *Cambridge Ancient History*, 1939.

prising the Hun Empire, followed by the Avars, who likewise centered their rule in the Carpathian Basin. At the same time a third wave is discernible, that of the Slavic peoples, who moved cautiously, in rather small groups. The Slavs were not primarily creators of political bodies of their own: they were not a military, much less a conquering race. Their tribes reached the Elbe River on the north, and the ridges of the Balkans in the south. In the twilights of the 9th century a new Ugrian people of Turkic organization arrived from the East in the Carpathian Basin: the Magyars.

Recent research has thrown lights upon the herdsman culture of the hard-riding, nomadic Turkic peoples. Heretofore they were regarded as a pillaging, devastating horde. Now we know that they had a well-developed social, political and military organization, enabling them to build great empires, and to employ strategic methods unknown in the contemporary western world. This warring form of life throve on the vast steppes stretching from the Carpathians to the Manchurian plateau: and whenever these peoples in their westward wanderings met with other forms of life, the inevitable results were desperate struggles.

Evidence indicates that the Turkic peoples were stockmen. According to Chinese historians they were always on the move "in search of grass and water." In their social life, the family, taken in its broader sense, was the judicial and economic unit, with communal livestock and pasture. The ablest among the heads of clans led the whole tribe as its chieftain, at least in matters of vital interests. The strong tribes undertook to organize the weaker ones, in this way forging an "empire" of their own. Since their mode of life was very similar, any tribe could join the "empire", yet retain its own customs, language, and separate entity; but it would adopt the name of the leading tribe. Thus the whole "empire" bore the name of the organizing tribe. For instance, everyone in Attila's empire was called a Hun, though it consisted of different peoples. The example of the Huns demonstrates that with the downfall of the leading people the "empire" crumbles, its place being taken by a whole series of races. Under the circumstances there was no other possible basis for political and social creations than this nomadic military organization.

From this vast, nomadic world came the Magyars. As regards their origin, life, and customs during the centuries preceding their entry into the Carpathian Basin, information may be found in contemporary Byzantine and Arabic reports and in mediaeval chronicles, the best source being the Magyar language itself. A branch of the Finno-Ugric family of languages, it differs altogether from the Indo-European family [Greek, Latin, Germanic, Slavic, Celtic, etc.]. It is most nearly related to the Finnish, though the Magyar vocabulary was supplemented by numerous Turkic words well before the 9th century A.D.

Popular belief places the Magyars among the Asiatic migrants. This is not altogether correct. The eastern-most fragments of the Finno-Ugric races mingled with the westernmost tribes of the Turko-Bulgar peoples. The Magyars may be traced to the intermingling of these two distinct races, and thus the Magyar language was enriched with Turkic elements while retaining its basically Finno-Ugric characteristics. The latter predominates in terms applying to family life, fishing, hunting, trading and the like; Turkic roots are found in words relating to animal husbandry, and to political and military organization.

The origin of the early Magyar people may be reconstructed as follows:

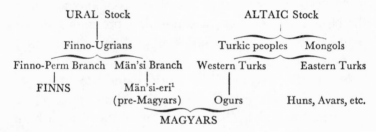

The merging of races that resulted in the Magyar people took place between the 1st and 5th centuries A.D. An Arabic writer notes that the Magyars had begun their southward migration from the Ural mountains before the end of the 5th century. During the following centuries they lived in the Caucasian region east of the Sea of Azov, again under the influence of Turkic neighbors. It is difficult to determine their exact whereabouts during this period; being a nomadic people, they were constantly moving, often a part of

[1]The name Magyar—in its original form Magyeri—comes from Män'si-eri (män'si = men).

empires founded by other Turkic peoples under whose name they were known. Thus the Magyars were variously called Sabyrs, Turks, Onogurs, the latter supplying the stem for Hungarus, Hungarian, Hongrois, Ungar.

During their association with these nomadic empires the Magyars patterned themselves almost exclusively after the Turkic model, becoming a well-disciplined, conquering race. The last empire of which the Magyars formed a part was the Kazar, with which they were connected until the middle of the 9th century.

During the Kazar period the Magyar chieftain, bearing the title "Kündü" was the leader of the entire people. After the break with the Kazar Empire, another chieftain of the rank of "gyula" gradually rose in authority. This gyula was the forefather of the Árpád dynasty.

During the second half of the 9th century, a Turkic people, the warring Petchenegs, exerted pressure on the Magyars, who then began their historical westward migration, severing all connections with the tottering Kazar Empire. From 830 to 889 we find the Magyars between the Don and the Dnieper. This region they named Levedia after one of their chieftains.

Previous to 830, some of the Magyar tribes broke away from the main body, and took no part in the migratory movement. These people called their country Greater Hungary (*Magna Hungaria*), and preserved their language to a remarkable degree. In the thirteenth century Father Julian, a Hungarian monk and one of the outstanding explorers of his day, visited them, and they had no difficulty in understanding each other. This tribe, however, disappeared soon afterwards under the tremendous onslaught of Mongol hordes.

Gradually forced westward, as far as the lowland that lies north of the Danube estuary, the Rumanian lowland of today, which they named *Etelköz* (Etel = river; köz = between, therefore "a plain lying between rivers"), the Magyars arrived within range of the conflict between the Byzantine Empire and the eastern peoples. While they fought the Bulgars as allies of the Greek Emperor, the latter deserted them just in the crucial moment when the Petchenegs launched a vicious attack against them. This forced the Magyars to unite under one leader and consequently they elected Árpád, son of Álmos of the Magyeri tribe, as their Prince. Following an ancient custom of nomadic peoples, the seven heads of the seven Magyar tribes cut their veins and mixed the blood in a vessel, thus sealing their loyalty to one another and to their ruler.

Árpád led his people out of their exposed position in Etelköz into the Carpathian Basin. The majority of the Magyars entered through the Verecke Pass, in the northeast of present-day Hungary. Three years before Árpád's entry, this country had witnessed a foray by Magyar warriors on their way to Svatopluk's Moravian principality, against which they were campaigning as allies of Emperor Arnulf.

Hungary has existed on its present site since 895, when the Magyars finally took possession of it as their

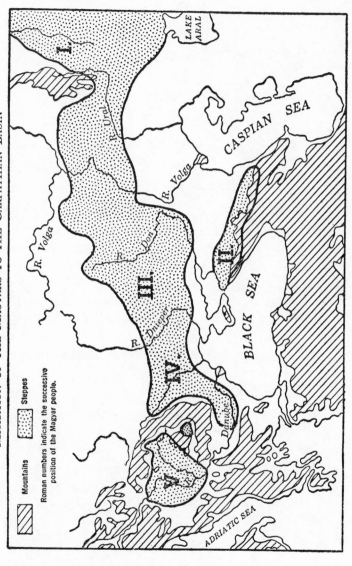

MIGRATION OF THE MAGYARS TO THE CARPATHIAN BASIN

Mountains

Steppes

Roman numbers indicate the successive
position of the Magyar people.

permanent home. According to mediaeval belief, which erroneously held them to be descendants of Attila, the Magyars inherited the Carpathian Basin as a legacy. This tradition of relationship between the Huns and Magyars, current as late as the nineteenth century, was nothing but a legend of the Árpád dynasty, preserved because of past dynastic associations with the Huns, and accepted by the entire people.

Of the seven tribes, the largest was the Magyar, after which the state and its inhabitants were named. The word Magyar, or Magyeri, is of Finno-Ugric origin. The second tribe bore the name of Nyék ("enclosed or forti-fied place"), probably of Turkic origin, since they fought in the forefront as tribes who joined the main body generally were obliged to. Such was the Kabar remnant which joined the Magyars after the dissolution of the Kazar Empire. The third tribe was known as Kürt-Gyarmat ("snowstorm", or "indefatigable"); the fourth, Tarjan (the name of a certain high office); the fifth, Jenő ("councillor"); the sixth, Kér ("giant"); and the seventh Keszi ("remnant", or "part"). All these are preserved to this day as place names. It is not definitely proved whether the Székely tribe, also of Turkic organization, came in with the Magyars or joined them after the conquest, having been left behind by the Avars. Be that as it may, the Székelys were a Magyar-speaking people, and have always considered themselves as Magyars.

According to contemporary historians, the Magyars, composed of one large body of Finno-Ugric people and several smaller tribes of predominantly Turkic origin, were a united, disciplined people. They believed in the super-natural mission of their ruler and his successors. As was customary with nomadic peoples, each tribe endeavored to trace its origin to some mythical animal (totemism) whose emblem they wore. The totem of the Árpáds was a legendary hawk, known to the early Magyars as the "turul".

To contemporary foreign observers the outstanding characteristic of the Magyars was their military power. Leo the Wise of Byzantium wrote of them: "This people abounds in men and is independent. Aside from their love of pomp and abundant life, their chief aim is to fight bravely against any invader". The Magyars, with their fast horses, were able to cover great distances in a comparatively short time: thus the heavily-armored feudal armies of the West were for a long time helpless against them. Among the Magyar's tactics, a favorite device was the hasty retreat, a successful ruse, for their strong flanks annihilated the charging enemy with disastrous arrow-fire. This explains their ability to roam over Europe for decades without encountering any effective resistance.[1]

Before the coming of the Magyars, the Carpathian Basin had never seen a lasting national régime. Nor was there a compact political organization or a larger body of people in 895. Since the fall of the Avars, the

[1]The opinion, that the Magyars are of predominantly Asiatic, Mongol stock can be dismissed in the light of anthropological research. Like all other peoples, they are a mixed race. Of skulls found in tombs dating back to the three centuries following the Magyars' entry into the Car-

Empire dominated the western border, and Bulgarian interests the eastern. In the mountains on the north li. ed Slavic peoples, ancestors of the Slovaks of today. There were also scattered Slavic settlements in Transdanubia, but these were too small to maintain their identity for long. In the east, in the present Transylvania, there were remnants of Bulgarian Slavs.

There is much argument about the priority of the Rumanians in Transylvania. Rumanians claim that they are the descendants of the Romanized Dacians of the emperor Trajan's day, who have lived uninterruptedly in Transylvania since Roman times. Many historians point out, however, that according to all available evidence, the Romans completely evacuated their Dacian settlements, and that from the third century to the twelfth, during the course of nearly a thousand years, not a single trace of the Dacians may be found in Transylvania—even if the Rumanians were their descendants. On the other hand there are chronological data concerning the Rumanians' gradual immigration into Transylvania from the twelfth century onward. The Rumanian language itself points to a long sojourn on the western, now Albanian, shores of the Balkan peninsula. Since the immigration, cultural standing and rôle of the Rumanians is sufficiently described in his-

pathian Basin, only five per cent are Mongolian. Even this small fraction is due partly to Avar remnants who were absorbed by the Magyars after their arrival. Another five per cent were Nordic, the majority of the remainder are classified as East Baltic. The low percentage of skulls of the Mongolian type found here, disproves the theory of Asiatic origin. The Magyars may rightly be termed a people of European racial composition.

torical sources, there seems little point in arguing about
hypotheses that cannot be supported by proof.

The Magyars first occupied the lowlands, gradually
spreading out into the valleys of the surrounding mountains. They encountered remnants of many other racial
migrants, and assimilated the smaller ones. This was
natural. In the British Isles there was a fusion of greater
number and longer standing, Stone and Bronze Age
men, Brythonic and Goedelic Celts, Angles, Saxons,
Jutes, Norsemen, Danes and Normans.

The tribe of the ruler, Árpád, was allotted the most
protected central zone in the vicinity of present-day
Budapest. The other tribes surrounded them, still maintaining the strategy forced upon them during their centuries of roaming, i.e., they established defensive outposts in the east, expecting further westward expansion
on the part of other peoples. The Magyars soon found
that instead of steppes and nomadic tribes, mountains
and peoples of different political structure were in their
way. For a time the Magyars took many military ex-
peditions, sweeping through western countries,—Germany, Italy, Switzerland, France, and even Spain.
These campaigns, causing people to fear the coming
end of the world, as shown by the pious chroniclers of
the Middle Ages, were not prompted, however, merely
by a desire for looting, as recent documentary proofs
bear out. This was the customary method followed by
mounted peoples of the age of the great migrations,
both to insure their own safety and to further political
alliance with their reluctant neighbors. As a result they

were able to conclude alliances with the principalities of Upper Italy, Bavaria and Saxony, all of which paid tribute to Hungary for a time. However, it was evident that since the possibilities of steppe-life were gone, the nomadic raids must come to an end.

The 9th century was undoubtedly one of the most crucial in the history of Europe. In addition to inner strife that undermined most of the states, three consecutive waves of pagan invasion threatened the very foundations of Christianity. The Norsemen, from the north, the Moors from the south and the Magyars from the east all arrived at a time when the Christian civilization of Europe was in its early stages. We have to bear in mind that it was barely two hundred years since only the most westerly fringe of the continent was Christian. The succeeding century saw the Germans join the fold. On the north and the east, hastily organized dioceses and military "counties" guarded the border districts against the Danes, Slavs, and the Avars, who then inhabited the territory of Hungary. In 796, Charlemagne defeated the Avars, but after the dissolution of the Carolingian Empire into three parts the expansion of Christianity was weakened. Four counties stood on the eastern border of Christianity; the most southerly, known as Ostmark, the forerunner of Austria, faced the assaults of the new arrivals, the Magyars. Its strength was insufficient against the latter's penetrating force. But the 10th century brought a revival of European resistance. Under its Saxon kings, the German Empire gained power. On the other hand, all Christianity became strengthened through the reform movement started in the French monastery of Cluny, France.

The defeat of the pagan Danes, as well as of the Slavs along the Elbe River, was a sign of the consolidation of the Empire. Immediately after his coronation in 962, Otto the Great founded the Archdiocese of Magdeburg with the aim that it would become a center from which the Gospel might be spread among the heathen. In the next year the first military conflict broke out between Germany and Mieszko, Prince of Poland. Bohemia was already under German influence. On the south-east, however, the Magyars proved so strong that the Emperor was glad if he could defend his domain, let alone launch an offensive against them.

Two decisive defeats were suffered by the rough-riding Magyar warriors. The first blow was delivered in 933 by Emperor Henry I on the down of Lech, the second by Otto the Great in 955 at Augsburg. These campaigns decimated Magyar manhood. Thus, Magyar paganism, like that of the Avars before them, faced disintegration; and it became more and more evident that the Magyars were doomed unless they gave up their nomadic habits and chose the plowshare instead of the sword.

The solution of this crisis was greatly helped by the religious reform movement of Cluny, one of the loftiest manifestations of mediaeval Christian universalism. It brought to the fore the idea of human brotherhood, establishing, at the turn of the millennium, the ideal of Christian unity and general peace. Up to the time of the

Cluny movement, conversion automatically meant incorporation into the Empire. The moral force of the Cluny reform made it possible for those inhabiting the Carpathian Basin to join Western civilization without losing their independence. Thus the eastern boundaries of East-Central Europe became the frontiers of European civilization, and its defense transferred to those peoples who were embracing Christianity at that time.

The acceptance of the Faith depended largely upon the hereditary chieftains of pagan tribes. In the case of the Magyars, Prince Géza or Geyza, a great grandson of Árpád, reestablished the authority of his family. Besides his achievements in unification, his move to tie his people's fate to Christianity proved a turning-point in Hungarian history. Hungary became an adjunct not of eastern Orthodox, but of Western European civilization, thus determining the country's character for the future.

Prince Géza's initiative was prompted by purely political intuition. He recognized the change of the European balance of power. But his son, baptized István (the Magyar form of Stephen), grew up to be a devout Christian. As King, he established the Christian Hungarian state, and with great political wisdom outlined the course to be followed in relation to other peoples in Europe. The first of the Árpáds to be canonized by Rome, he begins the history of European, Christian Hungary. Two principal factors contributed to the great change in the history of the peoples of East-Central Europe at the new millennium. These were: the reform spirit of Cluny and the newly established central power of the Princes. The Polish and Bohemian kingdoms also sprang into existence under national dynasties. The Hungarian House of Árpád became extinct in 1301, the Czech Przemyslides in 1306, and the Polish Piasts in 1370. The development of these three states may thus seem analogous, yet their respective political strength and measure of independence varied. Bohemia, for instance, even if autonomous, remained a part of the German Empire, while Poland won its independence from Germany only after considerable time had elapsed. In sharp contrast, the independence of the Hungarian state in the Carpathian Basin was complete. It successfully withstood the political and military interference of the Emperors, and unquestionably became the most substantial entity in East-Central Europe.

# II

## THE CHRISTIAN KINGDOM IN THE MIDDLE AGES

*The Age of the Árpáds*
*(1000–1301)*

Medieval legends picture the first Hungarian King as a pious, praying old man of colorless character, but this was only in the imagination of the good monks. King Stephen (997–1038), called the Saint, was a strong-handed, determined man. He ruthlessly broke up all opposition, both the pagan uprising in Transdanubia and the revolt against royal power in Transylvania. He proceeded along his prearranged path without hesitation, yet he was no reckless reformer, discounting tradition. He systematically established new institutions, gradually replacing the old with the new. He worked incessantly and sincerely for Christianity, but did not entirely destroy age-old customs. The old common law continued to prevail to some extent, and on Christian church walls one may find pagan motifs.

During St. Stephen's reign, the new, Western forms

of life were smoothly adjusted to specific conditions. The King was no mere imitator; he may have minted money after the pattern of his Bavarian father-in-law, but his two important codes of law express in greater part his own independent conceptions. No one state was his model; he merely built a typically Christian kingdom, adapting all good practice to peculiar Hungarian needs. Throughout the Middle Ages, his people recognized him as the great founder, sentimentally crediting him with all "good" institutions, including even many of later date.

Stephen was in his twentieth year when Géza died in 997. While his father saw in Christianity and in the Western orientation only a political weapon, Stephen accepted with heart and mind the new Christian culture. First he dealt drastically with his pagan relatives who refused to recognize his authority. Thus he suppressed by force an elder chieftain of the Árpád dynasty, who claimed, by the pagan custom of seniority, supreme authority and Géza's widow for himself. His own rule established, Stephen turned to the Pope for his investiture as a Christian King, and for his crown, the Pope alone having the power to confer the title, "King by the Grace of God," to the ruler of an independent country. Emperors had the right to confer the title of king only upon one of their vassal princes, and it carried with it no hereditary rights, being only for the lifetime of the person.

A special envoy brought the crown sent by Pope Sylvester II, together with an Apostolic Cross, to be borne before his royal person, in recognition of his organizing work. The Crown, the upper part of the present-day Holy Crown, was placed on the head of Stephen on Christmas Day in the year 1000. Since then, for more than nine hundred years it has been used in crowning all Hungarian kings, and it is even today the supreme symbol of authority.

Thus the Kingdom of Hungary was born at the opening of a new millennium. The time was favorable for the creation of a new, independent Christian state. That King Stephen grasped the opportunity points to a shrewd understanding of the European situation. The Emperor at that time was Otto III, a young and idealistic man who did not pursue his predecessors' policy of expansion but enthusiastically supported the "idea of Rome" and was in complete accord with the Pope. "They both clung with faith to the idea of a New Rome, a new universal Christian Empire embracing the entire world under the spiritual guidance of the Pope and the Emperor of Rome. But both stood aloof from the ecclesiastico-political imperialism of Charlemagne and Otto the Great, and from the idea of the spiritual and political subjugation of neighboring states. . . . Both labored for the realization of the peaceful co-operation of the Christian peoples, and they eagerly accepted as a new and powerful supporter of their endeavors the Hungarian Prince who had appealed to Rome for recognition of his royalty, and whose conscious and consistent policy of peace exactly fitted in with their own conception of universal peace."[1]

The organization of the Church proceeded parallel with that of the state. Many parishes and monasteries, eight dioceses and two archdioceses were founded. A testimony to his work in church organization is given by the first documents ever issued in Hungary. One of these describes the grants given to the Abbey of Panonhalma, which exists to this day.

The basis of royal power for more than two centuries lay in the vast domains of the crown, larger than the estates of anyone else throughout the land. The heavily wooded and mountainous outer fringe of the country, uninhabited for the most part, was also royal property. The crown lands were divided into counties (*comitatus*), each headed by a count (*comes*) or steward on the pattern of the French system. Their seats were fortresses, sometimes built on the sites of pre-Magyar, Avar or Roman strongholds. The counts meted out justice, enlisted men for military service when the King issued the command, directed the economic life of their respective territories and collected crops and revenue. Stephen himself established 45 counties, and the number rose to 72 by the middle of the 12th century. The central manager of all the estates was known as the royal count (*comes regalis*) whose office gradually developed into the position of Palatine, later to become the most important constitutional office in the Kingdom.

Clerics from foreign lands were of great assistance to

[1]B. Hóman, *King Stephen the Saint*. Budapest, 1938. p. 12.

King Stephen in his reform work. The most outstanding among these was the Venetian St. Gerard, known
to the Magyars as Gellért. In a pagan uprising, after
the king's death, Gellért was hurled from the hill that
stands in the center of the capital and subsequently
bore his name. A number of foreign knights, chiefly
German, Italian and French, also flocked to Hungary,
offering their services to the first Hungarian kings.
Some of them founded leading Hungarian families.

Occasionally the King sought the advice of his senate
*(senatus)*, composed of influential leaders of church
and the people, though his power was not limited by
this. His deeds were always governed by Christian
ethics, for he was no longer a pagan ruler but one
whose aim was to lead his people toward God; Stephen
outlined his principles in his "Admonitions" to his son,
Prince Imre:

"If you wish the honor of kingship, be peaceloving.
Rule over all without anger, pride or hatred, but with
love, tenderness, humanity. Remember always that
each one of us has the same standing: nothing exalts
a man but humility; nothing humiliates more than
haughtiness and hatred. . . . Peaceloving monarchs
rule, the rest only tyrannize. Be patient toward all, influential and destitute alike." Contemporary historians
testify that St. Stephen himself kept these rules. He
was merciful to defeated enemies, and provided a
haven for countless refugees from other lands. Among
these were the two exiled English Princes, Edward and
Edmund Ironside, who were given protection and a

home in Hungary. Edward, as the last descendant of
Alfred the Great, returned to England with his family
in 1057, as a pretender to the throne. According to
some historians, his wife was Agatha, the daughter of
St. Stephen, and Edward's daughter, St. Margaret of
Scotland, was thus allegedly the Hungarian King's
granddaughter.[1]

The new kingdom was capable of strong diplomatic
activity and successful military defence. Here, too,
Stephen pointed the way for his successors. His attention was not limited to the West, but was turned as
well to other Christian countries stretching eastward
from the Holy Roman Empire. With the dynasties of
these, particularly the Polish and Croatian, he maintained close family ties. His diplomacy embraced all
East-Central Europe, paving the way for closer relations between the peoples in the territory extending
from the Baltic south to the Adriatic.

With the untimely death of Otto III, an acute question arose over the relations between the nations of
East-Central Europe and the Empire. In the north,
Stephen's contemporary, Boleslav the Brave, laid the
foundations for the kingdom of Poland, but the Emperor succeeded in extending his feudal authority over
it. Bohemia was already a vassal state of Germany.
Emperor Conrad II had designs on Hungary, too, on
the grounds that Charlemagne had taken Pannonia
from the Avars at the end of the 7th century. He

[1]This much disputed theory is defended by A. Fest, The Sons of
Eadmund Ironside . . . at the court of Saint Stephen. Budapest 1938.

launched a campaign against them in 1030, only to be vanquished by the Hungarian army, which actually captured Vienna, and held it for a time.

King Stephen was the founder of a new principle of peaceful evolution, and his achievements have exerted a strong influence down to our day. During the forty-two years of his reign Hungary's position became stabilized. The fears of its western neighbors soon changed to admiration. Many a foreign chronicler saw the miraculous in King Stephen's actions, as if Providence had been behind them: "The Hungarians who but recently fought against Christendom and took thousands as prisoners, now treat Christians as their brethren."[1]

The trying times that followed Stephen's death proved best the strong foundation on which the Hungarian state had been built. All over contemporary Europe, royal authority was on the wane. In Bohemia, Poland, and the state of Kiev, authority did not remain unified in one King; but because the ruler in each case satisfied the claims of his nearest relatives with shares of the country, an aggregation of small principalities took the place of a unitary kingdom. This dangerously weakened the state, and, in the case of Poland, foreshadowed the loss of national independence. Since there was no established order of royal succession, similar difficulties arose in Hungary. According to the principle of seniority, the oldest male

[1]A. F. Gombos, Saint Etienne dans l'historiographie européenne du Moyen Age. Budapest 1938.

member of the dynasty succeeded to the throne. On the other hand, the kings wanted to assure the throne for their sons, preparing the way for primogeniture. The king during his lifetime often had to hand part of the country over to his brother and in a later period to his eldest son, who was called the "junior king". Though the German Emperors in the 11th century, and the Byzantine Emperors in the century following, attempted to capitalize on this state of affairs, Hungary's integrity and independence remained unshaken, unity and public morale becoming even stronger as a reaction to foreign intervention.

King Stephen I, whose son Imre died young, ignored his exiled pagan relatives and named his Italian nephew his successor. The short reign of Peter, son of Doge Orseolo of Venice, was attended by discontent among his subjects, and when he appealed to the Emperor for assistance, the dissidents recalled the exiled princes and placed one of them on the throne as Andrew I. Contrary to expectations, the latter did not approve the paganistic tendencies of some of his supporters, but followed in the steps of Stephen, working for Christianity. He was successful in repelling every German thrust, through the assistance of his younger brother Béla, one of the ablest strategists of his day. The latter succeeded Andrew, as Béla I (1060–1063), and utilized fully the advantages gained by the treaty of 1058, in which the German Emperor had to shelve all his feudal claims on Hungary. King Solomon (1063–1074), son of Andrew, followed next. He married the

Emperor's daughter, thus becoming a brother-in-law of the ambitious Henry IV.

This period exhibits the political tactics of the Hungarians, who used to all possible advantage the differences between the Empire and the papacy. The willingness of Hungary to follow the reform efforts directed by Rome had its political explanation. Pope Gregory VII had plans for the establishment of the Vatican as a world power. Henry IV of Germany was equally ambitious for himself. Hungary was divided into two factions. Solomon, as a dutiful kinsman, sided with the Emperor, while sons of the victorious King Béla, Géza and László, led the party that sympathized with the Pope. As these latter prevailed, Solomon was replaced by Géza I (1074–1077). Thus Hungary weathered the European crisis well and with added strength, a condition permitting her further expansion southwards.

The immediate results of all this were noticeable during the next two reigns. Kings László the Saint (1077–1095), and Kálmán "the Booklover" (1095–1119), consolidated peace and prosperity, and even ventured on further expansion. The Tirpimir dynasty of Croatia becoming extinct, the widowed queen invited her brother László, the Hungarian King, to incorporate Croatia into Hungary. László and his successor took care to preserve the autonomy of their new domain. For more than eight hundred years, up to the end of the First World War, Croatia, while under a royal representative called the Bán, enjoyed a separate constitutional freedom based on its own historical traditions.

King Kálmán extended his direct influence over the ports of the Adriatic, for which Venice competed down to the 15th century. Close political connections were also maintained with the Poles. The authority of the Hungarian state continued to grow, and the spiritual influence of the West became more pronounced, largely through the final establishment of Christianity. King Stephen, his son Prince Imre, and Bishop Gellért were canonized in 1083. King László founded a monastery for French monks at Somogyvár. The "Gesta Ungarorum", the nation's first historical treatise, lost in its original form, was written in Hungary at this time. László's three legal codes clarified certain issues relating to law and order, while Kálmán, with his up-to-date legal reforms embodied in some eighty-four articles, lessened the rigors of written law.

Besides the problems of the west, the defence of the eastern borders was a matter of no small concern. Nomadic peoples of Turkic organization—Cumanians and Petchenegs—urged in ever-renewed waves against the eastern bastions of the Christian Kingdom of Hungary. When they attacked the fortified border regions, they were met and defeated, then afterwards often accepted as settlers, converted to the Christian faith and taught the Western manner of life. King László was the great hero of these struggles with the pagan invaders. The "Illustrated Chronicle" describes one of his legendary engagements with the "Black Cumanians" thus:

"King László spoke to his knights: 'I will die with you rather than see these heathens carry off your wives and children into slavery'. Having thus spoken, he led the attack against the Cumanians. And God crushed these pagans before the Hungarians. Then the King called to his warriors. 'Let us not kill these people, but take them prisoner, and if they can be converted, let them live in peace with us.' " Many such colorful sagas prove the constant defence of the Faith undertaken by the Hungarians.

The middle of the 12th century was another trying period. King Stephen II (1116–1131), son of Kálmán and a Norman-French mother, Buzilla, was compelled to devote the greater part of his energies to adventurous campaigns. His brother, Béla II (1131–1141), married a Serbian Princess, thus strengthening Hungary's position in the Balkans. During his reign began the political penetration that later brought the northern part of this peninsula under feudal allegiance to the King of Hungary. These connections were continued when the two-year-old Géza II (1141–1162), was enthroned and the Palatine, Belos, exercised executive powers until Géza came of age.

During the turbulent decades in the middle of the 12th century, the political centre of gravity shifted from west to east. Emperor Frederick Barbarossa, however, never seriously threatened Hungary, even at the zenith of his power. The Kingdom of Hungary was considered a strong and wealthy one, and was so described by Cosmas, well-known contemporary Czech historian. An outstanding German historian of the period, Bishop Otto of Freising traversed Hungary with an army of crusaders in 1147, and was surprised at the great authority wielded by the Hungarian King. For to one coming from the West already infiltrated with the feudal system, this must have been a novelty. "The Hungarians"; wrote Bishop Otto, "obey their ruler to such an extent that they deem it a disloyalty even to whisper among themselves any criticism of his person . . . and should even the most powerful among the nobles offend him, the lowest servant of the court has power to place the offender under arrest, even if protected by his body guard." But the attention of the German historian was further arrested by the fact that the King never acted in an autocratic fashion, that he listened to the counsel of others, and that every important step was preceded by lengthy consultations. Nevertheless, Otto of Freising had little use for the Hungarians. He marvelled at the patience of God in permitting such a beautiful country, an earthly Paradise as he termed it, to be inhabited by such "ugly men, who speak such a savage language." Bishop Otto's antagonism must have been aroused in part by his brother's defeat when he attacked the Hungarians in the previous year.

The immediate problem of the time was unquestionably the conquering designs of Byzantium. Emperor Emanuel, on his mother's side a grandson of the Hungarian King László, dreamt of reestablishing the glory of Ancient Rome. He planned first to include Hungary in his domain, basing his claim on his relationship to the Árpád dynasty. During the second half of the 12th century, he launched no fewer than ten attacks in twenty-two years, and supported several pretenders against Stephen III (1162–1172). However, the danger of Byzantium's schemes for expansion proved to be but transitory. At the turn of the century, Hungary emerged stronger than ever before.

The reign of Béla III (1172–1196), saw the actual realization of the Árpád dynasty's efforts. Hungary was by that time the leading power in East-Central Europe, extending over all the Carpathian Basin. When Béla became engaged to Margaret Capet, daughter of Louis VII of France, his annual income, according to contemporary records, totaled 241,000 silver marks, an income equal to that of the kings of France or England. Political and economic stability fostered even deeper penetration of Christian culture and the maintenance of closer spiritual ties with the Western world. Foreign centers of learning, Paris for instance, were visited by a number of Hungarian scholars, who, upon returning to their homeland, were placed in key positions. The royal chancellery established by Béla III was conducted by Paris-educated priests. Lukács Bánfi who was Archbishop of Esztergom in 1158, and who played an important part politically, had been educated in Paris. He was a fellow student of Walter Mapes, the English scholar and satirist. The ·King's unnamed notary, known as "Master P." or "Anonymous", had likewise been educated in Paris. His History of the Hungarians,

"Gesta Ungarorum" describes in Latin the origin of the Magyars and their settlement in the Carpathian Basin. This work—one of the earliest histories of Hungary, is preserved to this day. Another link with the West was the establishment, on invitation, of the Cistercian and Premontreian monks. Hungary's culture in the Middle Ages, like that of the rest of civilized Europe, was predominantly Latin.

The Byzantine pressure had spent its force by the opening of the 13th century, during which the German Empire also lost most of its surplus energy for any Eastern undertaking. This situation resulted in the final elevation of the principality of Bohemia to the rank of a kingdom. Hungary, on the other hand, was tied down with internal problems, arising to a large extent from changes in the social structure. Although the King's authority still depended mainly on the great crown lands, these had been greatly reduced by generous grants to loyal subjects. The decrease in royal wealth brought with it a lessening of the King's influence. Imre (1196–1201), son of Béla III, went unarmed into the camp of some dissenters and none dared raise a hand against him; but his successor Andrew II (1205–1235), was in no position to check the growing influence of great land-owners, most of whom he himself had presented with more property, to no apparent good. As in other countries of contemporary Europe, another class emerged alongside the ever-greedy nobles. These were the smallholders, known as "the King's servants" (*servientes regis*), and destined later to form

the Commons. This class disapproved of the enlargement of already big estates, but welcomed the subdivi-
sion of crown lands whereby they themselves profited.
When central authority had thus been undermined,
parties with a thirst for power rose to leadership. General dissatisfaction with the government almost led to
an open uprising in 1222, to pacify which the King
issued his letter of rights known as the "Golden Bull"
(*Bulla Aurea*). Later jurists considered it one of the
fundamental pillars of Hungary's constitution, often
comparing it with the *Magna Charta* of England. Issued only seven years after its famous predecessor, the
Golden Bull of Andrew II refers to different social
circumstances, its closest resemblance to the English
document being in the limitations of royal rights and
prerogatives.[1] The Golden Bull eliminated many
governmental faults, and guaranteed the rights of the
smallholders. By narrowing the breach between the
upper and the middle classes, the *nobiles* and the *servientes,* the Golden Bull assured personal freedom and
other basic rights. The nobles were granted the privilege of resisting any illegal royal decree. From 1222
on, there was rapid development in the position of the
commoner class, one of its first practical signs being
the establishment of autonomous bodies of local government within the royal counties, which already at that

[1]According to some historians connections between the two countries at
that time explain this similarity. The Primate of Hungary was the guest
of Stephen Langton, drafter of the Magna Charta in 1220. Thomas,
Bishop of Eger, spent several months with some of the Barons of the
Magna Charta during the siege of Danietta, Egypt. I. Lukinich, A History
of Hungary, Budapest 1937. p. 63.

time had their elected judges. This was the beginning
of what was known for centuries as the *noble county,*
a self-governing institution playing an important part
in the national life of Hungary even as late as the
opening of the 19th century.

Owing to such social problems, the reign of Andrew
II appears less stable than the King's energetic efforts
merited. An example of the trying conditions under
which he had to exercise his duties was the expulsion
of the Teutonic Order of Knights (1125), who, fourteen years after their settlement in Transylvania,
threatened the central authority. The knights moved
from Transylvania to East Prussia and established an
independent political entity that grew to be a serious
rival to the Poles in the following century. It may be
mentioned that Andrew II led a Crusade to the Holy
Land in 1217, a Hungarian undertaking along the lines
of similar movements in Europe.

Andrew's son, Béla IV (1235–1270), was a studious
and straight-forward character. A conscientious, effective ruler, he first of all attempted to restore the
foundation of royal power, i.e., the crown estates. He
ordered an examination of royal grants, but before
this lengthy process could be completed, an onslaught
from the Tartars dealt Hungary her most serious blow
of the Middle Ages.

The designs of these Mongolians were first reported
by a Dominican monk, Father Julianus, who had been
sent to Asia in search of a tribe of Magyars separated
from the main body during their migrations three

hundred years before. The Cumanians, driven by the Tartars, also brought word of approaching danger, but only the King and his immediate advisers realized the gravity of this. Public opinion detested the immigration of the Cumanians who, though of Turkic race akin to the original Magyar settlers, were not so far advanced in Western ways. The country as a whole actually made only half-hearted efforts to stave off the threatening invasion.

The Tartars under Genghis Khan had built perhaps the greatest empire of any nomadic people. It stretched from China to the Carpathians. With their characteristically Turkic technique of attack, they destroyed the Little Russian state of Kiev, and then, in a mighty three-pronged advance, struck westward. Their northern wing penetrated Poland, their southern wing crushed southern Cumania, in present-day Rumania.

The Hungarians, bearing the brunt of the main Tartar attack, appealed for assistance in a last minute effort to stave off the inevitable, but in vain. On the plains of Muhi, between Budapest and Kassa, a desperate stand was attempted. The Hungarian forces, by now fully westernized and clad in heavy armour, were no more a match for the swift-riding, unending waves of Mongolians than were the armies of western countries against the pagan Magyars upon their entry into Europe. Since no assistance was forthcoming, and the Prince of Austria even capitalized on the plight of the Hungarian King by extorting ransom, Béla IV himself was obliged to take refuge on the shores of the

36    A HISTORY OF HUNGARY

Adriatic. The Mongolians wrought terrible havoc. Looting and burning the rich cities, during the winter they crossed the river into Transdanubia. An eye-witness, Father Rogerius, who lived through these terrible times in outlying forests, gives in his "Carmen Miserabile" a harrowing account of the wholesale murder and devastation committed by the Tartars, and the famine and pestilence that followed.

Owing to domestic trouble, the Tartar hordes withdrew after a year in Hungary. Some of the Mongols' other victims did not fare so well; Russia, for instance, suffered under their heel for a long time, and even the Grand Duchy of Moscow showed no signs of independence till late in the 14th century. Hungary, thanks to Béla's excellent leadership, soon recovered from its terrible experience. The country was literally rebuilt in a comparatively short time, and Béla IV deserves to be acknowledged as the second founder of his state. The first written document showing Hungary's solidarity with the civilized West of Europe bears the signature of Béla IV. It is in the form of a letter sent to Pope Innocent IV during the threat of a second Mongolian attempt at invasion in 1253. By urging a Crusade, not to the Holy Land, but to prevent another Tartar invasion, the Hungarian King pointed out to the Pope that the military preparedness of the Danube region was "all Europe's concern," as well as that of the Hungarians who fought alone, not getting any assistance, "except words".

The remaining years of the reign of Béla IV were

spent under the effects of the Mongolian invasion. As
it became evident that only fortified settlements were
able to offer resistance, the King shelved his radical
measures against the owners of large estates, encourag-
ing them rather to build fortresses, even though by this
he strengthened feudalism. Of importance were the
King's innovations in town development, and many a
Hungarian city dates back to Béla IV, who provided
them with self-government and privileges necessary
for their independent economy. His foreign policy likewise rested on the lessons of the immediate past; he
not only fostered his family connections with the Poles
and Ruthenes, forming a first line of defense against
a possible recurrence of the threat from Asia, but endeavored to draw Serbia and even Bulgaria into his
sphere of influence. This was to serve as the foundation of the defense-system against what later proved to
be a universal menace: the Mohammedan "holy war"
against all Christianity.

Béla IV, who by establishing connections with the
Neapolitan House of Anjou provided a future dynasty,
was the last outstanding monarch of the Árpád line.
His achievements reassert the main characteristic of
his predecessors: a determination to develop the country by raising it to Western standards, while assuring
peace for his people. His policy of settlement was likewise typical of the Árpád kings: he was able to settle
large groups of pagans, like the Cumanians, as well
as Christians from the West with equal success. The
policy of the Árpád dynasty is important in the light

of the medieval relations of Hungarians to other ethnic elements in the Carpathian Basin.

The elastic political organization of the Magyars in their nomadic stages made it easy for other peoples to join them. Later, the settled Hungarians upheld this tradition, thus making possible the peaceful cohabitation of other races. There was, however, a definite plan governing these non-Magyar settlements. Newcomers from the East, the Petchenegs for instance, were settled in the region bordering on Germany, where they manned the defence line wrought of natural and man-made fortifications known as "gyepük." Teutonic settlers were directed to the northern and eastern regions: from among these the "Saxon" settlements in Northern Hungary and Transylvania came into being. King St. Stephen's aforementioned "Admonitions" give a clue to his attitude toward newcomers, termed by him guests (*hospites*). "Assist them with good will, govern them with honor, that they may desire to stay with you rather than with others." This applied first of all to the knights from other countries, and while expressing a patient attitude toward migrant races, it does not mean that Stephen intended to establish what may be termed a "nationality state."

The Hungarians lived in the centrally located, level or moderately undulating, densely populated part of the Carpathian Basin, while the peripheries were occupied partly by other races. There were Slovaks in the mountainous northern region. Side by side with them, in the parallel north-and-south valleys, lived the

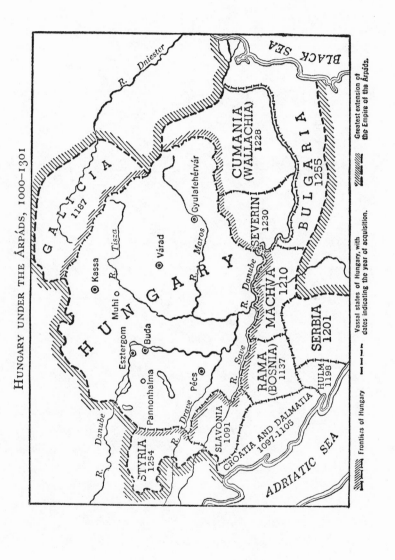

HUNGARY UNDER THE ÁRPÁDS, 1000–1301

R. Dniester

BLACK SEA

GALICIA
1187

CUMANIA
(WALLACHIA)
1228

BULGARIA
1255

SEVERIN
1230

Gyulafehérvár

R. Tisza

R. Maros

● Kassa

R. Danube

● Várad

HUNGARY

Muhi

Esztergom
● Buda

MACHVA
1210

SERBIA
1201

R. Danube

R. Save

RAMA
(BOSNIA)
1137

HULM
1198

Pannonhalma

Pécs ●

R. Drave

SLAVONIA
1091

R. Save

STYRIA
1254

R. Danube

CROATIA AND DALMATIA
1097–1105

ADRIATIC SEA

|||||| Frontiers of Hungary

– – – Vassal states of Hungary, with dates indicating the year of acquisition.

▨▨▨ Greatest extension of the Empire of the Árpáds.

Hungarian farmers. The *Drang nach Osten,* that eastward surge of Germanic peoples, touched Hungary too
in the latter part of the 12th century. This episode, one
of the most momentous in the medieval history of Germany, brought about partly by social, partly by political
causes, pushed the German language-line on the north
across originally Slavic territory from the Elbe River,
as far east as Silesia and Posen, to the very Baltic. The
German influx touched Hungary comparatively less. A
large group settled in the north on the slopes of the
Tátra Mountains, establishing such flourishing towns
as Késmárk, Lőcse, etc. Another, large group, found
a home in south-eastern Transylvania. These so-called
Saxons, hailing from Flanders, and the Rhine and
Moselle valleys, were granted rights by Andrew II in
1224, to establish their own autonomous administration as a unified political body called *"communitas."*
Due to these privileges, they have been able to preserve
to this day their original nationality and institutions.
Their autonomy was never in danger from royal authority, but rather from their own social development.
At times their leading families attempted to join the
Hungarian nobility. They wanted to convert the common holdings and the different Saxon settlements under their guidance, into private properties. But the
communal body persistently opposed all efforts to dislodge them from their privileges, safeguarded by royal
charter. The northern Saxon settlers, however, were
more scattered, and did not make full use of the rights
to exclusiveness granted them in 1271; this accounts

for the "Zipser" Germans of Szepes county who intermarried with the Hungarian nobility, playing an important rôle in the cultural and governmental life of
the country. It must be emphasized that immigrants
from the West were not always of Teutonic stock. Records show that many of the oldest inhabitants of the
earliest Hungarian cities, such as Székesfehérvár, the
original capital, and Buda, were French, especially
Walloons, and Italians. Rogerius gives a vivid account
of how these French town-dwellers fought shoulder
to shoulder with the Hungarians against the Mongols
when they attacked Esztergom in 1241.

In the southeastern mountainous portion of the Carpathian Basin, in Transylvania, the Hungarians and
in parts the Saxons, had already laid the foundations
of civilization amid the endless forest when the
first groups of Rumanians, then called Wallachians
(*Valachi*), appeared. These Rumanians were herdsmen, tending their sheep as they crossed the mountain
ranges. This made their infiltration difficult to control.
Their migration across the Balkans, from what is now
Albania, lasted several centuries. First they reached
the lowlands of the Lower Danube, the Rumanian
plain of today, where the Cumanians dwelt; then groups
of Rumanians drifted northward across the Transylvanian Alps where they found security and more
settled conditions.[1]

The presence of Rumanians in Transylvania is men-

[1]Louis Tamás, Romans et Roumains dans l'histoire de la Dacie Traiane. Budapest 1936.

tioned for the first time in 1210, in a document issued a number of years later. Traces of their more or less permanent hamlets and villages may be found only since the beginning of the 14th century. Though it was quite a task to extend the royal administration over these shepherds, the organizing of their settlements constituted a part of the royal program. Crown estates were designated for their systematic resettlement. Andrew III decreed in 1293 that "all Wallachians, whether to be found on noblemen's estates or on others' estates", should be settled on his own estate known as *Székes,* the territory of which is estimated between 45,000 and 65,000 acres. At that time then, Rumanians comprised but a small percentage of Transylvania's population.

Immigration continued in the following centuries, speeded up both by the Ottoman pressure and by a series of social calamities in Wallachia. After the 14th century, Rumanians settled not only on Hungarian crown lands, but also on private estates, where they established new settlements under leaders known as *Kenézek.*

The Hungarian peasant paid one-tenth, *tized,* of his crop in taxes; the Rumanians, living a more primitive life, were obliged to pay only one fiftieth of theirs. The *Kenézek* endeavored to enter the ranks of Hungarian nobility and to extend their influence as squires over the lower classes of their own people. The Rumanians never possessed that marked unity and political consciousness that characterized the Saxons, and thus they

were not in a position to withstand the enticement of
social development.

Social development also exerted a strong influence on
the ethnic elements coming from the East. The Cumanians, for instance, who arrived in the 13th century,
were settled in the Tisza Valley, on the great plains
of Hungary, between the Danube and the Tisza. In
1279, they were converted to Christianity and granted
a certain measure of autonomy. But soon their leaders
intermarried with the nobility, and their rank and
file with the Magyar peasantry, so that in a few centuries they were one.

At the end of the 13th century, nevertheless, the
presence of this pagan tribe caused difficulties, especially after Stephen V (1270–1272), when László
IV, the son of a Cumanian mother, ascended the throne.
During his short reign, the private power of the
feudal lords was in full swing, and a great part of the
lesser nobility was in their service. The King's authority could not compete with their influence and
party rivalries. The domestic crisis that developed
at this time continued for three decades until the Anjou
kings found a solution to it. It only made matters
worse that László, to escape from the responsibilities
of state, spent most of his time among the Cumanians,
claiming himself to be a descendant of Attila: he even
directed the historian Simon Kézai to rewrite his chronicles accordingly. The King did not possess enough
energy to restore political and social unity. His most
memorable action in the international field was the

decisive victory that he, in alliance with Rudolph Habsburg, won in 1278, over Ottakar II of Bohemia, who had aspired to conquer northern Hungary. This Czech king had made his political influence felt from Brandenburg to Austria. According to German historians, the reign of Ottakar II was of such a German character that his victory would have made possible the complete Germanization of Bohemia itself. Hungary's King László rose to the occasion and prevented Ottakar's aspirations by concluding an alliance with Rudolph of Habsburg; by this Hungary assisted in establishing the hegemony of the Habsburg dynasty in later centuries.

The death of László IV left but one male survivor of the Árpáds. Andrew III (1290–1301), grandson of Andrew II, who was born in Venice of an exiled branch, was the last of the national dynasty. As his Palatine wrote, "He was the last golden branch of St. Stephen's family tree. After his death the inhabitants of the country wondered with sorrowing hearts how they could find another ruler of the first king's blood."

The preceding pages have given only a short synopsis of the political and cultural achievements wrought during three centuries by the gifted Árpád dynasty. Through insight, and by systematic effort, this royal family brought about the consolidation of Hungary, determining its spiritual and political trend and its rôle in European history. Indeed, whatever happened in Hungary afterwards was built on the foundations laid by the Árpáds, who found a place for their nomadic people within the framework of a European state.

# III

## HUNGARY UNDER THE ANJOUS

*Hunyadi and the First Struggles with the Turks*
*(1301–1458)*

For years after the extinction of the House of Árpád
there was no power to break the influence of the feudal
lords or to force them to accept a central authority.
These so-called "little kings" built up their own territorial power in different parts of the country. Had
this state of affairs continued, Hungary, like Germany,
would have been broken up into small principalities,
a phenomenon not uncommon in Medieval Europe.

The feudal lords argued between themselves as to
whom to place on the throne of Hungary, favoring
now the Bavarian, now the Czech prince. The contender
with the best chances was the Pope's nominee, Charles
Robert of Naples, a scion of the House of Anjou, and
related to the Árpáds on the distaff side. He was from
the beginning championed by the lords of southern
Hungary and so was enabled to strengthen his position
in a comparatively short time. "The Hungarians would

not consent", states a contemporary document, "that the Vatican should provide a king for their country", but they were willing that the Pope's representative, Cardinal Gentile, should "confirm in the name of the Church one whom they elected according to their age-old custom".[1]

Charles Robert, despite his French ancestry, was the founder of the second national dynasty of Hungary. Charles, King of Naples, was his father; his mother was the sister of László IV of Hungary. The Hungarians themselves never felt him to be foreign, though with him the Western European conceptions were to become dominant, transforming, in an evolutionary way, antiquated institutions in accordance with the requirements of feudalism. Two members of the Anjou family rank among the greatest of Hungary's kings. There were Charles Robert (1307–1342), and his son, Louis the Great (1342–1382). Under them, Hungary became a great European power.

The 14th century was a flourishing age in East-Central Europe. The three major kingdoms of this region, namely, Hungary, Poland, and Bohemia, showed parallel though characteristic progress in the development of their national energies. An English historian has noted that French influence predominated in this century as against the German penetration of the preceding one: "Under their three dynasties, they developed not only feudal monarchies on the Western pattern,

[1] Papers relating to the Cardinal's mission are published in the *Monumenta Vaticana II*.

but national institutions and national cultures. . . .
They not only borrowed; they created; and their native
inheritances continued to differentiate their history
from that of the true West. None the less, their links
with the West grew closer and closer".[1]

Bohemia remained in the bondage of the German
Empire, but the Bohemian kings of the House of
Luxemburg, also of French origin, benefited by the
feud between the Habsburg and Wittelsbach dynasties,
and even won the title of Emperor for themselves.

In Poland Wladislas Lokietek, the organizer of national forces against the Teutonic Order of Knights,
was elevated to the throne through Hungarian assistance. The political successes of his son, Casimir the
Great (1333–1370), the last of the Piasts, were due in
part to Hungarian co-operation.

Hungary was not only completely independent but
had made its influence felt far into the Balkan peninsula. Organizing and directing the political as well as
the economic forces in that region, it spread its influence far beyond its borders and became a power to
be reckoned with throughout all East-Central Europe.
The diplomacy of the Anjous, following the path
marked out by the Árpáds, gained and even surpassed
their aims. Contemporary public opinion was expressed
in a document of 1330: "Among surrounding countries,
Hungary has become the queen". That is, Hungary
became the leading state, the *archi-regnum* of this

[1]C. W. Prévité-Orton in his "History of Europe, 1198–1378" (Methuen's *History of Medieval and Modern Europe,* Vol. III, 1937) pp. 402–403.

region, as she was termed by contemporary documents. At the time Charles Robert was crowned, there were still a dozen or so "little kings" in control of state affairs. It took years of effort and several major campaigns (e.g. 1312, 1317) to re-establish the central authority and to replace disloyal lords with more trustworthy ones. In this, Charles Robert followed the example of Béla IV, although he did not demand the return of the crown lands in their entirety. Thus the old order gave way to the new, for authority could no longer rest on immense crown estates. The aristocracy were given the task of keeping militias of their own, known as *banderia*, to be led into war under their own banners. The king and queen had their own troops besides, and the nobility of lesser means joined the royal forces individually but under the leadership of their respective county governors. Thus a new military system, satisfying the standards of medieval Europe yet based on Hungarian traditions, came into being and persisted for a long time to come.

Simultaneously, elaborate economic and financial reforms were carried out in 1323. The state treasury was made altogether independent of the large estates. The ancient crown lands and original counties provided only for the maintenance of royal forts. In the following period, the county was primarily a term for autonomous local body, headed by a sheriff (*főispán*) appointed by the king. The chief revenues of the crown at this time were the so-called *regalia*, i.e. customs, duties, direct taxes, monopoly on precious metals, etc.

Hungary enjoyed a unique monetary status under the Anjous. Formerly the rulers of Europe usually withdrew their silver coins each year, issuing others of inferior silver content. This *lucrum camerae* (profit of the treasury) was a source of continual uncertainty. Florence was the first city-state to shift to a gold standard. At the end of the 13th century its gold florins of unchanging value heralded a new era in the history of finance. Demeter Nekcsei, Charles Robert's economic expert and *magister tavernicorum*,[1] had the first Hungarian gold florins minted in 1325, and these were soon much in demand as currency even in foreign lands. Financial co-operation with neighboring countries, notably Bohemia, resulted in advantages to both countries, as Bohemia's silver production and Hungary's gold mining complemented each other. Up to 1338, Hungary experimented both with silver and with gold currencies; but then finally decided on gold as its standard.

The economic importance and financial security of medieval Hungary were greatly dependent on its vast resources in precious metals. The significance of this may be better appreciated if it is pointed out that at that time Hungary was the chief gold producer in Europe, supplying one-third of the whole gold of the then known world. The individual production of other European states was barely one fifth that of Hungary. In fact, the annual gold production of Hungary, some

---

[1] *Magister tavernicorum*, after the 13th century the outstanding financial authority, a state treasurer or minister of finance.

2,200 to 3,500 pounds, was unparalleled until the discovery of America, a factor in world history the significance of which cannot be overstated.

In conjunction with the financial reform, reorganization of gold and silver mining was likewise effected. Basing them on a new system of monopoly, Charles Robert established ten chambers of exchange, and nowhere else were precious metals permitted to be sold. This meant that from 35 to 40 per cent of the mined gold, silver etc., flowed into the royal treasury as revenue. The development in mining brought to towns in Upper Hungary and in Transylvania a permanent boom that reacted favorably upon industry and commerce. Commercial connections with other countries brought tangible results, primarily through the agreement concluded in 1335 by Charles Robert with Poland and Bohemia at the Congress of Visegrád, according to which commerce in transit was to be conducted directly, avoiding Vienna; thereby Hungary came into direct contact with a number of foreign centers of commerce.

This active and practical economic policy supported the diplomacy of the Anjous, whose full treasury was a safe foundation to rely upon. According to estimates based on contemporary documents, there were more than 21,000 villages, over 500 towns (*mezővárosok*) and 49 cities in Hungary at the end of the 14th century. The population numbered some 3,000,000 souls, not counting those of neighboring principalities connected with Hungary by feudal ties.

The kings of the Árpád dynasty had been the first to launch a diplomatic offensive for the co-operation of all Christian peoples of East-Central Europe. The Anjous followed the same foreign policy and successfully brought about the co-operation of most of the East-Central European or Carpathian nations. King Charles Robert, whose first wife was a Czech and whose second was a Polish princess, attempted in 1330 to smooth out the bitter Czech-Polish antagonism. Though Hungary had nothing to gain by this war, Charles Robert gave assistance to Poland on which the Czech King had made exaggerated claims. Then, having acquired the throne of Naples for his younger son Andrew, thus renewing Italian ties, he was able to arrange an armistice between Bohemia and Poland in 1335. In the autumn of the same year, the Bohemian and Polish kings were the guests of Charles Robert at his palace in Visegrád. Besides economic understandings, an agreement was reached for a common diplomatic front in many important matters relating to the future of East-Central Europe. This co-operation proved to be of great value; for a number of joint Polish-Hungarian military campaigns were launched in the east against Pagan invaders. This defensive system was further extended by virtue of an agreement reached in 1339 by which the Hungarian king, upon the death of Casimir of Poland, was to become the ruler of Poland. Such a personal union between the two countries actually came into being in 1370 when Louis the Great of Hungary became also King of Poland

Louis continued on the path laid out by his father, his ideal being King St. László, legendary figure of the struggles with the pagans. Louis was among the last of the great knight-kings, his contemporaries noting that "there was no other known to be as kind and noble, moral and lofty-spirited, friendly and straightforward". Even his Balkan policy, though along traditional lines, was woven through with religious motives, the desire for spreading Christianity, and converting heretics and schismatics.

A belt of feudal principalities on the South and Southeast protectively surrounded Hungary in those times. Charles Robert had endeavored to obtain the support of some of the former domains of Hungary, and tried to regain others lost during difficult periods. This defense system was of the utmost military importance during the coming centuries of Turkish conflict, and it served also as a balance among the principalities of the Balkan peninsula. Under the Árpáds the influence of the Byzantine Empire had counterbalanced that of Hungary on the Balkans; by the 14th century that situation underwent some changes, for the power of Byzantium was threatened by Turkey, and Hungary set no limitation to the evolution of the different Balkan principalities. The time for this, however, was not favorable for long; for Turkey soon put an end to all individual aspirations on the peninsula. Thus Tsar Stephen Dushan of Serbia (1332–1355), son of Stephen Uros and a Magyar mother, succeeded in organizing a strong state, only to have the Turks ruin it by the end of the century.

Hungary was able to retain the principalities (*bánságok*) of So and Ozora on her southern border, and that of Machva in northern Serbia, also relying much on friendly relations with Bosnia whose governor (*bán*) Kotromanić was related to the Hungarian king. It was also in the 14th century that the foundations of the two Rumanian principalities were laid under direct Hungarian influence. One of these, Wallachia, south of the Carpathians, was organized by Basaraba, a prince of Cumanian origin, after whom Bessarabia was named.[1] A number of Hungarian settlements, like Hosszumező, now Campolung, were signs of Hungary's ethnic expansion. Contemporaries called this territory Ungro-Vlachia, the westward portion of which was directly under the jurisdiction of Hungary. The son of Basaraba acknowledged his feudal dependence on the Hungarian king. East of Transylvania, where another Rumanian principality was in the making, Hungarian influence also made itself strongly felt. At the head of this principality, which later formed another nucleus of Rumania, Louis the Great placed the "voivod" Drágos.

Thus, beginning with Croatia on the south-west, and extending as far as Moldavia on the east, all peoples

[1]According to recent researches a large portion of the leading class of the Rumanian people was of foreign (Cumanian, Turkic, etc.) origin. The name "Rumun" (Rumanian) meant, until the 17th century, the serfs only and not the entire people. This shows that at the time when feudalism was introduced the leading class was still conscious of its non-Rumanian origin. Cf. L. Elekes' article in *Századok*, 1941.

EAST CENTRAL EUROPE IN THE XIVth CENTURY

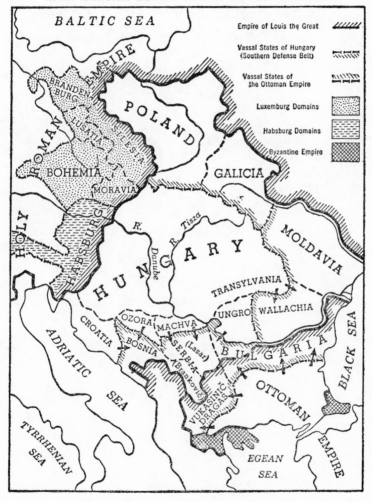

Empire of Louis the Great

Vassal States of Hungary
(Southern Defense Belt)

Vassal States of
the Ottoman Empire

Luxemburg Domains

Habsburg Domains

Byzantine Empire

BALTIC SEA

EMPIRE

BRANDEN-
BURG

LUSATIA

SILESIA

POLAND

BOHEMIA

MORAVIA

HABSBURG

HOLY ROMAN

GALICIA

MOLDAVIA

H U N G A R Y

R. Danube

R. Tisza

TRANSYLVANIA

UNGRO WALLACHIA

CROATIA

OZORA MACHVA

BOSNIA

SERBIA

(Lasar)

Brankovič

VUKASINC
DRAGAS

B U L G A R I A

OTTOMAN

BLACK SEA

EMPIRE

ADRIATIC SEA

TYRRHENIAN SEA

EGEAN SEA

of the northern Balkans belonged to this outer protective belt. To make this defense system complete against any possible attack from the rear, it was deemed necessary to thrust Venetian influence back from Dalmatia's shores to the other side of the Adriatic. Partly for this purpose, Louis the Great established an admiralty with some naval forces, and his successors maintained it until 1420. Bulgaria's western portion also became a province of Hungary.

As Louis was made King of Poland in 1370, and as he was able to bring about a co-operation of East-Central European and Balkan factors, his influence in Europe was considerable. True, Poland was tied to Hungary only through comparatively brief personal union; but the defensive system in the Balkans was not based merely on previous political traditions; it was the only possible alignment that could save the independence of these smaller nations from Turkish aggression. The reign of Louis the Great gave to these feudal units such security and peace that they long recalled his rule in the troubled years to come. A contemporary historian, John Küküllei (?–1396), wrote an entire chapter entitled, "The Calm and Peace of King Louis' Days".[1] He reveals that Louis, a true follower of God, was neither autocratic nor passionate in his rule, but was always the guardian of justice, *custos iusticiae,* himself taking pains not to attain anything by unlawful means. "He left his country and subject peoples intact in their respective liberties and customs, governing

[1]Thuróczy, "Chronica Hungariae" pars. III.

each with its own laws", and heroically defending them against enemies. The wise, practical policies of the Anjous guaranteed Hungary's hegemony by grouping some of the neighboring small peoples, without endangering their liberties and autonomous rights, into a protective system assuring common defense. This arrangement corresponded to the needs and conditions prevailing in the 14th century.

One single tragic episode marred the grand scale of this active diplomacy embracing all East-Central Europe. To avenge the murder of his brother Andrew, heir to the throne of Naples, Louis the Great led two victorious campaigns into Italy. While these were thought necessary to demonstrate Hungary's military and political preparedness, they necessitated expenditures that could better have been used at home. The campaigns had to be prepared for, diplomatically, as far afield as the British Isles and their cost was so great that the gold spent in Italy by the Hungarian army at once wiped out the contemporary gold crisis in all Europe! Had all this wealth been spent in East-Central Europe, the security of Hungary could have been protected for a much longer period. Yet at the time of the campaigns, the question of prestige was also important, both from a Balkan and from a domestic point of view. In the latter field, it prompted the King to reward the nobles who took part in his campaign, by reissuing the Golden Bull (1351), and even extending their privileges by the addition of *aviticitas*, i.e. the right of their relatives to inherit feudal holdings.

The four decades of Louis' reign were marked by a growth of political power and by the flourishing of arts and sciences. The high level of writing may be seen in the Illustrated Chronicle of Mark Káltai. The founding of a university at Pécs, in 1367, bore witness to the cultural trend of the times. Western centers of learning were frequented by large numbers of Hungarian students. One of the most impressive art relics of this period is the equestrian statue of St. George by the brothers Kolozsvári (1373). Such peaceful developments could be guaranteed only by a ruler about whom John de Cardailhac, patriarch of Alexandria and envoy of the Vatican wrote: "I call God to witness that I never saw a monarch more majestic and more powerful . . . or one who desires peace and calm as much as he".

This peace was threatened during the last years of his reign. The expanding Turkish power, driven by imperialistic aims and religious fanaticism, soon drew Louis' attention away from Poland. By the next century the Turkish problem had become the concern of all Christian Europe and the greatest possible menace to the Carpathian region. Coming from Asia Minor from the middle of the 14th century on, the military might of the Osmanli Turks systematically drove further and further into the Continent. In time, the feudal provinces of Hungary in the Balkans, because of their geographic position, began to feel the tremendous pressure. It is not surprising that the Bosnian, Serbian, Bulgarian and Rumanian border states shifted allegiance

56 A HISTORY OF HUNGARY

according to the balance of power. They knew that
only Hungary was able to defend them against the
powerful enemy, but in order to avoid continuous
Turkish raiding, they nominally accepted the over-
lordship of the Ottomans. Of course, the tremendous
and forceful penetration of the Turks could not be
estimated ahead of time by King Louis. Under him, the
Magyar armies fought off the Turks deep in Southern
Bulgaria, stopping their advance for ten years by a victorious campaign in 1377.

Unfortunately, like most of Hungary's great
monarchs, Louis died without a male heir. In fulfilment
of his wishes, his eldest daughter, Maria, inherited the
throne (1382–1395). The younger, Hedvig, was elected
queen of Poland as Jadviga (1384) and her marriage
with Prince Jagiello of Lithuania brought about the
union of this pagan principality with Poland. Thus
western ideals, both political and religious, penetrated
still further to the north-east. But the situation in Hungary was far from satisfactory. Lacking a strong hand to
master them, three major parties fought bitterly for political control, thus undermining the country's prestige
in the Balkans. The widowed queen mother Elisabeth,
together with the followers of the Palatine Garai,
wished to acquire a French prince as Maria's consort.
The nobles of the southern provinces again championed the Anjous, favoring their only male member
of age, Charles III King of Naples. When the latter
became the victim of an assassin the nominee of the
third party, Sigismund of Luxembourg, won the hand

Equestrian Statue of St. George

*by Martin and George Kolozsvári (14th Century)*

of Maria and with it the throne. In the diet of 1386, old followers and knights of King Louis the Great attempted to iron out party differences amicably. The government of Lackfi entered into a "league" with the new monarch, according to which Sigismund was to rule constitutionally, respecting the rights and freedom of his subjects. Otherwise they might rightfully rise against him, as set forth in the Golden Bull. Sigismund (1387–1437) was crowned the following year.

The most pressing problem of the time was the Turk's penetration into the Balkans. The Serbians suffered utter defeat at Kossovo in the spring of 1389; "Czar" Lazar himself perished and his son, vowing allegiance to the Sultan, presently fought against the Hungarians. It was at this time that the Turkish forces reached the boundaries of Hungary proper. Sigismund not only prepared his own army for defence, but also lined up Moldavia, Ungro-Vlachia, and Bosnia again, and was ready for an attack. In the spirit of the Crusades, the campaign against the Moslem invader reached international proportions. Far-away England sent ten thousand warriors under the command of Prince Henry of Lancaster, cousin of Richard II. France rallied no less than fifteen thousand troops led by John, Count of Nevers, cousin of the French monarch. There were numerous others of different nationalities, yet the bulk of the Christian forces was composed of Magyars.

At the fortress of Nicopolis, in western Bulgaria, then a vassal principality of the King of Hungary, the

Christian army met Sultan Bayazid's force. The decisive battle was fought on September 26, 1396, with the final victory for the Osmanlis who outnumbered the Christians two to one. Sigismund had wanted to make the attack with his Hungarian forces alone, because of their former experience with Turkish tactics, but the French demanded the honor and were utterly destroyed in a heroic attack. In spite of this, the Christian army was near victory in the second half of the battle, when the arrival of Serb reinforcements for the Turks turned the tide in favor of the latter. The catastrophe resulting from the lack of a unified battle plan made its depressing influence felt all over Europe, and forced Hungary to act on the defensive from then on.

Even in domestic relations there were consequences to be faced. Many of the lords, especially the knights of Louis the Great, were critical of Sigismund, pointing out that his personal characteristics were inferior to those of his predecessor. Although they were all with him in his campaign against the Turk, they disliked his favoritism and his extravagance. When, after the Nicopolis rout, he neglected the country's defence and turned to his personal affairs in the West, the dissatisfied Hungarian leaders had him detained in the Fort of Visegrád. In 1401, Sigismund again took over the reign and, though with some unlawful acts he again provoked dissatisfaction, he was finally successful in consolidating his power. He founded a society of knights, the Order of the Dragon, to fight Turkish invasion and serve as his own political machine upon which he could rely. Eventually this Order's influence became so great that not even the king could disregard it with impunity.

Sigismund's rule differed from that of the Árpáds and the Anjous in many respects, among them in his foreign policy. As the diagonal Hungaro-Polish conception, based on East-Central European policy, Sigismund's interests lay chiefly in a horizontal Central European direction, facing toward the German Empire. He concluded an agreement as to succession with the Habsburgs, and used the economic and military resources of Hungary to become emperor himself, thus uniting in his own person the rule of Hungary, Bohemia, and the German Empire. This political achievement placed Hungary in an entirely different position from that of later centuries; for Sigismund's power depended primarily on Hungary, and the Hungarian leaders played an important part in the international game of their monarch.

An outstanding issue of the day was the religious rift that arose out of the Council of Constance (1414), which deposed three popes and finally selected a fourth. Although the successful solution of this question was beneficial to Sigismund's prestige, (he concluded a pact with the King of England in Canterbury), the burning at Constance of John Huss, a disciple of Wycliffe and an outstanding figure in Czech religious and national history, roused the Czechs against Sigismund. The war which resulted dragged out for years owing to the Czech Ziska's new stratagems of war and his novel "wagon fortress"; Sigismund finally occupied Prague in 1436. Because of all these problems he did not use Hungary's political, economic and military resources primarily in the interests of Hungary, that is to say to launch an effective offensive against the Turk, but rather to help strengthen his position in Central Europe. Accordingly, the task of coping with the Turkish problem suffered a delay. The Tatar leader, Tamerlane, defeated the Sultan's forces in Asia (1402), and this situation could well have been utilized to advantage; but as Sigismund's ambitions lay in the West, he neglected the possibilities to consolidate his hold on the Balkans.

Sigismund's reign of five decades represents an era that brought many new elements into Hungary's life, preparing the way for the coming Renaissance. Even his mentality and character were a blend of the old and the new. Perhaps this accounted for his somewhat erratic, everchanging personality, so different from that of Louis the Great. The Czechs considered him a Hungarian, the Hungarians regarded him as a Czech, while he himself had no greater ambition than to become German Emperor. At the same time Sigismund knew that Hungary was his real support, giving testimony of this in 1429 in his angry words to the German Princes, "Though you may elect another as your Emperor, Hungary will suffice me, there is enough bread there while I live".

The first Habsburg on the Hungarian throne was Albert, Prince of Austria (1437–1439) who ruled much

in Sigismund's tradition. He died during preparations
for a thrust against the Turks. The latter had by this
time subjugated all Hungary's feudal territories to the
south, reaching the line of the Danube and the Save
rivers and threatening Nándorfehérvár (the present-
day Belgrade), strongest of all fortresses in the Hungarian defence system. The military situation needed a
strong ruler and thus Wladislas, King of Poland, was
invited, in spite of the fact that King Albert's widow
did not surrender the rights of Albert's posthumous son
László, later László V. Since a Polish-Hungarian union
was traditional, the alliance of the two nations against
the common danger was an obvious course to take.
Wladislas (1440–1444) undertook his duties with great
zeal, embracing the defence of Christianity, an ideal
generally accepted in Hungary by that time. According
to his royal declaration, "the boundaries both of Hungary and Poland touch those of barbaric peoples, and
thus these countries are bound to be the bulwark and
shield of the Faith, to the glory of God".

The outstanding, universally acknowledged hero of
this age was unquestionably John Hunyadi. According
to one version he was the son of Vajk, a Vlach *kenéz* in
south-eastern Hungary. The other version is that he
was the common-law son of Sigismund himself, his
mother later marrying Vajk. The large royal grants
seem to strengthen the latter version. Hunyadi received
a knight's education, at first in the courts of various
nobles, then at the royal court. By 1441, he was the
ruler of Transylvania, the richest man in the country

and holder of the largest estate, (some four million acres). Yet Hunyadi never used his unequalled position for personal ends. His chief aim was rather the military protection of the Christian world. One of the most brilliant strategists of all time, Hunyadi pursued an active defensive policy whereby he was able to keep the enemy beyond Hungary's borders. His victorious campaigns stopped the Ottoman advance on the threshold of East-Central Europe for another eighty years. His words show that he recognized the life-and-death character of the struggle against the Turk: "We can either free Europe from the cruel Turk's invasion, or we can fall for Christianity, earning a crown of martyrdom".

In 1443, Hunyadi succeeded in launching a successful attack on the enemy, followed, in the next year, by an extensive campaign as far as Bulgaria, restoring the rule of Prince Brankovic of Serbia. In view of such successes, the King was urged by the Papacy to continue the offensive. Young Wladislas, though he had already agreed to the terms for peace asked by the Turk, himself led, in the fall of 1444, the Christian forces into Bulgaria. Outnumbered five to one, the Hungarian army under Hunyadi still had good hopes for victory at the Battle of Varna, but the king with youthful impetuosity charged the enemy at the head of five hundred Hungarians and Polish cavalry, thereby losing his life on the battlefield and sealing the fate of the whole campaign.

It was only through the unusual ability and prestige

of Hunyadi that the disaster of Varna, "a second Nicopolis", did not upset the inner equilibrium of Hungary. On behalf of little László V (1445–1457), first seven royal commissioners, and then, following a decision of the Diet of 1446, John Hunyadi, Regent or governor-general, exercised administrative powers. Four centuries later Louis Kossuth was the second to hold this office, becoming Hungary's governor-general in 1849. Hunyadi never gave up the idea of active defense, chiefly for the reason that the Balkan peoples wavered, according to the balance of power, between a Christian and a Moslem allegiance; and so Hungary made efforts to hold these principalities within the orbit of the old protective system.

Preparations for a decisive showdown were pushed ahead feverishly by Hunyadi. Bishop John Vitéz well-known Hungarian humanist, admonished the young king: "Prove that you have the strength to accomplish the mission of the kings of the old and the famous Hungarian nation". The Turkish capture of Constantinople in 1453 shocked all Europe. Pope Nicholas V urged a crusade, entrusting its organization to Hungary, which more and more felt the necessity of outside assistance. The chancellor of the German Emperor wrote in 1444, "Hungary indeed is powerful and can boast of a strong army; but for the expulsion of the Turk from the continent a much stronger one is required". The era of the Crusades had gone, however, and Hungary realized that she had to carry the burden of defence alone. This is mirrored in Hunyadi's letter

written to the Pope: "We are in the sixtieth year of
the struggle against the Turk. And until now, only
one people has turned its arms against the enemy. We
only, left alone, have endured the fury of the battle."

The self-assured Sultan finally launched an attack
against the most important Hungarian outpost, the
fortress of Nándorfehérvár (Belgrade). The Turkish
army was supported by the fearful artillery that had
played a decisive part in the conquest of Constantinople. Anxiety gripped Europe as this mighty Asiatic
force approached, threatening the very threshold of
Christian civilization. The Pope ordered prayers in
every Christian land, the tolling of bells at noon re-
minding Christians to this day of the gravity of the
danger. A Franciscan monk, John Capistrano, hastily
organized some forces for a Crusade, and all of Europe
breathed a sigh of relief when Hunyadi, relying mainly
on his own troops, won one of his most brilliant victories, crushing the enemy's superior might.

General rejoicing was followed by a series of tragedies. First of all came the pestilence, that took as toll
Hunyadi and Capistrano. Then the eighteen-year-old
King, listening to the advice of the late Hunyadi's enemies, had the latter's elder son, László, executed. On
top of everything, the King went to Bohemia, where
he soon died. Thus the Hungarians turned to Matthias,
a younger son of Hunyadi, expecting him to continue
the tradition of national kings.

# IV

## THE RENAISSANCE POWER
## AND ITS DECLINE

### (*1458–1526*)

The great national states of the New Age became unified only from the 15th century on, under the guidance of absolutist national monarchs. By putting an end to the autonomy of feudal territories, these monarchs created unified states with a uniform economic system and a centralized administration. Thus Louis XI commenced, after 1461, the unification of an almost disintegrated France; Ferdinand II achieved like results in Spain; while in England, following the Wars of the Roses, the reign of Henry VII (1485–1509) was an introduction to the absolutism of Henry VIII. Similar phenomena were appearing all over Europe at the close of the 15th century. This evolution did not terminate with these almost simultaneously-appearing rulers but continued for generations after. These monarchs built up an efficient bureaucracy, entrusted the administration of justice to qualified judges, and introduced a new system of taxation. Furthermore, the king relied on a permanent army, thus breaking the political influence of feudal lords. Concurrently, the evolution of town life became more marked, and at the same time the position of the peasants was somewhat improved.

The expansion of national states ran parallel with the spread of Renaissance culture. The ideal for a ruler was soon to be set by the Italian Machiavelli in his *Principe*. The leaders of Italian city·states developed a veritable art of politics. They, and their contemporaries in Europe, were no longer governed by the old universal, Christian principles, but were guided by "utilitas regni" and "ragione di stato", the interest and benefit of the state.

While Western Europe proceeded along these lines of evolution, the development in Central Europe was not so complete. The city-states of Italy were not combined into a large territorial state in the way that the feudal provinces of France were welded into the French monarchy. They were modernized as separate entities. The German Emperor likewise was unsuccessful in uniting the numerous principalities under his rule, and had to content himself with building up his absolutist power in his own territory.

This national evolution soon showed its influence in East-Central Europe too, as did Renaissance culture, which, owing to close connections with Italy, struck roots early. One such Renaissance ruler was Casimir IV of Poland (1447–1492), who vanquished the Teutonic order of Knights; another, in many respects, was George Podiebrad of Bohemia (1457–1471). But the greatest expression of national absolutism was Matthias Corvinus of Hungary (1458–1490). He grew in stature in the memory of succeeding generations, for his name stood for great power, position, administrative efficiency, social justice and military strength.

When the eighteen-year-old Matthias, younger son of the famous strategist Hunyadi, returned from Bohemia to ascend the Hungarian throne, his position was somewhat similar to that of the first Anjou king a century and a half earlier. Political power was in the hands of the landed aristocracy, public life controlled by their pacts. Thus one of the stipulations of Matthias' election called for his marriage to Palatine Garai's daughter, as had been promised by the young king-elect's uncle, Michael Szilágyi. The latter was appointed regent for a term of five years during which the nobles did their utmost to tie the hands of the king in every respect.

Though the influence of the aristocracy in matters of domestic policy was enormous, especially as they were in a position to enforce the adherence of the lesser nobility, feudalism was never so strong in Hungary as, for instance in Germany, where the country was subdivided into small principalities. "The Hungarian Kingdom always enjoyed an unbroken continuity of territory such as in our own times is possessed only by several Great States of Europe."[1]

[1] The Cambridge Modern History. Vol. I. New York, 1903. p. 342.

Matthias, despite the fame of his father, was but a "homo novus", the descendant of a family of recent fame. His talent for statesmanship and his energy were first manifested during his successful efforts to limit the influence of the hitherto all-powerful lords. It was soon apparent that the young monarch had no intention of being led, nor of subordinating his political designs to the wishes of the landed aristocracy. He speedily disposed of those who had planned to act as his guardians, among them his own uncle, the regent-elect Szilágyi. When, in consequence, the Ujlaki and Garai families turned against him, scheming to replace him with the Emperor, Frederick III, Matthias promptly crushed the attempted revolt. With similar success, he cleared Upper Hungary of the Czech military bands that had disturbed the land for the last quarter century since the Hussite War.

Matthias's first task was to restore royal authority according to the best standards of his day. Through his financial and economic reforms, royal power became independent of feudal influence. The Anjou kings had once based the economic foundation of their power on the *regalia,* i.e., the royal revenue from mining, customs, etc. Now Matthias went further and in 1467 introduced a new system of taxation by which he was able to raise his revenue to almost a million florins yearly, a sum equivalent to the contemporary budget of England or France. The consolidation of financial conditions made possible the maintenance of a well equipped standing army, chiefly of mercenaries. This was the famous "Black Army", which won Matthias's victories and gave military weight to his diplomatic activities. Parallel with the creation of a central administration, Matthias freed the royal council and chancellery from the influence of the feudal lords and, instead of appointing the latter, often placed experts of humbler origin in leading offices. He did much to modernize courts and jurisdiction, and his legal reforms of 1486, affecting both civil and criminal law, are to be considered serious efforts at codification.

It was under Matthias that Hungarian towns began to develop into more or less significant factors, the King granting them autonomous rights and assisting them in consolidating their independence from the feudal lords. Though indirectly, Matthias also aided the serfs by limiting the power of their masters and preventing the tightening of their bonds. A characteristic sign of this evolution may be seen in the rights granted to large villages (mezővárosok, oppida)—which progressed rapidly from then on. Their inhabitants were given the privilege of settling their yearly feudal obligations to the landlords collectively instead of each person individually as heretofore. Since we know of about 800 such communities, this meant that a considerable part of the population was affected by raised standards. Retarding the upward surge of the magnates, Matthias favored the political self-assertion of the middle and lower nobility and the autonomy of their counties. Indeed, Matthias was the first educator of this social stratum, opening, by this fact, a freer path for the class under it. If peaceful times had followed Matthias, a prosperous and educated middle class would, undoubtedly, have risen out of this social layer.

The program of Matthias thus shows all the necessary elements of that of a contemporary absolute monarch, utilizing all available forces for the advantage of the state. Though upon his ascension he had promised to convene annually the feudal diet, where all noblemen could put in an appearance, such was not the case in reality. Under Matthias, the diets played only a formal rôle. The huge, tumultuous diets characterized by the "liberum veto", and resulting in complete disorder, which prevailed in Poland before its partitioning, and in slighter measure in Hungary prior to the catastrophe of 1526, were unimaginable in the time of Matthias.

As regards his foreign policy, Matthias, at the beginning followed his father's crusading spirit, as was expected of him. As the Pope greeted Matthias upon his ascension to the throne: "You are a heavenly gift that God has given not only to Hungary but to the whole Christian World." In his political correspondence, Matthias often referred to the sacrifices that "Hungary has willingly made for Christianity." Yet he was a realist too, and saw that the age of the Crusades had passed, that the national states of Europe, now developing, were engaged in furthering their own interests, and that he too, unless he would build his policy on illusions, must not forget that he could rely only on the strength of his own country. By this time, the last remnants of

Serbia were occupied by the Turk. To counterbalance
Turkish designs on Bosnia, Matthias launched a successful campaign in 1463, after which he built and
maintained a chain of defense works, to the south. He
went into action again in 1475–76, when he advanced
beyond the Save River to recover the important stronghold of Shabatz, then fortified by the Turks as a bridge-
head for future attack.

It was precisely his handling of Turkish affairs that
was misunderstood not only by his contemporaries but
by later historians as well. They claimed that by not
pursuing vigorously his father's policy against the Turk
he disregarded the dangers of the East for the sake of
his interests in the West. This, however, will appear to
be without foundation if one considers the circumstances from all angles of Matthias's position. Never
did he neglect the fortifications facing the Balkans, and
though he led only two large-scale campaigns this did
not mean inactivity. For instance, in 1474 the Hungarian army assisted the Rumanian Prince of Moldavia
against the Ottomans. It is true that Matthias's foreign
policy was not limited to the Turkish question, but this
could not have been expected of him, not only because
he could not be an exception among contemporary
rulers, who had grandiose diplomatic plans and many
ambitions, but chiefly because his main political and
military attention had to be concentrated on the German and Czech problems on account of the competition
of the growing Habsburg dynasty.

Many historians point out, moreover, that Matthias's

real purpose in endeavoring to unite Bohemia and Germany under his rule was to be able to strike a decisive blow at the Turk with an army sufficiently strong to drive them out of Europe.

It was clear that Hungary alone was incapable of carrying out this tremendous task, that the Western states no longer heeded the Vatican's exhortation to a final Crusade, and that the Emperor was rather satisfied that the Hungarian King should be occupied with Turkish affairs. Matthias wished to become emperor only in order to undertake a decisive offensive at the head of a powerful coalition against the Ottoman Empire.[1]

It is certain that Matthias never hesitated to resist an eventual Turkish attack with all the forces at his disposal. It was in his interest, moreover, to eliminate finally the Turkish menace, although for defense alone the Hungarian forces were sufficient, if adequately led. But the immediate reason why Matthias turned toward Austria and the Empire, seemingly neglectful of his father's traditions, was the continuous growth of the power of the Habsburg dynasty. The Habsburgs began at that time to lay the foundations of their future Central European Empire built of different territories and heterogeneous peoples. Matthias could not ignore the fact that Emperor Frederick III did not give up, even for a moment, his plans to acquire Hungary. Had Matthias left Frederick a free course and remained inactive toward this empire-building policy, he would

[1] E. Mályusz, Matthias Corvinus (Rohden-Ostrogorsky, Menschen die Geschichte machten, vol. 2.)

have virtually renounced the position Hungary had held until that time in Carpathian Europe. The only effective means of checking the systematic efforts which, in the long run endangered the very independence of Hungary, was to carry out a counter-plan. Indeed Matthias proved in his own day, more than a military and political match for the Habsburgs. It was due only to the uncertain times following the death of Matthias that, instead of his heirs, the Habsburgs were placed at the head of a new Central European Empire. Matthias was prompted by the genuine interests of Hungary to take the initiative in this unavoidable race. It is beyond doubt, therefore, that, despite occasional friendly negotiations, the differences between the empire-building Habsburgs and the last of the line of great Hungarian kings was unbridgeable and final. As a matter of fact this continuous antagonism in the fields of diplomacy and war dominates Matthias's foreign policy. At the very outset of his reign it became evident that Frederick III, and even Podiebrad of Bohemia, would leave no stone unturned to acquire the crown of Hungary. Deciding to deal with these predatory opponents separately, he concluded a peace with Frederick in 1463, largely because he had begun his domestic reforms and lost no time in preparing for the conquest of Bohemia. Here he was able to utilize a rift between the Pope and Frederick on the one hand and a rift between the Czech Catholics and Podiebrad, who relied on the Protestant Hussites, on the other. Encouraged by the Pope and by the Emperor who even

promised him the title of "King of Rome", Matthias,
with the aid of the Poles and Catholic Czechs, boldly
advanced to the annexation of Bohemia. He succeeded
in the decade after 1468; was crowned King of Bohemia; and took possession of Silesia, Moravia, and
Lusatia. But not for a moment did he contemplate in-
corporating these into Hungary. He promised to respect
the separate independent national life of each, though
he did introduce several up-to-date administrative innovations.

But such a growth of Matthias's power was by no
means in the interests of the Emperor, who in 1470 succeeded in forming an Austro-Bohemian-Polish alliance
against Hungary, the Czechs having offered the Czech
throne to Prince Wladislas of Poland. This coalition
threw Hungary into a difficult position and created
much dissatisfaction, especially among the friends and
partisans of the late John Hunyadi, who represented the
old anti-Turkish policy. When, in 1471, the Poles joined
the Czechs, dissident groups included such devoted
friends of the Hunyadi family as Bishop John Vitéz
and his nephew Janus Pannonius, one of the greatest
poets of his age. But Matthias easily frustrated his opponents' plans, emerging victorious also from his foreign
entanglements by finding allies behind the back of his
enemies and defeating at Breslau the combined Czech-
Polish armies. Having thus confirmed his conquests, he
was in a position to attack Austria itself.

To counterbalance the designs of the Emperor,
Matthias endeavored to form an alliance with France,

taking, one might say, the first step toward that policy which the French in succeeding centuries strove to direct against the Habsburg power. The basic conditions of this policy were that France's Carpathian ally should be strong enough to withstand the Habsburg power without Western assistance. Matthias not only felt equal to the Emperor, but could even show considerable success against him. "When it comes to power and authority", wrote Matthias "we are in no wise subservient to him, being his equal to such an extent that we do not fear him nor shall we ever fear him".

After 1477, he turned with vigor to the conquest of Austria. In 1478 he occupied the capital, Vienna and at the same time extended his domination over Lower Austria and Styria. He was unable however, to secure the title of emperor, which Frederick during his lifetime had succeeded in securing for his son Maximilian. Matthias, who attempted to nullify Maximilian's coronation, spent the last years of his life consolidating his position with undiminished activity, holding in his hand a great portion of his enemy's territory. Having but one son, the illegitimate John Corvinus, Matthias endeavored to assure the throne for him, but died unexpectedly in 1490 at the height of his power.

Matthias was one of the most outstanding figures in the whole history of Hungary. Few of his contemporaries understood his foreign policy but all admitted his ability as a ruler. Public opinion in the next century, already well acquainted with Turkish destruction, felt that Matthias's real purpose was the expulsion of the

Turk, and that he would have been capable of this undertaking even with his own forces alone were it not for the constant thwarting of his plans by the Emperor.[1] We see now that Frederick's plans were no immediate hindrance to a campaign towards the south-east. Yet, viewed from a distant perspective, it must be admitted that in the long run Matthias was right. He realized that either his power or that of the Habsburgs must disappear. How true were his fears is shown by the fact that barely a hundred years after his death the western part of Hungary the only part then left in Christian hands was under Habsburg domination.

Matthias was noted for his patronage of literature and the arts, and his court was one of the most magnificent in Europe. He was a great patron of the Renaissance movement in Carpathian Europe. At first he was surrounded chiefly by Hungarian scholars and churchmen; but later, after his marriage in 1476 to Beatrice, daughter of the King of Naples, Italian writers and humanists were brought to his court. Some of them, like Bonfini and Galeotti, wrote his biography and have left picturesque descriptions of his court life.

It is true, of course, that only the higher classes were influenced by the new cultural trend, but this was the case likewise in Western Europe. In his royal palace at Buda, rebuilt in French *flamboyant* Gothic and now enlarged in Renaissance style, a colorful and rich life was led. Matthias took great and justifiable pride in his

[1]Francis Forgách (bishop and historian, 1535–1577), *De Statu Reipublicae Hungariae.*

magnificent library. Volumes from this famous Corvinus Library are to-day treasured possessions of leading universities and private collections.

Part of his cultural program was the founding of the University of Pozsony (now Bratislava in Slovakia). As a result, humanistic conceptions did not diminish with the passing of Matthias, whose spiritual influence proved to be of a far more lasting character than his accomplishments in statecraft. This achievement of Matthias outlived Hungary's defeat and pointed the direction of cultural development for generations to come.

All Renaissance monarchs furthered the flowering of the national ideal. Hungary still felt herself to be the defender of Western Christianity. "This strong people, whose bones cover hills and vales in many lands, God sent to His people as a defender against the Great Turk, in order that the lands of the Cross may live in peace", said Osvat Laskai, a Franciscan monk, in one of his celebrated sermons. But this belief was colored largely by national pride. Matthias's popularity may be traced, to some extent, to his anti-foreign, one may say nationalistic policies. Indeed, humanist travelers all noted the proud, soldierly appearance of lower-class Hungarians, imbued with intense patriotism.

Nevertheless, the underlying aim of Matthias's political plans and military might was a populous and flourishing state, the result of the civilizing efforts of five hundred years. The proportion of Hungarians to other groups in the Carpathian Basin was never greater

than in this period. Most of the original Slavic and
Avar fragments as well as later Eastern arrivals such
as the Cumanians and Petchenegs, had already become
assimilated. On the other hand, the rôle of two factors
which in the following centuries greatly changed ethnic
conditions, had not yet begun. These were (1) the
devastation of purely Magyar districts by the Turks,
and (2) the influx of large numbers of Slavic and
Wallachian shepherd tribes from the Balkans. The bulk
of the Magyars, even at that time, lived in the plains
and on the hillsides, but their territory of settlement
extended far deeper into the south than in later centuries. This is borne out by a series of data preserved
in contemporary documents of revenues collected, list-
ing an imposing array of town and family names. According to these, the density of population was much
greater in the fertile central lowlands inhabited by
Hungarians than in the mountainous sections. In some
places the ratio was ten to one. This is best illustrated
in the 15th century royal ledgers of taxpayers, showing
altogether different returns in the counties of the plains
from in those of North Hungary, though the size of the
county was approximately the same. For instance, while
in the county of Pest situated in the central plains, there
were 4500 family farmsteads, in Heves County 5722, in
Somogy 11,085 and in Baranya County 15,018, yet in
mountainous northern Árva County only 301 farmsteads existed and no more than 791 in the comparatively prosperous Liptó County. It is evident that the

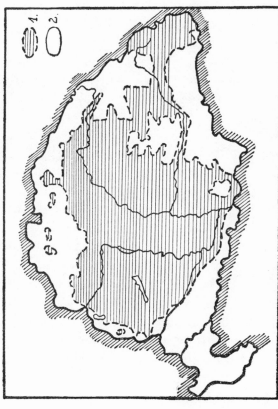

MAGYAR POPULATION IN THE CARPATHIAN BASIN
AT THE END OF THE 15TH CENTURY

1.
2.

*Based on a study by Dr. E. Mályusz in the "History of Hungarian Culture"*

1. Coherent Magyar settlements.

2. Other nationalities and uninhabited, mostly mountainous, territory.

bulk of the population lived on the plains, inhabited by Magyars.

The 150 years of Turkish occupation brought about a disastrous change in this respect. At the end of the 15th century, the population of Trencsén county in north Hungary was only one-fourth of that of Tolna in the Southwest; at the end of the 19th century, however, Trencsén surpassed Tolna county in population. This throws light on the devastation that took place during those years of occupation that laid waste the southern and central parts of the country. The population of Hungary at the turn of the 15th century was four millions, or about as many as in contemporary England. The Austrian Empire, together with Bohemia and Silesia, numbered about 5.5 millions, while France was a nation of 20 millions. By force of numbers alone, Hungary was an important factor. Of her four million souls, roughly 77 per cent were Magyar, forming an absolute ethnic majority in the Carpathian Basin, while the other 23 per cent were divided among several minorities whose leading class never faced any difficulties in entering the highest positions and taking an active part in state affairs. At that time, the problem of national minorities, as such did not exist anywhere in Hungary, and the livelihood of other nationalities was assured. While the diets in Hungary, as in other countries, tried to exclude foreigners from public office and the privilege of owning land, they officially stated that these were rights reserved "for the Magyars and those who have lived with them for a long time under the protection of the Hungarian Crown". The political and economic unity of the Carpathian Basin served the interests not only of the 77 per cent Magyars but of all those smaller ethnic groups who found security, protection, and livelihood in this region.

The reforms of absolutism were carried on in all Europe by the national dynasties for generations. Had Louis XI of France died without an heir, his life work could hardly have succeeded to the extent it did. King Matthias initiated a trend in Hungary which could have continued, provided strong successors had been at the helm. It was his tragedy, and the tragedy of Hungary, that no such heirs followed him. His illegitimate son John Corvinus, whose path Matthias had endeavored to smooth in his last years, was a weak and incompetent character, entirely unsuited for the rôle of Renaissance ruler. This, meant, for a while at least, the suspension of modern development. The conflict between the reactionary influence of the feudal lords, and the political traditions of Matthias soon became evident.

The magnates were out to smash Matthias's reforms and achievements and they were on the lookout for a ruler "whose locks they could hold in their hands", as one of them admitted. Royal elections, as manifested by the Polish example, were attended by much disorder, with ample opportunity for corruption whenever there was more than one aspirant to the throne. Besides, the conditions of the election generally tied the hands of any ruler from the outset. After death of Matthias, the majority of lords favored Wladislas, (1490–1516), King of Poland and Bohemia. Though a member of the House of Jagiello which had ruled Poland efficiently, and since the union with Lithuania had played an important rôle, Wladislas was not a man of backbone but was degenerate and physically unfit, his weakness and impotence being proverbial. Before he was elected, he gave his promise "not to bring in any innovations" (*nullas prorsus novitates*), i.e., he acquiesced in the nullification of Matthias's timely reforms. He soon lost the Austrian and Bohemian provinces; and since his disorganized treasury was unable to meet expenses, the famous "Black Army" the mainstay of Matthias's authority, was disbanded, and the antiquated system of medieval militia re-instated. The personality of the king, of such importance in the Renaissance era, had no influence, public life being maintained through private agreements of the feudal lords. The primary interest of the latter was to keep and enlarge their private power as landlords and their enormous holdings. The only check on them at the time was the lesser nobility (*Köznemesség*), an embryonic middle class, one might say, which just emerging politically, fought hard for its independence, influence and rights.

Matthias was the first mentor and educator of this class. But, just as the power-hungry lords were good material in the shrewd King's strong hand yet ruined the administration when left to themselves, so the lesser nobles, with little political experience and without proper leadership, were able to follow Matthias's "national" program only in a primitive way, with instinct and emotion to take the place of reasoned policy and executive experience. Their national feeling consisted mainly of hatred against foreigners, particularly Germans. They carried on heated discussions in the Diet, came into conflict with the lords, demanded more effective national defense, and, in 1505, decreed that never again would they elect a foreigner as their king. But all this legislation proved to be mere paper for power actually remained in the hands of the lords and the lesser nobility was not strong and mature enough to take over political leadership. First of all, some of their leaders were lords whose ambition or disappointment had led to their camp. Such was John Zápolya, voyvode of Transylvania, who unsuccessfully attempted to become related through marriage to the royal family. Even those capable leaders of non-aristocratic origin, such as the code-maker, Stephen Werbőczi, desired to become lords themselves.

Opposing the "court" party of the nobles, the commons represented the "national" party. Similar distinctions may be observed later on in Poland. Another typically East-Central European phenomenon of the time was the reaction against absolutist rule, together with the strengthening of the rights of certain classes. This development appeared simultaneously in Poland and Bohemia. In the latter, Czech aristocrats waged regular internal wars. The King of Bohemia and Hun-

gary was the same Wladislas and both Hungary and Bohemia were placed under Habsburg rule in 1526. In
Poland, under the sons of Casimir the Great, the magnates' power developed greatly and in 1505 the constitution known as "nihil novi" came into being; while
under Sigismund I the influence of provincial diets
strengthened.

After the death of Matthias Corvinus, kings of the
Jagiello House ruled over all East-Central Europe, but
were powerless to utilize existing advantages in the diplomatic and military fields. Thus the active modern
statesmanship of Matthias was followed by an era of
inertia; and as a result, both Hungary and Bohemia
"were quite outside the main current of international
policy from 1490 to 1527",[1] Matthias had waited in
vain for such an excellent opportunity to attack the
Turk as came ten years after his death with the Turkish-
Venetian War of 1500. Now the King preferred peace,
though here was an excellent chance to weaken the
Moslem forces, which by this time were much more
formidable than during Matthias's reign, when they
had not yet made sure their position in Asia. Another
neglected opportunity was the failure to join the Cam-
bray League concluded by the French King, the Pope
and the German Emperor among themselves for the
conquest of Northern Italy. According to the terms
of this pact, Hungary, provided she joined, was to receive Dalmatia, a splendid base for flank defense
against the Ottoman. In the struggle between the

[1]The Cambridge Modern History, vol. cit. p. 343.

Habsburg dynasty and Hungary, Matthias had emerged as victor, but his Jagiellonic successors, during their thirty-six years of rule, suffered a decisive diplomatic setback.

The Habsburgs had not given up the idea of extending their authority over Hungary and their active diplomacy brought about a marriage agreement with the family of Wladislas. According to this agreement, should the King die without an heir, the throne of Hungary would go to the Habsburgs. Whatever opposition the Jagiellonic kings might have shown, the Habsburgs were able to counterbalance it through their alliance with the eastern enemy of the Poles, the Grand Duke of Moscow.

The reaction of Hungary's leading elements had a serious effect on the social equilibrium of the country. While Matthias had assisted in the development of rural towns (*oppida*), there was now no authority to limit the power of the great landowners. The gradual deterioration of the situation was felt first, not by the lowest class, the poorest peasantry, but by those agricultural communities that had already emancipated themselves from their masters, settling their feudal dues with them annually. The landowners' attempt to force them back to a lower level, now resulted in the so-called "peasants revolt" of 1514. Headed by George Dózsa, a nobleman and soldier, leaders and priests of the privileged agricultural towns became the real supporters of this movement. Opportunity for this bloody revolt was given by the fact that Archbishop Bakócz, known as "the Hungarian Wolsey", obtained permission to draft a volunteer army for another Crusade. A good number of dissident peasants, inhabitants of the *oppida,* filled with bitterness at their new grievances, joined up and turned against their lords instead of against the Ottoman danger. After burning and devastating widely, they were, however, dispersed by the army of John Zápolya, who dealt mercilessly with the leaders. This social crisis undermined Hungary at a time when undivided unity and the pooling of all available resources were needed to show a determined stand against the coming Turkish onslaught.

He who examines the economic and social history of Europe will notice that in the early 16th century there was a similar trend of social evolution in the whole eastern half of Europe a trend in which Hungary inevitably shared.[1] It is regrettable, however, that the important codification of Hungary's laws, which exerted a decided influence on social and juristic life and on public opinion for centuries to come, coincided with this period when the general feeling was desperate because of the peasant uprising. Owing to the change in government, Matthias's codification (1486) lost its significance. The credit for a new systematic compilation of Hungarian law belongs to Stephen Werbőczi, the outstanding legal expert of his time and one of the leaders of the common nobility (*köznemesség*). His *Tripartitum* (or "Triple Code") became the basic authority in legal matters, even without the sanction of

[1]Cf. Chapter V. p. 109.

royal assent. Its value lies in the fact that it upheld the integrity of Hungarian jurisprudence even during the country's Turkish occupation and its resultant partitioning. But as was only natural, Werbőczi wove into his work the political concepts of his party, and so the *Tripartitum* bears the definite marks of that period.

In one respect, however, Werbőczi's legal compendium was, socially speaking, of equalizing value. It does not know any difference between the aristocracy and the lesser nobles, contrary to the fact that the masses of these were actually under the domination, or in the service, of the magnates. Werbőczi dealt with but one kind of nobility, *una eademque nobilitas,* whose rights and privileges he defined in classic terms. He endeavored to limit the powers of king, and according to his conception the king is elected by the nobles, who in turn invest him with royal powers through the act of coronation. The Holy Crown of St. Stephen is the symbolic source of all law and power, represented in reality by the nobles as its members, *membra sacrae coronae,* who, together with the king, exercise legislative authority through parliament. The latter principle, first clearly defined by Werbőczi, was the result of long development. As a matter of fact, it embodied almost republican principles, because, theoretically it did not exclude the extreme case that the nobility might not invest anyone with royal power, which meant that a king was not absolutely necessary.

The veneration of the Holy Crown dates back to early centuries, its placing ón the king's head marking a moral assent to his existing authority. It was only later, during the reign of weak monarchs, that the conception as defined by Werbőczi developed, naming the nation itself, i.e., the nobility, as the original possessor of the power of the state. At the beginning of the 15th century, this was expressed thus: "the coronation of any king always depends on the will of the citizens (*regnicolae*), and the effectiveness of royal power lies in their assent." This conception became generally accepted only after the death of Matthias. It is evident that for such privileges anyone of any nationality was anxious to join the body of Hungarian nobility. Thus the "nation political", i.e., the nobility, was not only powerful but, in its substance, unified. Socially, however, the Hungarian nation was split in two, nobles and non-nobles, as in other feudal countries of the time. The peasantry, handicapped by financial and servile liabilities, was retarded in its development for several hundred years. This naturally reflected not only on the peasantry itself but on the future fate of the entire nation.

The political crisis was complete at the death of Wladislas. His son, born out of the marriage with the French Princess Anne of Candale ascended the throne as Louis II (1516–1526). According to his contemporaries, he was considered a talented youth but was too inexperienced, too young, and too much under the influence of his courtiers to bring about any serious change in conditions in a short decade. The treasury was all but empty, sources of revenue being partly dried up and partly in the hands of others. Thus the maintenance of a defense system and military preparedness, at least to any practical extent, became impossible, no matter how spiritedly the commoners demanded the fortification of the southern regions, almost disorganized by that time. To remedy all this, Louis II would have needed to oust his corrupt government and rebuild the entire economic system.

Contemporary diplomats accredited to Hungary by other countries deplored this state of affairs in their reports. Arguing from their descriptions, some later historians claimed that the Hungarian nation was internally disintegrating even before its military defeat. This was not the case at all however. Only the leading group, holding the reins of government had lost its political competence and moral responsibility.

When, in 1521, a powerful Turkish thrust reached the southern line of fortifications, the government was in no position to render assistance to the outposts. One of the latter, Nándorfehérvár (the modern Belgrade), held out nevertheless for more than two months owing to the heroism of its small band of defenders led by a simple lieutenant. But there was no John Hunyadi to gather the nation's resources and drive off the attackers.

According to the reports of the envoys of Venice, the country's latent strength was unused, although Hungary was more rich and fertile than France. "If the King of Hungary were in a position to dispose freely of his country's natural resources and manpower", they wrote, "he could easily vie with any other ruler".[1] The bulk of the people, instead of revealing signs of decay, showed growing vitality as regards culture, religion and discipline, for the decaying influence of the upper classes had not reached down into the commonalty. It was only a complete bankruptcy of leadership that left the country undefended against outside attack.

In all East-Central Europe, at that time, modern development suffered a setback, in conjunction with the decline of central authority and the simultaneous increase of the nobles' influence. It is beyond doubt that if, for instance, Poland had lain in the path of the Turks, the catastrophe of Mohács would have been just as inevitable. It often happened in other parts of Europe likewise that social and political leadership failed, and some time had to elapse until those unfit for leadership were eliminated. In Carpathian Europe, however, risks were always greater, and there was no time for recuperation owing to the constant pressure of surrounding great powers. In this circumstance, one may find the real cause of the Mohács tragedy.

The papal nuncio, Burgio, characterized the situation as follows: "This country is in no position to defend itself, but is laid open to the mercy of the enemy. . . . How could it be imagined that it could wage war against the might of all Islam, when the king and the nobles are unable even to pay the skeleton army at the frontiers. . . . The nobility are broken up by

[1]Tommaseo (I.270) and Sanuto, *Diarii* 15–23. III.

party strife, but even if they would keep together, what could they do against the Turk without military equipment? They may attempt a single battle, but they will certainly lose out in the end. Where could they hope for assistance? From Germany, perhaps, where there is nothing but strife, and no more obedience in its subjects, neither executive authority?"

"I beg your Majesty, not to allow a limb of Christianity to be torn from its trunk", wrote Louis II to Henry VIII, the King of England. "We have been exhausted in the long struggle, all our strength is gone, and thus we are in no position to withstand the Turkish onslaught". He sent envoys to the courts of Europe, but they spoke in vain of the danger that threatened the Christian world. Hungary had become in recent decades diplomatically isolated; for the King of France Francis I, sought an eastern ally in the Turk against the Habsburgs and the road of that ally to Vienna led through Hungary.

The fateful attack struck Hungary in the summer of 1526. In that moment, everyone realized the gravity of the situation, but it was too late. The country was helpless, and the administration irresponsible and selfish. Yet, in the last minute, even if all hope had gone, everyone faced fate bravely. There was no common stratagem agreed upon. The young king, when the Sultan's armies broke through the southern defences and proceeded toward the heart of Transdanubia, did not even wait for the arrival of the auxiliary reinforcements, but immediately started off from Buda at the head of a

small army, together with his entire government, to
meet the onslaught. If he did nothing else, Louis set a
tragic example of courage; for his troops hardly exceeded 20,000, and the bulk of the Hungarian forces
were scarcely on the way from their bases.

On the plains of Mohács, he met the main force of
the Turks. It was August 29, 1526. The Hungarians
charged the enemy, who outnumbered them several
times over. The flower of the nobility, including Archbishop Tomori, in charge of the Hungarian army, together with other members of the hierarchy and a long
line of aristocrats followed their youthful monarch to
certain death. On that dark field, the Hungarian army
was virtually annihilated.

In the catastrophe of Mohács, where the political
leaders of the country atoned for their faults with their
lives, Hungary fell, after a century and a half of victorious defense against the Turks.

# V

## THE TURKISH ERA

### Struggle Against Foreign Domination
### (1526-1711)

For more than five centuries Hungary, as one of the leading states of East-Central Europe, had performed its rôle successfully between East and West. On the frontier of Christian civilization, it had stood on guard in the path of Asiatic and pagan expansion and, on the other hand, had maintained its independence. Even after the catastrophe of Mohács, it did not cease to fight. A defensive struggle against the oriental Great Power was the chief problem of Hungarian history during the next two centuries. But the country, partly subjected to Turkish occupation, did not possess sufficient military strength to assure the independence of the Carpathian Basin nor the cohesive dynamism that would have brought about the co-operation of other states in East-Central Europe.

The Habsburg dynasty gained in influence after the defeat of Mohács, since its assistance was deemed inevitable. But when later, foreign political and military pressure made itself felt, general dissension burst out in the form of desperate uprisings, all attempting a restoration of independence. Hungary was caught between two fires: she never ceased to be anti-Turkish; yet her attempts to throw off Austrian oppression gained her the reputation of being "rebellious". From Mohács to the insurrection of Francis Rákóczi II, nearly two centuries elapsed, which were characterized by the aggression of Islam. The latter was thrust back only at the end of the 17th century, after which Hungary, though maintaining her constitutional independence, was drawn, for another long period, into the claws of Habsburg imperialism, from which Kossuth tried to liberate her in 1848–49.

It should also be remembered that the fate of other peoples in East-Central Europe, was, to a certain extent, bound up with that of Hungary. The weakening of Hungary, after being for half a millennium a leading power, could not leave the fate of its neighbors, small or large, uninfluenced. Although the Serb and Rumanian provinces in the Balkans had already been occupied by the Turk, there was hope that as long as Hungary was flourishing, other East-Central European peoples would, in the long run, be able to withstand, by united effort, the Asiatic thrust. Thus the battle of Mohács not only sealed the fate of Hungary, but brought a turning point in the history of other peoples as well. The peoples of East-Central Europe successively fell under the hegemony of either Eastern or Central

European powers, even if their nominal independence, like Hungary's, was maintained. The Emperor finally vanquished the Bohemian uprising 1621. Poland, not immediately threatened by the Turk, withstood Imperial and Russian pressure, for a while at least: but finally, in the 18th century, owing to internal weakness and isolation, it was partitioned between Germany, Austria and Russia. The era beginning with the fall of Hungary, thus brought with it the almost unchecked spreading of Western or Eastern influences all over East-Central Europe.

The death of Louis II necessitated the election of a new king of Hungary. This sharpened antagonism between the two rival parties. The "court party" favored Archduke Ferdinand of Habsburg, the elder brother of the widowed queen Mary. He took the throne so much for granted, after the family pacts of 1491 and 1515, that at first he considered an election unnecessary. His Hungarian followers turned to him in the hope that being the brother of Charles V, powerful emperor of Spain and Germany, who also directed the fate of South America at the time, he would be able to secure sufficient assistance against Islam.

The "national party" on the other hand, had decided in 1505 that under no circumstances would it elect a foreigner as king, and it was consequently opposed to Habsburg influence. To this party belonged the common nobility headed by John Zápolya, "vajda" of Transylvania and the largest landowner in all Hungary.

He was the only one in Hungary with a self-contained and undefeated army and, except for some western portions, he literally held the whole country. He was crowned on November 10, 1526. Had he been a leading personality, he could have prevented his adversary from entering the country and so could have avoided the double election. The Turk did not attack for a time. Great statesmen recognize the never-returning moment when swift action brings its rewards. But Zápolya was not another Matthias Corvinus at the helm of the national party, but a helpless, hesitating, irresolute character, who was not a leader but a puppet of the movement. He was unable to consolidate his position. The opposition crowned its choice in the middle of December; and Ferdinand (1526–1564) took his time to organize his forces and then force his rival out of Hungary proper by next summer. John Zápolya found refuge in Poland and sought diplomatic connections, especially with France.

At that time, in the early 16th century, there began the undying rivalry between France and the Habsburgs. During this long struggle, the French tried to find allies in the East behind the back of the Habsburgs. This explains the French promises made to Hungarian revolutionaries in the following century. The idea of French-Hungarian diplomatic collaboration had come up in the time of Matthias. Post-Mohács Hungary, however, was no longer the same power; the French sought an alliance with the Turks, their interest in Hungary and Poland being but secondary. For a successful French-

Hungarian alliance, the ironing out of Hungaro-Turkish antagonisms was necessary, but Hungarian public opinion knew from long experience that dealing with the Turk brought no results, for the sole aim of Ottoman diplomacy was conquest. Yet exiled King John was persuaded to conclude an agreement with France (1528) and attempt a pro-Turk policy: these fruitless efforts were suggested to him partly by French diplomacy and partly by some of Zápolya's advisers of Southern Slav origin, who thought that their country's subjugation should serve as a lesson to Hungary that submission was inevitable.

From that moment, it became evident that King John had missed his chance ever to repulse his rival Ferdinand, and their civil war, lasting twelve years, proved that neither of them was able to dispose of the other. For the first time in its history, the country was torn into two parts as the result of a double election, the root of all misfortune: and the loss of a third portion of Hungary was soon to come, as the Turk took advantage of the unfortunate situation.

Until his death in 1540, John was upheld by Turkish diplomacy. In return, he was obliged to acknowledge the supremacy of the Sultan. Every Turkish thrust toward the West, even if directed against Ferdinand, struck into Hungarian fortifications, destroying life and property. Whenever Turkish or imperial armies passed through Hungary, the Hungarians bore the brunt. The Sultan supported John primarily because an Ottoman disliked the possibility of the revival of

Buda and Pest in Turkish Times

*An early 17th century engraving by George Houfnagel*

Hungary's unity. They still remembered well at Stamboul what a strong military power united Hungary had been and therefore they made it their principle to hamper at all costs, every attempt at the unifications of the severed parts of the country.

Hungarian statesmen recognized this danger from the beginning. Time and again the emissaries of both parties met secretly even against the intentions of the two contending kings, and attempted to work out a solution for the welding together of the severed parts of Hungary. These negotiations, begun some years after the elections, envisaged the securing of the throne for Ferdinand after the death of the childless Zápolya. The latter's confidante, Frater George Martinuzzi, a Franciscan monk of rare, far-sighted talents, also supported this plan. As a rule, the Peace of Nagyvárad (1538) put an end to the civil war, through the efforts of statesmen who remembered the happier past of the country.

But John, whose marriage with Poland's Princess Isabella brought him an heir, nullified the Nagyvárad agreement before his death. Sultan Suleiman, who so far as checkmated by the fear that a campaign against Hungary might smooth out the differences between the rival monarchies, finally found the time ripe for his plans. In 1541 he marched his armies into Hungary under the pretext of protecting the interests of the deceased John's son. He took Buda, the capital from which the Turk was not ejected for 150 years. In 1542, all central Hungary was under Turkish domination, and even a score of forts north of Buda fell into Turkish hands. All Hungary now expected its liberation by Ferdinand, who up till then had not made any serious effort to stop the Turkish advance. In 1542, he finally sent in an Imperial army, but it returned in shame without attempting any engagement. The attention of Ferdinand was primarily taken up with German and, in general, Western matters, while in the East he endeavored to quiet public feeling by means of promises. Thus the possibility of establishing another defense line on the south lapsed, and instead, Ferdinand concluded a pact with the Turk in 1547, humiliating himself to the extent of paying yearly taxes. From now on, the Sultan considered all Hungary his domain. To be sure, only the central part of Hungary was in his hands, while Ferdinand held the western portions, and in Transylvania Martinuzzi was attempting to organize national opposition. This monk-statesman worked for a unified Hungary also, but stipulated that Ferdinand should be in a position to defend Transylvania against the expected Turkish invasion. According to an agreement with Ferdinand, the deceased King John's son, John Sigismund, would have received Silesia and Lusatia in exchange for the transferred province. But the forces of Ferdinand were unable to defend Transylvania; the generalissimo of his mercenaries even feared for his life as in a foreign land; finally he had Martinuzzi, who was negotiating with the Poles, murdered. With this development, the former state of affairs was reestablished and the country's dissolution into three parts was maintained.

At first, Ferdinand had built forts for the defense of the northern and western fringes that were still in his hands, but after he was elected Emperor of Germany in 1556, his time was devoted to other matters. Instead of even attempting to drive out the Turk with the enormous resources and manpower at his disposal, he soon made another pact with the Osmanli, again at the price of tribute-paying. In the east, Transylvania, until now an integral part of Hungary, even if under the autonomous rule of a "vajda", gradually became independent. Its separate political entity was clearly developed by the 17th century, owing to unavoidable conditions brought about by the Turkish advance.

It is therefore necessary to examine the three parts of Hungary separately; then to explain the relations between the "western kingdom" and Transylvania and the question as to what extent their separation was influenced by religious matter; and finally to cast a glance at the territory under Turkish occupation.

Had the country been a unity, Ferdinand would, in all probability have lived in Buda, since the kingdom of Hungary was then of greater significance than the principality of Austria. It is noteworthy that Sigismund had gained the crown of the Holy Roman Empire through his reliance on Hungary. But now the country that had become part of Ferdinand's realm was no longer the great flourishing state of Matthias Corvinus. Western Hungary was but a shred of the whole. The

Emperor did his best for its protection, for otherwise he would expose his own provinces to direct danger. But in any case Hungary was in no condition after her defeat at Mohács to defend herself out of her own resources. Consequently, all these circumstances brought numerous infringements of Hungary's sovereignty and a curtailment of Hungarian interests and Hungary's part in the government.

Political evolution in Europe was still proceeding toward royal absolutism. Matthias had tried to inaugurate it through the establishment of a permanent army, centralized government offices, and the like. But what, during the reign of Matthias, had stood for strictly Hungarian interests, was now associated with a foreign power. The absolutism of the Habsburgs' day was directed against Hungary's national interests, the defense of which was in the hands of the feudal nobility. Feudal institutions, however, became rather outmoded by the 17th century. Ferdinand did not deliberately plan the destruction of Hungarian national independence, yet his measures greatly limited the sphere of action of the Hungarian administration. In the new central government offices (Court Council, Royal Chancellery and Royal Treasury) there were practically no Hungarians employed. The King did not live in the country permanently, his representative, according to the constitution, being the Palatine, who was, at the same time, the head of the army. But after the death of Palatine Bánffy, this office was filled but once, with Thomas Nádasdy, otherwise a procurator managed the affairs of state acting upon the king's instructions. Thus the foreign troops necessary for the defense of the frontiers were actually in the country but were not under Hungarian control. Its captain general was always a foreigner, just as the supreme military council at Vienna, functioning after 1556, could not show a single Hungarian member. The results of the campaigns against the Turk were unquestionably influenced by the fact that inexperienced officers supplanted, and even lorded it over, Hungarian generals seasoned in generations of war against the Turk.

Finances, excepting the taxes voted in the diet, were within the King's jurisdiction and Hungary's financial administration was subordinated to the royal treasury. Foreign affairs, too, were part of the monarch's prerogatives, an arrangement complicated by the fact that the King's interest was peace with the Turk, while active defense was that of the Magyars. Thus the sovereign rights of the Hungarian state suffered a threefold infringement, that is, in matters relating to finances, to foreign affairs, and to defense. To make things worse, the King was surrounded by foreign counsellors and his decisions were influenced by them. The diet, that is the representatives of the common nobility and towns in the lower house and the representatives of the lords in the chief hierarchy in the upper, knew well that the country was badly in need of defense, yet they were in no position to do anything but protest. The constitutional dispute concerning sovereign rights that arose at that time really came to an end only at the end of the

World War I through the dethroning of the House of Habsburg.

Defense was closely related to the problem of foreign support. Following the loss of the fortified zone in the south, the King was now bound to build, with the aid of the great landowners, a new line of strongholds. War expenses were thus continually rising, reaching the two million mark by the end of the century. As against the former almost straight line of natural defences difficult for a formerly united Hungary to hold, the new semi-circular and largely artificial system was much longer and harder to defend. The revenues of the treasury at this time were barely more than half a million, collected largely from mining royalties and customs. To this was added the war tax (*subsidium*), as voted by the Diet, totalling but a quarter of a million. Completion of the entire line of fortifications was impossible out of this sum, much less so since the financial administration of Vienna did not allot even the full income from Hungary for defense. Budgets being non-existent as yet, revenues were used mainly to fill gaps as they occurred, and so these estimates are only approximate. It is a fact, nevertheless, that owing to indiscriminate financial practises, the revenues and the Vatican's aid were improperly used and the expenses of the central administration, court and foreign affairs exceeded the total alloted for defense.

Transylvania, though it played an important part in Hungary's 17th century history, became an independent state only under Turkish pressure. No Hungarian of the 16th century would willingly have acquiesced in Transylvania's separation or renounced its unity with Hungary; but the ideal of unity could have been achieved in reality only if the Emperor had had sufficient forces to defend Transylvania against the invader, and the latter in turn regarded every attempt in this direction as a challenge. In every other respect, Transylvania, surrounded on three sides by the Ottoman power, and connected with Hungary proper only by a narrow corridor, could not defy the forces of the marauding Turkish aggressor. The idea of an independent Transylvania was not general at this time either, though the three nationalities inhabiting this area Magyar, Székely and Saxon had already arrived at a union for the purpose of political co-operation in the 15th century. Nevertheless, Transylvania emerges as an autonomous state only after the Turkish conquest.

Transylvania's independence was closely connected with the geographic and strategic conditions brought about by the Turk's advance. The separate existence of Transylvania was considered, therefore, by every Hungarian in the 16th century, as a necessary evil. They knew that the extinction of Transylvania would threaten the very existence of Hungary as a whole. Secretly they labored on unification even afterwards. The pact signed by Speyer in 1570 secured Transylvania for Emperor Maximilian, in the event of John Sigismund's death; but naturally the Turk made this impossible.

The first prince of Transylvania to possess really outstanding qualities was Stephen Báthory (1571–1581),
whose influence soon overstepped his domain's boundaries, for he was elected king of Poland in 1576. There,
too, as once in Hungary, Imperial and French factions
vied with one another, the latter's "national" party inviting Báthory. The new king immediately consolidated
his position against the Emperor, and, uniting Poland's
forces, was victorious in his campaign against Ivan the
Terrible, the first of Russia's monarchs desirous of extending his authority over Poland.

The idea of co-operation between East-Central
Europe's peoples revived once more in Báthory. After
vanquishing the Russian Czar, he made peace in order
to be able to force the Turk out of Europe, with the help
of the Vatican, and then to guarantee Hungary's independence from the Emperor once more. However,
Báthory, on account of his early death, was unable to
carry out his designs. It proved, indeed, to be a durable
and possible solution to come to terms with either the
Eastern or the Western powers while it was next to
impossible to unite all East-Central Europe's forces
against both of them.

The political antagonism between East and West became more complicated in the 16th century through
the introduction of religious problems. The Reformation, like many other spiritual movements, did not
reach beyond the eastern boundaries of East-Central
Europe, but, there, on the other hand, it made strong

inroads. The majority of Hungarians were Protestant by the end of the 16th century, but the Counter-Reformation of the 17th century reversed that proportion. While Catholicism was strongest in the section of Hungary under the Habsburgs, Transylvania was a veritable stronghold of Protestantism, with Calvinism leading.

Several members of the Catholic hierarchy lost their lives at Mohács, and with the decline of the state, the Roman church also declined. After this, the Reformation spread, especially by virtue of the principle of *"Cuius regio eius religio"*, according to which peasants were to follow the landowners' creed. Protestant missionaries, moreover, made great efforts to create and popularize national literature, by printing, education and school organization, generously aided by certain cities and lords. They cultivated the lower classes, too, and their simple language appealed to the peasantry. They ministered to the needs of every one, thus fulfilling a social mission.

In the west of Hungary, Emperor Rudolph, aided by the zeal of the Jesuits, succeeded, at the end of the 16th century, in retrieving Catholicism. But Transylvania remained Protestant; and there, the Lutheran, Calvinist and Unitarian churches took root beside the Catholic. Thus the problem arose as to whether these religions could exist peacefully side by side. It was the generally accepted principle in Europe in those days, fostered by most rulers, that there should be one single religion in each country or province, in order that the peace of the country might be maintained. Since the establishment of this system seemed impossible in Transylvania, the Diet of 1564 promulgated that *"pro quiete regni"*, for the sake of the country's peace, each town or province was given the free choice of its own religion. Although this did not signify complete individual religious liberty or tolerance, in the now accepted use of the word, yet it was a freer, one may say a more democratic solution, and something difficult to find anywhere else in those days. According to the Diet of 1571, three nationalities and four accepted religions, *receptae religiones,* were recognized in Transylvania, these being the Catholic, Lutheran, Calvinist and Unitarian. This unquestionably important solution reflects the tolerant rule Transylvania enjoyed under its Hungarian princes.

We may make similar observations in nationality problems. The peaceful cohabitation of the different races was not hindered, either in Transylvania or on the western fringes of Hungary. No trace of coercion is evident, comparable, for instance to the language law of Bohemia in 1615. In the language question, too, practical viewpoints were dominant. The upper classes spoke Latin and Magyar, while those of other origins, elevated to the nobility, found it to their advantage to learn Magyar, just as Magyars in the regions settled by other nationalities acquired their language. Regulations and by-laws of counties were issued in the tongue of the inhabitants in order that they might understand it, and no one ever thought to disturb this harmony at that time.

The population was divided primarily according to social and not national status. There were Magyars as well as foreigners among the peasants; and there was no obstacle to any worthwhile person being elevated to the Hungarian nobility, regardless of nationality. To mention only two examples from the 16th century: Nicholas Oláh, Archbishop of Esztergom, was a Rumanian; while the archbishop Anthony Verancsics, a prominent author, was of Southern Slav origin. The latter, in one of his works still extant, clearly states that the different nationalities always lived in unanimity *"concordibus animis"* with the Magyars, who never excluded them.

It is important to mention this, for Hungary changed from a strongly national state into one of more or less mixed racial population during the era of Turkish occupation. The migration of Rumanians into Transylvania continued, for her more advanced and peaceful conditions exerted a natural attraction. Their political self-consciousness, however, did not appear as yet, and therefore they could not play such an important part as the other three nationalities. The Calvinist Magyars, as well as the Lutheran Saxons attempted to spread Protestantism among the Rumanians. This had nothing to do with nationality problems, for the missionaries themselves urged the Rumanians to use, after the Protestant example, their own Wallachian tongue instead of the Old Church Slavonic of the Orthodox church. This resulted in their publication of the four Gospels of the New Testament (Brassó, 1561), marking the beginning of Rumanian literature. Another important work of the period is the Rumanian translation of the Bible (1581–1582) by Michael Tordasi, Rumanian Calvinist bishop, from the Magyar version of Gáspár Heltai. The education of Rumanians was indeed a tradition with the Hungarian princes of Transylvania. At the beginning of the 17th century, Gabriel Bethlen again had the Bible translated into Rumanian, while George Rákoczi I conveyed in 1641 his explicit wish to the high priest of Bihar "to preach to the poor Wallachian people in their native tongue". Another prince, Michael Apafy, instituted Rumanian schools at the end of the 17th century. Though the spread of Calvinism among Rumanians did not succeed, the literary and cultural results were beneficial to them, even if their influence was not felt in a wide circle.

The Turkish wars greatly influenced social development. In western Europe, large cities sprang up in this period, but in Hungary, the centre of home defense was the castle of the landowner, where he maintained a military force and reared up young men in the arts of warfare. Urban culture can only develop in secure, peaceful times. The period of Turkish warfare upheld the prestige of the landowner and the nobility, since home defense depended upon their economics and military preparedness. The distinguished families of this era, the Báthorys, Bocskays, Nádasdys, Rákóczis and Zrinyis were all great landowners. They were educated in the spirit of Italian culture, for the penetration of Humanism and the Renaissance did not cease with the defeat at Mohács. The nobles, as well as numerous writers of lesser means, studied mostly at the universities of Bologna and Padua; many went as far as France and even to England. The art of writing history was highly developed by three successive generations of humanists whose Latin works mostly contain the history of the period they lived in. Hungary, squeezed between Turkish and Austrian might, still upheld its direct cultural relations with the whole of Europe, steadfastly holding to its European perspective.

Unfortunately, conditions that strengthened the nobility did not improve the lot of the lower classes. The difference between the trends in social conditions in eastern and western Europe was already discernible at this time. In Western countries, independent peasant holdings came into being, while on the territory of Poland, East Prussia, Bohemia and Hungary, serfs were obliged to render financial and personal service, and their lot became worse as compared with that of the 15th century. In Hungary, no freer and healthier evolution was possible during the continuous warfare with the aggressor. Neither was the solution of the problem in the following century helped much by the fact that Hungarian peasants were better off than the peasants in many other parts of East-Central Europe. In East Prussia, for instance, besides increasing the peasant's obligations, the rulers not only took away his rights to free migration but were able to evict him from his home, and in some cases even to sell him. This was never the case in Hungary. The peasant in Hungary could not be evicted from his land, and the continuous living there of his family and successors was assured. Going farther east, in Russia, the noble had unlimited power over the life and death of his peasants. In the Rumanian principalities, as late as the 18th century, social oppression was of such a degree that it is characterized, even by Rumanian historians, as virtual slavery. In Hungary of the Turkish period, frequent elevation to the gentry, especially through military service, known as "life on the frontiers", with its freer social conditions, offered a way of improvement.

Life, as it was known before, changed radically under the Turk in the occupied central parts. The Christian populace was forced to the lowest possible standards of life, exploited and humiliated at every turn. "Disobedient and stiff-necked dogs" was the customary form of address in letters written by the Turks to the Hungarians. The people were weighed down by numberless taxes, new ones being invented for every manifestation of daily life. Administration was in the hands of the Turkish military ruling class, which had been rewarded by grants of land. But the new owners could hardly acclimatize themselves, for one day they received an estate in the Danube Valley, and on the next another in Asia Minor. Thus they cared no more than to exploit their possessions in the shortest possible time. The Turkish state farms, known as "khas", were in a more advantageous position. They served primarily as a supply base for the forces of occupation, with Buda, the capital, and Tenesvár, an important southern city, as centres of administration.

Continuous warfare likewise brought about the decimation of the civilian population. The Turk was strictly an occupying element, avoiding intermixture with the population. On the contrary he drove tens of thousands of Magyar slaves in long lines through the Balkans towards Asia Minor. At that time one could travel through the whole of Asia Minor, speaking Hungarian only. The annihilation of the population, following close upon the Turkish campaigns, took place in three phases. At the beginning of the 16th century, the Turkish attacks devastated the southern part of the country; the campaigns against Vienna laid waste the Transdanubian districts; and finally, toward the end of the century, the Tartar hordes destroyed all signs of life wherever they made their appearance. According to the degree and intensity of the desolation of the country itself, one may distinguish likewise three different regions as follows:

1. The southern area, thickly settled from the earliest times by Magyars, was exposed to Turkish attacks from the 15th century on. On the western edge of this area, in Somogy county, we may, from contemporary figures, trace the diminishing population. At the close of the 15th century, for instance, there were 11,000 homesteads, for each one of which we may estimate five persons. By 1534, the figure slumped to 7,300; by 1546, to

239; by 1596, to 193; and in another century to 106 homesteads. This means that out of a population of 55,000 only 530 remained in the country. In many places, after the Magyars had been extinguished, South Slav elements came in from the Balkans, adapting themselves to Turkish conditions and settling in their places. The change in place-names indicates this. Thus originated the nationality problem in the south of Hungary, to which wide attention has been given since the middle of the 19th century.

2. North of the former region, on the central plains, similarly occupied by the Turk but without systematic warfare, the Magyar population survived, but its numbers decreased and it was subjected to servitude. The old, medieval form of settlement changed, many localities disappearing. No new people migrated there, and the defenceless population, leaving their homesteads, flocked to the state farms, these "khases" supplying a somewhat better livelihood. Thus came about the extended "peasant towns", known as such even to this day, like Nagykőrös, Kecskemét, and Szeged on the Hungarian Plain. These paid their taxes in one lump sum and were likewise able to maintain a certain measure of autonomy. The Magyar peasantry, as soon as opportunity presented itself for a freer life, showed great capacity for self-government and even for commerce. These peasant towns, however, took over the territory of many villages left empty and destroyed since their inhabitants had fled. Kecskemét, for example, gained possession of the land belonging to 32 villages. The

TURKISH DEVASTATION IN HUNGARY

Numbers refer to the respective regions
described in the text (Chapter V.)

1
2
3
4

Pozsony

Kassa

Érsekújvár
1663

Eger
1596

Jászberény

Debrecen

Győr
1594

Buda
1545

Pest

Cegléd

Devaványa

Nagyvárad
1660

Kolozsvár

Kőszeg

Nagykőrös

Mezőtúr

Kecskemét

Hódmezővásárhely

Halas

Makó

Szeged

Kanizsa
1600

Pécs

Szigetvár
1556

Nagyszeben    Brassó

town embraced, at the time of its maximum holdings, 475,000 acres of uninhabitable territory. The people were forced to give up a more intensive agriculture and return to primitive stock-raising. The only market for their livestock, roaming the prairies, was in Austria. Farther to the east, Debrecen was another such peasant town, with well-established commerce for some time.

The original cities, like Buda and Székesfehérvár, all perished, and their medieval palaces were either burned or turned into barracks. As far as the erection of new buildings was concerned, the Turks built only barracks, jails, mosques and, occasionally, baths. Edward Brown,[1] physician to Charles II of England, who passed through Hungary at the end of the 17th century, gave a lamentable account of how Matthias's palace and famous library were destroyed under the Turkish occupation. He acknowledged that Hungary "hath given the longest stop unto the Turkish conquests and farther intrusions into the western parts of Europe." He saw that this meant hard fighting "though the Hungarians want not Ingenuity, Industry and sufficient parts for Learning and liberal Arts, yet have they been more addicted unto Martial Affairs than unto deep Learning". Brown also adds that "the Turkish power so much prevailing or threatening in these parts, it is vain to expect any great University beyond Vienna." There was no real persecution on a racial basis, the Turk even permitting a primitive religious life, not bothering much with the conquered who were already in servitude. Yet

[1] *A Brief Account of Some Travels,* London, 1673.

two distinct peoples, two distinct philosophies, faced each other.

3. Surrounding the central area lay a strip of land following the lines of defense. Magyar settlements suffered greatly here, too but survived in spite of numerous foreign arrivals. In every campaign, whole villages fled, each of them keeping the memory of a "small run" or a "big run". If there was a siege, long lines of ruined villages marked the vicinity. Nothing shows more the hardiness of the Magyar peasant than the fact that he returned again and again, though in the regions adjoining the Transylvania, Rumanian ethnic elements also made their appearance.

In this third belt, it became customary to pay taxes to the Turk as well as to the Hungarian administration. When the Turk advanced, taxes to the Hungarian government were reduced, yet the population continued paying it. As revenue, this was entirely negligible, yet the population regarded it as a symbol of the country's unity. Another like consideration was the maintenance by the nobility of the county system in occupied parts, even if this was purely symbolical. Writers of the day kept all their state rights in mind to such an extent that they referred to the two Rumanian principalities under Turkish occupation as feudal territories of the Hungarian crown.

With all the devastation brought about by warfare there began the decisive transformation that turned the preponderantly Magyar state of the Carpathian Basin into a nationality state. During the struggles of the Turkish era, the vital forces of the nation suffered; and the situation became worse with the colonization in the 18th century. Thus, because the Magyars opposed the Turks instead of joining them in their westward march against the Christian world, they tragically brought upon themselves conditions which, in the 20th century, were exploited by those who sought the dissection of Hungary and the Carpathian Basin. Under more favorable circumstances, the Hungarians could have reached a population of 15 to 20 millions by the 18th century, like other peoples numbering about four millions in the 15th. Hungary contributed this sacrifice, it can be squarely stated, not only in self-defense but also for the protection of all Europe.

All through the 16th century, Hungary fought the infidel to the last, as one man. The antagonism between them hardly abated even during intervals of peace. The cause of this may be found in the fact that the Hungarians had by then lived for five hundred years in a European atmosphere and possessed an adequate idea of the essential values of humanity, of contemporary European civilization. The Ottoman Empire's administration, on the other hand, was founded on Asiatic despotism. The military caste lived off the labors of the oppressed and despised Christian peoples, but they themselves were exposed to the unscrupulous despotism and the momentary whims of the Sultans. This was no fit life for a European. Even had the Turk not attacked incessantly there could hardly have been any basis for a

just peace, for the Magyars despised despotism. There
was a minimum of human freedom and rights without
which life was not worth living. A Hungarian staff officer wrote to the Pasha of Buda: "We are a free people,
with pride and honor, but you, Mustapha, are a miser-
able slave, with the rope around your neck every hour
of the day."

The lowest and the highest fought against the Asiatic.
Stories of the heroic defense that centered around certain forts are still being told. Nicholas Jurisich, for
instance, successfully retarded the Sultan's entire army
at Transdanubian Kőszeg. Another leader, Nicholas
Zrinyi led his whole garrison in a suicidal attack on
overwhelming forces of the enemy rather than allow
his fort at Szigetvár to be taken while a single defender
was alive.

On the other hand, distrust of the Austrian administration also grew steadily as the 17th century approached. Successors of Ferdinand, Maximilian (1564–
1576), as well as the latter's insane son Rudolph (1576–
1608), altogether neglected the interests of Hungary.
Not having known the country as it was before the
Battle of Mohács, they considered it as a fragment of
alien territory, good only to serve as a defense belt for
the Empire. They dispatched thither their own
strategists, who, naturally, were not successful on an
entirely new terrain. It was the confidants of the Habsburgs who spread all over Europe the calumnies about
the "recalcitrant" Magyars. From 1591 to 1606, the
Turk launched a long series of devastating campaigns,

against which the Imperial administration was pitifully helpless. From then on, the Hungarians became more and more convinced that not only the infidel, but also the foreign government, was an enemy. A contemporary poet, Peter Bornemisza, expressed the general feeling thus:

> "The haughty Germans persecute me;
> The infidel Turks surround me:
> Shall I again enjoy, and when,
> A residence in old Buda town?"

The Counter-Reformation, too, despite the protest of the Estates at the Diet of 1604 asking a *status quo* in religious matters, was forced upon the Magyars in places, and provoked a reaction. To make disillusionment complete, the government employed unscrupulous and baseless charges to indict wealthy landowners in order to secure their holdings. In one instance, even the acquittal of a Magyar landlord was subsequently falsified.

Such prosecutions fostered the anti-Habsburg movement which soon found an able leader in the person of Stephen Bocskay. Originally he too was a sincere partisan of "Western Orientation", favoring the closest cooperation with the Emperor against Islam, but was forced to flee to Transylvania by these methods of oppression. He led a successful campaign against the Emperor, and was consequently elected Prince of Transylvania in 1605. His political and military success helped him to form a new political conception.

To him, the independence of Transylvania was not merely the inevitable result of an unhappy political exigency. He regarded the existence of an independent Protestant principality, able to maintain, as far as possible, equally good relations with West and East, as a useful factor and a necessary good. A representative of the traditional western political outlook, George Thurzó, later Palatine, protested against the separation of the eastern territories from the mother country. In reality, however, it was not Bocskay who separated Transylvania from Hungary but the Ottoman imperialism. This is shown by the fact that later on, when Prince Gabriel Bethlen attempted to reunite the two parts, Stamboul protested. "We shall never cede Transylvania to Hungary", so went the Turkish answer, "for Transylvania was invented by Sultan Suleiman". Bocskay merely utilized the situation to the best advantage. He himself knew that a separate Transylvania was necessary only until a truly national sovereignty could again extend over the whole of Hungary. This he expressed in his political testament. Bocskay, from his own successes, arrived at new conclusions. The task of an independent Transylvania was to defend Hungary, including the western parts, against foreign, Austrian aggression. But at heart, Bocskay, as his opponents well knew, was never a pro-Turk, since Magyars, no matter how anti-Austrian they were, could never come to a lasting understanding with the infidel. The real reason why western Hungarian leaders opposed Bocskay's plans to maintain a separate Transylvania was the fear that this might weaken the idea of Hungary's unity, an idea that had never been relinquished. In the Peace of Vienna, concluded by Bocskay with the Emperor in 1606, he not only had his political success assured, but also successfully defended the rights of Protestants. Simultaneously he signed a treaty of peace with the Turk. Yet it was not Bocskay but his successors who made little Transylvania an important power. The most outstanding among these was Gabriel Bethlen, a son of noble but impoverished parents, orphaned in early youth. He was only fifteen when he witnessed the fall of Prince Sigismund Báthory, predecessor of Bocskay, a victim of his pro-Austrian political adventure against the Turk; and he actually witnessed the devastation caused by the mobs of Basta, the imperial generalissimo. He therefore fled to Turkey to avoid the oppression of the Imperial military autocracy. The very idea of taking refuge on Turkish soil was new and alien to the traditional feelings of the 16th century; but now it was an inevitable step. In the eyes of the Hungarians, the Turkish Empire was not only a sworn enemy and a constant aggressor, but also an unknown, heathen, Oriental power. They regarded its existence as God's punishment inflicted on a sinful world. Now as young Bethlen became acquainted with peculiarly Turkish conditions, he came to know his way about in Turkish administration, and discovered how to treat Orientals. He returned to Transylvania during the reign of Bocskay, and that Prince made good use of Bethlen's talents in diplomacy. Bocskay's successor, the young and irrepressible Gabriel Báthory, was indebted to Bethlen for his advice, which contributed to the success of his reign.

In 1613, Bethlen himself was made prince. Until then, Transylvania had been nicknamed "Fairyland", because its political conditions were unsteady and incalculable. Only a strong personality such as Bocskay, for instance, could enforce his constructive will upon it. Under the rule of Bethlen, Transylvania became a well-administered, economically consolidated, independent political factor.

The evolution of national absolutism in Hungary had broken down with the death of Matthias Corvinus. Now Bethlen, as a Protestant monarch, continued in his path. Contemporary English ideas made a deep impression on Transylvania. James I of England's book of instructions for his son was translated into Hungarian and widely read in Transylvania. The introductory poem to the Hungarian version was by Albert Szenczi Molnár, an outstanding figure in Hungarian Calvinist literature.

When, as a result of the Czech uprising, the Thirty Years' war started in 1618, Bethlen judged the time ripe for carrying out his plan for the reorganization of a united Hungary. As expressed in his Manifesto, the defense of religious and national liberty prompted him to fight. The Czech uprising was finally vanquished at White Mountain in 1621, yet Bethlen, who conquered the Habsburg-part of Hungary with a successful attack and was elected, in 1619, "Chief and Protector of the

Country", was able to sign a favorable Treaty in 1622, reaffirming the rights of the Protestants.

Bethlen's realistic policy was evidenced by his reluctance to have himself crowned, which would have brought him into conflict with the Emperor and the Sultan at the same time. Instead he assured security to Transylvania's rear, which he achieved by stimulated friendship and diplomacy.

Following his first campaign, Bethlen entered the anti-Habsburg coalition of power. England, France, the Protestant principalities of Germany, Denmark, Sweden and, in the southeast, Transylvania, had common interests against the Emperor. By the Treaty of Westminster in 1624, Bethlen was admitted, as a member with equal rights, in the anti-Habsburg coalition, created by the Pact of The Hague.

During the last three years of his life he devoted his attention to Poland. The tradition of Báthory was still alive, i.e. that Hungary and Poland should write their forces under the same ruler to maintain their position between East and West. But in 1629, before he could carry out his plans with Poland, he died. In his last hour, when he could no longer speak, he asked for a pen and scribbled the following: "If God is with us, who is against us? No one, certainly no one."

He could not attain his chief aim, the restoration of Hungary's unity. But he did unite the Protestant forces against the Emperor and by this step created historic traditions for later centuries. Without Bethlen, Hungary would, perhaps, have shared the fate of Bohemia. His greatness lies in the fact that in an era of Turkish inroads and of the Thirty Years War, he raised his country to the position of a European Power, safeguarding its political security and keeping alive, among its isolated people, vital intellectual and economic interests as well as the traditions of European civilization.

The national existence of Transylvania was established by Bocskay and Bethlen; and their successors continued in the same tradition. George Rákóczi I (1630–1648) attempted to preserve the achievements of Bethlen through careful, though simpler methods, and took over, in their entirety, his aims in foreign policy and his diplomatic connections. After he had signed a treaty with Sweden and France in 1644, he conducted a campaign against the Emperor, again, like Bocskay and Bethlen, as a member of a European coalition. In the following year, he was able to conclude a favorable peace, endeavoring in it to safeguard religious freedom as a right to be enjoyed even by the peasantry. This was a change from the old principle of *cuius regio*. The reason for this was that the Protestants of the West had sunk to minority position. Until their masters changed back to Catholicism, the lower orders also remained Protestant on grounds of the *cuius regio* principle. This situation brought about the fact that, during the Counter-Reformation, the lower elements were about to abandon Protestantism, together with their landlords. This explains the new standpoint.

In western Hungary, under Matthias II (1608–

1619), even the Palatines Illésházy and his successor Thurzó, were ardent Protestants. But the Counter-Reformation marched ahead, suiting the plans of the Emperor. The zealous Ferdinand II (1619–1637) helped Catholicism to final victory in his Austrian Provinces. In Hungary, on the other hand, it was not so much the pressure of Vienna's court as the dynamic personality of Peter Pázmány that most contributed to the successes of the Counter-Reformation. Pázmány, born a Protestant but educated by the Jesuits, chose the method of peaceful persuasion. With his magnificent sermons, he brought a long line of influential people back into the fold of the Catholic Church. He became archbishop in 1616, and did much to improve the discipline and standard of the clergy, as well as the status of education in general. In 1635, he founded the University of Nagyszombat, to be transferred to Buda in the next century, as the direct ancestor of Budapest University, known today as the "Royal Hungarian Peter Pázmány University of Sciences".

It was primarily the result of Peter Pázmány's action that by the time of Ferdinand III (1637–1657) the strong majority of the western part of Hungary was Catholic again. In his political outlook, Pázmány was devoted to the idea of a Western orientation. He steadfastly upheld the principle of a united Hungary, expecting its defense from the Infidel by the Habsburg king. He was worried about Transylvania, however, which he called the "beautiful bastion of Christianity".

He opposed the weakening of Transylvania, either in the political or in the military sense, a proposal seriously planned by the intransigent political leaders of western Hungary of the time, such as the Palatine, Nicholas Esterházy. During his twenty years of office (1625–1645), the latter never ceased to agitate for the expulsion of the Turk, with the aid of the Habsburgs. The Palatine Esterházy argued that Transylvania, built as a state upon conditions set by Stamboul, was therefore a formation not only retarding a truly national policy, but inimical to it. His greatest ambition was the completion of the defence lines and their proper supply, and with this in mind he drew up a plan for the reorganization of the country's military system, with which he wanted to begin a large-scale preparation for the expulsion of the Turk from Hungary.

As a result of the Turkish occupation, two distinct schools of political thought, indeed, two state administrations developed in Hungary. Transylvania attempted, as far as circumstances permitted, to perpetuate a living space for Hungarians between territories occupied by Turk and Austrian. In the western portion of the country, however, the principle of a unified Hungary and the expulsion of the Turk with Habsburg aid was upheld. The whole set-up of Transylvania, the high standard of its educational institutions, its capable leadership and constant cultural intercourse with Western Protestant countries made it an isolated outpost of European civilization on the east. Above it hovered the question mark, nevertheless, whether its

separate existence would not be hampered by the de-
cadence of the Ottoman Empire on one hand, and the
political reorganization following the Thirty Years'
War on the other. The Treaty of Westphalia in 1648
assured France's hegemony on the Continent, but, in
exchange, the German Emperor received freedom of
action towards the east. By now his power rested
primarily on Austria. With his rule of conquered Bohemia now secure, he was in a position to exert greater
pressure on Hungary. The Westphalian Treaty did not
guarantee Transylvania; and with the influence of the
Habsburgs even greater than in the time of Bethlen,
the outlook was none too bright.

Yet the situation underwent important changes even
in the western part of the country, under Habsburg rule.
Following Bocskay's campaign the statutes of 1608
confirmed the feudal constitution of the nobles, increasing the influence of the Estates. The towns in Upper
Hungary, as well as those in Transylvania, having enjoyed a privileged status and autonomous administrations since the Middle Ages, had not before allowed
nobles to settle within their limits. Thus, for instance,
it was possible for certain towns in Hungary, such as
those settled by Germans, to exclude Magyars altogether. In the middle 17th century, however, noblemen
were in a position to move freely into these towns and
exercise their privileges, which meant that they were
exempt from the town councils' executive powers. The
quieter era, lasting about one generation, at least as far
as Turkish wars were concerned, that began with the

ascendancy of Bocskay, likewise lightened the burdens of the nobility who usually bore the brunt of personal military service. Concurrently, the lesser nobility began its emancipation from the fetters imposed on it in public life by the magnates.

But relations between the Estates and the king underwent changes owing to certain outside developments. The tendency towards absolutist rule that had been evident in the Secret Court Council of Vienna, since the beginning of the century, revealed itself in ever greater intensity. Leading advisers of the monarch entertained an almost personal hatred against Hungary's constitution, since it was the most difficult obstacle to absolutist ambitions in the whole Empire. As soon as the influence of Habsburg might become stronger in the East, after the Treaty of Westphalia, this antagonism, until now a sentiment only, developed into a desperate political struggle. Not only did the position of Transylvania become more difficult by the second half of the 17th century, but even the western sections of the country were obliged not only to brace themselves for a final assault on the Osmanli, but at the same time to withstand the ever-growing pressure of Imperial absolutism. Both problems had to be dealt with soon.

Travelers passing through Hungary at the time depict a devastated, exhausted country, the once rich and happy land where the labors of many centuries had created an agricultural civilization now being disfigured by drifts of sand, unregulated floodwaters, and weedy abandoned gardens surrounding ruined homesteads.

Travelers were loath to visit such unknown regions, where intermittent fever and other dangers threatened. On the southern fringes of the fertile Hungarian Plain, toward the Balkans, not a single building was to be seen, every sign of life having been annihilated. Lady Mary Wortley noted in her diary, a little later that "indeed, nothing can be more melancholy" than seeing all the devastation.

The political forces of this Hungary, exhausted by the ceaseless strain, did not possess enough stamina to make a stand. The decline began in Transylvania. Prince George Rákóczi II (1648–1660), who took over the traditions and prestige of his predecessors, overestimated the possibilities and thus caused his own downfall. He was highly regarded even abroad; Oliver Cromwell greeted him as a defender of Protestantism; his French and Swedish connections were traditional; and so was his plan to become king of Poland. But he overlooked the changes in a Europe uprooted after 1648, and he attempted something that not even Bethlen had dared risk, i.e. securing the Polish throne by means of war, with the aid of Sweden. The unfortunate campaign ended in 1657 in a complete rout, and part of the Transylvanian army fell into the hands of the Tartars. This affair gave the Porte a magnificent excuse to check the rising power of Transylvania. In a "punitive" attack led by the Turk against the forces of Rákóczi, the latter lost his life, as did his successor John Kemény two years later, though he appealed in vain to the Habsburg Emperor for assistance. Transyl-

vania's independent political rôle was essentially finished. The indecisive Prince Michael Apafi (1662–
1690), was only a puppet in the hands of the Turks.

Emperor Leopold I (1657–1705), contemporary and
rival of King Louis XIV of France, ascended the throne
in the year of Transylvania's doom. His long reign is
identified with endless attempts to force absolutist rule
upon the country. At this time, the most outstanding
representative of Western political conception was
Nicholas Zrinyi, the last hope of Hungarian aspirations
in the century. Posterity recalls him chiefly as a poet,
for as a young man he eulogized the heroic death of his
great-grandfather in the defense of Fort Szigetvár
against the infidel. Some look upon him as a strategist,
for he was the first Hungarian military leader who carried on offensive campaign and who returned to the old
idea of active defense. Yet his contemporaries, Hungarians and foreigners alike, saw in him the predestined political leader. No one recognized Hungary's
position better than he, as is proved by his military and
political writings.

Zrinyi's ideal was the Hungary of Matthias Corvinus.
He saw the difficulties arising out of the fact that the
monarch was foreign to the country, and he worried
about the fate of Transylvania. Yet he realized and was
the first to realize, that the time had arrived for crack-
ing the domination of the Ottoman Empire in Hungary, and that therefore his country had to rely on
peaceful relations with its Emperor. Although the new
Grand Viziers were forceful men, and Turkish attacks

seemed to become more frequent and more vicious, all
this could not hide from Zrinyi the growing internal
weakness of the Ottoman Empire; and although
through the negligence of the Habsburg generalissimo,
Montecuccoli, two important fortresses, Érsekujvár on
the north, and Várad on the east, were lost, Zrinyi knew
that the situation was ripe for clearing the Turk out of
Hungary, provided all available energy could be directed to that end. Knowing that the Hungarians had to
rely only on their own resources, he worked hard on the
organization of a Hungarian national army, and steadfastly advocated unity, determination, and the necessity
of an early offensive campaign. His name re-echoed all
over Europe, his deeds aroused the interest of the King
of France, and many, even in the west, considered
Zrinyi the only one able to deal with the Osman problem, and as one "upon whom Providence hath devolved
the fate of Europe."[1]

But the attention of Vienna was fixed on the West,
on France, which, in turn, necessitated peace-making
with the Turk, thus foiling any active attempt on behalf
of Zrinyi. The plans of the Emperor concurred with the
wishes of the Sultan, who was anxious to shelve Zrinyi's
campaign. Between the two great powers, Turkish and
Austrian, the Hungarians were again left to themselves.
The court of Vienna did not waste any sympathy on
their decimation, especially since they proved such a
nuisance by blocking absolutistic schemes. In contrast
to this, French army officers who took part in the cam-

[1]The Conduct and Character of Count Nicholas Serini. London 1664.

paign of 1664 had nothing but praise for Zrinyi and his Hungarian patriots.

This attempt of 1664 to dislodge the Turk began victoriously, thanks to the genius of Zrinyi; but as soon as the leadership of Montecuccoli was forced upon the Christian forces, he countermanded every bold stroke. Under such circumstances, credit for the victory at Szent-Gotthárd was partly due to the French auxiliary forces. But even this was not exploited, as a shameful treaty followed it. The conditions of peace aroused country-wide resentment. Before the end of the year, however, Zrinyi met his death at a hunt. As Sagredo, the envoy of Venice wrote: "with the passing of Zrinyi, the Hungarians were left without counsel or leadership."

Finally, the attitude of the Vienna Court antagonized even its own adherents in western Hungary, the Catholics too turning away. The leaderless Hungarian magnates, Zrinyi's younger brother Peter, moreover, Francis Nádasdy, Francis Rákóczi and Francis Wesselényi, conspired and dreamed of a French alliance in 1671. This ill-organized political conspiracy gave the Court a welcome excuse to suspend the constitution and to introduce its absolutist rule immediately. Those responsible for the conspiracy drew death sentences from courts composed of foreign judges, and their wealth was confiscated. A plenipotentiary of the Emperor was placed at the helm of the administration, which unleashed unprecedented political oppression with "Bloody Assizes", exploiting every means for the moral and material destruction of the middle and upper classes. The Protestant faiths suffered most, many of their ministers being sent to the galleys, to the indignation of all Europe. To escape persecution, thousands fled towards Transylvania. The so-called *"Kurucok"* i.e. Crusaders, from the Latin *crux*, meaning "cross" engaged in guerilla warfare aimed at national defense, expressing, at the same time, the widespread national feeling against anything Austrian. The first leader of this movement was Emery Thököly, a landlord in Upper Hungary, who was forced to flee to Transylvania. Heading a ragged army of refugees known as *bujdosók,* he exploited the war that broke out between Austria and France, and, as an ally of the latter, he successfully attacked the Emperor's forces during 1678–1679. As an indirect result of this, the Emperor re-established the constitution at the Diet of 1681. He permitted the practice of Protestant religions again in the western portions of the country, but only in certain localities specially designated.

In their struggles, the *Kurucok* had no powerful Transylvania to rely upon, and so the outcome of their daring exploits depended largely on momentary oscillations of strength, that proved, quite often, disastrous. Thököly furthermore had to depend on the goodwill of the Sultan, though Zrinyi's warnings that it was high time and a good opportunity to expel the Turk became more and more cogent. When Kara Mustapha laid siege to Vienna in 1683, the Christian forces, aided by the army of the Polish King, John Sobieski, won a complete victory over him. This Turkish disaster marked the beginning of a sixteen year war of liberation, which resulted in the final collapse of Turkish domination over Hungary.

Buonvisi, papal nuncio to Vienna, was the soul of this prolonged campaign, and at last, in 1686, after almost one hundred and fifty years of pagan misrule, the town of Buda, capital of Hungary, was recaptured by the advancing Christian forces, commanded by Prince Charles of Alsace-Lorraine, with volunteers from Scotland and Italy. All Europe was impressed by this successful military campaign, in which the Hungarian nation, despite endless disillusionments, took a share well above its numerical proportion. The final victory over the Turk was achieved at Zenta in 1697, under Prince Eugene of Savoy. Within two years, the Treaty of Karlovic was signed, by which the Turks gave up all Hungarian territory with the exception of the border region of Temes.

Although the Turkish occupations, according to the plans of Zrinyi, could have been terminated a generation before, the unity of the country was re-established, nevertheless, with the aid of the Habsburg dynasty. This naturally resulted in the growth of the Emperor's influence and the Estates, in the Diet of 1687, agreed to accept the hereditary male succession of the Habsburg dynasty. Simultaneously, however, they abolished the clause of the Golden Bull of 1222 that gave the nobles the right to resist the king's unconstitutional decree. Only the problem of Transylvania had yet to be solved in order to bring about historic unity. Since the conditions that had produced Transylvania's separate existence had ceased, the continuation of her independent government was no longer necessary. After lengthy conferences in which Nicholas Bethlen, later Chancellor, who was very much at home in England, played an important part, Emperor Leopold I reached the decision that Transylvania was to be governed, by virtue of his powers embodied in St. Stephen's Crown, directly under his sovereignty but separate from the main body of Hungary.

The wars of liberation demanded great efforts and sacrifices from the exhausted nation. During all this time, the persecution of political suspects went on under the guidance of foreign generals, whose grip on the population became tighter and tighter. The liberated parts of the country belonged, according to the absolutist theoreticians, to the Emperor by right of armed conquest, *iure belli;* and all estates the ownership of which became doubtful during the long Turkish occupation, were likewise reallotted by a *neoacquistica commissio.* Descendants of the original owners, if they were alive, had to prove their rights by documents and long, costly processes of law. The majority of lands became the property of Austrian dignitaries either as rewards from their government, or as payment in lieu of overdue salaries.

It was at this time, that there began that colonization of abandoned lands which altered the ethnic

character of this part of the country in the following
century. Southern Slavs were brought *en masse* into the
newly-liberated territory as a result of Vienna's policy.
As soon as the scene of anti-Turkish campaign was
temporarily shifted to the Balkans, the Emperor issued
a manifesto inducing the Serbs, Albanians, etc., to fight
the Osmanli. But as soon as the Christian forces withdrew from the peninsula, the Turk unleashed a campaign of terror against the Serbs, who, led by Arsen
Cernojevic, the Patriarch of Ipek, sought and found
refuge in southern Hungary. About 36,000 Serbian families entered and were granted ecclesiastical autonomy.
Soon this immigrant population, placed directly under
the authority of the Vienna War Council, was exploited against the Magyars, since they were soon
incited to fight the Rákóczi uprising and derive benefits
for their alliance with the Emperor.

The systematic, relentless oppression that made itself
felt in the political as well as in the economic field,
greatly embittered the peasantry. Lexington, England's
minister to Vienna, wrote in 1697 that a rebellion had
again broken out in Upper Hungary, "declaring for religion, liberty and property." Whatever the issue may
be, "it is feared that if they (i.e. the Court of Vienna)
will not change the barbarous usage they show both in
religion and civil matters, the Hungarians will entirely
throw off, one time or another, the Emperor's domination."[1]

[1]Sutton, *Account of the Courts at London and Vienna at the Conclusion
of the 17th Century,* London 1851, p. 277.

The hope of the rebels lay in the person of Francis Rákóczi II, a nephew of Nicholas Zrinyi, and descendant of a prince of Transylvania, who at first tried to avoid any connection with the revolutionaries. He had received a thorough schooling in Jesuit institutions abroad, and his scholarly bearing predestined him to be the guardian of peace and a patron of the arts. As lord of Upper Hungary's largest estates, he was a loyal subject of the Emperor, his past not being marred by any political adventure. Yet the outrages committed against his people forced him to seek the alliance of Louis XIV of France. His correspondence was intercepted and he was detained, but escaped to Poland.

Up to now the whole affair was but a conspiracy of a magnate, something even the King of France was reluctant to be mixed up with. What made it a nationwide movement was the widespread desire to get rid of foreign oppression. Rákóczi's Manifesto, *"Recrudescunt vulnera"* (The Wounds Reopen), was addressed not only to the nobility but to the entire people, and his *"Pro Patria et Libertate"* standards were first borne by the peasants of Upper Hungary. Slovaks and Ruthenes, mountaineer folk of the area, were fighting side by side with the Magyars under Rákóczi.

Louis XIV, deep in the troubles of the Wars of the Spanish Succession, was glad to find an eastern ally in Rákóczi who by that time was in possession of almost the whole of Hungary. The uprising began under favorable conditions. The Estates elected Rákóczi as "ruling prince", and while England and Holland endeavored to mediate, the struggle went on relentlessly even after the death of Emperor Leopold. The latter's successor, Joseph I (1705–1711), was willing to conclude peace but Rákóczi could not trust him and demanded Transylvania as a guarantee of good faith. To this end, he attempted to arrive at a formal and mutual alliance with the King of France, in order that at the end of the Western European war, Hungary might be given an international guarantee. This was the main reason for the dethronement of the House of Habsburg at the Diet of Ónod in 1707. But Rákóczi's envoy to France soon found out that Louis XIV was only interested in the advantages he would gain through an alliance with Hungary. Soon after, when the Imperial forces were released from the Western front, the cause of the insurrection grew worse. Rákóczi himself was no strategist, and his brave generals knew more about swift guerilla warfare than about greater military conceptions. Besides this, the *Kuruc* forces, despite the organizing ability of Rákóczi, were not a regular soldiery, for they lacked officers, discipline and previous peacetime preparation, without which no army can make good.

With the defeats during the years 1708 and 1710, the *Kuruc* insurrection was doomed; but the Emperor also desired peace, and appointed John Pálffy, the most respected among his Hungarian followers as his negotiator. Rákóczi's general, Alexander Károlyi, arrived at decent terms in the Peace of Szatmár (1711) according to which everyone laying down his arms received

full amnesty, with a promise of constitutional and religious freedom. Rákóczi himself, with his entourage,
fled to Poland, then to France, and finally, when all
hope was gone, into self-exile in Turkey, leaving behind his family and all his wealth. There he died, in the
hamlet of Rodostó, in 1735. His work entitled *"Con-
fessions"* is proof of his noble character. Some of those
who followed him into exile stayed over in France to
become founders of the French light cavalry. Among
these was László Berchényi, Marshal of the Hussars.

While the insurrection failed in a military sense, its
political achievements were nevertheless great. By this
effort, Hungary assured herself of a political position
that made possible the following new period of peace.

# VI

## THE ERA OF RECONSTRUCTION

### (*1711–1825*)

A period calculated from the Treaty of Szatmár in 1711 up to the Diet of 1825 was known, until recently, as the Era of National Relapse. Those who witnessed the upswing of national principles and the victory of liberalism, considered this time as a long interval of enfeeblement in the national spirit, a period during which heroic warfare ceased yet new ideas did not arrive. As we can now judge it better, this was in reality an Era of Reconstruction, in which the grievous wounds of the Turkish era were healed.

Hungary had fought against Ottoman oppression for three centuries; and when this struggle came to an end, the Hungary to be rebuilt was no longer the rich country of Matthias Corvinus. During the latter's reign, the nations of Europe numbered but eighty million people, with Hungary's share at four million, not including acquired territories. At the beginning of the 18th century, Europe as a whole had almost doubled in population, yet Hungary's population was scarcely more than two and a half million, including its now numerous non-Magyar nationalities. These figures suggest the extent of devastation wrought by the Turkish occupation. This is the underlying cause why the Hungarians did not make themselves heard in the century of the founding of Capitalism and Commerce, since they were occupied with internal problems. They were obliged to build up settlements, to take care of basic economic conditions, and to rebuild civilization on the ruins of three centuries.

Aside from this, another important change had been brought about as a result of the Turkish occupation. Hungary was now subject to a foreign dynasty. Not even the uprising of Rákóczi could alter this. Thus Hungary was obliged to remain in the Central European system of the Habsburgs and to share the latter's fate, with Hungary's development made dependent on the policies of the Empire. In its relation with other peoples, Hungary could not, from then on, pursue any initiative for its scope of action was strictly limited.

On the other hand, the insurrection for a long time withheld the Austrian government from any attempt at oppression. Emperor Charles III (1711–1740), who ascended the throne in the year of the Treaty of Szatmár as well as his daughter Maria Theresa (1740–1780), avoided provoking open rebellion, knowing how difficult would be its pacification. Following the War of the Spanish Succession, the domination of the Habsburgs extended over Belgium and the northern provinces of Italy. To hold together this vast territory, a crazy quilt both geographically and ethnically, was indeed a tremendous task. Therefore the statesmen of Vienna concentrated on their Western possessions, a policy which in turn necessitated peaceful conditions in the East. This explains their apparent willingness to grant concessions to the Hungarians.

As a result, an era of compromise followed, a change from continuous conflict. As opportunities for another insurrection faded, this state of affairs was welcomed by the Estates, who were in control of domestic administration. In this particular respect, there was not much change from the 16th century in Hungary, in contrast to the conditions in Western Europe, where the monarchs were able to break the political power of the Estates and to introduce an absolutistic rule that unified state economy as well as administration. A classic example of this type of rule may be found in France under Louis XIV. England, on the other hand, had progressed one step farther by the end of the 17th century for as a result of the Revolution of 1688, the English finally instituted the parliamentary form of government, under a definitely limited monarchy.

By the beginning of the 18th century, it seemed to be evident that this latter form of government, as tried out in England, had a better chance to succeed than an absolutist system. This contributed to the turning of European philosophers against political despotism and religious intolerance, as causes of national weakness.[1]

[1]G. M. Trevelyan, *The English Revolution,* London, 1939 (Introduction).

In Central Europe, though absolutism was maintained, a new ideal developed, known as "Enlightened Despotism", in which the monarch was supposed to exercise his power for the good of his subjects. Disciples of this ideal like Frederick II of Prussia and Joseph II of Austria considered themselves first servants of the state. This type of absolutism was, unquestionably, on a higher level than the despotism of Emperor Leopold I at the end of the 17th century. The state now went as far as considering social problems and demanding tolerance in religious matters.

For a considerable time in Hungary, the administration of the Estates merely endeavored to uphold existing conditions instead of introducing reforms. It did not take very much notice of social and economic problems, because its roots were in the Middle Ages. It could not refer to advanced models as did absolutism and clung to old traditions based on the legal principles laid down by Werbőczi two hundred years earlier. The nobility could not pay sufficient attention to the lower classes because the nobles themselves, fighting personally through long centuries, had greatly diminished and were in difficult economic circumstances.

Specific Hungarian interests and Hungarian sovereign rights were often at stake, for the monarch considered the welfare of Hungary no more than was necessary for the Habsburg Empire. There was however no choice but to submit, irrespective of injustices suffered, since the country was badly in need of a period of peace.

Political reorganization was of great importance in the early 18th century, and settled questions until 1848 and, in some respects, to the end of World War I. The succession of the male branch of the dynasty had already been accepted under Leopold I. In 1711, Charles III was the sole male member of the House of Habsburg. As early as 1713, Charles announced in Austria the dynastic law known as *Pragmatica Sanctio,* which regulated the right of succession of his daughters and the daughters of his two elder brothers who had already died. But in the case of Hungary, he had to secure his daughter's succession by separate legislation. To win the good will of the country, Charles III was careful to adhere to the conditions of the Szatmár Treaty, summoning the Diet, which in turn elected John Pálffy as Palatine. The King declared his wish to govern the country according to its laws, saying that he would defend its integrity and would respect the privileges of the nobility, who were exempt from taxation. In such matters, the monarch kept true to his principles according to which "Hungarians are to be deprived of their assumption that they are under German domination." The successful, final campaign against the Turk, led by Eugene of Savoy in 1717, recovering Temesvár and the southern provinces, and taking even Belgrade, made a good impression. This helped in the appreciation of Habsburg assistance.

The first three articles of the Act of 1723, containing the Hungarian *Pragmatica Sanctio,* assented to the succession of the female line of the dynasty in Hungary.

Every ruler however, was to be obliged to take an oath
that he or she would observe the constitution and the
laws of independent Hungary, and that the two countries, Austria and Hungary, were to be considered connected, *"indivisibiliter et inseparabiliter"*, and as owing
mutual assistance to each other against external aggression, *"contra vim externam."*

Hungary, according to this Act, preserved her independence, though no provisions were made as to her
share in matters of mutual interest, such as defense. A
serious setback was suffered by the nation in this respect. For mutual defense, the customary muster of
the nobility was insufficient according to the standard
of modern warfare, and had to be augmented by a
permanent army. For the maintenance of this, a general war tax, known as *contributio* was introduced.
The permanent army, however, despite its numerous
Hungarian contingents, was under the command of the
Vienna War Council, with no Hungarian member, in
spite of the fact that the chief commander of the Hungarian army had always been the Palatine. The Emperor's court constantly suspected the Magyars and
stationed a large number of foreign troops in Hungary.
The upkeep of these troops was allotted to the peasants,
but its command was beyond the control of the country's
administration. Owing to mutual mistrust, a Magyar
could hardly ever reach the higher ranks in the army
or obtain important positions in the government.

The higher offices of the newly reorganized administration were made dependent on the Vienna Govern-

ment, without being responsible to the Hungarian Diet. Among the central government offices *(dicasteria)* in Vienna, the Royal Court Chancellery was the highest, and through it decrees of the King were passed to the Hungarian Deputy Council *(consilium locumten-entiale)* which exercised executive power in Hungarian internal affairs. The president of the latter was the Palatine, his seat being at first Pozsony, and later on, Buda. Its officials were dependent on the king, who issued his orders upon the advice of the Viennese councillors, to the frequent detriment of Hungarian constitutional law. On such occasions, the Deputy Council in Hungary faced an awkward choice between protesting to Vienna against royal decree of sending out the order and taking chances on its refusal by the autonomous counties and cities.

One of the main obstacles to an efficient administration was the shelving of the Council's power. It could not command the army and had no say in matters relative to customs duties, colonization, commerce, or the management of royal revenues. Since the 16th century economic affairs had been handled by the Hungarian Royal chamber depending directly on the Vienna Court Chamber, over which the Hungarian Diet had no power, its only function being to vote on taxation. Such a procedure was bound to be followed by dire consequences, and Hungarian sovereign rights suffered. The central authorities of Vienna gained a strong influence in Hungarian affairs, passing order after order against the interest of the nation. In the time of Maria

Theresa, all matters relating to the Hungarian state were under the direction of the Vienna State Council. The political significance of all this was not properly realized by the Hungarian Estates because in the medieval system of administration the control of financial, military and foreign affairs belonged to the personal rights of the king. Thus, according to the letter of the constitution, no legal harm was done to Hungary's sovereignty.

The integrity of the country was not left unharmed either. Transylvania was maintained as a separate principality, directly under the King. It was evident that with the passing of the Osman danger, there was no need for Transylvania's separation. But Habsburg scheming did not welcome any strengthening of Hungary. Thus the Estates petitioned in vain, (1723) for the reincorporation of Transylvania; although, with the passing of the 17th century, any political significance of Transylvania as a separate entity became a thing of the past, in spite of the tradition of Bocskay and Bethlen.

In Croatia there was no need to disturb the old ties even after the common Turkish danger had passed. The Estates of Croatia supported the Hungarians in their struggle against absolutist rule. Whenever problems concerning the entire realm of the Hungarian crown were at stake, the Croats naturally had their right to speak. The Hungarian Estates, on the other hand, did not interfere with the internal affairs of Croatia. Thus, until the end of the century, when new nationalism began to stir, there were no difficulties in Hungaro-Croat relations.

A serious blow to the integrity of Hungary was that the territory regained from the Turk at the Treaty of Passarovic (1718), was not returned to the country, no matter how often this was urged by the Estates. The Banat, a province between the rivers Danube, Tisza and Maros, was placed under the military rule of the Imperial staff. On the site of numerous devastated Hungarian villages, newly settled Southern Slavs known in those days as Rascians, occupied large portions of this part of the country. Thus the southern strip of Hungary, a territory reaching from the Banat to the west through Bácska County as far as the Croatian border, was organized into a "military frontier zone", something utterly unnecessary from a strategical point of view. All this was not arranged against any foreign enemy. Since the time of Leopold I, the Viennese court entertained the idea that the Hungarians should be weakened through foreign colonization and by conniving with the newcomers. This policy was responsible for turning the Serbs against the Magyars during the Rákóczi insurrection. Marshal Eugene of Savoy once shrewdly remarked that the "anti-Hungarian feelings of the Rascians had better be kept warm". Prince Kolowrat, Premier of Austria, explained to Maria Theresa in 1748 that the Serbs had to be governed separately because they could be used as an armed force against the Hungarians only if they depended directly on Vienna. It is customary to bring up the Southern Slav question at a later date, yet it is closely related to the Imperial policies of the 18th century. As a result of deliberately antagonizing small peoples against each other it was made *a priori* impossible that later, when nationality problems appeared, a peaceful agreement could be reached, no matter how advantageous this might be for all concerned. Perhaps in no other phase is the fatal shortsightedness of the Imperial policy more evident than at this time, when fear of the Hungarians prompted them to lay the foundations of movements that later destroyed the Monarchy itself.

In the last years of the reign of Charles III, disappointment reached even greater proportions. In addition to the reasons already outlined, an unsuccessful campaign was waged against the Turk in 1737–1739, during which the gains of previous campaigns were lost including Belgrade and northern Serbia. The costs of this unfortunate war were enormous and it was the task of Maria Theresa on ascending the throne in 1740, to allay her subjects' disillusionment.

Both Austrian and post-World War Hungarian historians have acknowledged the Queen's outstanding personality, her feminine charm, her human sentiments based on religiousness, and her psychological skill in the treatment of her subjects. Her qualities were revealed as soon as she ascended the throne. All Europe's attention was focused on the fate of the Habsburg Empire, which had been left without a male ruler. Emperor Charles III had not been very successful in preparing a smooth path for his daughter's reign.

Frederick II, King of Prussia, offered to defend the
Habsburg Empire against its enemies, but wanted the
transfer of Silesia, one of the richest provinces, as his
reward. Maria Theresa refused this solution, a refusal
which set the well-trained Prussian armies marching
against Silesia. Bavarian forces, allies of France, attacking Austria from the West, were already in Bohemia. Austria seemed defenceless, and the Queen
lacked outstanding statesmen and trained strategists
who could have been a match for Frederick. While
England sympathized with her, Maria Theresa realized
that effective assistance could come only from Hungary.

In the spring of 1741, at the first Diet in twelve
years assembled, the Queen came before its members
in person and not only disarmed the recalcitrant Hungarian nobles but even won their enthusiastic support.
The scene is often referred to in history: Maria Theresa,
dressed in mourning, carrying her small children, delivered a stirring address to the nobles gathered at
Pozsony. She confided that everyone had deserted her,
and that she had to rely on the chivalry and loyalty of
the Hungarian nobles and their military assistance.

Had the traditions of the Rákóczi uprising still been
alive in Hungary, the Queen's psychological instinct
would not have been sufficient to win co-operation for a
common defense. Had another struggle for liberation
begun as forty years before, Austria would, perhaps
have been doomed. But, apparently, the Hungarians
had given up the idea of armed insurrection, and had
accepted the solutions offered by the Treaty of Szatmár.

Rákóczi's son, Joseph, had turned up on the Turkish side some years ago; but had not created the expected impression. The Hungarians did their best to arrive at some peaceful arrangement with the Austrians, as the former were badly in need of it. More than a century passed before they again took up arms, in 1848, to defend the rights of the nation.

The Treaty of Aix-la-Chapelle (1748) which terminated the warfare, gave Silesia to Frederick, yet the Habsburgs were upheld as a great power. Antagonism between Prussia and Austria soon burst out again in the Seven Years War (1757–1763), ending in a *status-quo* (Treaty of Hubertusburg) which left Silesia in Prussian hands. In all these campaigns, Hungarian regiments stood their ground excellently; and though Hungarian strategists were again pushed into the background, a few of their outstanding deeds merited Europe's attention. Such were the cavalry attack at Kollin, led by General Francis Nádasdy, and the capture of Berlin, Prussia's capital, by General Andrew Hadik (1757).

Maria Theresa was well aware of her indebtedness to Hungary, and publicly expressed her gratitude on a number of occasions. She attached the port of Fiume to Hungary, thus providing an exit to the Adriatic. She also returned the county of Temes in 1779, although its southern portion was retained as a frontier zone. The Queen endeavored to preserve harmony to the end, yet the differences between the Estates and the Court continually increased, chiefly on account of the latter's economic policy. All in all, despite foreign wars, the forty-one-year reign of Maria Theresa provided the long desired period of consolidation, during which the country regained its strength. The conditions of this comparatively peaceful existence were not always advantageous; but at the time, the Hungarians were in no position to choose.

As has been mentioned, the population of Hungary in 1720 hardly exceeded the two-and-a-half million mark, with 1.16 million of that Magyar. The annihilation had been worst in the southern districts, which were directly in the line of every Turkish assault. This flat, fertile section of the country was originally densely covered with Magyar settlements, dating back to the earliest times. Now, while in the western counties the population reached the figure of 100,000 per county, in the south it had shrunk to between 3,000 and 5,000 souls. Colonization appeared to be the most urgent task. From the reserves of the Magyar people, hailing mostly from the western counties, regeneration proceeded at an almost miraculous pace. By the beginning of the 18th century, the population was tripled in this manner in several districts in the Lowlands. This was partly due to the return of inhabitants from the western regions and partly to natural increase which was highly augmented by the return of peace. The vitality of the Magyar people showed itself in the younger generation, who vigorously recommenced farming on the ruined countryside.

The greater part of the territory regained from the

Turk was transferred to the Crown as most of the families who had once owned it had died out. The King distributed enormous tracts of land among his courtiers, his foreign generals, high dignitaries, and the hierarchy. Land was plentiful, the treasury empty, and as a result the monarch paid the overdue salaries of many of his officials with Hungarian estates. One of the serious consequences of this was the transfer of the country's agricultural wealth to foreign ownership. Only a few Magyar families were in a position to buy up newly acquired estates from these foreigners, some of whom were glad to turn their lands into cash. It was on the other hand a sad blow to the land distribution of Hungary that the number of large estates increased to the detriment of the middle-sized ones. In the county of Baranya, for instance, there were 540 smaller estates in the time of Matthias Corvinus; two centuries later there were six large estates (two secular and four ecclesiastical), and only eighteen medium-sized ones. Consequently the abundance of large estates in Transdanubia and other parts of Hungary were not so much the outcome of Hungarian land policy as the result of large 18th century donations by the Vienna court.

Settlers were placed on these great estates, owned partly by the Crown and partly by individuals. This made the lot of the Magyars worse instead of better. After being decimated by foreign wars, they were now excluded from these settlements, as Emperor Charles preferred foreign immigrants, mostly Germans. He issued a proclamation to the people of the Rhineland promising them privileges if they migrated to Hungary, the "destroyed bulwark of Christendom." These immigrants received land, buildings, live-stock on long-term payments and at nominal figures, and their industry secured a good living for them in Hungary. No Magyar was ever favored so lavishly; in certain respects, his legal status was even inferior to that of the newcomer. Whenever a Magyar settlement came into being, it usually did so in spite of the wishes of the government, and not with its assistance. The German newcomers, on the other hand, had every chance to make good. Literally hundreds of German villages came into being at this time, populated chiefly by Catholics from Southern Germany. All the German settlements to be found around the Hungarian capital were founded at this time. The large body of Germans in Transdanubia (in the counties of Tolna and Baranya) settled on the estates of foreign generals and the hierarchy. The territory was nicknamed "Swabian Turkey". Other Germans were settled in the counties of Békés and Szatmár, beyond the Tisza.

From then on, there were two types of German settlements in Hungary. Those of medieval immigration, largely town folk, were already acclimatized to conditions and identified themselves with the Magyars, except for the so-called Saxon in Transylvania, to such an extent that they fought side by side with the Magyars in the coming reform movement and the revolution of 1848. The other group were the 18th century agrarian immigrants who just got accustomed to the new country within a hundred years. Later on, many families of this latter group assimilated themselves to the Magyars. But the bulk of the German minority in post-war Hungary dated back to the 18th century colonization.

There were other great migrations in Europe at that time. Such was the flight from France to Prussia of the Huguenots, who, belonging to the middle class, not only greatly enriched Prussian life but soon accepted both the language and the customs of their new country. In contrast to this, Hungary received mostly farmer immigrants enjoying state protection, who tenaciously preserved their racial characteristics. A policy of this nature was bound to create national minorities. This was especially the case where the resettling of the original Magyar population was retarded for political reasons and every chance was given to foreigners, who, in turn, changed the whole ethnic aspect of the regions concerned. A good example of the official Austrian attitude is reflected in the colonization policy of General Mercy, first governor of the Banat of Temes, who settled 21,000 Rumanian and Serbian families in return for their enlistment. When the swamplands around Temesvár were canalized and the city rebuilt, French from Alsace, Spanish, Italian, Czech and Bulgarian, as well as German immigrants were brought in. Even politically undesirable Viennese were deported there in the second half of the century. Only Magyars were discouraged as being untrustworthy from the Habsburg point of view. Maria Theresa established in 1766 a special colonization committee in Vienna. The official colonization brought chiefly Germans to Hungary. But naturally also some smaller groups of the Slovaks living in the mountainous north were established as new settlements in the lowlands, as in the Békés County. While the Slovaks however, had lived inside Hungary from the earliest times, those non-Hungarians who were to be found in the south were mainly newcomers.

During the Turkish occupation, Southern Slav and Rumanian elements increased considerably in the southern parts of the country. Contemporary travelers were shocked to see the backward and primitive conditions in which these peoples existed. They did not take into consideration that their backwardness was mostly due to the fact that they had lived under Turkish rule, which made civilized conditions impossible for any non-Mohammedan. The Serbians, for instance, lived in mud huts, half underground, and had never heard of schools or public security. The lack of hygiene and the power of superstition were so great that a bloody rebellion broke out when the kissing of the deceased by the villagers before burial was banned by the military authorities.

The authority over the Serbians was at first in the hands of the Vienna military authorities, and was later transferred to the Court Chamber. Their organization into regiments assisted in establishing order. In 1741, the Vienna administration invited Arsen Cernojević, Patriarch of Ipek, to transfer his seat to Karlowic (north of Belgrade), not long liberated from the Turkish yoke. The Patriarch soon became not only the ecclesiastical head of the Serbs, but their political leader as well. Their Orthodox faith separated them from both the Magyars and the Germans, and it was not long before they complained against military administration. Though they lived intermingled with many other ethnic elements, they demanded autonomy for themselves, referring to privileges granted to them by Leopold I. Their demands were found exaggerated even by Vienna, though the Serbs did not cease to figure prominently in Habsburg plans as loyal supporters against possible Magyar uprisings. Vienna hoped to hold in hand all the different South Slavs. At the end of the 18th century, however, the first Russian emissaries, advocating a great Pan-Slav empire with the Serbs as its southern outpost, made their appearance on Hungarian soil. From the time of Peter the Great, the Czars had had their eye on the Balkans, and their intrigues henceforth became notorious.

In Transylvania, too, ethnographic conditions changed. The economic situation of the Saxons took a turn for the worse, and it was due only to a constant influx of newcomers that their number was saved from decrease. The lot of the Székelys became darker when the Vienna government forced them into "border militia" under foreign Austrian officers. This was unbearable to the Székelys, who had always been a free people. In 1763, the Austrian recruiting mission, from which Székely men had escaped to the forests, ejected the women and children into the winter cold and then in the night massacred a number of people at Mádéfalva where they had taken refuge. Many Székelys, realizing that they had no chance and no one to whom to apply for help, left their country for Moldavia and Bukovina.

Ethnographically, moreover, the growth of the Rumanian population was an important change. Of the half million people inhabiting Transylvania in 1700, the Rumanians did not exceed fifty per cent. By 1763, the proportion of Rumanians had risen to fifty-eight per cent. The Saxons, in the meantime, dropped from twenty to twelve per cent, the Magyars managing to uphold their proportion of about one third of the population. The increase of the Rumanians, it is believed, was not so much due to their natural prolificity as to continual infiltration. For a people composed chiefly of herdsmen, this was achieved without any difficulty through the Carpathian Mountains separating Transylvania from the Balkans. From Transylvania proper their continued westward surge brought them deeper and deeper into the plains, and finally resulted in their political demands by the 19th century.

The gradual change of ethnic conditions explains the beginnings of the nationality problem that appeared later. At the time of Matthias Corvinus, Magyars in the Carpathian Basin represented a majority strong enough to form a base to develop a national state. During the long Turkish occupation, however, hundreds of old town and village sites were uprooted, leaving deserted tracts where foreign settlers often started life anew. The continuous and varied immigration and infiltration of the different ethnic elements resulted in some places in ethnic conglomeration arousing wide attention in the 20th century.

First among economic tasks was the resumption of production. Wherever the Turk had been in control, agriculture had been retarded by several hundred years. The Magyars were thus obliged to do the same pioneer work over again with which they had civilized the land in the Middle Ages. For a few years, they produced without proper care and fertilization, the land having lain fallow for so long. But after a time, the soil became exhausted, and the inhabitants drifted from one place to another. Livestock raising had degenerated during the Turkish era also. Droughtland and marshes found in the Middle Ages mostly around the Cumanian wastes, now extended over a great part of the Lowlands between the rivers Tisza and Danube. Only the raising of livestock was feasible, and this made it necessary for the population to lead a ranch life. It is since then that the wastelands reached such proportions that though greatly reduced, they are a problem even to this day. Remnants of this sandy *puszta* attract and fascinate the modern traveler, who is often unaware of the fact that populous settlements once inhabited the now lifeless prairie, and who takes the famous *puszta* as a preserved part of medieval Hungary.

This alone shows that while Europe was about to launch social changes of great importance, in Hungary even primitive conditions of life had first to be re-established. This work was carried out mostly by the peasantry who had passed through the Turkish period under the conditions in which Werbőczi's code had left them. They could not essentially improve their circumstances even in the 18th century. That their conditions were slightly better than those of their counterparts in East Prussia, for instance, does not alter the fact that social development in Hungary was stagnant for over two centuries, a stagnation through which not only the peasants but the whole social structure suffered. One must not forget that, naturally, social development in Hungary was related to that of all East-Central Europe, and should be compared with that of other countries of that region. The peasantry endured its fate with comparative patience, resisting only when the landlord demanded more than his legal due. Maria Theresa first of all wished to abolish such practices with her order-in-council (*Urbarium,* 1767), regulating the relations between landowners and peasants. In this order, she entrusted the control of living conditions to the Deputy Council, and set the minimum of land (sixteen to 40 yokes according to the quality of soil) to be allotted to peasants. All this was important, though it did not mean a radical improvement, since the Vienna Court even failed to institute what it carried through in Bohemia, i.e. the distribution of Crown lands among the impoverished peasantry.

By that time, the Hungarian peasant looked at the future with apathy. Gregory Berzeviczy, an eminent economic expert and writer, wrote in 1804 a treatise on the psychology of peasants (De Indole Rusticorum), in which he stated that the Magyar peasant was utterly "diffident" and suspicious towards everything that came from above, whether it be an official matter or otherwise. This suspicion, together with a gift for endurance, was the result of centuries of experience. Similar, or even more marked attitudes may be found in every country where feudalism lasted long, as it did in the whole of East-Central Europe.

The greatest factor in the country was the landed aristocracy. According to Hungarian law there was no difference between nobles, yet in practice the authority of the magnates was naturally much stronger. Indeed at the beginning of the 18th century, only they had any serious political influence, the lesser nobility not attaining a say in affairs of state until later. Comparatively speaking, nobility was one may say, more democratic owing to the large number of nobles who enjoyed the same fundamental privileges. The percentage of nobles was much higher in Hungary than in Western countries. Of the three types of nobility, i.e. (1) The magnates, or aristocracy with great estates, (2) common nobility, with medium-sized estates, and (3) minor nobility, "walking in moccasins", as they were called, the latter alone for a time could not attain a word in public life for want of educational and material advantages.

In an era when in France the Tiers Etat grew to such proportions that it was soon ready to take over leadership from the nobility, in East-Central Europe, even in Hungary, only the middle strata of the nobility were in a position to insist on new ideas in opposition to the magnates. At the end of the century, this stratum, however, attempted to wrest leadership from the aristocracy, thus becoming the Hungarian counterpart of the French Tiers Etat.

In an age when the bourgeoisie had already begun to play a decisive rôle in the West, in Hungary only the skeleton of a middle class was in existence. This belated development is sufficiently explained by the previous two centuries and by the anti-Hungarian trends of Austrian economic policy.

One of the most awkward problems that the Austrian government had to face was its war debt, which piled up ominously with each campaign. This debt amounted to 70 million florins in 1711, 100 million florins in 1740, and by 1767 had reached the staggering total of 260 million florins. The Court endeavored, unsuccessfully, to solve the problem by founding a state bank *(Universal-Bankalität)*. As the situation became more unbearable, economic experts in Vienna began to complain that Hungary did not participate in due proportions in the expenses of administration and suggested the increase of the tax rate, although 2.5 million in war taxes were already paid annually. The Estates did not give their consent to this, since the peasants were unable to bear a greater load. Then the Court demanded that the hierarchy and the nobility should contribute. The hierarchy had actually

paid some taxes since 1725. When the Habsburgs lost
Silesia, Count Haugwitz proposed to the Queen the
taxation of the nobility. The Estates of the Austrian
provinces were actually forced to pay taxes for a ten-
year period. But the Hungarian nobility stuck to its
guns and in 1741 passed an Act to the effect that Tax
exemption belonged to the fundamental rights and
liberties of the nobility.

It is beyond argument that with this action the nobility hindered national evolution, and at the same time
damaged the reputation of the country. The distribution of the public burden was undoubtedly unjust, although somewhat better, in comparison, than in many
East-Central European countries. This however, does
not alter the fact that the demands of Vienna were
wholly excessive and unjustified because Hungary already contributed substantially to the maintenance of
the Habsburg Empire. But the treasury officials of
Vienna credited Hungary only with direct taxes, voted
by the Diet, whereas mining revenues, customs duties
and other *regalia* flowed directly into the treasury without authorization from the Estates. These sums were
used at will for debt payments, current expenses of the
Court, and maintenance of the army and administration. The support of the army was a further considerable burden to the populace. Thus Hungary contributed to the maintenance of the Empire proportionately to a very considerable extent (about thirty-
eight percent of the total expenditure), more than the

share Hungary had to pay by virtue of the 1867 Compromise with Austria.

Regardless of this, the Court applied its new economic policy to Hungary in an extreme form and regarded the country merely as a colony to be exploited for the benefit of the Austrian hereditary provinces. As a result, the manufacturing enterprises (silk, textile and metal plants) founded in Hungary at the beginning of the 18th century were forced out of existence. A few industrial experiments by English interests likewise had to be discontinued. Hungary had to restrict itself to supplying Austria with raw materials bought at very low prices, while exports beyond Austria were ruled out by exorbitant taxes. With the partitioning of Poland in 1772, the province of Galicia was joined to Austria, thus making difficult the export of Hungarian wine to the north. Simultaneously, customs barriers prohibited the importation of industrial products from countries other than Austria and Bohemia, whose new factories prospered by the Hungarian market. In 1762, all matters pertaining to commerce were placed under the authority of the *Kommerzienrat* (Board of Commerce) of Vienna.

Such a procedure was naturally followed by dire consequences, seriously hampering Hungary's economic development. The country was left as a purely agricultural economy, even though its natural resources, especially in the Uplands made it likewise suitable for industry. The development of the middle classes was retarded. The nobility, as everywhere else, considered a public or military career its true calling, as had been its practice for centuries. This does not mean however, that the Magyars had no talent for carrying on business and commercial enterprise. On the contrary, there were quite a few examples of their successes in this field. It was rather the Austrian economic policy that ruined commerce and industry, although its encouragement would have hastened the disappearance of the nobility's influence. The Court, fearing a possible alliance of Turkey with Prussia, was willing to give economic concession to the Porte. These, among other things contributed to the fact that much of Hungary's existing commerce passed into the hands of Greek and Armenian merchants, coming from Turkey.

Previous to the American Revolution,[1] England regarded its colonies in a like manner. "England was still in the grip of mercantile and protectionist theories of the old type. She still regarded her colonies primarily as markets for her goods, and the trade of the colonials as permissible only so far as it seemed consistent with the economic interests of the mother country."[2] According to Egerton, the incidents of 1765 and 1767 hastened the clash between England and America, but "that the crisis must sooner or later come, unless Great Britain altered her whole way of looking at her colonies, seems equally certain".[3] The relations between Austria and

---

[1]Colonel Michael Kovách, a Magyar officer fighting in Washington's army, gave up his life for the cause of American Independence at Charleston, South Carolina, on May 11, 1779.

[2]G. M. Trevelyan, *A History of England*, London 1939, p. 551.

[3]Egerton, *The American Revolution*, p. 4.

Hungary were much worse. Hungary was never a colony of Austria; but not a distant continent, but a convalescent state pitted against a neighboring Great Power.

Every characteristic of the Magyar people—languages, culture and independent history—was different from that of Austria: but not much could be done. Hungarians, though realizing the trend of European development, understood that their economic and social problems were, as Berzeviczy wrote, a *Concatenatum Systema,* a system which could be altered only as a whole. It was the intellectual élite, the writers, who began to work out plans for a general reform, trying to bridge the gap between upper and lower classes. This is one of the great traditions of Magyar literature.

Hungary's cultural connections with the West were not severed even in the darkest times. The youth of the Turkish era found its way to Italian, German and Dutch universities, and visited France and England. As soon as political pressure abated a little, spiritual life was immediately on the upswing, as during Prince Bethlen's rule in Transylvania. A general improvement, however, was not possible until the comparative consolidation following the close of the Ottoman occupation.

The era of consolidation came with the 18th century in which cultural life was, in many respects, influenced by the close political ties connecting Hungary with Habsburg Austria. Vienna was then the only great city of the Monarchy, and there the Hungarian magnates built palaces and participated in the court life of the Catholic Habsburgs. The loyalty of the Hungarian hierarchy was obtained by the piety of the dynasty. This was the last phase of the Catholic restoration in Hungary. One state, one religion, was the popular slogan in Europe; Louis XIV expelled the Protestants from France not long before.

The high clergy considered Hungary, too, a Catholic state. Only naive persons, however, could hope to crush Hungarian Protestantism with simple administrative devices. Charles III, while he did not heed the extremists, regulated religious life by his *Carolina Resolutio* in 1731 according to the Catholic viewpoint. The former rights of Protestants were abolished and Leopold's strict restraints upheld. No Protestant services could be held, except at specially designated localities. A Catholic oath was demanded from those entering the civil service, which made it practically impossible for a Protestant to serve in such offices. All this made the Protestant minority very bitter and irreconcilable towards the Habsburgs, something that left its mark centuries to come.

From the standpoint of Hungary's interests, the repression of Protestantism was a serious loss. Protestantism had produced great and worthwhile achievements in the political and spiritual life of Hungary. The elimination of this creative force was a loss to the whole country. For a while, the Court of Vienna prohibited Protestant students from visiting universities in Western Europe, mostly in the Netherlands and Switzerland. This was a deliberate attempt to curtail Hungarian culture as is shown by the fact that during a sixteen-year period after the lifting of the ban, no fewer than seven hundred Hungarian Protestant students went to colleges abroad.

Generally speaking, the education and culture of 18th century Habsburg Central Europe, Hungary included, was of a religious and Catholic character, with Latin as its accepted language. It determined the style of architecture, too, producing the style known as Baroque. This style went parallel, naturally with a special way of thinking, as different phenomena of an age seem to be correlated. The ideal of this era is the religious, loyal man who respects authority and whose passions are restrained by discipline and obedience. His speech, like his dress, is noted for colorful, rich figures. This conception, favored by the Habsburgs both in the cultural and political fields, cannot be simply ignored as foreign. The Catholic school of thinking manifested in Hungary was partly based on Hungarian tradition.

Contrary to examples in France and Austria, where the principle of authority was fully accepted, the Estates of Hungary defied absolutism and remained firm to the constitution irrespective of their loyalty and gallantry to Maria Theresa.

In educational reform, the Jesuit fathers played a conspicuous rôle. The colleges of Nagyszombat, Kassa, and Kolozsvár were in their hands and they organized secondary education extensively. By 1773, when the order was dissolved, they had forty-one high schools and were the beneficiaries of a good number of church and private funds. They developed education to a higher level, bringing up three consecutive generations of young nobles in the classical Catholic-Latin spirit. True enough, the Jesuit school system, based on the *Ratio Studiorum* of 1591, was in some respects obsolete at the end. Latin instead of the national language predominated; and historical, natural and political sciences were scarcely represented. On the other hand however, no other body was qualified to do better under contemporary political circumstances.

Such quasi-ecclesiastical training, which brought up students on the examples of early Christian heroes and the medieval saints of Hungary, was bound to strengthen Catholicism. Thus the conception gained ground that Hungary was a Catholic country, the domain of the Holy Virgin, *Regnum Marianum*. The Jesuit fathers expounded that King St. Stephen offered his state to Mary, who now defends the country and its good people, as she had liberated them previously.

In the second half of the century however, an avalanche of novel ideas gained ground. French writers directed a drive against dogma, superstition, and religious intolerance. They condemned absolutism and propagated the rule of Reason. Free research could refer to a Newton in England. In Hungary, Maria Theresa's pious administration was yet in power when, as first herald of a new era, the American Declaration of Independence surprised the Old World. Hardly a decade after the Queen's death, the French Revolution broke out. Trailing behind the trends of the day, the cultural conditions of East-Central Europe looked a little archaic. In the previous centuries, Hungary had not had to rely so much on the cultural contribution of the Habsburg Empire. The antecedents of 18th century ideas were present in Hungary too. Protestants had brought home English Puritanism and the rationalism of Descartes in the 17th century. One of the Lutherans who visited the University of Halle, Matthias Bél of Pozsony, wrote a monumental work on the geography and ethnography of Hungary in 1746. In 1765, an educational committee took over cultural matters from the church. A wider reform was made possible by the confiscation of the wealth of the disbanded Jesuit order. The *Ratio Educationis,* made public in 1777, was mainly the work of the Hungarian Joseph Ürményi. Hungary's school system was made uniform, the country being divided into nine educational districts. Elementary schools employed all the other tongues spoken besides Magyar. In secondary and higher education, Latin was the language used. One drawback of the new school system lay in its application according to Austrian standards, which left their mark on it.

This age, usually referred to as the era of *L'Europe Française,* was noted for the general influence of French Literature, ideas and manners, from which no civilized European nation escaped.

When Prince Kaunitz, the leading statesman of

Austria returned from Paris and brought with him the secular spirit of the literary salons, the old pious conceptions were seriously undermined. Hungarian aristocrats residing in Vienna followed the fashion, became estranged from their national traditions, and came under the spell of French culture through the Vienna Court. In the Theresianum College, founded for young noblemen, no fewer than 117 Hungarian students were enrolled up to 1772. Returning to their estates, they followed the French pattern and set up literary salons, collecting French books by the thousands. Voltaire, who ridiculed the backwardness of humanity with such caustic irony, was their favorite author. The deism of the French philosopher, not denying the existence of God yet discarding ecclesiastical regulations and dogmas, was accepted by them. Freemasonry, spreading from England and counting numerous members in Hungary, assisted in the popularizing of new ideas. The first lodge was set up in Vienna in 1742.

The young generation was all for the new ideas, and, unlike their fathers, who read religious and Latin works, they propounded Enlightenment according to the French philosophers who claimed to terminate the "dark" age of humanity. But while the aristocracy simply accepted the fashionable ideas found in every metropolis at the time, there was a younger set who attempted to apply reform ideas to Hungarian conditions, in an endeavor to serve the advancement of their country. Here again writers were in the forefront; outstanding among them was George Bessenyei, who

as a member of the Queen's Hungarian Noble Body-
guard went to Vienna in 1765 and studied French,
acquainting himself with the ideas of his day. Therefore he and his circle might be referred to as the "generation of 1765".

In the Hungarian past, Bessenyei saw not only pious
saints but warlike pagans as well. He condemned any
religious intolerance. His ambition was to raise the
standards of Hungary, to make its people happier, towards which he considered the first step the cultivation
of the national language and literature. This was behind his plans for the foundation of an Academy of
Sciences. With him this was a national problem, but
not a one-sided one. He and his friends desired to "show
that they were of service to their country and to humanity as well". Their favorite author was Montes-
quieu, who had also visited Hungary and who in his
work, *Esprit des Lois* referred to the opposition of the
Hungarian nobility to the absolutist Austrian rule. In
his footsteps, Bessenyei and other young Hungarian
guard officers were devotees of constitutional monarchy. The work of Bessenyei and his circle was supplemented by those Hungarian Protestants who went
beyond Vienna, traveling to Western lands, there to
get into direct touch with the trend of the times.

One of the most gifted members of the new generation was Joseph II himself, son of Maria Theresa, who
ascended the throne in 1780. As crown prince, he
waited impatiently for the time when he could carry
out his reforms. His ambition to serve the common

good, and his dashing personality made him an outstanding character among Habsburg monarchs. Abandoning the cautious methods of his mother, he proceeded to discard all that hindered the execution of
his political aims. According to his thesis, a monarch
has the right to make his subjects happy even against
their own will. He attempted to change backward
conditions almost overnight, issuing a legion of decrees.
He himself wanted to direct and carry out every important task. He traveled about incognito, clad in
shabby clothes, to secure first-hand evidence as to what
should be done. Yet his colossal political experiment
ended in failure as the enormous mechanism he wished
to build out of his empire rested in his person, and
died with him. The greatness of his intentions and the
sincerity of his convictions, however, demand acknowledgment.

So that he should not be bound by an oath, he did
not permit himself to be crowned King of Hungary
for which he was nicknamed "the hatted king". He
abolished the religious orders and placed their wealth
under state supervision. In 1781, he issued his Decree
of Tolerance. In this, he condemned coercion of conscience and terminated barriers hindering the religious
life of Protestants. With the example of England before him, he was about to abolish the exemption from
taxation hitherto enjoyed by the nobility. Since the
nobility controlled the counties which sent two Deputies each, with instructions, to the Diet, Joseph II first
aimed at the destruction of the county system. He

divided the country into ten districts, with a royal commissioner heading each. He improved the lot of the peasantry lifting them from under the jurisdiction of the nobility. In order to institute general taxation, he ordered the surveying of lands. In a word, he tried to carry out such reform plans as would have been realized with the greatest success by a national king. Though the radical overthrow of traditions aroused widespread discontent in the counties, Joseph II nevertheless had many sincere Hungarian adherents.

The policy of Joseph II was bound to fail, because he wanted to weld into a single unified centralized state Europe's most heterogeneous political organism. In 1784, he made public his language decree, in which he stated that Latin heretofore used in Hungary was no longer suitable for official transactions and must be supplanted by German, inasmuch as that language seemed to be the most expedient medium and also because of the German character of Austria. He gave his officials three years to conform; otherwise, they would lose their positions. The Emperor was primarily concerned with practical aspects rather than national discrimination, for he believed that through simple administrative measures he could solve the greatest problems of his composite Empire.

As a consequence, however, discontent became general. In Belgium a revolt broke out; in Hungary the county administration defied the execution of the royal decree. The military campaigns of 1788–1789, waged against the Turk, in alliance with the Empress Catherine of Russia, turned into a rout. Joseph II became mortally ill on the Turkish border. Almost on his death-bed, he revoked all of his edicts with the exception of that affecting the peasants and that concerning religious tolerance, reservations which proved his moral courage. He died a few weeks later, on February 20, 1790.

When the Diet of 1790–1791 convened, the atmosphere was filled with anti-Austrian reaction and with news of the French Revolution. Hundreds of contemporary writings attest to the excitement that reigned in political life. The younger generation had already taken the American Declaration of Independence and the Declaration of Human Rights as their ideal. Members of the Diet, however, belonged to the generation of 1765, and did not plan radical social changes; but on the other hand they presented political demands of an almost revolutionary character to the Court. The Hungarian nobility arrayed before the Habsburg monarch all the new concepts they had learned from French books.

According to Rousseau, the people and its ruler originally arrived at a contract *(Contrat Social)*, and should the ruler abuse his prerogatives, the contract would become void and a new agreement would be necessary. The Hungarian nobility regarded itself as the people, and since, according to their interpretation, Joseph II had broken his pact, the succession of the dynasty had become invalidated and a new contract was necessary, that is, a new constitution limiting the powers of the king. The nobles referred again and again to the English example. Several treatises were published comparing the English and Hungarian constitutions, noting that both were directed against royal encroachments. Though social conditions in England differed from those in Hungary, yet the traditional struggle to gain political independence showed some similarities. Traditions and revolutionary ideas were strangely intermingled in the mind of the nobility. The efforts of Joseph II had evoked nation-wide reaction, turning the attention of politicians to the defense of the mother tongue.

To counterbalance these movements in Hungary, Leopold II, successor to his elder brother, introduced the political police system then prevalent in Italy, together with its dreaded stool pigeon practice. Paid writers attached the "uncultured" Magyar nobility that dared to oppose the "civilized" German administration. By an even more serious measure, Leopold, true to old Austrian practices, incited the Serbian immigrant population against the Magyars. At the so-called "Illyrian" Congress, the chairman of which, acting as royal commissioner, was a confidant of the court, antagonism was fanned to a high pitch. The Magyars were branded as disloyal to the ruling house and territorial concessions were demanded. Prince Kaunitz clearly defined his principles: the stronger the Magyar attempts at securing the nation's unity, the more necessary it was to institute the methods of *divide et impera*.

The revolutionaries among the nobility sought an

ally in the person of King Frederick William II of Prussia, who was no friend of the Habsburgs. Some were thinking of inviting the Prince of Weimar to the Hungarian throne, so that Goethe almost became the minister of Hungary's king. But Austria arrived at an understanding with Prussia, and the plans were frustrated. The nobility were compelled to accept a compromise which resulted in the reinstatement of the constitution. Act 10 of 1791 decreed that in spite of the Sanctio Pragmatica, i.e. the continued succession of the Habsburg dynasty, Hungary was *regnum liberum,* an independent state, "which is not subject to any other state or people." According to Act 12, the king can no longer govern through decrees but only in conformity with duly passed laws. The Diet despatched several committees to prepare the necessary reform legislation, and these set to work in earnest. Nevertheless, no radical results were to be expected as a total discard of feudal conceptions was necessary for tangible reforms. The nobility held firmly to its old practices in the peasant problem, though they respected the reforms of Maria Theresa.

A section of young intellectuals got beyond that, however. Thirty years after the arrival in Vienna of Bessenyei, a conspiracy of "Magyar Jacobins" was uncovered in 1795, resulting in the execution of the leaders and the imprisonment of many sympathizers. Members of this generation of 1795 were mostly writers, barristers, educators and professional people. Of these, Joseph Hajnóczy was the most outstanding political thinker. He, like his friends, demanded the abolition of all feudal privileges. According to a pamphlet by George Belnay, human beings were free by nature and the peasantry were the class on which the whole nation was based. Among the writers, we find young Francis Kazinczy, a prominent figure in the revival of Magyar literature; likewise the poets Francis Verseghy and John Bacsányi, the latter threatening the aristocracy with the French example.

This group of youthful idealists, mostly under twenty-five and lacking political experience, was caught in the net of an impostor, Ignace Martinovics. Originally a monk of Southern Slav ancestry, he was one of the Habsburg secret agents, and a writer of anti-Hungarian pamphlets. After the death of Leopold II, when Francis I ascended the throne in 1792, these dubious elements were out of a job. The former agent provocateur soon worked himself into the confidence of the radicals, advertising himself with the lie that he was entrusted by Robespierre to organize a revolt. He founded two secret societies, one of which, known as The Reformers, propagated the aspirations of the common nobility; while the other, called the Society for Freedom and Equality, propounded revolutionary ideas. Members of both societies barely numbered one hundred, and thus they had little importance. Their sad significance lies in the fact that Martinovics, when seized and cross-examined, tried to defend himself with a long series of lies, uncovering, as it were, a momentous plot in which many officials of high rank were supposed to have taken part. These series of accusations intimidated the 22-year-old Prince Alexander Leopold, Palatine of Hungary since 1791. The Palatine, younger brother of Francis I, who until now had looked with good will on the Hungarian reform movement, fell under the spell of suspicion. In the spring of 1795 he therefore submitted a memorandum to the King in which he advocated absolutism and the preservation of the old feudal system. In the words of Alexander Leopold: "more enlightenment and the widening of knowledge are of no benefit to the common people . . . " The views of the Palantine made a lasting impression on the King, who was of weak mental ability, yet of a stubborn nature. Francis I, after the early death of his younger brother, during his whole reign faithfully followed the suggestions contained in the ill-fated memorandum. When the new century arrived, Hungary still suffered under the iron grip of an absolutism left behind by another age.

An echo of the efforts of Joseph II was to be heard also in Croatia and in Transylvania. The Estates of Croatia struggled with united effort with the Magyars against absolutistic rule. Their leader, Nicholas Skerlecz, asserted publicly that unbreakable ties joined Croatia to Hungary. The attitude of the two countries clashed, nevertheless, in two points at least. The Catholic Croatians refused to accept free practice for Protestant religions. Furthermore, they were against the gradual substitution of Magyar and Croatian for Latin as the official languages in Hungary and Croatia re-

spectively. According to them, the Constitution pre-
scribed Latin as the official language, and this was
not to be changed. Later antagonism is traceable to
these two differences on which, true to Habsburg
policy, Francis I was all too eager to capitalize. Joseph
II likewise transformed conditions in Transylvania
with a stroke of the pen. In a period of excitement,
two Rumanian peasant leaders returned from Vienna
with the tale that the Emperor had persuaded them
to incite a riot among their kin in Transylvania. A
bloody uprising followed, whose undertones were not
national but social. It is true that similar uprisings had
taken place in other countries before, but at the end
of the 18th century the brutalities were more conspicuous. The rebellion was finally crushed by the soldiery. This painful incident had no connection with
the development of Rumanian political opinion; at
most, it illuminated the stage of their social development.

Under the Habsburgs, Transylvania, once a stronghold of Protestantism, had become predominantly
Catholic. The Church did its best to win the Rumanians from the Orthodox Church to the Uniate.
This union with Rome was one of the most important
chapters in the cultural history of the Rumanians.
It was through the Rumanians in Transylvania that
inhabitants of the principalities of Wallachia and
Moldavia (united in 1861 and declaring their independence as Rumania in 1877) came into contact with
European ideas. It was their Greek Catholic bishop

Klein (who Rumanized his name to Micu) who in 1730 first referred politically to the theory advanced by some writers that the original inhabitants of Transylvania were, supposedly, the Rumanians, as descendants of Trajan's Roman settlers and the Latinized offspring of the Dacians. It is really not as important as generally thought, whether or not this hypothesis can be substantiated. What is important is that this theory proved a potent force in the formation of a Rumanian national consciousness, which, together with Western ideals developed in Transylvania and eventually reached the Wallachians, i.e. Rumanians in Wallachia and Moldavia.

Rumanian political conceptions were the result of the activity of the faculty of the Balázsfalva Greek Catholic seminary in Transylvania. Two priests of the Uniate Church, George Sinkai and Samuel Klein, were particularly instrumental in organizing the Rumanian intelligentsia into the first group that was capable of manifesting a Western mentality. These two clergymen, after spending some time in Rome and Vienna, became officials of the University Press at Pest and there worked out the so-called Dacian-Roman theory as a political principle. This theory, which became the foundation of national consciousness, placed emphasis on certain similarities to Latin which they found in the Rumanian language. They were responsible for changing the Cyrillic alphabet to Latin characters. The *Supplex Libellus Valachorum,* asking for the acknowledgment of the Rumanians as the fourth "nation" in 1791, was also the work of priests of Balázsfalva.

The reign of Francis I (1792–1836), wasted a full generation, as far as Hungary was concerned. By that time, it had become evident that the old feudal system was altogether out of date, for its interests did not coincide with those of the nation. Instead of pressing for her liberation from a colonial status, Hungary kept her agricultural position in a time when the launching of industrial enterprises and of social reforms were of the utmost necessity. On the other hand, the monarch could easily judge from the French example that his position was secure only as long as the nobility was in existence. Francis I hastened to encourage his Hungarian subjects to preserve their constitution at a time "when the whole world has gone mad".

Maintaining the appearance of the old constitution, absolutist rule weighed on the country. Francis I administered the most important matters in secret, often with the counsel of irresponsible courtiers. Among these latter were many avowed enemies of Hungary. Police rule characterized the uncivilized, low level of this administration. No modern writings were permitted to enter Hungary, censorship and relentless book-hunt choked cultural life. A system of stool pigeons demoralized public opinion. The Emperor's distrust went so far that he suspected his younger brother Joseph, who as a Palatine, lived among the Hungarians and understood them much better.

The first fifteen years of the 19th century were filled

with the Napoleonic wars. Napoleon subjugated almost the whole of the continent, conquering Austria several times, forcing it out of Germany and finally reducing it to Austria proper. The Holy Roman Empire thus ceased to exist and Francis adopted the title of Austrian Emperor (1804), with the rights of Hungary upheld.

As the French war was Austria's affair, Hungary did not meddle in its foreign ramifications; yet Hungarian troops took an active part in it, in accordance with the mutual assistance agreement. When Napoleon took Vienna in 1809, the militia of the nobles was summoned, but though they fought bravely they faced heavy odds and were defeated near Győr. Their system and equipment were obsolete compared to those of Napoleon. In a manner that had been waited for in vain by Rákóczi, the French Emperor now issued a proclamation in Vienna urging Hungarians to elect a national king, for the hour of their ancient independence struck. The translation of Napoleon's proclamation was likely the work of Bacsányi, one of the Jacobin conspirators of 1795. Having no confidence in the permanence of Napoleon's new order, Hungary left the French call unheeded. Following the defeat of Napoleon, the absolutist rulers of Germany, Austria, and Russia formed the Holy Alliance (1815), which endeavored to hinder national and democratic movements. This period often named after Prince Metternich, the foremost statesman of Austria, consisted of thirty-three years of reactionary administration.

The French wars ruined Austria financially. The state debt amounted to 338 million florins by 1789, and then up to 676 millions by 1811. Faced with this situation the Vienna treasury issued paper banknotes at an alarming rate, and at the same time attempted to maintain the full face value of the notes by force of edict. Since there was no gold reserve behind it, however, the purchasing power of the florin continued to drop, again starting the presses in Vienna; so that by 1811 no less than 1060 million florins of paper currency was in circulation. In the same year, these issues were called in at a discount of eighty per cent, the new issue of banknotes totaling 220 million. All this took place without consulting Hungary, although the country's economies suffered heavily through these manipulations. During the wars, the Hungarian Diets kept supplying the Empire with army replacements and taxes, the latter finally in metal, as demanded by the treasury. The Diet protested in vain that such economic measures, made without their assent, injured the sovereign rights of the country. Finally, the monarch suspended the Diet entirely from 1812 until 1825.

This helps to explain why modern nationalism could appear only in a restricted way. The beginnings of nationalism reach back to the Middle Ages when racial consciousness was fanned by the common interest of defense against foreign aggression. By the 16th and 17th centuries the struggle with the Turks had developed Hungarian national feeling considerably. Yet in practise this feeling could not find its full expression in all phases of political life. In Western Europe, absolutism succeeded in unifying state territory and centralizing economy, defense and administration; and when, after American and French patterns, the people gained their political rights, they could take over a ready-made national frame. Such an advance facilitated the realization of great political and spiritual achievements. But in Hungary, at the beginning of the 19th century, these results had not yet been obtained. Foreign absolutism had not only neglected the country's unity, but had also sacrificed it to foreign interests. The experiments of the patriots of 1790 and 1795 could not clear the way for a realization of national demands in economic and social fields. Accordingly the national spirit could not achieve tangible expression except in some rather abstract forms, in sentiment, and, because of literary influences, in fostering the native tongue. This accounts for the frequent mention of the language question, the importance of which was often expounded by the Estates.

For the time being, national aspirations had only one important way to find expression and this was provided by the language question. In 1791, Magyar was made an optional subject in the schools and in the following year a regular one. In 1805, the Estates were permitted to address the Deputy Council in Magyar, to be used, as in addresses of the Diet, alongside of the official Latin. Such request sounded almost naive in an age when modern languages were in universal use. Francis Kölcsey, a distinguished contemporary poet and the author of the National Anthem, made a note in his diary of a remark made by an Englishman who passed through Hungary in 1825: "Your freedom gentlemen, is a joke. You fight for the use of your own language. Even wild tribes can boast of that right through nature."

Those who advocated the use of Magyar as the official language meant no harm to the interests of other nationalities living in the Carpathian Basin. The nationality question had not yet appeared in Europe, and Hungarians did not realize the importance of the problem which later became so serious. It was Vienna and its foreign rule against which the Language Act was directed. In the Diet of 1825, the epic poem of Michael Vörösmarty, dealing with the occupation of Hungary by the Magyars, aroused such enthusiasm that immediately schemes were discussed as to how the national language could be made dominant in official and educational life. But that Diet was still unable to pass reform measures. The Estates protested against economic exploitation, but the King easily disarmed them with fresh promises that he would, from then on, really keep within the laws.

One old plan, however, did materialize: on November 3, 1825, a young aristocrat, Count Stephen Széchenyi, donated a full year's income for the foundation of the Hungarian Academy of Sciences. This act is the first gleam of the Reform Period.

# VII

## THE REFORM PERIOD

### (*1825–1848*)

In the first half of the 19th century, the greatest problem of Hungary was how to discard her antiquated institutions and catch up with the West. The foregoing chapters have examined the conditions that retarded Hungary's development. The chapters that now follow will show that in Carpathian Europe Hungary became one of the outstanding advocates, a *centre du rayonnement*, of the new ideas, and that she fought with the most forceful momentum for liberty when Reaction already prevailed on the whole continent.

The greatest obstacle in the path of reform was the international situation. The French Revolution in July 1830 had continent-wide effects, but the Holy Alliance of the Austrian, Russian and German rulers jealously guarded the old *status quo*. The gradually awakening peoples of East-Central Europe found themselves in the political system of Eastern or Central European great powers. In the south, the Ottoman power was slowly weakening in the Balkans; and the different small Slavic and Rumanian principalities had just begun to achieve a sort of semi-independence. There the four hundred years of foreign misrule had not allowed even such social and political advancements as were by now regarded obsolete by the Hungarians. In the north, Poland was divided between three great powers, and the 1830 attempt at liberation had been unsuccessful. Bohemia, strongly Germanized, could not check absolutism. Under Habsburg rule, Hungary was the sole survivor united, with its constitution intact, and ready for modern political initiative.

The question was, how strong was Hungary for such an initiative. An important factor was the increase in population, numbering some twelve million souls before the War of Independence began in 1848. This increase, as if to balance the centuries of devastation, was proportionately greater than in any other part of Europe. As far as the economic situation was concerned, agriculture had gone ahead during the French wars but as soon as prices slumped after the war and inflation set in, a serious crisis developed. This undermined the position of the aristocracy, who, living in Vienna, were totally unprepared for the blow and were at a loss as to how to manage their estates. The aristocracy lived too completely within the sphere of court influence to be able to take over the nation's leadership in an age of almost revolutionary advancement.

The peasantry, without political consciousness, was

THE REFORM PERIOD 187

in the same position as before. Reforms sometimes
made the peasant's lot worse; if, for instance, a county
decided on a road-building program, this meant an
increase in the load already crushing the lower classes.
The conditions of all the peasantry were not on a
uniform level, yet, even the more prosperous rural
communities felt the consequences of the obsolete economic system. They had to rely on agriculture, and
this demanded almost superhuman efforts during the
growing season and harvesting but none during the
winter. Abundance came in good years, and starvation
when crops were poor. A rational utilization of human
effort and natural resources was unknown. The obligations of the peasants remained as before, though from
1836 on these obligations could be bought off. Previous
to 1848, some of the landowners arrived at a final
agreement with their peasants, who were thus in a
position to obtain their freedom.

The middle class, or *bourgeoisie,* representing the
new ideas in Western Europe, was as yet undeveloped
in Hungary, parallel with the absence of large-scale
industry and commerce. Dependence on Austria
brought with it the most serious consequences in this
respect particularly. While the hereditary provinces and
Bohemia fared well industrially, Hungary, owing to
her resistance to absolutist rule, was still, for the most
part, only a provider of agricultural products. Her
cities, including Pest, which barely exceeded 50,000
in population, were mostly agrarian in character. The
slowly emerging minor industries of Hungary com-

prised distilleries, silk factories, and sugar manufacturing plants. The first flour mill was established in 1836, on the American pattern. Commercial enterprise, as in every country where feudal influence prevailed, was partly transferred to foreign hands. A large number of orthodox Jews entered Hungary from Galicia, annexed to Austria after the dismemberment of Poland. They were granted the rights of free settlement in 1840. By this time, they numbered about a quarter of a million, three times their total in 1785.

Only the common nobility was consequently in a position to play the part of the Western middle class in national life. Managing their own homesteads, they did not feel so much the economic crisis as the aristocrats, and benefited from the comparatively peaceful years. Altogether, there were some 700,000 of the nobility in Hungary in the decade previous to the revolution of 1848. The minor nobility, called "moccasin nobles", *bocskoros nemesek,* could boast but little political vision, for they were not much better off than the peasantry. Nevertheless their attitude greatly influenced the outcome of political issues. At first, the administration was successful in signing them up against the reform measures by threatening them with the loss of their charters, without which they would have nothing to distinguish them from the peasantry. Later, Kossuth was able to swing them over to the reform party by playing on their antipathy to the aristocrats.

Political leaders came from the ranks of the economically independent common nobility. These *bene pos-*

*sessionati,* owners of from one to nine thousand acres of farmland, were well qualified to grasp the spirit of the times and matters concerning the legislature. It naturally took time before this group, facing the resistance of the official machinery serving the reaction, was able to effectuate current spiritual trends. But it absorbed these ideas to such an extent that the generation responsible for the achievements of 1848 produced one of the most distinguished groups of leaders in all Hungarian history.

The man who did most in arousing public opinion and pointing it towards reforms was Stephen Széchenyi, the young aristocrat who in 1825 had endowed the Academy of Sciences. Széchenyi (1791–1860) inherited from his parents a deeply religious temperament and a sensitive personality. His father, Francis had founded the National Museum in 1802. His education did not differ from that of other young aristocrats living under the spell of the Vienna Court. At the age of seventeen, Széchenyi joined the army and took part in the Battle of Leipzig (1813) against Napoleon. The superficial and reckless court life, however, could not satisfy his budding talents, and the young captain of the Hussars early decided to devote his life to the advancement of his country. Just as in the diary which he kept from early youth he wrote with the utmost frankness about himself, so in his works he wrote about his country without eulogies and with unusual sincerity, no matter how uncomfortable the truth might be. He demanded sincere self-criticism, and ridiculed noblemen lazily enjoying their privileges. He was the first openly to ridicule the popular saying, "Extra Hungariam non est vita", branding it as futile chatter.

Széchenyi was already far from feudal traditions. He considered the interests of the nation as a whole and worked for its future without class distinction. He made his first visit to England in 1815. "We must admit the high standard of this country", he wrote, adding, "with the conditions of life in such a free state, with its manners and customs, I fully agree." And the obstacles against Hungary's evolution? "We, well-to-do landowners are the chief hindrances to our country's progress," he wrote. The nobleman, unfamiliar with conditions abroad, "appraises his country above its value", is unwilling to effect innovations and improvements, has no real idea as to what liberty consists of, and confounds it with the privileges of the nobility. The Hungarian nation is, nevertheless, entitled to a brighter future, and "may rise to any heights, for spiritual and physical powers are latent in its youthful bosom. . . . It has but two enemies, Prejudice and Conceit."

Széchenyi attacked this conceit with arguments, sarcasm, and practical examples. While, according to public opinion, the sole reason for any economic trouble lay in the policy of the Court, Széchenyi maintained that the ill will of Vienna did not exonerate the nation from its own faults. "It is not the King's fault if we are poor farmers and waste our beautiful estates", he

Count Stephen Széchenyi

*Lithograph by Francis Eybl, 1842*

wrote. As a typical example, he cited viniculture, pointing out that while it was true that the Austrian customs policy played havoc with Hungary's wine exports, it was also true that the Hungarians did not use the remaining small possibilities. With better management, high quality wines could have found a good market in England. But the Hungarian wine producers were not willing to acknowledge this, because they were convinced that whatever they did was the best. Széchenyi charged his compatriots with always being ready to blame others without seeing their own faults, and of not exploiting every avenue of endeavor. He made conspicuous his peoples' shortcomings, many of which had been summarized as early as the 17th century by Nicholas Zrinyi: conceit, self-admiration, daydreaming and an ephemeral enthusiasm that is of no value unless coupled with endurance.

To counterbalance and eliminate this, Széchenyi offered a moral program for Hungarians, striving to raise the standard of "public enlightenment". "The number of educated heads is the real power of a nation", wrote Széchenyi. "Not fertile valleys, mountains, ore and climate make strength, but mind, which uses natural resources intelligently." His program served national aims; he wanted to modernize his country, which he called the Great Fallow. He tried to teach his people to see realities instead of following an "emotional policy" which only favored national shortcomings. But he did not lose sight of the fact that a nation is but a part of humanity. Through the advancement of his country, he wanted to "conserve a nation for humanity in its original individuality."

In his first important book-length essay entitled *Credit* (*Hitel*, 1830), soon followed by two others, *Light* (*Világ*, 1831) and *Stadium* (1835), he tried to apply his views to Hungary's conditions. He maintained that the privileged classes were responsible for its backwardness, and the fact that, owing to the "obsolete and rusty system," neither land nor work nor capital were of any value, because there was no confidence, no credit. All this was caused by the feudal system, with its entailed property, based on peasant labor.

The sale, and even the mortgaging, of farms was virtually impossible because, by the law of family entail (Ősiség, aviticitas), alienation of land was illegal so long as any scion, however distant, of the original owning family survived, and in default of such heirs the property automatically escheated to the Crown.

According to Széchenyi the constitution exempting the nobility from all taxation should be amended, the bad tariff system remedied, and commerce assisted.

He mercilessly dissected the faults of the nobility, because his humane and religious conscience turned him against social injustices. He pointed out that nine million peasants, "the most numerous part of the population and that deserving the chief attention," were patiently carrying every burden, though they were "the provider and hope" of the nation. Széchenyi saw "with joyous feeling" that in England all men were equal before the law, and he asked his nation to see that "every one receive his share of human rights." While the legal thinking of the nobility could not emancipate itself from the letter of the old laws, Széchenyi fought for the whole country, the whole people, his eye always on the future. He concluded his first great work with these words:

"The past has slipped out of our grasp, but we may yet own the future. Why should we bother then with useless reminiscences? Instead, let us work for a glorious dawn for our homeland through determined patriotism and faithful unity. Many think that Hungary is a thing of the past; I like to believe its greatest achievements lie in the future."

He pointed out that free government had made England great. And while former writers had drawn parallels between the constitution and political conceptions in England and in Hungary, Széchenyi pointed out the differences between social conditions in England and in Hungary in an attempt to eliminate these. He knew well that this was impossible with simple regulations. He therefore endeavored with sharp criticism and ruthless frankness, to change the whole mentality of the educated classes.

His love for his "poor little homeland" did not restrict him in uncovering its faults, for he did not consider anything dear to him as necessarily better than anything else. "I am loyally devoted to you", he wrote, "despite your sandy wastes and your haughty inhabitants."

While examining the most complicated national problems, Széchenyi did not neglect to demonstrate the benefits of his program in small political matters. In addition to his activities as an author, and in the highest sense of the word, an agitator, he was very active in social, economic, and technical fields. Most of the successful economic achievements of this era were due to the initiative of Széchenyi. He did not miss opportunities, seemingly of the slightest importance, to influence people. After the Diet of 1825, when he was engaged in popularizing horse racing and the raising of thoroughbreds, he wrote in one of his letters: "some of my friends would surely not like it if they found out that it was really they, and not the horses that I endeavor to train . . ."

It was Széchenyi, too, who first saw the future of Budapest. At that time, Buda and Pest were two separate and not very significant cities, the Diet being held in Pozsony. In Széchenyi's imagination they were to become the future modern metropolis, the representative capital of Hungary, a fitting successor to the Buda of Matthias Corvinus, and a cultural center that would lure Hungarian magnates back from Vienna. It was Széchenyi who founded the society which adopted the aim of connecting the twin cities with a permanent bridge. It was due to his influence that the Diet passed a resolution in 1835 that everyone, even noblemen, should, without any exemptions, be obliged to pay toll on the proposed bridge. The Suspension or Chain Bridge, a majestic structure designed by the English

Clark brothers, was completed in 1848, and is in use even today.

Széchenyi endeavored to shift the center of political activity to Hungary proper. In order to give an opportunity for the exchange of opinions, he founded, on the pattern of the English clubs, the National Casino (1827), which was copied by similar clubs all over the country.

With the engineer Paul Vásárhelyi, Széchenyi began the regulation of the Lower Danube, carrying out measures which, by the end of the century, made possible shipping as far as the Black Sea. Another of his achievements was the regulation of the meandering river Tisza, a regulation through which large tracts of marshy land were made available for farming. He developed steamboat traffic on Lake Balaton; he was instrumental in the establishment of the Danube Steamship Co.; and he took an active part in other enterprises too numerous to record here.

The echo of Széchenyi's works was tremendous, much more so than that of any other Hungarian writer up to that time. Conservative elements, as expressed by Count Joseph Dessewffy's *Analysis,* a reply to Széchenyi's *Credit,* were alarmed at his severe criticism, and charged him with seeing only the bad points and "defaming" the nation. On the other hand, the lesser nobility, which was above the peasantry chiefly through the very privileges that the "Count of Pest" fought, received his reform ideas in many places with antagonism, not being broadminded and educated enough to grasp them. Volumes of *Credit* were publicly burned in some localities. But all this could not put an end to Széchenyi's influence. Everyone read his works and the discussions thus arising, even if his adversaries led the argument, helped to spread his ideas. Whether for him or against him, no one could disregard the problems of reform.

Széchenyi had undertaken a tremendous task and the results of his efforts already began to show in the thirties. Though the Diet of 1830 was largely conducted in the old manner, his new concepts soon swept through the political field. As far as the language question was concerned, Act 8 of 1830 provided that government officials and barristers in Hungary should know the Magyar language. Though not even the Long Diet of 1832–1836 could pass the social reforms, Széchenyi could already count among his followers such outstanding men as Francis Kölcsey and Francis Deák. Among the new achievements, conditions of the peasants were somewhat eased, for it was now possible for them to buy off once and forever, through contract, the services they were supposed to render. Yet the Conservatives thwarted substantial reforms with the old excuses, i.e. that sudden changes might bring dangerous reverses, and that full freedom should be granted the lower classes only gradually and after proper education to forestall possible disturbances. The most serious opponent of any reform measure, however, was the Austrian administration, which attempted to silence the reformers at any cost. It therefore incited the minor nobility against the representatives of the reforms, precipitating violence in a number of counties. After the Diet, the mutual distrust between the government and the Estates grew greater. The danger of this lay in the fact that the reformers had gradually come to the conclusion that they could achieve the necessary social and political changes only in open opposition to the administration.

Széchenyi himself was careful not to disturb the "mixed marriage", as he termed the relations that tied Hungary to Austria. He knew that the nation was unable to cope with both tasks at once, and that domestic reforms were entitled to preference. In public opinion, however, the old antagonism and mistrust against Vienna's absolutism was kindled anew.

Even Baron Nicholas Wesselényi, a friend of Széchenyi's youth, his companion in travels abroad, and one with whom he had made a romantic vow to fight jointly for their country's future, disagreed with Széchenyi's stand and leaned more towards public opinion. In his book, *Wrong Judgements* (*Balitéletek*), he used a much stronger tone than did Széchenyi in writing against the selfishness of an "officialdom that grows fat on the peasantry". It was primarily Vienna that Wesselényi accused for blocking every attempt at amending the constitution. With rare foresight, on the contrary, Széchenyi had planned first to strengthen Hungary within the Empire, seeing to it that the energies indispensable for domestic reforms should not be fatally divided. The administration, on the other hand, did everything in its power, especially with its arbitrary rule after the Diet of 1836, to strengthen the belief that no reform whatsoever could be realized with its assent.

One of the principal shortcomings of the central Austrian government was its disregard of the fact that the fate of several peoples depended upon its actions. It neglected the problems of the Empire as a whole. Maria Theresa, with her fine instinct, recognized in the 18th century that with social and educational measures of a general nature, the different peoples within the state may be benefited. The forced centralization of Joseph II, as well as his attempts at Germanization, evoked widespread dissent. During the reign of Francis, on the other hand, no new concepts, much less programs, were considered for the solution of these pressing questions. The fact that the creation of a uniform German state out of the Habsburg Empire was impossible, was proved by the time of Joseph's death; it was then evident that this program was dead, yet its faded traditions were evoked again and again. These remnants of political "Josephinism" cropped up in the forms of the so-called "system of stability" maintained by Francis I, a system characterized by lack of ideas and by a struggle against the modern trends of the early 19th century.

There was an obvious opportunity, for instance, for the reform of customs regulations, in order that the several peoples might feel that at least some joint interest attached them to the Empire. But instead, the

THE REFORM PERIOD 199

Court for another three decades attempted the suppression of every such endeavor, and paid no attention to these practical problems. The thinking of Prince Metternich was typically 18th century. It was his mouldy idea that it was the common interest of the King and the Estates to join forces to block every social improvement.

Following the death of Francis I, under the imbecile Ferdinand V (1835–1848), the old reactionaries continued to rule. Metternich, after whom the régime was named, turned most of his attention to foreign affairs, domestic problems being relegated to a so-called State Conference, composed of Habsburg princes and Kolowrat, the avowed enemy of the Hungarians. The president of this Conference was Prince Louis, uncle of the king. These leaders viewed the spread of liberal ideas with great concern and would have gladly placed the whole continent under police supervision. Thus the administration obstructed everything, but was unable and unwilling to achieve anything.

After 1836, the leaders decided that they would take strong measures against the reformers. They condemned Nicholas Wesselényi for the publication of the proceedings of the Transylvanian Diet. They arrested Ladislas Lovassy, a university student and a leader in students' political groups, and sentenced him illegally to ten years' imprisonment. Lovassy went insane in prison, and the case caused public indignation. Even greater disapproval followed the incarceration of Louis Kossuth.

Louis Kossuth (1802–1894) was born into a Lutheran family of the lesser nobility in the county of Zemplen. He finished law school in nearby Sárospatak, and secured a position in the county offices. As proxy for an absentee aristocrat, he took part in the Diet of 1832–1836, and attracted much attention by his talents. Until then the general public had not received any detailed information about the Diet's proceedings; and Kossuth, to remedy this, published the *Diet Bulletin,* written and copied by his young friends in longhand. The administration looked upon this venture with misgivings and when Kossuth followed it up by publishing the *Municipal Bulletin,* a résumé of political activity in the counties, he was sentenced in 1837 to several years of imprisonment. In spite of his youth, he was a well-known man by that time, and his colorful summaries of addresses delivered by members of the Reform Party were widely read. His condemnation enhanced his popularity even more. He did not waste his time in prison, but read, studied, and learned English from the Bible and Shakespeare. When he was set free in 1840, he was soon recognized as a leader in public affairs, and proved worthy of the trust placed in him.

At the Diet of 1840, it was evident that the government, by its violent persecutions, had been successful in making the desire for reforms stronger than ever. Already by that time even the sages of Vienna were ready to admit their blunders and accepted the assistance of young Hungarian Conservatives led by Aurel Dessewffy, Samuel Jósika and Antony Szécsen. As a matter of fact, these young Hungarians were the ones who, instead of the government, worked out a general program attempting to save the Empire by harmonizing its interest with gradual reform measures. Their "modern Conservatism" fought almost hopelessly against a traditional Germanizing tendency. The last-minute attempt failed, because the administration called upon them far too late, when slow procedures were of no avail, especially when those in charge were not willing even then to make serious concessions. What would have caused enthusiasm in 1830 as a sign of the administration's good will, was definitely too late in 1840 and could no longer merit the confidence of the bulk of the population.

The Christian reformism of Széchenyi undermined preconceived opinions and furnished a plan without affecting the legal and political relationship with Austria. However, the radical Liberalism that swept the country from the West, coupled with the stubborn attitude of the government, prepared a new platform in which one of the most important issues was the complete political freedom of the country. Just as in Germany young intellectuals created a Young Germany against the police rule, and a similar movement was afoot in Italy, so in Carpathian Europe a Young Hungary came into being.

Not only through the perusal of foreign literature, but through travel and personal experience did the new Hungarian generation learn its lesson. Some of them ventured as far as America, like Baron Majthényi, for instance, who as early as 1812 studied economic improvements in the New World. The enthusiastic Alexander Farkas Bölöni visited the United States in 1831, describing it as "a happy fatherland" where "everyone is equally born into freedom and independence." Bölöni's travelogue reached two editions within one year, and was considered valuable and practical by such men as Széchenyi. His account dealt particularly with the political institutions, educational system and social order of the United States, and contained numerous observations of interest. According to Bölöni, "the eyes of Europe and Humanity are turned on America, since in the Old World Liberty wages a hopeless fight with Oppression."[1] Another contemporary Hungarian traveler to America was Charles Nagy, mathematician and astronomer, who gained the friendship of President Jackson.

To study new principles in application, and modern political institutions, many went to England and France. One of these young Hungarians who sought examples abroad was Bartholomew Szemere, later premier of the republican government in 1849. The views of this young generation are perhaps most typically reflected in the travelogue of Joseph Irinyi, a barrister, who wrote with great respect of the English and with admiration of the French. In his words: "That parliamentary government is good, that is a truth not only for England and France but for the whole world."

[1]Bölöni, Farkas Sándor, Utazás Észak-Amerikában, 1834. Other Hungarian authors who wrote on the United States may be found in Eugene Pivány's Hungarian-American Connections, 1927, Budapest, pp. 32–33.

The young generation was mostly under the influence of such contemporary French writers as Thiers, Victor Hugo, Lammenais, and others who thundered against oppression and advocated the rights of subject peoples. Francis Deák remarked that the young people used Lamartine's *History of the Girondists* as their Bible. Morris Perczel, general in the War of Independence in 1848, noted in his recollections: "We derived our political philosophy from the history of the French Revolution."

Many foreign books sold well in Hungary in those days. Among these were de Tocqueville's *History of North American Democracy* and Sparks's *Life of George Washington* which were translated into Hungarian. As a typical anecdote, it is related that Balogh, a member of the Diet for Bars County, educated his little son with such lessons: "Who was the greatest man in history?"—"George Washington." "What is the best form of government?"—"A Republic." "What is your conviction?"—"I am a democrat."[1]

As expressed by Daniel Berzsenyi, one of Hungary's outstanding poets: "Our democracy should not be that of lawlessness and recklessness, but one of wisdom and human understanding, like that of George Washington. This is the finest victory of civilization, something writers should furnish the groundwork for, provided they wish to be the schoolmasters of humanity."[2]

[1]Edward Sayous, *Histoire des Hongrois,* Paris, 1875, Vol. 11.
[2]*Complete Works,* 1864, p. 202.

So new ideals and faith in liberty swept with great force through Carpathian Europe. Thus did the generation of 1848 prepare for its future rôle, all knowing that a change was bound to come. As young Kossuth prophesied to Deák, at some time and in some manner, "either through a European revolution or through war," a break-up was inevitable.

Louis Kossuth was the real leader of the young generation. As soon as he was set free from prison, he founded in 1841, a daily newspaper *Pesti Hirlap* in which he propagated his liberal theories with remarkable literary talent and unprecedented success. It was not the news in the *Pesti Hirlap* that was mainly read, but the editorials of Louis Kossuth. These were impulsive, colorfully written articles, which appealed to the imagination and sentiments of the widest public and proved to be far more popular than the writings of Széchenyi. In general, his political platform coincided with that of the latter and advocated the abolition of feudal privileges, equality before the law, and numerous other more or less important reforms such as improvement in prison conditions, that were just as timely in western Europe. Kossuth was a past master in illustrating the existing injustices with such a vivid style and appropriate examples that all his readers became ardent supporters of his drive for a change. Thus Kossuth, as the greatest Hungarian journalist, was able to control the sentiments of the public, and it was not long before all saw in him the competent political leader sent by Destiny in a struggle for human and national liberty.

Instead of beginning with practical details, he first of all aroused the public's wrath against feudalism and its representatives, Austria and the aristocrats. Many saw in this the essential difference between Kossuth and Széchenyi, and believed that the root of their later antagonism lay in the difference that Széchenyi planned to carry through the reforms with the aristocracy at the helm, while Kossuth relied on the cooperation of the common nobles and the large number of impoverished minor nobility. Certainly Kossuth did not trust the aristocrats and wrote in the *Pesti Hirlap* that the reforms will be carried through "with them or by them, if they like, but if they are not willing, then without them or even against them." Széchenyi, on the other hand, had no confidence in the political ability of the minor nobility, while Kossuth took advantage of the latter's hate for the aristocrats, thus winning a populous class for the reform.

The real cause of the rift between Kossuth and Széchenyi was, however, of another nature. Széchenyi did not want to aggravate the problem of relation between Austria and Hungary. He realized that the nation was in need of inward strength, and that any acute crisis in its relations with the Habsburg Monarchy would precipitate a constitutional or even a military struggle in which the odds would be against Hungary. Kossuth, on the contrary, drew the logical conclusions of the avalanche of Liberal thought and placed the political freedom of his country as the first aim of his policy. Though not even he entertained until 1848 the idea of separation from Austria and the overthrow of the dynasty, yet he never shrank from tackling this problem as well. Kossuth himself later on characterized his feud with Széchenyi thus: "Széchenyi roused our nation from its slumber, then he attempted to utilize the energies thus produced for improvements in some restricted and purely economic fields. For the carrying out of these he hoped to get the consent of Vienna. In a word, he did not consider the inclusion of the nation's constitutional interests in his sphere of activities and disagreed with anyone who wished to do so. . . . I took up this problem, for I not only wanted the people in the fatherland to be free, but wanted to see the fatherland liberated too."

Széchenyi, while he fought for reforms, was against revolutionary methods and every one-sided political theory. He could not believe the nation strong enough for domestic transformation and for a struggle against the political and military might of the dynasty at the same time. Széchenyi wished to see economic advancement precede everything else, while Kossuth favored national independence first. Yet this dispute on the order of succession was not of merely academic value. Széchenyi dreaded the pressing of this kind of political topic, in fear lest a catastrophe would strike his country as a result of estrangement from the dynasty.

General opinion did not side with Széchenyi, branding his anxieties as far-fetched. This was due to a large

extent to Kossuth's exploitation of the popular opposi-
tionist mood and anti-Austrian feeling, winning the
following of the rank and file for himself. Széchenyi
did not hesitate to bear the onus of unpopularity, fearing for the fate of his country and judging that Kossuth's bold policy would automatically thrust Hungary
into a disastrous clash. In his work, *The People of the
East (Kelet Népe,* 1841), he severely scored Kossuth's
activity. Széchenyi admitted the talents and idealism
of his opponent but simultaneously accused him of an
excessive desire for popularity, and warned that his
reckless agitation would lead to revolution. The re-
current criticisms of Széchenyi discouraged even his
own friends, among them the moderate Francis Deák.
Kossuth, on the other hand, spoke of Széchenyi, his
senior with great respect in public. It was he who once
called Széchenyi "the greatest Hungarian", and by
showing such deference he was able with all the more
effect to present his views in the discussions they carried on publicly in the press.

Széchenyi attempted to point out that the government, after all, was willing to make concessions and
that the reforms could be realized in collaboration with
Vienna. He saw great danger in the mutual suspicion
that on the one hand the government was working
against the Hungarians, and, on the other hand, that
Hungary in her turn was preparing for revolution and
separation from the Habsburgs. But opposition was
also fanned by the clashing of economic interests. One
of the foundations of Kossuth's anti-Austrian attitude

lay in the fact that official Vienna's conception of economy still considered Hungary only a colony. This was why a change in economic connections with Austria, as well as the development of industry, was deemed necessary. Until then, the Monarchy was not a unified customs territory. As soon, however, as the German principalities under Prussian leadership joined in a customs union (*Zollverein*), there were statesmen anxious to attach the Monarchy to it, which was an impossibility as long as the latter was cut up by inside customs barriers.

Under such circumstances, the Court was willing to abolish the customs barrier between Hungary and Austria. But Kossuth and his followers saw clearly by then that just as a German customs union naturally and primarily served German interests so Hungary's customs policy should aim at specific Hungarian requirements. The crystallization of these questions was partly due to a German economist, Friedrich List, who visited Hungary and carried on propaganda for the customs union between Hungary and the Monarchy. His work, *Das Nationale System der Politischen Oeconomie* (1841), emphasized the German protective customs union and impressed Kossuth to such a degree that he became an out-and-out devotee of a Hungarian customs system entirely independent of the rest of the Monarchy. It was with this aim in view that an Industrial Protective Union, a Society for Factory Establishment, and a short-lived Hungarian Commercial Society came into being. The general mood in Hun-

gary was expressed by a boycott against goods made
in Austria and the likewise protected Bohemian industry. It was at this time that credit facilities and
banking made a start. The Inland Savings Bank of
Pest was founded in 1840, soon to be followed by the
Hungarian Commercial Bank of Pest. The problem
of railroad building also provoked controversy. There
were only two short lines in operation by 1848; and
Kossuth favored lines built in a direction towards Fiume
and the Adriatic in order to divert Hungary's exports
by routes outflanking Austria.

The Diet of 1840 passed laws qualifying the peasants
to own land and to buy their freedom. Tax exemption
of the nobility, on the other hand, was not abolished,
not even by the Diet of 1843–1844. The explanation
of this may be found in the fact that the minor nobility
was not yet gained over to the cause of reform, defeating at election the devotees of general taxation.
Even Francis Deák was defeated at the polls; and
the Diet passing only a single law of importance, that
in regard to the use of the Magyar language.

Modern requirements and ideals naturally brought
about a struggle between the Magyars, who demanded
the acceptance of their national tongue, and the Austrian bureaucracy, who persisted in the use of Latin
and German. In Hungary, Latin was almost a second
mother-tongue, without the knowledge of which early
Hungarian historical literature is difficult to compre-
hend. Official business was conducted in Latin and
the educated classes spoke this tongue fluently as late

as the beginning of the 19th century. Indeed, Hungary was the outstanding representative of Latin culture in Carpathian Europe. It was quite natural on the other hand, however, that at a time when every Western country adopted its national tongue, the conditions of a new era demanded the general use of Magyar instead of the dead Latin. But as the ideas of nationalism swept Europe, they did not stop with the Magyars, for neighboring peoples reacted to it similarly, in proportion to their self-consciousness and cultural advancement. In the Carpathian Basin, the Magyar race had lost its earlier absolute majority of seventy-six per cent and by this time the total of other individually smaller nationalities exceeded it, as a result of the large-scale foreign colonization in the 18th century. Thus the national spirit, awakening many peoples, placed new problems in the path of their peaceful co-existence. Those who are of the belief that the national spirit of the Slovaks or Rumanians, for instance, came into being as a reaction against alleged Magyar oppression, minimize the significance of national development. The awakening of nationalities was a phenomenon enveloping all Europe. This is the cause of the nationalistic movements which followed Hungary's initiative and ran parallel with it in East-Central Europe.

These national movements in East-Central Europe passed through two distinct phases. The first could be termed a cultural stage, for it was characterized by the cultivation of the past, history, literature and linguistic studies, by means of which national consciousness was strengthened. In its second phase, the national movement advanced to political demands insisting that a nation or fragment of a nation should exclusively rule over a certain territory which it felt belonged to it according to its nationalistic aspirations. The protection of racial minorities within the state was, naturally, not yet in the air; just as, in the religious disputes two centuries earlier, the territorial principle was taken for granted.

Hungarian nationalism, resting on old traditions in state affairs, soon got over the first phase and presented Austria with political demands. By the beginning of the 19th century, several Slav nationalities reached the first phase in this process. Their self-consciousness was bolstered by the feeling that they were akin to that great body of eighty million Slavs, pushed to one side by historical developments, but generally characterized, according to the appraisal of the German poet, Herder, as a clear-minded, innocent people. John Kollar, a Slovak Lutheran clergyman living in Pest, devoted a lengthy epic poem to the glory of the Slavs,[1] and emphasized the spiritual unity and reciprocity of Slavic literatures, passing judgment upon other peoples. From among the representatives of this cultural Pan-Slavism, many, especially the Czechs, looked upon Russia, the mightiest nation of them all, as the embodiment of their ideals. Tsarist imperialism gladly accepted this rôle for its own interests, if for no other reason.

[1] Daughter of Slava, 1827.

In its second phase, however, the literary and sentimental Slavism resulted in the blossoming out of an
individual national consciousness in every branch of
the great racial family, large and small, and thus
worked for their disintegration instead of for their
unification. It is sufficient to point to the example of
Russia and Poland, to illustrate the great antagonism
that separated Moscow from the Slavic peoples of
Carpathian Europe. Consequently literary Pan-Slavism
turned into separate, individual national movements,
in Croatia, Slovakia and Bohemia. While Magyars in
the early 19th century remembered and evoked their
medieval glory; and while the Rumanians warmed
to the hypothesis of a Daco-Roman origin, so among
the smaller Slav peoples a similar inspiration may be
detected in their dream of a Great Slav Empire. As
a psychological motive every people apparently needed
some tradition, a more less sentimental factor in building and strengthening national feeling.

Among the Slovaks of northern Hungary, the outstanding figure in linguistic and literary activities were
the poet, Louis Stur, and Joseph Hurban, a Lutheran
minister. In the case of the Serbs and Rumanians,
while the bulk of them lived outside the Hungarian
border, forerunners and literary representatives of the
new nationalistic thought often studied and worked
in Hungary. Among others, Vuk Karadzic, collector
of Serbian folksongs, found haven in Hungary. The
University Press of Pest was the headquarters for
Serbian and Rumanian publications in Cyrillic char-

acters. Young scholars graduating from the college of
Balázsfalva, Transylvania, emphasized the importance
of the Rumanians' Latin extraction as against ecclesiastical connections with Orthodox Russia, having concluded a thorough reform of the Rumanian language
with that point in view. Many of them were in the
Hungarian civil service, employed by Hungarian scientific organizations, or tutors in the homes of Magyar
aristocrats, like the two outstanding Rumanian writers
of this period, George Sinkai and Peter Major, for
instance. The spirit of nationalism was in fact trans-
planted into the Rumanian provinces of Transcar-
pathian Wallachia and Moldavia from Transylvania,
the latter Hungarian territory supplying the founder
of the first significant school of Bucharest, George
Lazar. The new ideas were spread everywhere by the
unfolding intelligentsia. This accounts for the fact that
Rumania and Serbia imported, so to speak, their movements of national renaissance from their kindred resident in Transylvania and the Bácska-Bánát region
of Southern Hungary, for the simple reason that higher
social conditions within the Monarchy favored the rise
of an educated class.

The decisive question at the time was, what would
be the relation of these national awakenings to the
Habsburg Empire. In principle at least, the German
character of the Empire was still maintained, by the
administration, hindering however linguistic and literary endeavors only in case they seemed to involve
political implications dangerous to Vienna. Thus the

administration was benevolently neutral towards the Czech movement, not anticipating political opposition from that region, which was well acclimatized to absolutistic rule. Even the slightest Magyar cultural endeavor, on the contrary, was looked upon with suspicion, and regarded as very dangerous; for Hungary had always despised and resisted absolutistic rule and Vienna dreaded their separation. Hence Vienna insisted on the maintenance of Latin as the official language, especially since it hoped to have the nobility on its side, whose traditional means of expression was likewise Latin. The Court feared that the introduction of Magyar would foster a democratic spirit. Therefore, from 1790 to 1830 the Magyars could not get any greater concession than that their language should be taught as an ordinary subject in the schools. In 1830, it was finally decreed that officials should know Magyar, except in Croatia. It may be remarked that the Magyars, in their turn, did not appreciate the now unfolding movements of their own national minorities for they conformed to the then dominant European trend of having the language of the majority accepted. But the culture of the minorities is not underrated if one points out the fact that it was still in its infancy and time was needed until it succeeded in gaining attention and consideration. The Hungarian poet Berzsenyi pitied their backwardness and expressed his desire for them to understand also Magyar in order that through it they might come closer to civilization.

Hungary had no free hand to act in nationality

questions, in any case. The Magyars were not fight
against the other nationalities but against Austria.
They wanted to strengthen their nation in order to be
able to cope with an alien absolutism. Indeed, they
were always on the defensive against the government,
which suspected every Hungarian movement, and only
the Hungarian ones, as being politically dangerous.
This caused Vienna to incite against Hungary, the
Croats, who had lived through long centuries in collaboration, sharing common interests with the Magyars. Austrian policy was a true expression of the old
*divide et impera* principle, which pitted one people
against the other, thus preparing antagonism between
them and bringing about the dissolution of the very
hope for Carpathian Europe's unity. While Metternich
still considered the Slav and Magyar movements equally
dangerous from the Empire's point of view, his successor Kolowrat, of Czech descent, attempted to use
all the Slavs of the Empire to break the democratic
movement of the Magyars.

He believed that the unified Southern Slavs would
serve the dynasty's imperial interests against Hungary.
The "Illyr" movement of the Croats, led by Louis Gaj,
received official assistance, as it was not directed against
absolutism. Kolowrat, nevertheless, did not recognize
in time that the different Southern Slavs were working for their own cause, too, instead of bolstering Austrian imperial schemes. Unknown to him, a plan to
bring about a Southern Slav federation of states had
already made its first appearance in Serbia.

Magyar-Croat relations, accordingly, depended upon the struggle between the Hungarian reform party and the Vienna administration. At the negotiations regarding the question of language, both Magyars and Croats showed excessive sensitivity. Kossuth made it clear in 1842 that, as far as Hungary was concerned, the official language could not be any other than Magyar. At the provincial Diet of Croatia, the discussion might be conducted in Latin or Croat. But nobody could demand, said Kossuth, that the Hungarian Diet speak Latin or Croat. Act No. 11, passed by the legislative session of 1844, went a step farther, however, by prescribing instruction in the Magyar language as a regular subject in the secondary schools and colleges of Croatia. This scheme proved to be impracticable, and resulted in nothing but complaints. Contemporary debate in the press, both Magyar and Croat, gives a clear view of the national sensitiveness of both parties.

It goes without saying that the Magyars, like every other nation in Europe, did not recognize the trend of the nationalistic movement. Pan-Slav ideals caused nervousness, and the Magyars, viewing the problems from a political standpoint, became aware of Russia's imperialistic designs. The "Summons" (*Szózat*) of Wesselényi (1843), dealing with nationality problems, warned the country against the threat of Russia. He, too, shared the opinion then prevalent that if everyone living in Hungary, minorities included, would have equal rights guaranteed by a liberal amendment of the constitution, the nationalities would not lend an ear to the agents of Absolutism. Wesselényi considered the attractive force of Liberalism very highly, and the latter proved to be a truly worthwhile means of gaining the co-operation of the bulk of the German minority in Hungary as well as the better part of the Jewry.

The whole complex problem, together with the illusions of the Magyars and others, was viewed from a higher, humanistic level by Francis Deák and especially by Széchenyi, as was proved by his address in 1842 to the Academy of Sciences, of which he was president. Széchenyi explained that in the language question the young and small nations suffering from growing pains, so to speak, are the most sensitive. "Do not do to others", he said, "what you would not wish done to you." He also cautioned them to respect the feelings of other nationalities: "If one speaks Magyar, it does not necessarily mean that he is Magyar in his feelings". Széchenyi urged that a desire for unity is of far greater importance than the question of what language should be spoken.

The Liberal opposition was not united sooner than a decade before the revolution. Kossuth and his followers were agitating in the counties, Kossuth being a believer in autonomous administration for the counties as a constitutional guarantee against absolutistic excess. Another group of young politicians, however, known as the "Centralists", argued that administration through the county system was obsolete. This group took over the *Pesti Hirlap* from Kossuth and waged a publicity campaign for the establishment of a Liberal constitution based on strictly Western European lines, with a government responsible to parliament. Outstanding in this group were Joseph Eötvös, eminent author of social novels, the historian László Szalay, and Sigismund Kemény, perhaps the greatest Hungarian writer in his day.

The Court of Vienna realized by this time that it would be impossible to refuse every measure of reform. It did endeavor, however, to approach the vexing problems through the young Conservatives. Of the latter, Count George Apponyi, vice-chancellor, attempted after the Diet of 1844, to organize a strong government party, being given official aid in the form of administrators despatched to every county to displace the Liberal opposition there. This again evoked unanimous resistance, strengthening and unifying instead of weakening the forces of the opposition. In the meantime, Széchenyi published his *Fragments of a Political Platform* in 1847, in which he defended the unpopular cause of the Conservatives, again painting the future in dark colors with his usual pessimism. Nevertheless, the advance of the Liberal opposition could not be blocked. Francis Deák was able, through extended negotiation, to have a uniform Liberal platform accepted by the factions of the opposition. The main demands of this were responsible government, a parliament elected by popular ballot, uniform taxation, a free press, and the reincorporation of Transylvania.

With such antecedents, the last feudal Diet of Hungary opened in Pozsony, November 12, 1847.

# VIII

## REVOLUTION AND WAR OF INDEPENDENCE

### (*1848–1849*)

The Era of Reform broke trail for Hungary's modern transformation, something the educated classes and the political leaders had longed for for a number of years. The last steps on this long journey were facilitated by the impression created all over Europe by the French Revolution in February 1848. The events in Paris found an echo in a series of political movements through all Europe. These were mainly of a social character in the West and strongly nationalistic in the eastern parts of the Continent. The significance of 1848 in France was different from what it was in Carpathian Europe. In France it was primarily a socialistic movement followed by the restoration of a bourgeois government, and then by the *coup d'état* of Napoleon III and the establishment of his personal rule. In Carpathian Europe, conditions which had been attained in the West in 1789 were brought about in the year 1848.

Louis Kossuth was the first to realize the continent-wide importance of these upheavals, and in the succeeding period he dictated to his nation the requirements of the age with suggestive force. More and more people saw in him the representative of both human liberty and national interests. In the Diet, the power of Conservatives and Liberals was at first about balanced. The Conservatives, supporting the government, gained strength, for they too advocated reforms, and gained the support of Széchenyi who prepared a vast railway building program. Kossuth, on the other hand although he enjoyed the confidence of some members of the Upper House, among them Count Louis Batthányi, found his most enthusiastic followers among the younger elements. In spite of this, he protested in vain to the Vienna government against the sending of its "administrators" to the counties, and its attempt to prevent the election of Liberal candidates.

News from France finally settled the issue, the Liberal opposition gaining victory in a few days. With their insistent backing, Kossuth had already, on March 3, demanded a change of the system, with a modern constitution not only for Hungary but for Austria as well. Owing to the hesitation of the Upper House, this memorandum did not reach the King before revolution broke out in Vienna on March 13, overthrowing Metternich and establishing a parliamentary government. On the following day Kossuth incorporated the full Liberal platform in his text, to which even the Upper House now gave its consent. A joint delegation of the Diet was sent to Vienna to submit the memorandum to the King.

With the news of the Paris and Vienna revolution, the youth of Pest was likewise stirred to action. Their leaders were mostly writers of humble origin, Alexander Petőfi among them, the greatest lyric poet of his time, whose poems, burning with the spirit of human and national liberty, have been translated into many languages. These young men, most of them barely thirty, were impatient advocates of radical reform, who thought that the deliberations of the Pozsony negotiations were too tedious and finely spun. On March 15, they held a bloodless demonstration, had a platform consisting of twelve points, similar in its essential demands, to that of the Liberal opposition, printed without permission from the censor. In the same way they circulated a stirring revolutionary poem by Petőfi, destined to become the "Marseillaise" of Hungarian liberty.

But Pest was not a metropolis comparable to Paris, and was unable either to organize the whole country overnight or to secure, following the French example, the political leadership for itself. The capital city turned republican; but it could not swing the country, which remained loyal. The working out of the reforms and their execution was left in the hands of the Diet. The Ides of March, however, as interpreted by the youth of 1848, have been to this day revered as the symbol of the new ideals and of liberty, and have become one of the chief national holidays of Hungary.

The Vienna government was partly taken by surprise and partly intimidated by these events. In Pest, Archduke Stephen, successor to the late Palatine Joseph, nicknamed in Vienna the "Old Rákóczi" because of his Hungarian sympathies, tried to persuade the King to fulfill the wishes of the nation as soon as possible. Indeed, there was no time for delay. The King heeded the warning and accepted the demands, naming Count Louis Batthyány the first Hungarian Premier on March 17. The entire program of the reform era was now put through as legislation in three short weeks, Ferdinand V sanctioning the bills on April 11. The foundations of a new Hungary were ready, and the great struggle against feudal institutions had ended in a victory.

The change was indeed remarkably swift, almost revolutionary. This peaceful "revolution", however, did not upset the legal order, and was terminated with the signature of the King. The national-liberal movement had achieved its aims, having presented the country with a modern government and modern institutions. It seemed as if Hungary had arrived at the threshold of a golden era in which nothing would disturb its peaceful evolution.

The legislature of 1848 did not effect any change in Hungary's relations with Austria. The *Pragmatica Sanctio* of 1723, assuring the hereditary succession of the Habsburg dynasty was naturally left untouched, so much so that the Compromise of 1867 between Austria and Hungary was, in fact, based upon the legislation of 1848, with some necessary supplements. The bills passed in 1848 did no more than transform Hungary, which, according to Act 10 of 1790 was a "regnum independens", from a feudal into a democratic state, assuring it a form of government of a Western European character. They established an "independent, responsible ministry", through which the King exercised his executive powers. Without the countersignature of the ministry no decrees of the king were valid. Representatives were elected to parliament for three years and all citizens above 20 years of age could vote, provided they had a certain grade of education or paid taxes above a certain level. The freedom of the press and the long-desired full re-incorporation of Transylvania were declared.

One of the most important provisions was general taxation, which wiped out the privileges of the nobility together with feudal burdens and liberated the peasants. By this, the peasant masses were immediately won for the cause. This social reform made Hungary able to carry out the great military and political effort that was soon to follow. The Hungarian peasantry still cherishes, as an historic tradition, the respect and devotion it owes to "Father Kossuth". The nobility hastily renounced its privileges without definite assurance of compensation. State indemnification of landowners, referred to by the previous legislation in a single sentence, was taken up by parliament at the end of 1848. By that time, however, the military defense of the country proved to be of greater importance and, at the suggestion of Francis Deák, the whole problem was

postponed with the remark that it would be selfishness
to negotiate such matters under the circumstances. Unquestionably the economic crisis that beset a part of the
nobility in the following decades found its origin in this
period. On the other hand, the swift application of the
law probably saved the country from acute social
trouble.

It soon became evident, however, that the very problems left untouched by the legislature of 1848, such as
the one concerning Hungary's relations to the Austrian
Empire and, on the other hand, the nationality question, involved possibilities of political complications.

Beneficiaries of the old order, die-hard partisans of
absolutist rule did not for a moment acquiesce in the
new order, despite royal assent. The stalwarts of old
Austria, generals, aristocrats, dignitaries and bureaucrats, steadfastly believed in the idea of the total
Monarchy. In the Hungarian April legislation they saw
a deadly blow to the unity of the Empire, and though
the new order was made binding by royal assent, they
considered it as the serious beginning of Hungary's
secession. Their anxiety seemed to be justified by Hungary's intention to have her finances placed under her
own management instead of under the court of Vienna.
This, however, was not the result of any basic change
in the legal relations of the two countries at all. It was
a natural consequence of the democratic reforms
effectuated by the Acts of 1848. In a feudal state, military affairs, finances and foreign affairs are directly
under the jurisdiction of the monarch. In a democracy,

however, the responsible government is entrusted with their management. In feudal Hungary, as the king was a foreigner, these matters were in the hands of a foreign administration. Liberal Hungary endeavored to take these affairs out of the king's direct influence.

Thus, from a strictly constitutional point of view, there was no change in the relations between Austria and Hungary. But in reality there were a number of problems which the two countries had to solve jointly. These were termed later, in 1867, "common affairs". Count Paul Esterházy, the former ambassador to London, and minister of "foreign affairs" in the Batthyány cabinet, had just begun negotiations concerning these common problems, when events upset peaceful procedure. The charge that Hungary intended to destroy the Monarchy with the legislation of 1848, is without foundation. In Batthyány's cabinet there were some, Széchenyi and Deák especially, who were ready to go to any lengths for peaceful co-operation. Not even Kossuth, who was minister of finance, and the most intransigent member of the cabinet, contemplated separation from Austria at the time.

But adherents to the old order were already, even in the Spring of 1848, preparing for a counter-revolution. What dangers lurked behind such a dangerous move, not only for Hungary but for the whole Habsburg Empire as well, were partly recognized even by the diplomatic envoys of Western countries to Vienna. The solutions of 1848 improved rather than marred the reputation of the Monarchy abroad. Palmerston of

England, and two French ministers for foreign affairs, Bastide and de Tocquille, were for the Habsburg Monarchy in its modernized, constitutional form, especially as a counterbalance to Russia. The divergent nationality movements which threatened to disrupt the Monarchy were looked upon with misgivings by the French, but the legislation of 1848 was acceptable to them.

Blackwell, England's agent in Hungary, reported early in 1848 that the Austrian cabinet was endeavoring to render the Hungarian government dependent upon them, though this might develop into turmoil, or perhaps armed conflict.[1] The French ambassador, de la Cour, accused Vienna of a "deplorable policy" which wilfully upheld the "inner division" of the Monarchy, leading to rivalry and racial antagonism between different parts of the Empire.[2] Thus the very circles that were anxious for the maintenance of the Monarchy were the most surprised to see the Vienna court's secret attempts at counter-revolution and the fanning of dangerous antagonism. With the flight of Metternich, however, Kolowrat was left without a competitor and found collaborators in War Minister Latour and the latter's followers for the restoration of the old order. On March 20, Kolowrat handed in a memorandum warning about the "Hungarian danger". He advocated

[1]*English State Papers, 1848–49*. Correspondence respecting the Affairs of Hungary, pp. 674, etc.

[2]In his report of June 7, 1848, published in the author's article, "French and Hungarian Foreign Policy in 1848." *Századok* (Review of the Hungarian Historial Society) 1938.

the making of a Croatian-Hungarian rapprochement impossible, and the blocking by the appointment of a royal commissioner, of every attempt at the reincorporation of Transylvania. It was through the suggestion of Kolowrat that Baron Joseph Jellachich was made Ban of Croatia as early as March 23. To every instruction of Hungary's Palatine or government, Jellachich countered with the argument that the revolution upset Croat-Magyar relations. In him, the Croats saw a patriot, the Magyars a political rebel. In fact, Jellachich was regarded by Kolowrat and his Vienna clique as a tool in their hands to poison Magyar-Croat relations.

With the assistance of War Minister Latour, Jellachich began to arm in earnest. Early in June, the Palatine began to suspect that the Ban's insurrection was fomented by secret influences emanating from the highest circles. He rushed to Innsbruck, where the Court had fled before the second Vienna revolt in May. He persuaded the king to have both Jellachich and the Hungarian premier summoned to Innsbruck in an attempt to reach a settlement. The Croat Baron, however, did not heed the order of his monarch, who thereupon issued a manifesto declaring Jellachich's movement illegal. It did not take long, however, to persuade the King to forgive him and revoke the manifesto. Finally, on June 24th, Premier Batthyány and Jellachich began to negotiate. The head of the Hungarian government was most conciliatory, offering the satisfaction of all of Croatia's national demands. Jellachich, as a Croatian patriot, found this acceptable in a tête-à-tête meeting; but as a tool of the counter-revolution, he also demanded the centralization of military and financial affairs again in Vienna, something that was exclusively of counter-revolutionary interest. On behalf of Hungary, Deák and Szemere worked out a bill, guaranteeing far-reaching independence and privileges for Croatia. A Hungarian cabinet meeting on August 27 was even ready to acquiesce in some form of federation. The Magyars did everything possible for a peaceful solution to serve the interests of both nations. All these plans were frustrated, however, by the counter-revolutionary movement that had the blessing and assistance of the innermost circles within the Austrian government. These served no aims but those of the counter-revolution, which coldly and deliberately engineered a conflict in order to regain, with the help of the Imperial army, the rights that the Magyars had won in the April legislation.

The counter-revolutionary movement did not try to find allies only in the Croats. The events in the spring of 1848 re-echoed among other peoples of Carpathian Europe. As the Croats wanted a separate ministry in Zagreb, March 25, other nationalities also appeared with political demands. These smaller peoples had just about that time arrived, after a cultural preparation, at political nationalism. They did not aim at gaining minority protection as we understand it now, but at obtaining certain territorial autonomies within which they could force their own national conceptions upon others. In fact these autonomies were to be national states in a nutshell, offering, naturally, even less minority protection for other ethnic elements living there. It goes without saying that to allay the antagonisms brought about by the effect these nationalisms would have been a difficult task under any circumstances. Nevertheless it seems probable that the peoples of Carpathian Europe could have found a peaceful solution among themselves, at least a better one than that brought about by the Austrian government with its systematic policy of *divide et impera*. The incitement of small peoples against one another resulted in a general conflict in 1848, the direct responsibility for which must be placed at the door of the counter-revolutionists.

In the southern parts of Hungary, as has been pointed out, the Serbs had been resident immigrants for about a century and a half. Referring to the privileges granted them by Leopold I, they demanded an autonomous Serbian territory governed by a "chief" (*voyvoda*). The Imperial government supported this claim also, for reasons already known. On the other hand, the Serbian government of Belgrade assisted this scheme for its own interest, minister Garashanin, a number of years before, having completed his plan of a great Serbian union to the detriment of the Monarchy. The congress of Hungary's Serbs on May 13, 1848 demanded nearly full independence and, in the meantime, emissaries of Belgrade worked hard to whip up feeling for an uprising. The clash did not occur because of the failure of negotiations between Stratimirović and Kossuth, but because neither Vienna nor Belgrade was anxious to reach a peaceful settlement. It is interesting to note that at the time when the French minister to Vienna, fearing for the fate of the Monarchy, welcomed the Hungarian military measures against the Serbian uprising, the Austrian consul Meyerhofer in Belgrade, in his reports to Vienna, rejoiced that Serbia would be only too glad to help the rebellion. The counter-revolutionaries were quite unable to see that the Serbian scheme was really pointed at the Monarchy. The Hungarian government came to terms with the Serb minority on June 16, 1849, after their excessive territorial demands were turned down even by Austria. This agreement assured protection of minority rights, giving a guarantee for higher education as well as other school and church affairs.

The mass of Slovak and Ruthenian people did not follow the example of other nationalities and held out with the Magyars who championed Liberal legislation. As once in the struggle of Rákóczi, many of them fought side by side with the Magyars, the Hungarian army numbering some 40,000 of their troops. However, several leaders of the rising Slovak intelligentsia, Stur, Hurban and Hodža, for instance, sympathized more with the Czech movement, feeling their Slovak people too weak to emphasize their independent nationality. In March, the Czechs too demanded a separate ministry for Bohemia. Later on, a Slav Congress tried to harmonize the interests of the different nations of the Slav race. Finally a revolt on June 12 broke out in

Prague, only to be crushed by Prince Windischgraetz. From then on, the Czechs joined the Austrian parliament in Vienna. Their leader Francis Palacky, the historian, professed so-called "Austro-Slav" views, claiming that Austria would have to be invented if it did not already exist.

The Rumanians of Transylvania passed resolutions similar to those of other national movements, at their meeting at Balázsfalva (Blaj) on March 15 and protested against reunion with Hungary. The Rumanians in the Principality of Wallachia followed the example of their more advanced kin in Transylvania, but Russia soon crushed the midget revolt of Bucharest. It was not long before the Saxons as well as the Rumanians became tools of the counter-revolutionists of the Habsburg court, the latter inciting the nationalities against the unarmed Magyar and Székely population in bloody guerilla warfare. There were negotiations between Kossuth and some Rumanian leaders of Transylvania, but these were finally handicapped by the events. Later in the summer of 1849, the Hungarian parliament passed a Nationality Act submitted by Bartholomew Szemere, then prime minister, which was based on the principle that in a democracy the desires of all elements of the population have to be satisfied. As a matter of record, this was the first legislation in all Carpathian Europe which aimed at the welfare of nationalities by assuring them modern minority rights.

The counter-revolutionary movement prepared for civil war, utilizing the small peoples as tools. Against it the only counter-measure worth speaking of was the resistance offered by Hungary, the strongest representative of Liberalism in 1848. Everything depended, therefore, upon the shaping of the relations between Austria and Hungary. Against the reform legislation of April, two strong movements were afoot: the counter-revolution in Austria on the one hand and the radical republican movement in Hungary on the other. The latter was fed by ever-increasing and more or less justified, suspicion toward the governing clique in Vienna. The more apparent their anti-Magyar attitude and open military preparations against Hungary became, the more widespread in Hungary became the republican conception which demanded the breaking off of relations with Austria. Although in the spring this party was insignificant, Kossuth terming it "a dwarf minority", by the autumn Deák already realized the impossible position of the Batthyány cabinet between the two extremist movements.

For the consolidation of a Constitutional Monarchy, the collaboration of the Vienna and Pest governments was essential. Premier Batthyány of Hungary did his best to assure this; but Vienna made no distinction between the radicals and Batthyány, and by disavowing him compromised his peaceful endeavors. With this attitude, the Vienna statesmen played right into the hands of their worst enemies, the radicals. This was the reason for the breaking off of relations. England's agent, Blackwell, reported to London as early as the spring that the "republican spirit" of Pest "can only be counteracted by the Austrian government lending its support to Count Batthyány's ministry." He also noted however, that a "strange infatuation" had taken hold of Vienna, which might easily lead to disaster. The French ambassador likewise considered the policy of the Hungarian premier a right one. When revolution broke out in Milan and the army of Piedmont rushed to its assistance, resulting in an Austrian request to Hungary for aid, Batthyány promised this, for under the *Sanctio Pragmatica,* assuring mutual assistance, he was obliged to. Nevertheless popular feeling was for Italy, for the Magyars admired their fight for liberation. On July 21, even Kossuth demanded free institutions for the Italian people in return for Hungary's assistance. Batthyány did everything to maintain peaceful relations with Austria but his position became hopeless as soon as the Croat armies of Jellachich, openly supported by the Imperial government, launched an attack against Hungary in September 1848. The premier, having tried in vain to negotiate with Vienna, resigned. The Palatine had no more success at negotiations either. Finally he arranged for the dispatch of the Imperial general, Count Lamberg, as royal commissioner to negotiate peace with Jellachich. Count Lamberg's appointment, however, happened without asking the assent of the Hungarian ministry and therefore was unconstitutional. The already intense feeling ran amuck of the masses, and resulted in the lynching of the emissary in Pest. The last possibility of peace vanished. Jellachich moved against Pest and there was great concern as to how the country, threatened by Imperial forces from every direction, could defend itself.

But Kossuth was there, almost the personification of national defense. He it was who first realized that the nation must prepare for any eventuality. In a famous address to parliament on July 11, 1848, he asked for a home defense army of 200,000 men "because the motherland was in danger", and this was unanimously voted. It was Kossuth, too, who provided the necessary financial arrangements. Without him the crisis in September would have ended in disaster. When it became evident that a break with the Imperial government was inevitable, leadership automatically fell on his shoulders. On September 21, Parliament entrusted the duties of government to a Home Defense Committee under the chairmanship of Kossuth. The political instincts of the nation now found expression in Kossuth, who encouraged, recruited, armed, and prophesied victory.

The first sign of this victory was that a Hungarian force of recruits defeated Jellachich's army and forced it to retreat towards Vienna. Two young Hungarian officers, Arthur Görgey and Morris Perczel, outflanked and captured a large part of the Ban's force.

On October 5, the third revolution broke out in Vienna, led largely by students who sympathized with the Hungarians. Urged by Kossuth, the Hungarian army attempted to break through the forces of Prince Windischgraetz which besieged Vienna. As might have been expected, the undrilled *Honvéd* (home defense) troops were defeated at Schwechat, near Vienna, on

Louis Kossuth

*Lithograph, 1848*

October 30, and were obliged to withdraw to the frontiers of Hungary. Vienna capitulated before the Prince. Kossuth then entrusted the command of the army to thirty-year-old Arthur Görgey. Görgey, educated at the Military Academy of Ulm had served for some years as Hussar officer in the Imperial army, leaving it for studies in chemical science. He was to become the outstanding military genius of the War of Independence.

Being a lawyer and a statesman, Kossuth would not have been able to conduct large scale military operations alone. On the other hand, there could be no doubt that Windischgraetz was about to attack Hungary. In Transylvania and in the south, the Imperial forces openly supported the revolt of the minorities. As a sad chapter in the events of 1848, Rumanian terrorists waged a guerilla warfare of murder and pillage against undefended towns and families. These sanguinary acts of brutality had many victims among the Magyar population of Transylvania.

From west and east, north and south, Imperial forces appeared ready to crush the hemmed-in Magyar defences. It was Görgey who forged from the varied, hastily recruited elements a well-disciplined army. The former officers were at first apprehensive, for their oath tied them to their King, who as emperor ordered Austria's armies against their country. This dilemma was dealt with in a Hungarian declaration on November 26 which stated that Hungarian officers were fighting for the constitution sanctioned by the King himself, and thus they, and not their enemies, were the ones who followed the King's genuine intentions. Thus Hungarians maintained that they fought for the established legal order. When the new Austrian cabinet of Schwarzenberg forced Ferdinand V to resign, and his cousin Francis Joseph succeeded to the throne, the Hungarian parliament declared the resignation illegal.

The offensive campaign of Windischgraetz against Hungary started in the middle of December. Görgey slowly retreated before overwhelming forces. Knowing that the public wished to hear of some success, Kossuth constantly urged the young general to attack; but Görgey was not willing to expose his army, and with it the Hungarian cause, to a defeat. Kossuth already began to feel that he misjudged the young strategist, who did not share his optimism and made sarcastic remarks about politicians meddling in military affairs. When Perczel's separate army corps was defeated through the daring and inconsiderate orders of Perczel, Görgey retreated to Pest, from which the government had fled to Debrecen, in the eastern part of the country. A peace delegation, sent to Austrian headquarters at the insistence of former premier Batthyány, returned without results, because Windischgraetz was unwilling to talk to "rebels". At the staff conference of January 5, 1849, it was decided that Perczel's troops should move east to defend the government, while Görgey should lead his forces to the north, to distract the attention of the Austrian main forces.

Windischgraetz, moving into Pest, seriously believed

that he had put an end to the Hungarian resistance and this he naively reported to Vienna in boasting bulletins. In Pest, he approached a few Hungarian aristocrats in an endeavor to restore the order of 1847. This was another naive plan, for at that time the Schwarzenberg cabinet of Vienna was preparing for a new, totally absolutistic form of government.

Hungarian resistance, thought hopeless in January surprised the world in the spring. The January crisis was so serious that Görgey was obliged to issue a manifesto in order to assure the unity of the army. The officers, while ready to fight for the constitution of 1848, feared that the republican spirit was gaining ground and were unwilling "to go into sheer revolution." Görgey's manifesto stated that the "army would remain loyal to its oath", and would defend, against any outside enemy, legal order and the constitution sanctioned by the King. This declaration augmented the lack of confidence which the Debrecen government already felt toward Görgey. After all, every one began to realize that negotiations between Hungary and Austria were impossible, as the Vienna government refused to consider any mediation. Through Count Ladislas Teleki, on a diplomatic mission to Paris, Kossuth invited General Dembinsky, of Polish revolutionary fame, to become commander-in-chief of the Hungarian forces. Görgey, however, demonstrated his strategical talents in a model winter campaign, proceeding east through Upper Hungary and tying down large Austrian forces. He not only saved his army but also improved its morale, discipline and fighting ability, and his soldiers adored him. Having successfully negotiated the difficult mountainous terrain, he attacked from the rear the army of General Schlick, who had broken into Hungary from the north and in February he joined the Hungarian forces newly organized by Kossuth. In the meantime, the Austrians in Transylvania were being severely pounded by a diminutive Polish strategist, General Bem. One of the faithful admirers of this daring old soldier was the poet Petőfi, who served as his adjutant. The success of Görgey and Bem turned the tide and afforded an opportunity for a Hungarian offensive to regain the heart of the country. The organization of war materials and replacements was secured through Kossuth's energetic management, but on the military field only a unified high command could have successfully undertaken a general offensive. The new generalissimo, Dembinsky, under whom the seasoned army of Görgey was also placed, soon demonstrated his inability to conduct offensive warfare on unfamiliar terrain. Bem was a born strategist, and had won the confidence of the Hungarian officers in spite of being a foreigner. With Dembinsky, who proved to be vain and impetuous, it was different. He could give no clear account of his plans and his orders were contradictory. The Austrian attack at Kápolna, on February 26, struck his forces by surprise. His units got mixed up and could not force a decision, though their fighting abilities remained intact. When Dembinsky gave orders for a retreat in divided columns, his army was exposed to new dangers which provoked open criticism from the officers. They declared that they could no longer trust Dembinsky, and that their confidence was in Görgey. This step cannot be considered a simple piece of insubordination, for sincere anxiety for the country's future prompted their action. Kossuth, hearing the first news, hastened to the front with the thought that he would have the recalcitrants shot. A personal conference, however, convinced him of the situation and he saw it again demonstrated that Görgey was an outstanding soldier and a true patriot. Kossuth saw also that the intrigues of radical republicans at Debrecen against Görgey were baseless. It was about that time that Görgey wrote the characteristic words about Kossuth; "Only Kossuth has real faith in the Revolution. He is indeed a classic character. What a pity he is not a soldier . . ." The two great personalities sealed a friendship again and shortly afterwards Görgey's phenominal spring offensive began.

In this large-scale campaign the newly-born, young army, and its generals Klapka, Damjanich, Gáspár and Aulich performed their tasks excellently. The Imperial forces, comprising crack regiments of Austria, one of the military Great Powers of contemporary Europe, were soon thrown back beyond Pest from where not so long ago the haughty Prince had sent glowing dispatches to the Emperor. Leaving in the capital only sufficient troops to fool the enemy, Görgey turned north, and winning another battle at Nagysalló, led his troops in a great semi-circle toward Komárom, to the southwest, cutting off retreat for the bulk of the Austrian army. Reports of the new generalissimo Welden clearly indicate in what condition the disorganized Imperial troops reached the Austrian frontier from which Görgey had commenced his retreat six months before.

But in the meantime political changes of great significance took place. Following the Battle of Kápolna, Windischgraetz, in his naive way, had sent a new bulletin to Vienna reporting the termination of all Hungarian resistance. This happened just before Görgey's spring offensive. On March 4, the Vienna Court issued a new constitution which, discarding the Acts of 1848, established a unified and a centralized Empire, with Hungary embodied as a second-rate province, Transylvania again completely separated, and a Serbian "voivodina" (something novel and unheard of until then) created on the southwest. This manifesto, published at the temporary seat of the Court at Olmütz, Moravia, confiscated Hungary's independence.

In response, at the end of the victorious spring campaign, Kossuth was about to dethrone the Habsburg dynasty and to proclaim full independence. As he wrote to Bem: "The last possibilities for an agreement have gone, and we may just as well fight to the end." From among former associates of Batthyány, a very cautious "peace group" was formed at Debrecen, seeking to maintain the legislation of 1848 and to enlist the support of Görgey. Their influence, however, was insignificant compared to the respect commanded by Kossuth. While the peace group considered it dangerous to keep on fighting against the overwhelming power of the

Habsburg dynasty, their opponents on the other hand pointed out that negotiations could not begin without the willingness by the other party.

Kossuth, who wanted to rush things on account of the peace group's activities, confided to the general staff that a proper answer should be given to the dynasty's manifesto. Görgey, on the other hand, explained his anxiety over abandoning the principle of the defense of the Constitution of 1848. He pointed out that this would not only endanger the country's international situation, but would also affect the morale of the troops, fighting, according to their views, for laws to which the King had given royal assent. With many already celebrated victories, Görgey knew well that he had difficult problems yet to solve. The young general appraised conditions with the sceptical eye of a scholar; yet he was, first and foremost, a soldier, who feared for the morale and the unity of his troops as the result of political changes. As he had once written that Kossuth was no soldier, so Kossuth felt that Görgey would never make a politician that he could never win over this ironic, often pessimistic soldier for his future plans. On the other hand, a Declaration of Independence was a logical result of Kossuth's love for freedom, because, according to him, this involved the liberation not only of Hungary, but of all East-Central Europe as well.

On April 14, 1849, in the Calvinist church at Debrecen, the Declaration of Independence was approved with enthusiastic cheers. This document, which exercised such a lasting spiritual influence for the next half century, stated, among other things, that "the dynasty has forfeited its right to the Hungarian throne. We feel ourselves bound in duty to make known the motives and reasons that have impelled us to this decision, in order that the civilized world may learn that we have not taken this step out of overweening confidence in our wisdom, nor out of revolutionary excitement, but that it is an act of utter necessity, adopted to preserve from utter destruction a nation persecuted to the limit of a most enduring patience."[1] Giving an account of the events leading up to the war, the Declaration also related the more important phases of the struggle. Concurring with the dethronement of the Habsburgs, Kossuth, with the unanimous approbation of the Parliament at Debrecen, was named Governing President, "under obligation to render an account of all acts". Kossuth appointed Szemere as premier and the latter furnished a republican platform.

The Declaration of Independence expressed the desire and will of the nation, as personified in Kossuth to active freedom; but it also confirmed Görgey's anxieties. The political upheavals of 1848 had by this time quieted down all over Europe. In France, Louis Napoleon, who later became emperor, was president. Austria had soon succeeded in crushing the insurrection in Italy. England and France had from the beginning favored a constitutional Habsburg Monarchy. "Unfortunately their heads are still filled with ideas of a

[1]The American Declaration of Independence of 1776 served, partly, as an example in the drafting of the Hungarian Declaration.

strong Austria", wrote Francis Pulszky, the London representative of the new Hungarian government. Palmerston, in spite of all his sympathy toward Hungary, told Pulszky that the Magyars should reconcile the Habsburgs "because in the frame of European State system it would be impossible to replace Austria by small states", Austria being "a European necessity and the natural ally of England in the East".[1] The diplomacy of either England or France would not have done more than offer its good offices for a compromise, but neither the Hungarian nor the Austrian government was ready for this.

As surmised by Görgey, both officers and men were affected by the change in politics. Political arguments had arisen before the offensive was ended. A group of officers demanded that Görgey should sever his relations with Kossuth and his followers, and, declaring himself military dictator, should move his troops to the western frontier and should immediately seek some agreement. Görgey was of the belief that the government had acted hastily, yet he himself was unwilling to force political decisions. He was absolutely unaccustomed to this field, which was quite foreign to him, and he tried to avoid the issue. First of all, he wished to spare his army from political arguments. Therefore, he published a stirring proclamation to his soldiers, inspiring them to continue fighting for freedom against the "dynasty that had broken its oath." Thus

[1]A. W. Ward—G. P. Gooch, The Cambridge History of British Foreign Policy 1783–1919. Vol. 2. 1923. p. 320.

he accepted the Declaration of Independence, which naturally expressed his own feelings too, though he was aware of its political complications. He accepted it because otherwise he would have had to repudiate Kossuth, whom he too considered the irreplaceable leader of the national cause. Had he turned his back on Kossuth and sought a compromise with Austria, the unyielding attitude of the latter would have left him in a situation far worse. At the same time, however, Görgey could not share the optimistic plans of the government and would have liked to see the Declaration revoked, which was of course impossible. From this time on, the antagonism between the great statesman and the great strategist grew deeper and deeper. Görgey was under the impression that the government had committed an error as far as the army was concerned. The radicals at Debrecen, on the other hand, accused him of designs to make himself military dictator and claimed that he was a traitor to the cause of liberty. This was the foundation of that false rumor which circulated for decades, that the struggle for liberty was lost on account of Görgey's treason. Secret documents made public in 1918 thoroughly refuted these accusations.

Instead of pursuing the beaten enemy on the Austro-Hungarian border, Görgey, bowing to the will of Kossuth and of the public opinion, returned to besiege Buda, the capital. Many writers point out that this was a grave mistake. Others state, however, that it would have been unwise to order the Hungarian army, ill-supplied and exhausted after a swift campaign, to a new major offensive. Another important reason was that a part of the officers wished to be near to the western border for political reasons. Nevertheless Buda was occupied, after a rather long siege, in a single stroke on May 21. The public hailed Görgey as a great victor, but he saw that he had lost much valuable time. He kept on repeating bitterly that this was the end of his luck. On the north, a crack Russian army of 200,000 stood poised for a thrust into Hungary. When the army of Windischgraetz was defeated, Austria applied to Russia for aid. Tsar Nicholas I had promised Emperor Francis that he would support the Habsburg dynasty. The Tsar considered himself the defender of the Holy Alliance, and dispatched his troops on the pretext that the Hungarians and Poles had launched an international revolution which had to be crushed. Under the leadership of Prince Paskievich of Warsaw, an army of 200,000 descended upon Hungary. With these, the forces opposing an exhausted Hungarian army of 152,-000 and 450 cannon was swelled to 370,000 men and 1200 cannon.

On the western frontier, in the Vág Valley, the advancing Hungarian troops attacking again in the middle of June, found themselves opposite strong Russian columns. This necessitated shelving the offensive, and Görgey, gathering his army at Komárom, suggested the grouping of all forces around Komárom in order to strike a decisive blow at the real enemy, the Austrian army, before the main body of the Russian divisions could arrive from the northeast. The cabinet council originally approved of this plan, but later, at Kossuth's suggestion, ordered the army to withdraw, together with the government, to the Southern part of Hungary. By this time, Kossuth's trust in Görgey was shaken. The latter fought an indecisive battle at Ács (July 2) against superior forces. Görgey personally led a heroic cavalry attack, himself heading his best Hussar regiments, and suffered a severe head wound. Some believed that he had sought death on the battlefield.

The odds against the overwhelming forces of two major armies surging from every direction could not have been counterbalanced in the long run even if Görgey had been appointed commander-in-chief of all Hungarian armies. By this time, however, the antagonism of the leaders had grown so bitter that only Görgey's popularity with his troops saved his actual position. The main army, under the leadership of Dembinsky and Perczel, retired towards the south-east, the government having been moved to Szeged.

The wounded Görgey, after his plans for a general offensive at Komárom were frustrated, marched in a great arc toward Arad where he was to join the main body. By outwitting the Russians, he proved for the third time that he was a strategist of superlative ability. During the long and arduous march, he was able to keep all his troops in high spirits and only one wing suffered a minor reverse. Kossuth's commissioner, after visiting Görgey's camp, reported on July 31: "After so many vicissitudes, the army is still in good spirits. Görgey is their life and soul, ready to save the country in unanimity with you, dear Governing President." Görgey marching as fast as he could, arrived in Arad on schedule only to find that the main army, under Dembinsky, numbering some 60,000 men, had, in spite of the plans, moved on to Temesvár. There the new generalissimo, Joseph Bem, the Polish hero of Ostrolenka fame, took charge, since his own troops had been previously annihilated by the Russian army which broke into Transylvania. Bem immediately contacted the Austrians and suffered a decisive defeat.

Görgey's plan, as revealed to Kossuth on August 10, was to attack the Austrians with all available men, provided he could effect a junction of the remaining armies. At that time, there was as yet no news about the main army. Görgey declared that if the main army was safe, he would attack the Austrians; if it was defeated, he would surrender. The sad news of defeat was not long in coming, leaving no other way out but capitulation. On the next day, Görgey requested Kossuth's resignation and the transfer of authority entitling him to make the necessary arrangements. Kossuth fled to Turkey, first hiding St. Stephen's Holy Crown near Orsova. On August 12, the war council decided on surrender, but to the Russians only.

Görgey's position was hopeless. He had barely 30,-000 overworked men at his disposal. The rest of the Hungarian army had perished, through no fault of his; and Görgey wished no glory for himself at the bloody price of the life of these remnants. When sunset came on August 13, on the plains of Világos, near Arad, Görgey for the last time inspected his brave warriors. Following the laying down of arms, the orderliness of which again demonstrated the high morale and discipline of the *Honvéd* forces, only the fortress of Komárom was able to hold out against the combined Austro-Russian forces. Its defender, General Klapka, capitulated in October.

Surrender was purposely made to the Russian army only, for it was common knowledge that there was rift between the Imperial and the Tsarist general staffs and both Kossuth and Görgey believed they could secure concessions through Russian mediation. The government had previously endeavored to seek contact with the Tsarist general staff without positive success though the Russians apparently showed sympathy, not hiding their dislike towards the Austrians. After the surrender at Világos, Paskievich suggested amnesty to the Austrian cabinet, Tsar Alexander II sending his own son to Vienna to prevail upon young Francis Joseph to apply "rightly interpreted mercy". Despite Paskievich's reports to the Tsar that "Hungary is at your Majesty's feet", the fate of the country was really in the hands of Prince Schwarzenberg and the Austrian generalissimo Haynau, already ill-famed for his cruelty in the Italian campaign. Haynau was bent on revenge and declared that he would see to it that the Magyars would not attempt any revolution for a hundred years. The Russians allowed the entertaining of hopes they were unable to back up. All that the Tsar's mediation could bring about was the sparing of Görgey's life, and the latter was interned in the Austrian town of Klagen-furt. The intervention of France and England was of no avail, Haynau had the former premier, Louis Batthyány, and thirteen high officers executed (Arad, October 6), and they thus became martyrs of national and human freedom. More than a thousand officers were imprisoned and the rank and file of the defeated army were pressed into service in the Austrian Imperial forces. The majority of Hungarian leaders fled abroad as émigrés and continued to work for the country's cause. Hungary lay open to the violence of foreign despotism.

# IX

## ABSOLUTISM AND EMIGRATION

### (*1849–1867*)

With the defeat of Hungary, the strongest champion of contemporary modern ideas disappeared from Carpathian Europe. The country was helpless against plans to merge it finally into Austria, and it was equally undefended against the bloody revenge of the Austrian generals. According to adherents of absolutism, "Hungary had lost its constitutional institutions by open rebellion and revolt", and as in the case of military conquest, the occupying forces were entitled to impose on her any rule at will, without any consideration for historic rights. This so-called *"Verwirkungstheorie"* was equivalent to the denial of the existence of the Hungarian state. They endeavored to cut the country into fragments, with the intention of destroying its unity. Thus Transylvania was separated, then Croatia and the port of Fiume were sliced off, and finally, an entirely novel district (*Vajdaság, vojvodina*) was created in the

South, comprising the four counties of Bács, Torontál, Temes and Krassó-Szörény. It would be misleading to think that they wanted to satisfy the nationalities with such an arrangement. To be sure, the Serbs had asked for such "vojvodina" as a distinct territorial entity, but they had no desire to have it run by the Austrian military command.

The autonomy and separate Diet of Croatia were also lost. Not even the Transylvanian Saxons were granted their previous autonomy. As Francis Pulszky said, "the nationalities who were allies of absolutism in the past struggle received as reward the same treatment meted out to the Hungarians as punishment". Another contemporary Hungarian writer, Antony Csengery, aptly remarked that "all nationalities now received equal rights to become Germans." The separated portions of the country, put under the direct jurisdiction of Vienna, were governed without exception by an Austrian administration. The remaining central part of Hungary was subdivided into five districts.

As soon as Haynau's terrorism quieted down, even civilian administration followed the pattern of the armed despotism initiated by Count Schwarzenberg. From 1851 on, Archduke Albrecht was head of the state as governor. Under him, an enormous, sprawling and costly bureaucracy was set up, with an army of political police which had, as its chief task, the control of the Hungarian public and the checking of every popular movement. The evil genius behind this huge organization of intimidation was Alexander Bach, after

whom it was named the "Bach System". Originally a
barrister and agitator in the Vienna Revolution, he
turned overnight from a radical orator into an unquestioned master of censorship, intrigue, denunciation
and a colossal machine of political informers and con-
cocted trials—as Imperial minister of internal affairs.
He planted Hungary through and through with his
trusted Austrian and especially Czech officials. These
were derided and hated by the downtrodden Hungarians, who nicknamed them "Bach's Hussars". The
bureaucracy they established was characterized by corruption, lack of intelligence, and extremes that bordered on the tragi-comic. There was no constitution,
for even the one decreed in March 1849 was revoked.
Imperial orders and so-called patents were in vogue.
Young Francis Joseph, ascending the throne at the age
of eighteen, could not break with the system.

What was most detrimental to the country was the
fact that the rapid development in all phases of economic, political and cultural life which had seemed so
promising in 1848 was in many cases fatally throttled.
The great generation of 1848 was dead, executed, imprisoned, scattered over the face of the earth, or retired
from public life. Széchenyi was in a hospital for the insane at Döbling, near Vienna; for his mind had given
way in the autumn of 1848, when he saw that the
catastrophe of which he had warned his people was inevitable. Together with Count Louis Batthyány, many
outstanding leaders had been executed. The poet Petőfi
had died on the battlefield of Segesvár in the cause of

liberty, thus fulfilling a patriotic desire expressed in one of his lyrics. This was the fate of many promising members of his generation. And those left alive returned home long after broken by Austrian prison life, or emigrated abroad. Many never returned.

Kossuth himself spent the rest of his life in voluntary exile. Some committed suicide in their desperation. Premier Szemere went insane. The interned Görgey was ruined for life by baseless charges of treason heaped on him by his republican enemies. One could enumerate many examples of how a whole outstanding and talented generation was wasted in tragedy. This generation could have successfully led Hungary in a peaceful advance, but now its remnants were forced, at best, to fight for their ideals on foreign soil, scattered over the world from Turkey and Italy to America.

Those who starved out the next destructive seventeen years at home brought about, with the wise and patient leadership of Francis Deák, the last great achievement of that generation, the Compromise with Austria in 1867. But the exiles who returned after 1867 had lost precious years of their lives, their energies already spent. Soon after the Compromise with Austria, Deák died, without leaving a worthy successor to carry on his work in the right spirit. It is with these tragic circumstances in mind that one should approach the period of forty-seven years from 1867 to 1914.

During the absolutistic era, losses were suffered by the educated classes in every respect. A certain temporary economic crisis was inevitable in any case be-

cause of the change from a patriarchal system to hastily
growing capitalism without any interval of transition.
Material sacrifice, and devastation by military operations made the situation extremely difficult. The victors
simply burned some seventy millions worth of banknotes issued by Kossuth. Landowners, on the other
hand, received a certain compensation, as provided by
the legislation of 1848, but in installments only and with
great delay, provided they could prove their political
trustworthiness. And if they did receive anything—the
Patent of 1853 promised thirty per cent—it was in the
form of five-per-cent bonds of land amortization. Customs barriers between Austria and Hungary were
abolished in 1850, but heavy land taxes and excise duties were imposed on the Hungarian population, together with all kinds of public levies. Within a decade,
direct and indirect taxes were raised a thousand per
cent! Changed conditions would have required extensive credit facilities for new investments, but no care
was taken of this. The economic experience of the educated classes was rather antiquated in comparison to
demands of the vast new problems. They tried to keep
their old standards but were at a total loss as to how to
deal with the situation, and the uncertainty could not
be remedied soon for there was not sufficient economic
education. The higher strata of the peasantry, which
should have joined the middle class, were in an even
more neglected position, credit facilities and co-operatives being introduced only after 1867. The lower
strata though liberated from feudal burdens were with-

out leaders, their political consciousness more or less undeveloped, following events simply from a sentimental viewpoint. They were faithful to the memory of Kossuth and his social achievements, though their political rôle was restricted to passive resistance.

Thus leadership was left to the remnants of the generation of 1848. But, besides economic distress, there were other troubles. Foreign occupation was bound to make its ill-effects felt in all phases of life. Public opinion, deprived of any real action, began to see the expression of patriotism in wearing national costumes and by other such external demonstrations. The best elements wrapped themselves in seclusion. Those who accepted commissions from the oppressors, were ostracised. This passivity and the spiritual depression strangled all life. There was no sign of the dynamic activity and the widespread interest that had characterized the previous generation. Students did no longer travel to the West. Education served but one purpose, to school spineless individuals for absolutism and even that in foreign language. Owing to all these circumstances, the standard of education of youth was much inferior to that of the previous period. Young people were brought up in a boundless hatred against everything Austrian. This explains the general feeling in the second half of the century.

What political trend was possible under such conditions? Three distinct platforms had hastily followed each other in the past few years. The first was based on the old constitution of 1847; the second considered the

April 1848 legislation as its standard, and the third, radically differing from the others, accepted as its foundation the 1849 Declaration of Independence. During the new period, all three trends found their partisans.

Those aristocrats representing the Conservative party in the reform era were now called Old Conservatives. They endeavored to secure autonomy for Hungary within the framework of the Austrian Empire. According to their plan, Hungary was to return to the pre-1848 constitution, as far as her relations with Austria were concerned, although naturally with modern social changes put into effect. Among other measures, they wished to regain the local administration of the counties. Though they had the best opportunity among the three groups, owing to their aloofness from revolutionary activities and their family connections with the Austrian ruling class, the platform they tried to popularize through pamphlets and memoranda had only seemingly more chance than the others. The dynasty was for the time being unwilling to grant any concessions, great or small. Thus the activity of these Old Conservatives was of more importance in the social, literary and scientific fields, to the survival of which they really contributed.

Between the Conservatives and the other extreme of the total independence platform of the 1849 émigrés, there was Francis Deák, steadily proving his principle that the April 1848 legislation was constitutionally speaking still valid. Many could not imagine that those who were ready to frustrate the execution of the 1848 legislation by force of a counter-revolution would ever consent to grant the rights contained therein; but Deák witnessed the exertions of the administration with stoic calm and unshaken faith. His perseverance aroused confidence throughout the nation. He was responsible for the "passive resistance" against the administration, the only possible attitude amidst oppression and the troubles that it brought. Deák was a courageous pessimist, not a man who based his calculations on illusory hope. He was a scholar versed in the Latin classics, and nothing could swerve him from the path that he had learned was the right one. Just as Kossuth's stirring orations were a true mirror of the nation's sentiments, so Deák's attitude sprang from that strength and endurance without which the Magyar people could not have survived in the troublesome centuries.

Around Deák were gathered the outstanding authors who had not emigrated, among them the novelist and philosopher, Joseph Eötvös, the historian Francis Salamon, and the editor of the *Pesti Napló,* Sigismund Kemény. In the tragic days following the defeat, when self-knowledge was needed and when there was a search for scapegoats, it was the pamphlet *After Revolution* (1850), by Kemény, which pointed out the moral from past events. He quoted examples, proving that while every power from England and Russia desired the maintenance of Austria, the Declaration of Independence could not be carried out by the Magyars single-handed. He also observed that the people, whom he did not find to be revolutionary, should be led back to the conceptions of Széchenyi. Such an attitude was denounced as defeatism by those who anxiously awaited the return of Kossuth and his followers. Kemény asserted that his aim was nothing else but "to make a sober and sincere estimate of mistakes and sacrifices, amidst the ruins of the country."

The most intransigent platform was professed by the émigrés. They steadfastly maintained the aims of 1849, planning to regain the position defined in the Declaration of Independence, even at the cost of another revolution. This party never gave up the fight against Austria. It considered itself the rightful representative of the nation, with the Declaration of Independence as the "fundamental law" of Hungary. It was not 1848, but 1849 that they wanted. Kossuth, too, was faithful to this standpoint until his death. The émigrés attempted to exploit every opportunity, real or imaginary, which occurred in international politics, hoping to gain allies for the liberation of Hungary. "Should everyone in Hungary give up the ideas of 1849, the émigrés cannot do so," wrote Kossuth in 1861.

But these political exiles had first to be organized. Thousands of the refugees had fled towards Turkey after the catastrophe, finding refuge at first in a concentration camp at Viddin. Spreading false reports of the beginnings of an international revolution with Kossuth as its spiritual leader, Austria and Russia demanded his extradition. Sultan Abdul Medjid, however, was influenced by the assistance of England and

France which led to a naval demonstration at the Dardanelles. Premier Palmerston realized that it was not in the interest of England to let Russian influence increase in Turkey. Finally the Vienna government acquiesced in the internment of Kossuth at Kiutahia, in Asia Minor.

But by this time, the cause of Hungary, hitherto unknown, was already well appreciated. The successful spring campaign and the lone heroic struggle against two major powers gained the sympathy of public opinion in Western Europe and America. The Hungarian diplomatic agents, becoming émigrés, did their utmost to capitalize on this. Against the meddling of Russia, they sought the intervention of the Western powers. The French, under the influence of previous Polish emigration to that country, were apt to appraise affairs of East-Central Europe from a more or less Slavic viewpoint. László Teleki, Paris representative of the émigrés, was unable to secure any promises but those of the left wing democrats. England, too, under realistic Palmerston, shirked official recognition. Francis Pulszky, Kossuth's agent to London, however, was successful in making excellent social contacts and influential friends, such as Richard Cobden, Lord Dudley Stuart and Lord Landsdowne.

The Magyars really did very well in the English capital. Editorially, *The Times* sided with Austria, but a number of pro-Magyar writers counterbalanced this.[1]

[1]Henningsen, *Kossuth and the Times*, 1851.—J. Smith Toulmin, *Parallels between England and Hungary*, 1849, and *Louis Kossuth*, London, 1852.

It was not uncommon that at popular meetings copies of *The Times* were burned in public because of its anti-Hungarian stand.

Public opinion in the United States also became acquainted with Hungarian affairs through news about the struggle. In Hungary's desperate fight for freedom, Americans saw a defense of their own principles. In their eyes, Hungary was a representative of the cause of liberty. The first links between Kossuth and America date back to December 1848, when Kossuth conveyed through secret channels a confidential letter to W. H. Stiles, U. S. minister to the Court of Vienna, requesting him to mediate with Prince Windischgraetz, who was about to issue orders for the attack on Hungary. The Prince, however, was unwilling to negotiate.[1]

Following the Declaration of Independence, Kossuth appointed an emissary to Washington. The U. S. government, on its part, sent A. Dudley Mann to Hungary on a special diplomatic mission. According to President Zachary Taylor, in case Hungary was able to survive the uneven onslaught, there was no reason why its independence should not be acknowledged. Should Hungary's struggle for freedom be successful, the U. S. A. would gladly establish economic, commercial and diplomatic relations. Thus, after 1848, America was the first power to indicate its readiness to consider Hungary as an independent sovereign state.

A. Dudley Mann, however, could not get farther

[1] W. H. Stiles, *Austria in 1848–49,* 2 vols., New York, 1852.

than Vienna, and dispatched his reports from there.[1] These were published in parts in 1850, precipitating a threatening note from Ritter von Hülseman, Austrian chargé d'affaires at Washington, to the U. S. government. This gave an opportunity for Daniel Webster, in his second term as Secretary of State to write his celebrated diplomatic note, known as the Hülseman Letter. In this note he expressed his views on up-to-date state administration, refuted Austrian interference, and, in defense of Kossuth's cause, stated that had Austria disregarded the diplomatic character of Dudley Mann's mission, this would have resulted in grave repercussions on America's behalf.

The real leader of the émigrés and the personification of the Hungarian cause in the eyes of the world, was Louis Kossuth. It was only natural that the London émigrés should try everything within their power to have him released from Turkey. At first they expected assistance from Palmerston, and when this was not forthcoming they planned his abduction. Then, at the proposal of Senator Foote of Mississippi, the United States invited Kossuth as its guest, as once they had invited Lafayette. Consequently, the U. S. Navy's steam frigate *Mississippi* was sent to Smyrna. This noble gesture enabled Kossuth to leave Turkey on an American gunboat. He could not land in Italy, but his admirers lit bonfires on the mountains surrounding the Bay of Spezia. The

[1]His reports were published in *Senate Document No. 279*, 61st Congress, second session. Cf. Curtis, *Austria and the United States 1848–1852*, Northampton, 1926, and Piványi, *Hungarian American Connections*, Budapest, 1927.

French government did not permit him to go ashore
in Marseilles because public opinion hailed him as
Europe's champion and demonstrations were feared.
On October 23rd, 1851, when Hungary's exiled leader
arrived in England, enthusiastic crowds greeted him at
Southampton. Kossuth stayed barely a month in England, but during this short period he captivated public
opinion. He received greetings and addresses by the
score; these, now among documents in the Archives in
Budapest, give a vivid testimony to the Hungarian sympathies of England's citizens at that time.

Kossuth's tour of England was a great success. He delivered his first address in the City Hall of Southampton. The following day, he spoke to representatives of
the English press, giving an account of Hungary's
struggle and pointing out that it was in the interests of
the Liberal countries to see that a foreign power should
not interfere with the domestic affairs of any nation. According to the *Memoirs* of General Klapka, who accompanied Kossuth on his English tour, Cobden stated
publicly that not for years had the English heard an address comparable to Kossuth's speech. On October
29th, after being greeted in London by the Lord Mayor,
Kossuth gave another address in the Guild Hall. He
spoke at meeting after meeting and received almost an
endless number of deputations. The cities of Manchester
and Birmingham issued special invitations for him to
speak. Kossuth's popularity and influence were not restricted but reached all classes of the population of England. Some prominent men in public life addressed,

already during the War of Independence, a memorandum, probably worded by Lord Fitzwilliam, to Palmerston as Prime Minister, recommending the Hungarian
cause for consideration. But the lower classes also sympathized with Hungary. When the Austrian generalissimo, Julius Haynau, visited London some years later,
workers of Barclay and Perkins Brewery attacked him
and only the arrival of the police saved the sanguinary
"hyena's" life.

Kossuth made a deep and lasting impression in England. According to Justin McCarthy, a contemporary
author,[1] . . . "The failure of the Hungarian rebellion,
through the intervention of Russia, called up a wide
and deep feeling of regret and indignation in this country. The English people had very generally sympathized with the cause of the Hungarians." Kossuth was
received "with an enthusiasm such as no foreigner except Garibaldi alone has ever drawn in our time from
the English people. There was much in Kossuth himself,
as well as in his cause, to attract the enthusiasm of popular assemblages . . . He was undoubtedly one of the
most eloquent men who ever addressed an English
popular audience . . . He had mastered our tongue
as few foreigners have ever been able to do, but what he
had mastered was not the common colloquial English
of the streets and the drawing rooms. The English he
spoke was the noblest in its style with which a student
could supply his eloquence: Kossuth spoke the English

[1]Justin McCarthy, *A History of Our Own Times,* London, 1879, Vol.
II, pp. 109–110.

of Shakespeare. He could address a public meeting for an hour or more with a fluency not inferior seemingly to that of Gladstone, with a "measured dignity and well restrained force that were not unworthy of Bright, and in a curiously expressive stately, powerful, pathetic English, which sounded as if it belonged to a higher time and to loftier interests than ours . . ."

On December 4th, 1851, the great exile reached the shores of America. A few days previously, the President of the United States, in his annual message to Congress, recommended the arrival of Kossuth to the nation's attention, stating that it was impossible for the people of America to witness with indifference the principles of freedom attacked.

Kossuth was received in New York with triumphal honors.[1] The diary of the Pulszky couple who were in Kossuth's entourage, contains many interesting observations on contemporary American life, and can hardly find expressions to do justice to the royal reception afforded them. It was an unforgettable sight they wrote, when all eyes turned towards the flag-bedecked avenue through which Kossuth rode on horseback, accompanied by General Sandford and his staff, after their inspection of the guard of honour. Meetings and demonstrations followed one another. Kossuth's personality really lived in the minds of the English-speaking world until the 20th century. In the United States alone, several hundred volumes of books, articles and poems were

---

[1]*Report of the Special Committee of the City of New York for the Reception of Governor Louis Kossuth,* 1852.

devoted to Kossuth. Such illustrious authors as Matthew Arnold, Elizabeth Browning, Garrison, Griscom, Lowell, Massey, Swinburne, Whittier and a host of lesser American and English poets were inspired by his patriotism. Bryant and Longfellow often referred to him in their prose. The editorials of Horace Greeley on Kossuth, appearing in the New York *Tribune,* are masterpieces of American journalism.[1]

In slightly more than seven months, by the middle of July, 1852, Kossuth delivered over five hundred addresses in America. His activity is well shown by the territory he covered during this time, reaching Boston in the north, Wisconsin in the west and New Orleans in the south, quite a performance considering the slow means of travel in those days. In Washington, he was received by one of his most enthusiastic friends, Senator H. Seward of New York, who became Secretary of State under Lincoln. Kossuth was officially introduced to the Senate and the House of Representatives, and was invited to address the latter. This exceptional honor had been previously bestowed on General Lafayette in 1824, and since then only on Count Albert Apponyi, Hungary's representative to the Interparliamentary

[1] Eugene Piványi, *Op. Cit.,* Budapest 1927, pp. 43 etc. Of the extensive Kossuthiana in the United States we can mention only a few here: Ph. Skinner, *The Welcome of Kossuth,* Phila. 1852. W. L. Crabal, *Letter on Kossuth and his Mission,* N. Y. 1852. Rev. B. F. Tefft, *Hungary and Kossuth,* Phila. 1852. Headley, *The Life of Kossuth,* Auburn, 1852. *Kossuth in New England,* Boston, 1852. His major addresses were edited by F. M. Newman, *Select Speeches of Kossuth,* New York, 1854. A complete collection of documents relating to Kossuth's visit in the United States has recently been published by D. Jánossy, *The Kossuth Emigration in America,* Budapest 1940, Hung. Hist. Society.

Union, in 1911. Daniel Webster took a prominent part in the congressional banquet in honor of the "nation's guest" which was held under the chairmanship of William Rufus King, Vice-President of the Republic. The chairman, in introducing Kossuth, said that "Hungary had proved herself worthy to be free". Kossuth then delivered one of his characteristic addresses: "I most fervently thank you for the acknowledgment that my country has proved worthy to be free . . . I feel proud of my nation's character, heroism, love of freedom and vitality, and I bow with reverential awe before the decree of Providence which has placed my country in a position such that without its restoration to independence, there is no possibility for freedom and independence of nations on the European Continent. We will live free or die like men; but should my people be doomed to die, it will be the first whose death will not be recorded a suicide but as a martyrdom for the world. . . . But I look to the future with confidence. . . . Now matters stand thus: that either the continent of Europe has no future at all, or its future is American republicanism. . . . I am aware that this future is vehemently resisted by the bayonets of Absolutism, but I know that though bayonets may give a defence, they guarantee no seat for a prince. I trust in the future of my native land, because I know that it is worthy to have one. . . . and whatever may be my personal fate, so much I know, that my country will preserve to you and your glorious land an everlasting gratitude." Daniel Webster then rose to say that every

American would like to see Hungary, "when she becomes independent, embrace that system of government
which is most acceptable to ourselves. . . . The first
prayer shall be that Hungary may become independent
of all foreign power, that her destinies may be entrusted to her own hands and to her own discretion."

Yet Kossuth's sole aim was not to create a favorable
impression. Neither did he seek popularity; nor did he
intend to settle in America as some thought. His rôle in
the United States was in accordance with his political
ideas, which were based on an idealistic conception derived from contemporary liberalism and adapted to
American viewpoints. Hungary's hastily recruited defense forces had defeated the standing army of Austria,
only to be crushed by the Russian steam roller. Kossuth
attempted to prevail upon both England and the United
States to stop Russia's meddling by intervention, thus
assuring "fair play" to Hungary in a coming struggle
with Austria. Kossuth emphasized that there ought to
be a natural community of interest among the democracies. This solidarity should take practical forms whenever an absolutist power endangers another state's independence. Therefore it was Kossuth's aim to have
the United States declare that in such a case America,
in understanding with England, would intervene in
order to block the lawless intervention. This principle,
aiming at assisting the smaller nations, was labeled
the policy of "intervention for non-intervention". Nothing was further from Kossuth's intentions than to meddle in the internal policies of the United States, but

he was convinced that this system of mutual security would assure the success of his plans involving Hungary's future.

Kossuth discussed this topic in several of his speeches which merited country-wide attention. He pointed out that Absolutism, represented by Russia, and Democracy, are enemies, and therefore there is "necessary antagonism between despotic Russia and republican America." The checking of absolutism was primarily in England's interest, but was America's concern too for "if the League of Despots becomes omnipotent in Europe, it is certain that the commerce of Republican America will very soon receive a death blow on the other side of the Atlantic." The growth of Russia and the extension of its influence over the Balkans must be stopped. "I came to the United States," said Kossuth in Columbus, "relying upon the fundamental principles of your great Republic, to claim the protection and maintenance of the law of nations against the armed interference of Russia."

Kossuth also strove to show that Hungary possessed the conditions necessary for a democratic evolution. "Hungary can look back on a continuous existence of almost a thousand years", he stated, "and through all this long time, amid all adversities, there was no period when the people of Hungary did not resist despotism." The spirit of self-government is a "fundamental feature of our national character. . . . We have preserved it throughout the vicissitudes of ten centuries."

He pointed out that he expected the reconstruction

of Europe by means of the application of the American idea of federalism. "Happy is your great country, for being so warmly attached to the principle of self-government. . . . Your principles will conquer the world. . . . The respect of state rights in the Federal government of America will become an instructive example for universal tolerance, forbearance and justice to the future States and Republics of Europe. . . . Smaller states will find security in the principle of federal union, while they will preserve their national freedom by the principle of sovereign self-government." Washington was one of the idols of the younger Magyar generation of Kossuth's time. "I have studied the history of your immortal George Washington and have, from my early youth considered his principles as a living source of instruction to statesmen and patriots."

Although Kossuth naturally could not achieve his political aim, i.e. the acceptance of the "intervention for non-intervention" principle, his American tour was not in vain. On the contrary, it was a tremendous success and made a unique impression. Indeed, in him the American public saw not only the representative of Hungary, but also a universal leader of world freedom. Kossuth did good service by making known the world over not only the fate of his own country but also the existence of conditions in Carpathian Europe affecting the fate of the whole Continent. One can safely say that Kossuth gained more friends abroad for his country's cause than all the generations before and after him. And this was truly the result of Kossuth's personal efforts. Even those sympathized with him who did not subscribe to his political ideology. The Legislatures and Governors of Indiana, Pennsylvania, Ohio, Massachusetts, Vermont, Rhode Island, Wisconsin, Michigan, Iowa, Maine and New York approved in the most explicit manner the policy recommended by him to the Union with respect to foreign affairs. The dying Henry Clay too, though differing in his views from the policy recommended by Kossuth, wished to see him and to express his sympathy with the cause Kossuth represented. R. C. Winthrop likewise admitted the rare impression that Kossuth, with his personality, made on all classes of Americans. "A wandering exile, from the banks of the Danube, embarks for America. He comes to pray a great and powerful people to aid and avenge his downtrodden country. He speaks. And within one week from his first uttered word, the whole heart and mind of this vast nation is impressed and agitated. . . . Kossuth will be remembered by many of us, as he has been received by us all, with the kindness, the respect and even the admiration, which a man of real genius, of marvellous eloquence, of indomitable energy . . . struggling against fate and in a holy cause, could never fail to inspire."[1]

Some of the Magyar émigré lived in the United States. They were composed mostly of intellectuals, army officers and professionals, rather than farmers. The first Hungarian settlement, New Buda in Iowa, was founded by a prominent exile, László Ujházy,

[1] Francis and Th. Pulszky, op. cit. Vol. III, pp. 184–7.

former Lieutenant-Governor of Sáros County, who, like several other Hungarian refugees, later entered the American foreign service. Most of the émigrés had seen many a battle during the Revolution and were ready to show their devotion to their new home by signing up with Lincoln's army in the Civil War of 1861. Their numbers were not large, the number of Hungarians in the States being hardly more than three thousand, but these few hundred volunteers represented a per capita proportion probably not reached by any other nationality in the United States. Among the Hungarians, there were two major-generals, five brigadier-generals, fifteen colonels and numerous officers of lesser rank serving in the United States army. Their military achievements were outstanding. It was Hungarian officers who organized the Lincoln Riflemen so named by special permission of the president. Major-General Samuel Stahel-Számvald received the highest decoration for valor, the Congressional Medal of Honor. He played a decisive part in the battle of Piedmont, Virginia, June 5, 1864, and was one of the officers especially trusted by Lincoln. Before coming to America, Stahel-Számvald was a bookseller and friend of Petőfi, and had gained his military experience in the 1848–49 War of Independence. According to General David Hunter, "for the final happy result this country is much indebted to his services." Also distinguishing himself was Major-general A. Asbóth, one-time adjutant of Kossuth, who accompanied him into exile in Asia Minor. His gallantry in the Battle of Pea Ridge helped to save the day for the army of the North. Charles Zágonyi, commanding officer, formerly of the Hungarian hussars, led the memorable cavalry attack at Springfield, Missouri, October 25th, 1861.[1] Thus did the political émigrés from Hungary express their gratitude for America's interest in their cause.

Returning from the United States, Kossuth lived in England, where he was in touch also with the Italian revolutionary leader, Mazzini. Hungarian émigrés seriously expected a new revolution to break out in Hungary. Kossuth, after he had gained world-wide sympathy, awaited the opportunity to launch another War of Independence. At first, the Crimean War (1854) seemed to bring the desired chance, since England took action against Russia; but Austria preserved her neutrality at that time and thus the Hungarian question did not come to the fore.

During his preparations against Austria and Russia, Kossuth and some of his friends sought the collaboration of leaders representing East-Central Europe's small peoples. He endeavored to reorganize Carpathian Europe into a federation of small states, the peaceful cooperation of which would be attempted through new formulas. Kossuth, as early as 1850, had expressed the opinion that a "Hungarian, Polish, Croatian, Serbian and Rumanian federation could not only guarantee the independence of these peoples, but would be the strongest bulwark against any Russian attempt." Hungarian-

[1] Eugene Piványi, *Hungarians in the American Civil War*, Budapest, 1913. Edmund Vasváry, *Lincoln's Hungarian Heroes*, Washington, 1939, containing 110 biographies and bibliography.

Polish relations were good, many Poles having fought with the Hungarians in the 1849 campaign. One of the outstanding Polish émigrés in Paris, Count Worcell, who was later on in correspondence with Kossuth, published as early as 1849, articles claiming that the place of small Slavic peoples living in the Carpathian Basin was within historic Hungary, for Pan-Slav ideologies would always lead to foreign domination.

As far as Hungary's nationalities and neighbors were concerned, Kossuth reasoned that the example of 1848 proved to everyone that Austrian absolutism merely exploited the aspirations of the small nationalities. He was of the opinion that if the nationalities, once misled by the common enemy, were given complete freedom, they would, in the future, be satisfied to live in an independent Hungary. He pointed out that "nations of the lower Danube region would be able to form only second-rate states, even if they succeeded in uniting all their nationals—(the Rumanians their kin in Transylvania for instance—) their independence would always be exposed to danger and necessarily subordinated to foreign influence."

Such were the ideas preparing the way for the plan of a Danubian Federation, which underwent considerable alteration from 1851 to 1862, when I. Helfy, a journalist intimate with Kossuth, made it public. Klapka had stated in 1855 that Poland should be revived and that Hungary should sign an alliance with its Rumanian and Southern Slav neighbors. In 1859, the general negotiated with Rumanian Prince Cuza in an endeavor to bring about Hungarian-Rumanian-Serbian co-operation for a possible imminent war. In accordance with Kossuth's 1862 plan, the Rumanian principalities of Moldavia and Wallachia, as well as Croatia and Serbia, were to have a share in the proposed federation. They were to conclude a close alliance, and would have jointly managed foreign and financial affairs as well as commerce and defence. The common council of these states would have resided alternately in the capitals of the respective countries. Hungary was to grant generous minority rights to the nationalities, each county having the privilege of deciding its own official language according to the proportion of its inhabitants. "In heaven's name, I beg my Slav and Rumanian brethren," wrote Kossuth, "to throw a veil over the past, and to rise, hand in hand, for our common freedom."

This was the first serious draft of attempts that endeavored to bring together the smaller peoples in Carpathian Europe. With this, Kossuth simultaneously drew the consequences of the Declaration of Independence, viz., that if Hungary was to separate from Austria, she had to draw closer to her smaller neighbors. The greatest obstacle was in the circumstance that the mentality of these peoples was not ready for such collaboration, even if Austria's grip could have been broken. In any case, Kossuth's plan, the granting of autonomy to all nationalities, would have meant certain sacrifices on the part of every people, including the Magyars, for the greater cause. The other peoples, however, wished no renunciation of rights, but on the contrary desired the extension of their national sovereignty and territorial domain in much larger measure than before. Such plans as those of Kossuth could never have won over the Serbs, for instance; and to this day no similar plans could escape the basic weakness that the interested peoples themselves, individually and collectively were not willing to accept any of them. Very few realized, anyhow, that plans of this sort have to be based on historic and economic units. Kossuth anticipated his time by urging the settlement of minority problems not exclusively on the territorial basis, which, in territories of mixed nationalities, is quite impracticable, but on the basis of autonomous communities, similar to that of churches, within historical units.

The first real opportunity for the émigré planners was in the conflict of 1859. Prime Minister Cavour of Piedmont, the champion of Italian unity, made a pact with Napoleon III during the summer of 1858, according to which he was to receive France's aid against Austria, in return for which he would part with the city of Nice and the province of Savoy. He also received assurances as to the neutrality of Prussia. At that time, Austria was totally isolated diplomatically, the long Austro-Russian understanding having been terminated since the Crimean War. Russia had begun in earnest to organize the Orthodox peoples of the Balkans under her own protection, something that Austria could not tolerate. Antagonism between the two powers was so great that in 1858 the French approached Russia with a direct invitation to a secret alliance against Austria. This alliance, which among other things has acknowledged Hungary's independence, was refused by Russia, for it did not bring her closer to her real aim, the possession of the Dardanelles. Prussia was against Austria, too, for the latter blocked attempts to bring about German unity under Prussian hegemony.

The Hungarian exiles took an active part in the preparations. Kossuth personally negotiated with Napoleon III. The French Emperor asked him, as a man who enjoyed great popularity in England, to use his influence in securing England's neutrality. Kossuth, Teleki and Klapka formed the "Hungarian National Board", and organized a Hungarian legion in Italy, with official blessings. The Italo-Hungarian co-operation could look back upon years of effective work. Already in 1848–49, Colonel Monti's Italian Legionnaires had fought in Hungary's War of Independence. A part of the Hungarian Legion in Italy distinguished itself in the famous operations of Garibaldi following the war. Austria attacked Italy in 1859, but suffered defeat from the combined Italian and French forces on the battlefield of Solferino and lost the province of Lombardy. However, an armistice and peace treaty followed quickly, and thus the hopes of the Magyar exiles were frustrated.

The military fiasco, economic troubles and corruption made the position of Austria's administration untenable. The over-developed bureaucracy used up tremendous sums, the yearly deficit amounted to two hundred and thirty-eight millions, public debt rose to twenty-three hundred and sixty millions, having been doubled since 1848. In 1857, Minister of the Interior Bach attempted to defend his system in an anonymous pamphlet intended for use abroad, to which, in a similarly anonymous work, Széchenyi, who had regained his health, answered *(Ein Blick,* 1859), creating a nation-wide impression. The reappearance of Széchenyi in public life was simultaneous with the strengthening of Magyar opposition, of which the Emperor had occasion to convince himself when he met stiff resistance in trying to crush the ancient autonomy of the Protestant Churches 1859. Consecutive blunders weakened Austria, but Hungary, too, suffered an irreparable loss in 1860 with the death of Széchenyi. The great statesman regained his mental powers, but could not survive the persecution of the police and committed suicide.

The new period beginning in 1860 revealed the weakness and decline of absolutistic rule. The *Imperial Diploma,* issued in October, 1860, renounced the system of centralization and absolutism, restoring the "historic individuality" of states and provinces. With this, the institutions known from pre-1848 times, i.e. Council, Chancellery, etc., were revived. This change corresponded with the platform of the Conservatives, some of whom, like Szögyén, Majláth and George Apponyi, took an active part in preparing it. The government remained under an Imperial cabinet, headed by Ritter von Schmerling.

The *Patent* of February, 1861, completed and partly

amended this system, establishing a central parliament
with 343 seats; of these, 169 were allotted to the Austrian provinces, 85 to Hungary, 54 to Bohemia, 26 to
Transylvania and 9 to Croatia. It was soon found, however, that the efforts of the Conservatives were fruitless
and that this modified system of government merely
eliminated some of the excesses of the Bach administration, without touching its substance.

In the Hungarian Diet of 1861 there was a very
strong Liberal opposition to the Conservative aristocracy. Although not altogether cohesive, this opposition
professed the 1848 legislation as its platform, with
Francis Deák as its recognized leader. The more radical
wing was unwilling to negotiate with the Emperor according to the rules of the Diet, considering Francis
Joseph unconstitutional. They were for sending resolutions to the monarch, thus earning their name, the
Resolution party. Deák's standpoint differed only in
form and it was finally approved. Deák in two consecutive memoranda gave the opinion that Hungary
would stand on the constitutional platform of 1848.
Contrary to the opinion of the Court, he maintained
that there was never a complete union between Hungary and Austria, but only a personal union in the
person of the monarch. Therefore the government was
bound to reinstate the rights contained in the 1848
legislation, together with a responsible cabinet, and the
emperor would have to be crowned king of Hungary
and swear a constitutional oath before he could be
considered a rightful ruler. Deák pointed out that

Hungary could not renounce its claim to its own constitution even if another despotic rule was the alternative. "It is possible that troublous times are ahead, but we shall endure", wrote Deák, "in order to save the constitutional liberty inherited from our ancestors."

Francis Joseph did not accept this argument and dissolved parliament. Another police rule followed, with two conspiracies soon to indicate the growing bitterness of the people. The Conservatives again attempted to intervene, proposing certain amendments to the 1848 legislation so that the monarch would accept it. Deák and his circle were eager to come to terms but unwilling to give up any of their legal ground. At Easter, 1865, an editorial by Deák appeared in the *Pesti Napló,* stating that Hungary was ready to harmonize its legislation with the security of the Empire, and acknowledged that there are "common affairs", such as defense, finance, and foreign affairs, which should be negotiated between the two countries by mutual agreement. This conciliatory yet firm tone expressed the sentiments of the majority of the Magyar population.

There was a long road yet to be covered in arriving at final terms. Jurists of Austria still maintained their pet principle, according to which Hungary was never a sovereign state under the Habsburgs. To one of them, Lustkandl, Deák himself replied in an essay *Data on Hungarian Public Law* (1865), proving that legally the country was independent, since 1526, in every respect. The grievances were, really, mostly of practical nature. Generals from Austria still considered Hungary

as a militarily conquered colony. In 1865, Francis
Joseph would not hear of accepting the legislation of
1848 as the basis for negotiations, but sought some middle course between the Austrian conception of *Verwirkungstheorie* and the principle of Hungarian constitutional continuity.

The war of 1866 brought a decision in this matter.
Austria suffered a defeat from the Prussians under Bismarck. This was the last appearance of the Hungarian
émigré party in European politics. Bismarck gladly
consented to the organization of a Hungarian Legion
under Klapka. But Hungary's independence was not
achieved. It was in the interest of Bismarck to conclude a hasty peace treaty with Austria. Thus the participation of the Hungarian Legion was used chiefly
as a scarecrow against the Vienna cabinet.

With the defeat of Sadowa, only seven years after
Solferino, Austria was squeezed out from Italy and
Germany as well. The dynasty was now in a more
conciliatory mood, since Austrian territory had shrunk
sufficiently so that Hungary had become the larger
half of the Monarchy. Yet Deák did not demand more
than before, steadfastly holding to the foundations laid
down in 1848. The Empress Elizabeth, consort of
Francis Joseph, also urged her husband to come to
terms with Hungary. After negotiations lasting more
than six months, the Compromise was thoroughly prepared, an agreement which formed the basis of the
Austro-Hungarian Monarchy for a long period, ter-
minating only at the end of World War I. Julius An-

drássy received a commission to form a cabinet in February 1867. After passing Act XII, ratifying the Compromise, on June 8th, the coronation took place in Buda with all the ancient rites. This promised a reconciliation between Hungary and the Habsburg dynasty after a struggle of three and a half centuries.

# X

## THE ERA OF DUALISM I

*Political and International Issues*

*(1867–1905)*

During the four centuries that joined Hungary and Austria from 1526 to 1918—from the castastrophe of Mohács to that of Trianon—the last fifty years comprised the most balanced period. This era, beginning with the Compromise of 1867, is known as the Era of Dualism, because its foundation was Act XII of that year which determined the independence, parity and equality of the two countries and the forms of their cooperation. This compromise, attempting to solve the problems that had accumulated since 1526, was considered by its authors as unchangeable, basic law.

The substance of the Compromise was built upon the principles of *Sanctio Pragmatica* of 1723, according to which the two states had a common ruler and were obliged to assist each other in national defense. In reality, however, it was the system of laws of April 1848, completed by institutions relating to the "common

affairs", for the planning of which there had been no
time in 1848. Deák and his colleagues could justly refer to the fact that they carried out the real meaning
of the 1848 laws in detailed form.

The Compromise of 1867 re-established parliamentary government not only in Hungary but in Austria as
well. It assured Hungary's "constitutional independence involving public law and autonomy." As a consequence of the principle of mutual defense, war,
foreign affairs and finance were considered as "common affairs" and their management entrusted to "joint
ministries." These ministers, however, were not responsible to some central parliament, the existence of
which would have endangered Hungary's independence. Instead, the parliaments of both countries elected
committees, "delegations" of equal size which sat once
a year alternating between Budapest and Vienna. As
a rule, they attended to their business through correspondence, meeting only for voting when three ex-
changes of letters were insufficient to arrive at a settlement. In this manner they could not assume the aspect
of a third parliament. It was this committee that fixed
the budget of the "common affairs". These expenses
were proportionally divided between the two parts of
the Monarchy by the so-called Quota Committee.
Hungary at first shared thirty per cent of the budget,
a figure which later rose to thirty-seven per cent. Commercial and customs agreements were to be renewed
every ten years on the basis of new negotiations.

The Austrian State Bank was also "dualized" in

1878, and known from then on as the Austro-Hungarian Bank. Several practical innovations resulted, among them the unification of currency. As regards matters of defense, the "constitutionally sovereign rights" of the King were acknowledged to the extent of reserving for him both the leadership and inner organization of the army: while supplementary drafts, recruiting and determination and change of the defense system were within the scope of parliament. The Compromise as a legal solution was a proof of Deák's genius and it is a remarkable example of close collaboration between two countries under modern conditions.

True, the Compromise of 1867 did not bring the complete independence visualized in 1849. But its significance is to be measured by the relations previously existing between Hungary and Austria. Foreign absolutism had for centuries attempted to weaken Hungary's independence for reasons evident from its very nature. The feudal system placed important matters in the hands of the king, and since the king himself was a foreigner, his orders were carried out by foreigners. Since 1526, there had always been "matters of common interest" which, according to Premier Julius Andrássy, "were taken care of previous to 1867 without us and against us, but now we too have a say about them with those whom also they concern." The foreign dynasty sometimes determined to thrust Hungary into a state of dependency in which it was impossible to acquiesce. In consequence the country endeavored to restore its rights through armed insurrection. The

tragic end of the War of Independence proved that
Hungary alone could not wage war against the combined forces aiding Austria and the dynasty's auxiliary
resources. After that all methods of repression were
brought into play at the same time. There was no more
hope either for the success of another revolution, nor
for essential diplomatic assistance.

Pioneers of Italian and German unity were eager to
help the Hungarian émigrés, but, naturally, only as
far as it benefited their interests and they were unwilling to discuss any matters beyond their immediate
objective. "We had to realize," wrote Pulszky, "that we
could be of no influence upon our country from
abroad." Neither could "passive resistance" continue
long, for the extended immobility of a nation is preg-
nant with danger. The only possible solution seemed
to be a peaceful agreement with Austria which could
assure basic rights on a more lasting basis, since it did
not depend on momentary military successes. On the
other hand it is also true that this Compromise did not
suit the requirements of a self-reliant nation, conscious
of a dynamic development that demanded complete
independence and sovereignty.

The solution of 1867 brought it about that both
countries became automatically interested in each
other's domestic affairs. It was lamented especially at
the end of the century that the nation was not in exclusive control of its own affairs, the ones complaining
being members of the generation that followed Deák,
who did not witness the difficulties encountered by the

latter and his collaborators. It was another problem
whether it was wise to tie Hungary's future to a state
like Austria, the disintegration of which Kossuth had
prophesied with such rare insight. But Austria was
strenghthened by the very fact of its agreement with
Hungary, so much so that a long period of peace lay
ahead of it. At any rate, there was no other choice
but to accept the existing political structure of Carpathian Europe, and take that system as a basis, for
there was no practical possibility of replacing it with
any sort of Danubian Confederation. No doubt, Hungary derived many benefits from the Dual System,
mainly the integrity of her territory, safeguarded by a
major power's military and political prestige. But even
if we consider the drawbacks of the personal union with
Austria, the fact remains that under the circumstances
the Compromise was the only possible solution.

Francis Deák himself did not accept any cabinet
post, yet he was the authority behind the government
of Julius Andrássy which was composed of some brilliant members of the generation of 1848, including
Joseph Eötvös. He also gave real weight to the so-called
Deák Party, which was founded by one hundred and
seventy politicians in 1866. Numerous émigrés returned
from abroad, such as General Klapka and Perczel,
Francis Pulszky, Michael Horváth the historian, and
Stephen Türr, Garibaldi's collaborator, and became
adherents of the Compromise in which they saw a continuation of 1848. It was, however, a serious blow to
the popularity of Deák's achievement that Kossuth, in

an "open letter" published in May, 1867, accused him of surrendering the nation's rights. With unbroken consistency, Kossuth remained until his death faithful to the Declaration of Independence of 1849. Kossuth saw "the peril of the nation" in the dualistic solution, since he considered it detrimental to "the conditions of the existence of the Hungarian state." This letter was the first in a long line of public utterances which Kossuth "the hermit of Turin", sent unceasingly to his followers, to cities, and to public institutions from his voluntary exile. Kossuth lived alone, far from his country, but his voice again found its way to Magyar hearts. Much as the Compromise of 1867 was a necessity, memories of the War of Independence still lived on in the large mass of Magyar people, together with the desire for an independent state life, without being tied together with another nation. The Magyar population, chiefly in the large agrarian cities of the Central Plains, thought of Kossuth as a national idol who personified every social achievement and the national glory of 1848. On the other hand Kossuth continually attacked and made unpopular the Compromise which meant breaking with his political platform. His agitation was the greatest asset of the left-wingers, later known as the Independence Party. The latter, of meagre following just after the Compromise was signed, grew to be of considerable importance by the end of the century. Though in fact its foundations were based on 1849, it called itself the Party of 1848, for it considered itself the rightful heir of all the traditions of that great year.

It was thus that Andrássy's cabinet was thrust between two fires, being received by unpopularity on the one side and by difficulties created by Austrian officialdom on the other. In Austria, too, the parliamentary system was built up, but functioned with difficulties. The Czechs kept themselves aloof, some of their leaders anticipating support for their pan-Slavic ideas from Russia. In Austria real power was left in the hands of the generals and the aristocracy, who were in favor of a centralized Monarchy instead of the Compromise. These, under the leadership of Archduke Albrecht, caused serious troubles in matters of mutual defense, for instance, it was only with the greatest difficulty that Andrássy was able to secure a separate Hungarian *Honvéd* defense force established in addition to the "joint army", as provided by the Compromise. Provisionally, this defense force was organized without artillery and a similar body, known as the *Landwehr* was set up in Austria. Military problems, especially the German language of command in the common army, gave occasion for heated disputes later, at the end of the century. Andrássy had quite a difficult time also in connection with having the southern military frontier abolished and returned under its civil administration, since the advocates of a centralized Monarchy insisted on its separate existence, following the old traditions of using it, whenever necessary, against the Hungarians.

The solution of the Croatian problem was of special importance. Parallel with the negotiations leading up to the Compromise, negotiations with the Croatians were conducted, though temporarily without success. The Croat National Party was adamant in support of the principle approved by the Diet of 1861, according to which it had no other bond with Hungary except the person of the monarch. Following the election under the control of the viceroy Baron Rauch, the new Diet, under government pressure, accepted the so-called Croat compromise in 1868. It was Deák's view that the Croats should be given concessions. Hungary thus renounced possession of the countries of Lower Slavonia. Croatia gained both territorially and in the field of autonomy. The head of this autonomous administration was the "Ban", accepted by the king and responsible to the Hungarian government, directing affairs with the aid of the Zagreb provincial Diet. Internal affairs, justice, and education were attended to independently. Matters of defense and finance were "joint" with Hungary and therefore there were twenty-nine Croatian members in the Hungarian parliament who were entitled to use their own tongue during debates. The language of command in the Croat defense forces was also Croat. Of mutual expenditures Hungary shared 93.56 per cent, Croatia 6.44 per cent. Beyond doubt, the 1868 Compromise modified in 1873, was advantageous to Croatia, assuring it a free and prosperous life. Yet just as the Compromise of 1867 did not satisfy the Hungarians, so it was evident from the very nature of national movements that the Croatian national parties, led by Starcevic and Bishop

Strossmayer, would strive for an even greater measure of independence. The majority of the Croatian people were behind these national movements, the counterbalancing of which with mere economic favors was not easily possible. Miletic, leader of the Serbian irredentists, also sided with the Croats. Bishop Strossmayer was thinking of the federalization of Austria. Until 1918, the relations between Hungary and Croatia were, nevertheless, governed by the legislation of 1868 and 1873.

The position of the Hungarian government party was none too easy. The extreme left, the Independence Party was not very strong as yet. The middle-left wing, which developed from the radical Resolution Party of 1861, was more dangerous. Kálmán Tisza, the shrewdest political organizer in contemporary Hungary, was its head. In 1868 he set forth his platform in the "Paragraphs of Bihar", demanding a separate Hungarian army as well as separate commerce and finance. With this program he too intensified the antipathies against the 1867 Compromise, chiefly among the educated gentry, who were the mainstay also of the Deák Party. The latter was not very active and well organized. The Compromise was the last achievement of the great generation. Eötvös passed away soon afterwards, and then Deák, who had already retired from private life.

In 1871, Andrássy took over the direction of the Monarchy's foreign affairs. Under his successor Lónyay, and under the two successors of the latter, the

weakness of the government party became more pronounced. Due to the organization of the new administration, financial burdens accrued. Losses also piled
upon the state on account of its policy in connection
with new enterprises, especially railroad building,
brought about by the hasty growth of capitalism. In
the election of 1872 the Deák Party won in 245 con-
stituencies, the Tisza Party in 116, and the Extreme
Left in 38. But the disintegration of the government
Party was only stopped in 1875 by Tisza who amalga-
mated it with his own middle-left-wing Party, thus
creating a "Fusion." Simultaneously, he put the "Paragraphs of Bihar" on ice, and accepted the system of
1867. No doubt the political equilibrium of the country
was greatly served by this denial of principles, assuring the further unhampered existence of the dualistic
administration. Tisza's premiership of a decade and a
half 1875–90, signified a quite distinct era and his
political party system outlived its founder many years.

The long-lived Liberal Party, the result of the 1875
Fusion, was maintained by the constant organizing
efforts of Kálmán Tisza, and wielded its power for
decades, almost monopolizing political life. Other
legislators on the 1867 side organized only smaller fragments of parties, dwarfed by the tremendous majority,
and chiefly centering around some strong public personality who could not find his place in the Government
Party or crusaded against parliamentary corruption.
The turning of the situation into such channels was
largely due to the problem of the relations between

Austria and Hungary and the constant quarrels between the arguments of 1848 and 1867. Owing to this,
no well balanced system of two parties, as in England,
could develop, to alternate with and control each other.

The government, insisting on the Compromise of
1867, was widely unpopular and often under attack. On
the other hand, the 1848 or Independence Party continually acted as an opposition, drafting, with public
approval, those national demands which went beyond
the Compromise, and continued its agitation against
the system of 1867. What took place was not that all
parties accepted the Compromise and, with that common basis of principle launched their activities according to their different domestic platforms. On the contrary, in principle all the parties were Liberal without
exception, but represented different degrees of opinion
in public law. Pitted against each other were the followers of the 1848 to be more correct, 1849 ideas and
the advocates of 1867, vehemently arguing this topic,
all their attention being occupied with the relations
between Austria and Hungary and the question of their
eventual modification. Besides creating general uneasiness, these legal feuds diverted attention from other,
more important problems, as, for instance, cultural
evolution, social and economic reforms, and nationality
questions. Peoples were first of all interested in whether
national desires could ever overcome the obstacles of
the Compromise, or on the other hand whether the
position of the unpopular government might ever be
rendered secure. The assertion that all these were mis-

takes, belongs to any sincere appraisal of the era. The appearance of a party with a platform of an essentially social and cultural character, would have been a great relief. Under the pressure of such a party, the other parties founded on mere differences of public law, would most likely have disintegrated into Reformers and Conservatives. However, no such thing took place. The cabinet and party of Tisza may be looked upon as a representation of the educated, better-to-do higher classes, which at the time did not seriously contemplate any social change whatsoever.

Beyond the change of the Compromise, the 1848 party was in no position to offer a comprehensive platform either. Some of their leaders, especially Daniel Irányi, a lesser star of the great generation, sincerely professed democracy, striving for the secret ballot. The chief demands of this party, however, as manifested in their platform of 1871, were for the abolition of the Compromise. They were for a separate army and separate finances, virtually the complete separation of the two countries. They acquiesced only in the principle of a personal union, that the monarch should be one and the same. In this, they contradicted their idol Kossuth, who protested against any solution in which the Emperor of Austria would be the King of Hungary. Foreign observers saw advantages for Hungary in the system of dualism, but the Hungarians themselves, at least the general public opinion, considered it insufficient and defective.

The desires of the 1848 Party could have been

realized only by uprooting the Compromise system, and this was possible only through revolution, another War of Independence. The Compromise was unchangeable without a break with the monarch. Francis Joseph strictly adhered to Dualism, however, for in this system he saw security for his Monarchy, which was considered both in England and France as an element necessary for a European balance. Francis Joseph supported the political rule of Tisza, the Calvinist nobleman from the Hungarian Lowlands, for his rule was the bulwark of dualism. The king adhered to dualism in accordance with his oath, but demanded that others keep it just as faithfully. Conditions rendered any armed Hungarian uprising futile, but it was not seriously contemplated by the 1848 partisans either. Times and men differed from those of the era of Kossuth. The mere hatred of 1867 could not have defended the country. As a consequence, no matter how many members the Party of Independence could boast, it could have taken over the administration only against its own principles, for otherwise it would risk an armed conflict.

Such circumstances explain the long régime of Tisza's Party and the efforts which aimed at the maintenance of his government at any price, against the unquestionable majority opposing it. Primarily, the administration, an unpopular but necessary rule artificially sustained, attempted to control the elections. This purpose was served by the Election Act of 1874, more narrow-minded than the previous one, limiting the right to ballot to six per cent of the population. An-

other measure with similar aims was the distribution in
1877 of electoral districts in such a manner that where-
ever the majority of the population followed the Independence Party, as in the Hungarian Central Lowlands, it took about ten times as many voters to send
a representative as against the non-Magyar districts
where there was no danger of a victory for the 1848
platform. This arrangement, detrimental chiefly to the
purely Magyar districts, was due to the feud between
the government and public opinion, retarding free
political evolution and sometimes resulting in controlled elections.

Consequently, Kálmán Tisza labored under trying
conditions to sustain his majority party and with it
Dualism and balance. His government was denounced
by many, contemporaries and later observers alike, for
its subjective policies. In fact Tisza surrounded himself with his personal followers, and members of families with middle-sized estates played the most important rôle in his party. These took part in many a
blossoming industrial enterprise, though shirking active
management owing to their traditions, often leaving
such leadership to financiers of Jewish extraction. The
one-sided, nay monopolistic, rule of the Party, and the
fact that membership sometimes proved to be lucrative,
was not favorable for the preservation of political convictions. In Tisza's party many petty persons were
carried over from term to term, which enabled the
premier to have his influence made dominant.

But no matter how tightly Tisza held the reins in his

hands, he could not escape becoming unpopular. At the time of the renewal of the ten-year agreement of commerce and customs with Austria 1878, Tisza was obliged to accept the proportional quota of Austrian state debt, contrary to the demands of the 1848 party for an independent customs territory. Owing to such circumstance several members quit Tisza's cabinet, Kálmán Széll, who had successfully balanced the budget, being among them. A number of young parliamentarians, like Dezső Szilágyi and Albert Apponyi, son of the Conservative chancellor, George Apponyi, headed a smaller Conservative party and established in 1878 the so-called United Opposition, known from 1892 on as the National Party. This group emphasized that it would retain its support of the Compromise but, not being able to evade the influence of legal arguments, it propagated the "amendment" of the Compromise, the organization of an independent army, for instance. But there was no possibility for half-way measures, since there was no hope for the transformation of the Compromise. Thus, those not wishing to share unpopularity, likewise later joined the Independence Party like Apponyi.

One of the favorable consequences of the Tisza government's stability was that it made possible the foreign policy of Julius Andrássy, since 1871 in charge of the Monarchy's foreign affairs, independently of the sentimental desires of public opinion. The Hungarians hardly noticed that for long centuries past he was the first Hungarian at the helm of a Great Power's diplomacy, and one who attempted to direct the foreign policy of the Monarchy with consideration also for Hungary's interests. Andrássy was unquestionably one of the outstanding statesmen of his time, demonstrating the many-sidedness of the generation of 1848, to which he also belonged.

It was Andrássy who, as Hungarian premier, foiled in 1870 the plan of the Austrian generals, ready to avenge their defeat of 1866, to lead the Monarchy against Prussia in the latter's war with France. In such an event, Andrássy expected Russia's intervention, which could have been fatal to the Monarchy. In the case of a victory, on the other hand, Austria again would have meddled in German affairs and its preponderance would have disturbed the system of Dualism which, according to Andrássy, under the circumstances satisfactorily assured Hungary's political interests. Likewise, in the defence of Dualism, Andrássy in 1871 frustrated the federalization of Austria as planned by the Hohenwart cabinet. This plan would have granted a prominent political rôle to the Czechs, enlarging the dangers of pan-Slav and Russian interference.

The fundamental principle of Andrássy's foreign policy was apprehension of Russian expansion. He considered relations with Russia as the greatest diplomatic problem of the Monarchy. As a member of the 1848 generation, he remembered the invasion in 1849 by Russian troops, and shared the anti-Russian feelings of his Hungarian contemporaries. Yet no such sentimental reasons, but sound recognition of the international situation, guided his foreign policy. He did not want stiffly to resist Russia, for his foreign policy tried to avoid all possibilities of a clash. Simultaneously, he did everything in his power to counteract Russian threats.

The shadow of Tsarist imperialism was now cast upon Hungary not from the east, but primarily from the Balkans. There the power of Russia exerted, through its Slavic and Orthodox religious connections, its ever-increasing influence on some smaller peoples just liberated from the yoke of a waning Turkey. Already Kossuth was aware that whenever the Turk would be obliged to clear out of the Balkans, the peoples inhabiting the peninsula would be thrust under Russian influence. In Serbia, where Turkish rule was already more or less nominal only, Russophile nationalists exiled, in 1858, the Pro-Austrian Prince Karageorgevic and replaced him with an Obrenovic. In 1861 the two Rumanian principalities were united, Charles Hohenzollern being made ruler of the new state in 1866 and crowned King of Rumania in 1881. There were continuous atrocities and clashes between the Slavs and the Turks on the Balkans. Since the scheme of Garasanin became current, the Serbians fought for a Greater Serbia, their wrath involving not only Hungary, but Austria, the whole Monarchy. This in itself shows what a shortsighted policy of the Vienna schemers it had been to antagonize the Serbs against the Hungarians. Andrássy realized that parallel with the Russian pene-

tration in the Balkans the Serbs might acquire Bosnia
and Herzegovina. The Porte would be unable to defend
these provinces, partly inhabited by Mohammedans.
Then the southern Slavs of the Monarchy might revolt
with Russo-Pan-Slav assistance. Yet Andrássy did not
rigidly challenge Russian plans in the Balkans. Like
Bismarck, who consolidated Germany's international
position through Russian connections (Three Emperors' Pact, 1881), one may say that Andrássy also fought
with seemingly Russophile methods against Russian
expansion and the weakening of the Monarchy. To prevent the Balkans from being totally and exclusively
dominated by Russia, he concluded a pact with Russia,
which did not block its plans on the Balkans but at the
same time assured new privileges to Austria. Andrássy
thus solved the problem of the disintegrating Turkish
state in the Balkans by having its legacy divided between the rival great powers, of which Russia was the
more aggressive, the Monarchy being more on the
defensive. Andrássy did not obstruct the development
of Serbia and Rumania; rather, he desired to keep on
good terms with them. Yet, in 1876–77 he arrived at an
agreement with Russia that after the retreat of Turkey, the Monarchy was to receive Bosnia-Herzegovina.
Russia, on the other hand, was given southern Bessarabia. Andrássy was not led by any desire for territorial expansion in the Western Balkans. His step was
simple self-defence. He wanted to build a bulwark
against Russo-Serb desires for conquest. Thus Andrássy
was able to cut an opening in the Russian sphere of im-

perialism which surrounded the Monarchy in a semi-
circle.

In 1877 war broke out between Russia and Turkey.
The cause of the Turks was very popular in Hungary,
where public opinion was anti-Russian and saw in the
Turks the people who had given asylum to exiled
Kossuth. The Hungarians did not appreciate Andrássy's
policy and openly demonstrated for Turkey. The Monarchy, however, did not enter into the conflict, although advised to do so by Lord Beaconsfield, representing the traditional anti-Russian policy of England.
The war ended with a Turkish defeat. The independence of Serbia, Montenegro and Rumania were assured.
Russia, however, wanted to get rid of the agreement
concluded with Austria and in the Treaty of San
Stefano in 1878 there was no mention made of Bosnia,
which the Porte could not hold much longer, owing
to the unsettled conditions in the Balkans. Andrássy,
taking advantage of the Anglo-Russian antagonism,
took up the matter at the Congress of Berlin, where,
upon the suggestion of England's delegates, occupation
and administration of Bosnia and Herzegovina were
entrusted to the Austro-Hungarian Monarchy, the latter immediately carrying out its obligations in 1878.
Andrássy had to frustrate also the large-scale and spectacular military operations planned by Archduke Albrecht and the Austrian general staff. On the other
hand, he had to defend himself against criticisms of
Hungarian public opinion. The latter was now against

the occupation of Bosnia for fear of an increase in the Slav element in the Monarchy.

Andrássy was guided by considerations of defense against Russia when, in 1879, he accepted Bismarck's offer of an alliance. In this Vienna agreement, the Monarchy and Germany promised mutual assistance to each other against Russian encroachments, but were to stay neutral in case the contracting parties were attacked by any other power except Russia. The Monarchy's system of foreign policy was later developed along these lines by Foreign Minister Count Kálnoky, who in 1882 added Italy in a tripartite alliance. In 1881, Milan Obrenovic, ruling prince of Serbia, joined this group and in 1883 the Monarchy concluded a defensive alliance with Rumania.

Though the later co-operation of the Central Powers grew out of this tripartite alliance, it would be erroneous to think that the international situation which led up to the First World War was a natural result of Andrássy's policies. From 1890 on, international policies changed radically. After Bismarck's fall, England, too, became estranged from Germany. Andrássy would not have consented to such a grouping of powers which united England, France and Russia against the Monarchy and Germany, without the support of Italy. As Andrássy's system rendered security in his time, changed times would have demanded new solutions. The last Hungarian, however, who exerted decisive influence on the Monarchy's foreign policy, had no successor of equal quality.

Tisza's government fully supported the foreign policy
of Andrássy, but it faced ever-mounting domestic difficulties. Among common affairs, the army question
gave occasion for the hottest arguments. The Compromise provided only a weak Hungarian *Honvéd* defense
force, the real military body being the joint army. Its
German language of command, and the frequent arro-
gance of its foreign officers were considered by the
Magyars as an insult to their national sovereignty.
Only a few Magyars took part in the management of
this joint army, partly on account of the Austrians'
lack of confidence, partly through the Magyars' dislike
of the old Austrian spirit that saturated it to the core.
Foreign officers, stationed in Hungarian towns, often
provoked incidents with their tactless behaviour. These
aroused wide comment, not only in the press but in
parliament as well. One such incident was the bedeck-
ing with a wreath of General Hentzi's statue in the
fortress of Buda by General Jansky, military commander of Budapest. Since it was Hentzi who had
bombarded defenceless Pest in 1849, public opinion,
already irritated, was outraged by this act, condemned
also by Tisza, but praised by Archduke Albrecht, commander-in-chief of the joint army.

Under the influence of such events, the Hungarians
who felt the system of 1867 too miserly, endeavored to
amend the defense measures of the Compromise, for
the army was indeed a foreign body, almost another
state within the state. But there was not the slightest
hope for such an amendment. In Austria every party

and every shade of opinion, even Crown Prince Rudolph, whom the Hungarians believed to be their
well-wisher, would have changed the Compromise in
only one way, namely to the detriment of Hungary.
Thus, under the circumstances, the attitude of Francis
Joseph, who was against any change in the Compromise, was still the best. The crisis reached its peak in
1899 when Tisza, on pressure from Vienna, forced the
passage of a new Defense Bill. According to this, the
contingents of recruits were fixed for ten years. Among
the stipulations objected to was the one affecting would-
be officers. Those of the intelligentsia who served their
one year of training were compelled to take their
officers' examinations in the German language, and,
if they failed, had to serve another year. This Bill
caused street demonstrations, and perhaps only the
news of the tragic death of Crown Prince Rudolph
saved the Monarchy from another internal crisis. Tisza
realized that he could no longer head the administration, and soon, in the spring of 1890, offered his resignation which was accepted.

Tisza, despite his parliamentary majority, was
ousted by public scorn, his one-sided party rule having
long caused a strong reaction. The system Tisza introduced, however, assuring an artificial balance in public
life through the top-heavy political machine of the
Liberal Party, prevailed for another fifteen years. The
Opposition, the Independent Party especially, gaining confidence through the fall of Tisza, now attempted
to bolster its weakness with noisy agitation and the

foiling of every plan of the government. During the premiership of Count Szapáry, they frustrated the centralization of the administration, partly because it would, against Kossuth's principles, have done away with the county system. From then on the fight was again joined for or against the Compromise.

At the time political leadership was in the hands of the sons of the generation of 1848. Some of the outstanding parliamentarians were the young Andrássy, Apponyi and Stephen Tisza, son of Kálmán, all well qualified and with a European viewpoint, but lacking the social and economic touch, or overwhelmed by problems of the moment and by the debates on legal principles. As a result they neglected to recognize the necessity for sweeping practical reforms, though great strides might have been made during the following quarter of a century that preceded the first World War. In his memoirs, later, old Apponyi himself admitted that under the influence of 1848, social and nationality problems were allotted secondary importance only, and were subordinated to debates on principles. In those days, when he was chairman of the National Party, he demanded "amendments in accordance with national achievements". This feud on abstract legal questions continued, centering especially around army matters, and hence resulted in distrust between the dynasty and the nation. The corps of Austrian officers aggravated the situation by proving with their behaviour that their mental attitude had not changed since the days previous to 1867.

An attempt was made to sidetrack endless political debates by injecting reforms of church problems. Liberal conceptions demanded modification of the relations existing between State and Church. It was at this time that in France the church was separated from the state. In Hungary, too, the introduction of civil marriage had been urged for some time, especially by Protestants and the Liberals of the 1848 Party. Up to that time, however, only church marriages had been allowed. The reform was to weaken the state protection of the Roman Catholic Church then prevalent. The introduction of this question into parliamentary proceedings was not to the liking of the strongly religious King, who consented to it only for political reasons, trusting that the Compromise Party would be strengthened by it. Indeed, the debate diverted attention for some time, for the government party as well as a good part of the independent opposition favored it. The majority of the Party of Independence voted for the Bill, a smaller group, headed by Gabriel Ugron, against it. Alexander Wekerle, successor to Count Szapáry and an eminent economic expert who consolidated state finances, actually had the measure passed with a substantial majority, and the Upper House, though reluctantly, adopted it in 1894. The Act declared civil marriage obligatory, introduced state registration, and made possible the intermarriage of Christians and Jews.

The attempt, however, to put an end to debates on governing principles was unsuccessful. As a result of

parliamentary proceedings, a Catholic People's Party
was formed under the leadership of Ferdinand Zichy,
emphasizing the social problems of the poor classes as
against legal debates. While the latter exhausted the
energies of the Hungarian legislature, matters were
perhaps still worse in Austria because of the differences
between the German and Slavic factions. From time to
time, they were compelled to resort to the use of
Paragraph 14, known as the "safety valve" of the
Austrian constitution. In certain cases, it enabled suspension of parliament and the conduct of government
without it. However, just as it was unsuccessful in dis-
arming the feud between representatives of '48 and '67
in Hungary, with the introduction of the church reform,
so there it was a futile attempt to soothe the antagonism of nationalities in Austria by experimenting with
the secret ballot. From all this, foreign observers arrived
at the conclusion that the inner structure of the Monarchy was shaken. Simultaneously the international
position of the Monarchy took a turn for the worse and
it seemed that there was no one who could replace the
talents of Andrássy.

In the premier's office Wekerle was soon to be succeeded by the energetic Baron Dezső Bánffy. Though
the latter was already assured of a parliamentary majority, he conducted the elections with such violence
that general indignation followed. The returns were
287 seats for the Liberal Government Party, as against
48 independents, 37 of Apponyi's National Party, 20
of the Catholic People's Party and 7 of Gabriel Ugron's

group, formerly Independents. The administration applied restrictions against the Catholic People's Party, and, since many of its supporters were Slovaks in Upper Hungary, anti-Magyar propaganda exploited this as if measures were directed against the nationalities. As a matter of fact the election, employing a powerful political machine, drew merited condemnation from the whole Hungarian public.

It was not long before the energies of Bánffy were found too weak to withstand the attacks of the Opposition. The Austrian parliament being out of commission, the King in 1898 made an agreement with the Hungarian government that the economic contract of the two countries, about to expire, should remain in force automatically until the time when constitutional renewal would be possible. This prompted filibustering on the part of the Opposition, as a result of which the government's authorization of the next year's budget was voted down and a state of "ex lex" prevailed. When the cabinet attempted to get this authorization at a party caucus, a faction of the government party itself saw impairment of parliamentary procedure and, under the leadership of Julius Andrássy jr., left the party. Thus Bánffy's government was defeated in 1899.

The new premier, Kálmán Széll was just the opposite of his predecessor: a conciliatory, peace-seeking character, champion of the middle course, who took over government with slogans of reason and fairness. He succeeded in having not only Andrássy and his followers return to the party fold, but in securing the amalgamation of Apponyi's National Party as well. The government won out with a substantial majority at the next election, without resorting to force. This unity, however, did not prove to be lasting for, when at the end of 1902 Baron Fejérváry, minister of defense, submitted his plan for raising the annual army contingent, a Bill unavoidable in an arming Europe, the political storm broke out anew. The plan would have augmented the joint Austro-Hungarian forces by 22,000 men each year and the Hungarian defense militia by 18,000 men, which was far from being a serious measure of rearmament. But the Apponyi faction of the government party, and especially the Independence Party, would give their consent only upon the granting of several conditions. The Independence group asked above all for the use of Hungarian as the language of command. Several, the young Andrássy among them, realized that the replacing of German commands with Hungarian would antagonize the nationalities. Francis Joseph, however, during the war games held in 1903 at Chlopy in Bohemia, in his order to his troops, himself declared that he would not tolerate any attempt to touch the unity of the army. So there was no hope for concessions, though public opinion constantly felt that German words of command meant harm to national sovereignty.

One should bear in mind that this was an era of militant nationalism, when even the smallest Balkan countries of recent creation schemed for conquest and the enlargement of their national power. It is not sur-

prising, therefore, if Hungary wished, instead of conquest, the rounding out of its own national life. The
Independence Party, headed by Francis Kossuth, the
returned son of the great exile, could count on the full
support of Hungarian public opinion. It attacked the
government in parliament and the young generation
echoed this with street demonstrations. The methods
employed by the Opposition included every variety
of obstruction, filibusters among them. One section of
the government party, headed by Stephen Tisza, the
strongest character of his time, recognized the possibly
grave consequences of this, for it sabotaged every serious
legislative endeavor and endangered the solemnity of
parliamentary procedure.

The cautious passivity of Kálmán Széll turned out
to be a failure, and he too resigned. After the Liberal
Party had accepted the king's royal prerogatives in
army matters as constituted in the Compromise, including the language of command, Stephen Tisza was
named premier in 1903. He soon proved himself a
determined and purposeful statesman. By openly opposing parliamentary obstructionism, he was never
popular, losing the support of Apponyi and his followers; but when Austria's premier Körber launched
an attack against Hungary's constitutional rights, a
step usually resorted to by Austrian politicians to bolster
their waning popularity in Austria, Tisza sternly rejected this as "interference by a distinguished foreign
dilettante". His personality was eminently suited to
restore order. In 1905, Tisza had, through informal

balloting, which was not quite in accord with the letter of the usual parliamentary procedure, stricter House rules accepted, an act which was very bitterly resented by the Opposition.

It is impossible not to admit that formalities instead of principles were given too great an importance even by Andrássy, who left the government party, though he was inspired by conceptions deserving of respect, i.e. that the inner workings of parliament be assured freedom. In the Spring election of 1905 Tisza and the Liberal Party, the latter after thirty years of domination, were defeated. The majority party became a minority as against an Opposition group of 229 members in which Kossuth's Independents were represented by 159, and other parties by 70 legislators. The coming to the fore of the Independents was the most remarkable change. Now that it had acquired a majority, there was great speculation as to how it would be able to realize its platform, for the secret of its popularity and success had lain in its being in opposition. It was also a problem as to what forces would assure continuation of the Compromise policy after the defeat of a party of three decades' experience.

Yet these questions bothered few. The nation had but recently celebrated, in 1896, its one thousandth anniversary of the occupation of the country by Árpád's horsemen, and looked with unperturbed optimism into the second millennium, expecting a revival of the splendor of King Matthias Corvinus. The previous paragraphs have viewed developments with a critical eye, but contemporaries looked upon their age as one of prosperity, happiness and security. The future appeared to be bright, and the problems of the present capable of solution. Everyone was proud of the admittedly great strides forward made possible by recent Liberal reforms. But a historian cannot fail to recognize the failures of this altogether too optimistic period, and especially the lack of consideration for social and nationality issues.

# XI

## THE ERA OF DUALISM II

### Social, Economic and Nationality Issues
### (*1905–1914*)

During its forty years of leadership, from 1875 to 1905, the Liberal Party ensured a political balance, based on the Compromise, thus fulfilling an important task. On the other hand, however, it did not devote enough energy to problems of the social development of the country. This omission was all the more serious because the continuation and further development in every field of the platform of 1848 after the Compromise should have been very necessary, for the tragic end of the War of Independence and the subsequent foreign oppression brought about not only a political but an economic and social crisis as well.

In the second half of the century, however, Hungarian public opinion was occupied primarily with the complications of Austro-Hungarian legal relations. The parliament, elected on a rather limited franchise, debated mainly questions of an abstract character, for everyone trembled for national independence, really or supposedly threatened by the recent enemy, Austria. In the field of joint affairs, real or suspected dangers against national liberty aroused an uproar many a time; and matters of spectacular interest (but often also of diminutive importance) were given such predominance that really significant issues were lost sight of. This was the psychological influence of the situation after the Compromise on that generation whose younger years were spent in the era of political oppression.

One of the outstanding political figures of the pre-World War period, Count Albert Apponyi, wrote of all this in his memoirs with noble sincerity. During the ascendancy of the Liberal party, there was no serious interest in social problems, simply because "not a single member's election depended on the ballot of workers". The policies and social outlook of the Party were decided by its members, and these were mostly of that part of the old, well-to-do stock of educated noblemen that had retained its wealth. This stratum had played the rôle which in France, for instance, was performed by the bourgeoisie, the Tiers Etat. In Hungary, it took a longer time for the middle class to become wealthy and independent enough to be able to assume leadership and wrest the initiative from its landed predecessors.

The Liberal Party was characterized by Conservative Liberalism, professing the principle that no development was to be interfered with beyond the granting of equality before the law. It refused to interfere even when this would have meant positive assistance and protection for the lower classes. It allowed free passage for the sudden growth of Capitalism, but for a long time it left agricultural and industrial laborers to their fate. It did not occur to it to introduce state mediation in their behalf; it was not familiar with their problems and surrendered them to the different left-wing, radical, and socialist unions that blossomed out at the end of the 19th century. This misconception prevailed, characteristically, in the peasant questions. The peasants, though they came into possession of their dwellings and lands through the abolition of privileges, were not only at a loss in their new circumstances, but were left alone without any guidance. The poorer section of the peasantry, with little or no arable land, found employment until the end of the century in large scale government works projects, such as building railroads and canals. During the following two decades, the total length of railroad tracks was quadrupled and whatever complications resulted from private enterprise in this respect, the completion and establishment of the State Railways in 1880 eliminated them. The great plan of Széchenyi, a centralized system of communications reaching the farthest points of the country, was finally realized. A general reduction of fares during the tenure of office of Gabriel Baross, minister of communications, increased traffic. Another important plan of Széchenyi, the regulation of rivers and the building of canals, was also finally carried out, making new acreage available for farming. Irrigation, much as it belonged to this conception, and would have been of enormous importance to the arid central plains, did not materialize even then. When, at the end of the century, these large public works were completed, marginal agricultural labor lost its outstanding source of income. This caused, among other effects, the movements of so called "agrarian socialism."

The better-off peasants, farming on from 60 to 100 acres, were eminently adapted to become an active factor in political and social development. But since these very people were the most enthusiastic supporters of Kossuth, the government was against them instead of for them. This stratum could have been strengthened by the poor peasantry joining it when it had acquired smaller or larger tracts of land; but the system of large estates checkmated all such efforts. The majority party holding the partly justifiable opinion that, under the existing traffic and market conditions, the large estates have a better chance to produce and to sell, and more capital to invest, rather tried to conserve the large estates;—two-thirds of the entailed property dates back to that time—resisting every attempt that would have changed prevailing conditions. The reformers, like Louis Ecsery, championed the leasing of small tracts to individual farmers instead of renting whole blocks of large estates to entrepreneurs, mostly Jewish business men, who in turn exploited both soil and labor. But the expropriation or division of landed properties was not suggested at that time, because public opinion was made to believe that all official intervention would be injurious. A few reform-spirited landowners made a study of the homestead system in America, launching a movement to prevent further disintegration of small farms. But the leading class not only did not acquaint itself with the material conditions of the peasantry and its social problems, but viewed these with an antiquated and patriarchal attitude.

Under such conditions, it was no wonder that, although some of the well-to-do peasantry in the rural towns of the Great Plains could demonstrate remarkable ability and almost miraculous results in livestock raising and fruit farming, essential reforms in production and in land distribution were, generally speaking, not carried out. According to a modern expert, about one-third of all arable land in 1890 was in the hands of owners holding estates above 1000 yokes (1422 acres). Of the total 36,000,000 yokes under cultivation (without Croatia) 3,768 estates comprised about 12 million yokes. At the same time 1.3 million diminutive farmsteads of less than five yokes each comprised 2.2 million yokes. In other words 53.6 per cent of the total number of farms held 5.8 per cent of the area under cultivation. Between these two extremes, farmsteads of from 10 to 100 yokes (of sufficient size to ensure a livelihood) were comparatively not so numerous, representing 36 per cent of the number of homesteads and 37.5 per cent of the total area under cultivation.[1]

A rather substantial change in this matter took place

[1]Michael Kerék, A Magyar Földkérdés, (*The Hungarian Land Problem*) Budapest, 1939, pp. 64-5.

in Carpathian Europe after the first World War, when Hungary and the so-called Succession States instituted their land reforms. This, however, except in Hungary's case, was mainly based on political and nationalistic considerations. The newly formed states distributed the lands of Magyar owners, among non-Magyars, although millions of Magyars were within their borders.

Despite its rapid industrialization, Hungary remained substantially an agrarian state, having continued its traditional production of wheat of good quality. As to quantity, it closely followed the crops of the U. S. A. and Russia, with a yearly production average of nearly 200 million bushels. Thus it not only supplied Austria but also was able to export abroad. As long as world price of wheat was sufficiently high and American competition did not assume prohibitive proportions, Hungarian grain growers throve on this export. But when, around 1890, wheat-producing areas overseas grew enormously, and, besides the United States, Canada and Argentina entered world competition, a substantial slump of price resulted, seriously hampering Hungarian farming. Since more than half of Hungary's population earned its living by agriculture, the drop in the price of wheat in world markets was a serious blow to Hungary as a whole.

The phenomenal growth of the American economy and the ascending prosperity of the U.S.A. prompted a flow of emigration from the eastern and south-eastern parts of Europe to the New World. In 1871, only 119 persons left Hungary for the U.S.A. By 1882, this number rose to 16,000 for that year, and by 1904 to 70,000, only to rise still further in the following years. Many of these left Hungary for no other reason than to acquire capital with which to purchase sufficient land to maintain a livelihood in the country of their origin. A part of them, 161,513 to be exact, achieved this aim and returned during the period of 1908–1930.

Quite a number of Americans of Hungarian origin are living in the Western hemisphere, most of them in the U.S.A., together with their second and third generations. They have become sincerely assimilated to the language, life and ideals of their new homeland. According to the 1920 American census, almost 500,000 Americans declared Magyar as their mother tongue, i.e. about 0.5 per cent of the total white population. The states in which they are most numerous are Ohio, New York, Pennsylvania and New Jersey respectively, each one of which has a Hungarian population of over 50,000. More than two-thirds of the American Hungarians, however, dwell in the large cities, with New York 76,575, Cleveland 42,134, Chicago 19,405, Detroit 16,240, and Philadelphia 8,060 leading.[1]

[1]Ivan Nagy, *Hungarians of the Five Hemispheres,* Budapest, 1935. Imre Ferenczi, *International Migration,* 2 vols. New York, 1929, to 1931.

Géza Kende, *Hungarians in America,* 1583–1926, 2 vols. Cleveland, 1926.

Hungarians in America maintain numerous societies of their own among which the four most important are the Verhovay Benefit Association, the American-Hungarian (Bridgeport) Relief Federation, the American-Hungarian Reformed Association and the Rákóczy Sick Benefit Society. These four have a combined membership of 57,459, with capital stock exceeding 3.8 million dollars.

Professionals from the second and third generations show interest in

Just as rising wheat prices during the first years of the Compromise improved living conditions, so the drop in price caused economic grief. By introducing protective customs duties, wheat prices were again stabilized and the depression abated somewhat previous to the First World War. Hungarian agrarian products found a market primarily in the Austrian half of the Monarchy, in unprecedented quantities.

The agrarian population found itself in distress at the end of the 19th century, especially on the Great Plains, where the rural proletariat realized the possibilities of improvement, provided the large estates were broken up and redistributed. The agrarian Socialistic movements, beginning in 1891, were far from Marxist ideology, for instead of demanding the abolition of personal property they were out to establish individual small estates. The classes higher up were taken by surprise by such a movement, and, unable to grasp the situation, were ready to term it the work of "agitators". Scattered conflicts took place when the government refused, in 1894, to grant a charter to a

postgraduate courses in Hungary's universities, the annual number of American-Hungarian students studying overseas averaging about forty.

But it was not farmers alone that came to the U. S. A., especially since the First World War ended. On the faculties of universities and colleges in the U.S.A., one finds many Hungarians of specialized training. Of professional people, especially physicians, engineers, architects, musicians and artists, there are literally hundreds of Hungarians all over the U. S. A.

American-Hungarians maintain two liberal dailies and some three dozen weeklies, the latter serving the local needs of Hungarian communities. There are numerous periodicals, chiefly in the religious fields, which promote the cause of the major denominations.

There are about 85,000 Hungarians in Canada and a total of 50,000 in South American countries.

socialist club, and again later, in 1897, when the harvesters on large estates in several counties struck for higher wages. The movement managed to take shape in some sort of organized form, one among them being known as the Federation of Agrarian Workers, at first incorporated as a section of the Budapest Socialist Party, later becoming independent. Two of its leaders, William Mezöfi and Andrew Achim, himself a peasant, were elected to the Hungarian parliament.

It goes without saying that all social problems could have been solved more easily at that time than later. One of the causes of failure in this respect was unquestionably the lack of information among the upper classes, who buried themselves in debates over legal and constitutional principles. Many who devoted their time to the problem endeavored to remedy the situation with sympathy and good will. Credit is due to Count Alexander Károlyi, who established the first Farmers' Co-operatives. Thanks to his initiative, a Central Credit Society was founded in 1898, soon to branch out into thousands of locals all over the country in order to satisfy the credit needs of the peasantry. It was Károlyi, too, who was responsible for the establishment of Farmers' Mutual Insurance Co-operative companies as well as the marketing and distributing co-operative *Hangya* (Ant), still one of the pillars of the Hungarian rural economy. Another distinguished figure of the social movement of the period, was Ignace Darányi, for twelve years minister of agriculture. Among other reforms, he had passed in

1898 the Industrial Workers Sick Benefit and Unemployment Bill, making state supervision of labor contracts compulsory. He also provided small garden acreage and lots for city workers in the low income brackets, being the first to promote slum clearance in Hungary. Among his varied activities, Darányi promoted the crusade of Edward Egan, an economist of Irish parentage who endeavored to free the impoverished Ruthenian peasantry of Carpathian Ruthenia, partly from the pressure of large estates and partly from the usury of eastern Jewry filtering in from Galicia.

Perhaps the greatest change in the era of Compromise, however, was effected by the development of industry and commerce. Parallel with the development of capitalism in all Europe, factories, banks and concerns of all sorts came into being, facilitating the growth of capital. The country, formerly exclusively agrarian, now began to become partly industrial in character, though competition on behalf of the older Austrian industry hampered it. In the case of textile manufacturing, however, state subsidies helped to overcome such difficulties. Other branches of industry, which enjoyed some measure of immediate success, were processing of agricultural produce, such as flour milling (utilizing Andrew Mechwart's roller system, later to be adopted in America), sugar refining, distilling, and leather tanning. In the decade previous to World War I, both private and state enterprise in Hungary could boast of an excellent steel industry and the manufacture of agricultural as well as of other machinery.[1]

All these brought a natural change in the social structure as well. Gradually the number of industrial employees grew, though it could never reach the number of agricultural laborers. The organization of industrial workers was not aided by the government either, and so they established their own trade unions, adopting the Marxian platform of the Austrian Social Democrats in 1890. Membership in the Hungarian unions did not pass the 100,000 mark until after the turn of the century.

But a change of greater significance was brought about by Jewry gaining ground in unprecedented proportions. Jewry had played an important part in capitalism everywhere in Europe. The position of Hungary and of all Carpathian Europe was different, however, because of the large number of Orthodox Jews who were newcomers from Russia's Southwest. Owing to their foreign tongue, the Yiddish-German jargon, their heterogeneous mode of living, their contrasting habits and especially their different outlook of life, they constituted a distinct nationality and presented a problem of assimilation. Within two centuries, their proportion to the rest of the population rose from 0.5 per cent to 5 per cent. In 1785, there were only 75,000

[1]The reputation of the Hungarian electrical industry, recognized to some extent in South American countries, dates back to this era. Kálmán Kandó, manager of the Ganz Electric Works, was the first to utilize high tension electricity as railroad energy. Contracting first for the electrification of mountain railroads in Italy, he initialed an ever increasing export of Hungarian electrical and railroad supplies.

Jews in Hungary; in 1840, their number was already 241,000, i.e. it had trebled within 50 years. In 1870, they numbered 550,000; in 1900, 835,000; and before the First World War, almost 1,000,000. This enormous increase was the outcome of a steady flow of immigration from the East, partly from Galicia and Russia and partly from Rumania.

Wherever feudalism continued to exist for a longer time, commerce easily slipped into Jewish hands. In pre-1848 Hungary, for instance, Jews made it a point to set up their grain and wheat business in rural centers, near large estates. The generation of 1848 considered it only natural that these Jews be emancipated; but already Széchenyi and then Deák urged the closing down of the eastern frontiers. Some of the Hungarian Jews played an important part, some as publicists, both in the era of 1848 and among the émigrés. It would have been in the interest of this assimilated class that the influx of their foreign ghetto co-religionists be stopped. Hungary was, however, altogether too liberal in this matter; the eastern gates of the country were left wide open and Hungary's economic prosperity attracted new masses of orthodox Jewry from its primitive surroundings beyond the Carpathians. Their first generation settled in the northeastern counties of Hungary; the second and third moved to the cities, preferably to Budapest; the fourth generation in many cases migrated further west to other countries. In this procedure, Hungary mostly lost the assimilated European-type educated Jewish element, and received instead ever new waves from the east, raw and un-assimilated as they were. This resulted around 1880 in a short-lived movement of anti Semitism, instigated by Victor Istóczy and a few members of parliament. They demanded regulation of immigration, but public opinion failed to realize that the mass influx of foreign-speaking Jewry was creating not a religious but a nationality problem.

All such changes had a marked influence on the evolution of the middle class. It is too often pointed out that in the era of the Compromise the rôle and influence of the middle nobility, which had been re-sponsible for the constitutional achievements of 1848, was left untouched, with the possible exception that during the régime of the Liberal party many of them found employment in the administration and civil serv-ice. However, as has been shown in previous chapters, owing to the catastrophe of 1849, the generation of 1848 was unable to provide worthy successors. The generation of Kossuth, even if its leaders were largely of noble ancestry, initiated a democratic trend and began the creation of a new intelligentsia composed of city people, peasants, and the minor nobility, with a keen interest in industry and commerce.

A new and active generation could easily have ab-sorbed the non-Magyar elements joining the middle class; but this generation, as a result of the catastrophe of 1849, broke down. The influence of the national disaster left its mark chiefly on the educated middle

class. Only part of the common nobility preserved its
leading rôle in this class; other parts lost their wealth
and social standing and, falling in social status, intermingled with the lower classes. Even at this time, the
ideal followed was the life of the rural squire, and
almost everyone was anxious to copy this gentry type
of living, whether or not he had anything to do with
the nobility. This attitude struck foreign travelers passing through Hungary at the end of the century. But
the task which the fathers would not carry out in
1848-9, the generation of their sons, weakened in
wealth, number and education, was equally unable to
accomplish. This task was to unify and amalgamate a
new middle class, national not only in language but also
in instincts, politically trained and democratic in its
aims.

At the turn of the century this middle class was still
a conglomeration of different elements. Economic prosperity facilitated the assimilation of the town-dwelling
Germans and Jews, at least in name, language and
costume. The often incriminated "magyarization" of
the nationalities proper was well nigh impossible and,
for instance, in the case of Transylvania's Rumanians,
the case was sometimes reversed, the original Magyar
settlers losing ground in some places. The proportion
of Magyars grew primarily in towns and cities. Leadership in business was entrusted to the ever-increasing
Jewry, which was soon to assume larger proportions in
intellectual professions too, with great numbers of
physicians and lawyers.

In the administration, not only descendants of
medieval German settlers but foreign bureaucrats as
well, brought in by the absolutist rule, had easy access
to the highest offices. That their assimilation was possible is beyond doubt, but it is equally true that assimilation as a process needs more time than was
imagined by contemporary Magyar public opinion. According to an English scholar, it involved dangers even
in America that "tradition might not suffice to absorb
the vast body of alien ideas pouring into the country
with the host of new immigrants", and "it was the
size of the blocks of alien culture . . . which constituted the problem . . . There is a limit to the
amount of foreign stock which can be taken up by a
nation in a given time."[1]

The problem of the Hungarian middle class was to
digest the great mass of newcomers, and to retrieve
leadership in its own land in the spiritual as well as
in the material fields, in literature as well as in economics. There were relatively few guardians of the
genuine traditions, as in the great generation of 1848,
the "folk classicism" of an Arany or the frankness of
a Petőfi in literature; the European perspective of a
Széchenyi, Kossuth or Deák; the liberal attitude of an
Eötvös toward the nationalities. In literary criticism,
these traditions were kept alive by Paul Gyulai's "Review of Budapest", which spread Western culture and
propagated national realism as against popular illusions but at the same time idealism as against ma-

[1]Julian Huxley, *We Europeans*, Conclusion.

terialism. They represented Magyar political traditions which the hastily transformed foreign intelligentsia could hardly follow even with the best of intentions. Historians and scholars, like the physicist Roland Eötvös, son of Joseph Eötvös and inventor of the magnetic torsion balance, arrived at tangible results. But the majority of the intellectual class passed through a moral crisis searching for "Magyar" peculiarities in architecture, literature and everything else, only to prove the uncertainty of its instincts. They considered Gypsy music as genuinely Hungarian, although it was never that, and had no idea of the original Magyar folk music of old, which has but recently been revived. In a similar manner, they were unable to find the proper modern form of the old attitude towards the nationalities, which had assured tolerance and common benefits to every ethnic element of the Carpathian Basin for long centuries, although this form was presented to them as a result of the lesson of 1848, by Kossuth and Eötvös. The assimilated ones became the noisiest advocates of "magyarization" and those who resented the latter procedure really quoted, for condemnation, the slogans of these Hungarians. Thus the anti-German Eugene Rákosi-Kremsner, himself of German parentage, was the one, who, in the editorials of the daily *Budapesti Hirlap,* was advocating a policy of creating "thirty million Hungarians". So was Béla Grünwald, the instigator of the "magyarization" of the Slovaks. Stephen Tisza, on the other hand, even if he was not for democratic reforms, pointed out that "the nation preserves its very characteristics" by respecting the rights of others.

The era of Compromise was undoubtedly an era of spiritual crisis, so far as the newly forming intellectual class of Hungary was concerned. And when Hungarian traditions and powers of assimilation slowly asserted themselves at last, and the first signs of recovery began to appear, another catastrophe, the First World War, was already at the threshold.

Many authors, English and French among them, have condemned Hungarian policies in the era of dualism, accusing Hungary of oppression of its national minorities. The majority of works dealing with this subject appeared to be on the side either of condemnation or of defense. During, and following, the First World War, a multitude of propaganda pamphlets were published according to which the Magyars were a nation of "born oppressors", while the different nationalities were innocent, gentle and defenseless people. Magyar nationalism, they argued further, was brutal; Rumanian, Czech, or other nationalisms, on the contrary, were human and reasonable. On the other hand, Magyar works attempted to forget about all past mistakes and errors.

The preceding chapters endeavored to point out that the influence of nationalistic ideas disturbed the centuries-old peaceful coexistence of several peoples of East-Central Europe, and that national movements there went through similar phases of an analogous development. The difference between them was nothing more than that peoples of a greater historic past, more advanced traditions and more self-assured leadership, like the Magyars, for instance, reacted more quickly to the new ideas. Similarly, in the era of dualism, one has to consider under what influence and in what manner these national movements were continued, what effect they had on the mentality of the respective peoples, and what relation they bore to each other. It is rather childish to approach either pro or con this maze of problems with the same sentimental arguments which at that time were themselves the typical expressions of the national movements in question.

The generation of 1848, utilizing the experiences of the War of Independence, made a compromise with Austria, and attempted to arrive at a settlement with the national minorities. This was the motive of Deák and Eötvös in creating the Bill of Nationalities in 1868. In this they attempted, in a true Liberal spirit, to balance the security of the state with the principle of free development for the nationalities. Both these statesmen evidently wished to settle this problem in accordance with all fairness and the requirements of the day. Eötvös was one of the outstanding contemporary writers of political philosophy, having devoted several of his books to the question of the equal rights of nationalities. In his voluminous work, *The Reigning Ideas of the Nineteenth Century,* he revealed with shocking clarity where European developments would lead. He pointed out that the three leading ideas of the day, Liberty, Equality and Nationalism, clashed with each other in the long run, and that without sufficient balance this would lead to disturbances, social revolutions and war. The principle of nationalities embodied in itself the destruction of the existing states of Europe, to be followed by what he called Caesarism, a sort of state absolutism, menacing the achievements of Liberalism.

The Nationality Bill of 1868 stated that "all citizens of Hungary compose one nation, politically speaking an indivisible unified Hungarian nation, in which every one, no matter to what nationality he or she should belong, enjoys equal rights before the law." Accordingly, the idea of the "political nation" did not recognize any difference or privileges based on the racial background of its citizens. The official legislative and parliamentary language was Magyar, yet in dealing with the lower spheres and offices of administration every one may use his mother tongue. The bill was explicit in stating that its aim was to serve every one's freedom and cultural advancement.

It was due to the very nature of nationalities movements that the initiatives of Deák and Eötvös were not successful. Both parties looked upon their ideas with suspicion. The nationalities, or rather their radical leaders, wanted no Minority Protection, the idea of which was still in its infancy, but they wanted large tracts of territories, sliced off the country, tracts in which they could enforce their own nationalistic ambitions on the mixed population living there. The Slovaks, for instance, wished to be the ruling nation in Upper Hungary; the Serbs demanded a separate district in the South of Hungary; and the Rumanians clamored for the separation of Transylvania. For this reason, they did not accept the Nationality Bill of 1868, but adopted passive resistance instead. Their model for the time being was Croatia, because it enjoyed autonomy and practiced sovereign rights. The Croats in their turn demanded complete separation from Hungary and full independence. Nationalism at that time was quite unable to separate itself from the territorial principle, every nationality wishing to establish its own exclusive sovereignty, without consideration for others living in the same area.

It would primarily have been the task of the Magyars to prove, through a continuation of Deák's proposals, that it was possible, by initiating modern minority protection, to assure free development for the culture of the minorities, and to prove that this would not disturb the historic, economic and political unity of the Carpathian Basin, but would rather serve the interest of all and not of a single people. But the direction indicated by Deák was not accepted by Magyar public opinion either. It has been pointed out above that in other fields, too, the traditions of the generation of 1848 did not survive in their pure form. It was the same with the nationality question as well, in the application of which Magyar public opinion came more and more under the influence of contemporary foreign

ideas. It was at this time that the Prussians set themselves to strengthen the German elements in what
had been Western Poland. Some writers expressed the
opinion that a state possessed the right to assimilate
its national minorities and that a people forming a
strong state is supreme and does not have to bother
with "inferior" minorities. According to one of the contemporary experts on Austrian nationality problems,
Gumplowitz, only nations with an historic past could
create a state, and one had better be patient about
the idioms of other smaller peoples, for sooner or
later they would meet their fate of assimilation.[1]

German writers, generally speaking, placed the Magyars above the other surrounding peoples, Slovaks,
Rumanians, etc., advising them, however, occasionally
to accept German culture in order that they, too, might
become a ruling nation. Since 1870, there were charges
published against the Magyars that they "oppressed"
and partly assimilated their own German minority; as
a matter of fact, the assimilation of the Germans living in Hungary was entirely voluntary. Several plans,
on the other hand, advised the forging into a greater
unit under German leadership of all these smaller
peoples. This unity appeared in their minds in various
forms, and was generally referred to as *Mitteleuropa*.
According to the German geographer Partsch, this
Central Europe was a natural unit "with a well marked
outline and an independent destiny", embracing everything from the Netherlands, including Belgium, to the

[1]Das Recht der Nationalitäten. 1879.

Balkans, including Serbia.[1] In his definition, all the rest of Central Europe, except the farthest portion of the Balkan peninsula, "consciously or unconsciously, willingly or unwillingly, belongs to the sphere of German civilization". This conception would have resulted in the erection of a great Central European political organism, with about 130–150 million inhabitants as an economic unit. An outstanding exposition of this plan and of its many problems was published by a remarkable expert, Frederick Naumann, in 1916. This work, *Mitteleuropa*, pointed out that all the peoples in question would be benefited by such close collaboration.

It was only natural that the newly emerging Hungarian middle class was strongly influenced by contemporary nationalist ideas. Several authors, for the most part newly assimilated, accused Hungary of weakness and extreme indifference, demanding an energetic policy against the minorities. On the other hand, those who felt a certain anxiety, wished, for this very reason, to strengthen the position of the Magyars partly through assimilation.

Thus, the initiative of Deák and Eötvös was not continued, let alone developed further. But the question then is, how did this abstract theory work in practice and to what extent was the dream of assimilation carried out. Those bombastic journalists and politicans who were for "magyarization" provided excellent material for anti-Magyar propagandists to denounce. The literary circle of Paul Gyulai, as guard-

[1]Partsch, Central Europe. [English ed.] Oxford, 1903.

ians of the true traditions, constituted their only opposition. But just as that era was unable to recognize
political realities and placed importance on appearance,
so in the nationality question, by emphasizing formalities and pursuing illusions it was unable to achieve
effective assimilation. On behalf of the lower administration, many an insignificant, yet to the sensitive
nationalities painful, incident took place in connection
with the use of the flag, the coat of arms, and the
Magyar language. The best explanation for this is to
be found in the supersensitiveness and jealously of both
parties including the Magyars, who themselves had to
struggle continuously for their own sovereignty and even
the use of Magyar for commands in the army.

The desire to assimilate was prevalent chiefly in
education, where it attempted to secure a wider and
more intensive teaching of the official language. To
this end, a number of measures were passed which
were certainly not worth the reaction they caused, both
among the nationalities and abroad. As regards education, one of the most important protective means of
the minorities was the autonomy of the Greek Orthodox
and Greek Catholic religions, untouched throughout
all this period. After the Compromise, almost 100 per
cent of the elementary schools were sectarian. The
spread of the Magyar language was possible among the
minorities only through the establishment of new state
public schools; yet the proportion of the latter in 1884
was only 5 per cent, and in 1908, 15 per cent, while
the sectarian elementary schools were left untouched.

The educational act of 1879 made instruction in the Magyar language compulsory, and also required that teachers of minority schools should be able to speak and write Magyar. An amendment passed by parliament in 1883 provided for instruction in Magyar grammar and literature in the two upper grades of minority high schools. The greatest resentment was caused by the act of 1907, sponsored by the minister of education, Albert Apponyi. This act provided for further free education in elementary schools; but in raising the salary of the teaching staff it wanted the minority schools to ask for a state subsidy, yet granted this only to those minority schools that taught certain subjects in Magyar. Both the Greek Catholic and Greek Orthodox churches were so strong financially that such measures did not constitute a serious threat. It now appears naïve to assume that the learning of the Magyar language during the school year would result in the pupils becoming Magyars. Nothing shows better the failure of such an educational policy than the fact that several German and Slovak villages near Budapest, settled in the 18th century, have preserved their mother tongue to this day. Indeed, it was not wise to abandon Deák's ideas for the sake of innovations of doubtful value, which had only the appearance of real violence and could be exploited before the world as a proof that the Magyars were "oppressors". Just as in social questions, so, too, in the nationality problem, the leaders of the era did not recognize the right policy to follow.

The leaders of Rumanian and Serbian minorities in Hungary were eager to have territories only partly occupied by them joined to Rumania and Serbia proper, whence they originally migrated into Hungary. For a certain time, these desires could not be completely eliminated through minority protection, since the aim of contemporary nationalistic movements was the establishment of their own exclusive sovereignty. But as the Croat and Slovak peoples had all lived within the boundaries of Hungary, attempts could have been made, without touching the unity of the country, to foster the independent national development and thus hold them at a distance from Serb and Czech influences respectively. Among the Slovaks, there was always a trend against Czech literary influence. This could have been given assistance, but for the Hungarian government's fear of Pan-Slav agitators and Russia's plans with them. In 1875, Premier Kálmán Tisza had three Slovak high schools closed, and banned the activities of the literary society Matica of Turócz-Szent-Márton (Turciansky Sväty Martin), of which Hviezdoslav-Országh, a great poet of the Slovaks, was also a member. Besides, the Slovak Lutheran clergy failed to have a separate diocese set up. Slovak intellectuals thus lapsed into passive resistance. The Czechs, on the other hand, displayed greater activity, expecting the growth of their own political influence from the popularization of the myth of Czecho-Slovak unity. The "literary reciprocity" soon penetrated into the social and economic fields, with the Czechs dominating. The society known as Ceskoslovenska Jednota, founded in 1896, nurtured this conception. The real leader of this movement was Thomas G. Masaryk, professor at the university of Prague, who reared his students in "realism" and liberal principles. The Slovak national movement showed inactivity, leaving leadership to others.

The Croat-Hungarian relations somewhat reminded one of Austro-Hungarian affairs. The agreement of 1868 was, there too, assured by the Croat National Party (1873–1906) and, as with Tisza's Liberal party in Hungary, its success at the polls was due to a rather restricted franchise and was similarly unpopular. The independent movement was represented by the party of Starcevic, which was not only against Hungary, but against any connections with any other state. Nothing shows more clearly the shortsightedness of Hungary than the actions of Ban Khuen-Héderváry, who, between 1883 and 1903, purposely favored the Serbian minority in Croatia and willingly gave them concessions strengthening the influence of Serbian deputies in the Croat National Party. This policy continued afterward, too, assisting, in fact, the schemes directed against the Monarchy. Later on, the Starcevic Party, headed by Anton Frank, gave up its struggle for complete independence, aiming at a sort of three-fold state under the Habsburg dynasty, with Croatia as a separate kingdom. The peasant leader, Stephen Radic, later shot in the Yugoslav parliament, was then in touch with the Czechs, with whom he drafted a plan of federation in 1902. When, after the defeat of the Hungarian Liberal Party, the Croation National Party met a similar fate, the Hungarian Coalition arrived at an agreement with a Croat-Serb coalition signed at Fiume in 1906, unconsciously strengthening Serbian influence.

Hungary's relations with her Serbian minority seemingly involved fewer complications. But the leaders of the Serbs, Miletic and his followers, were in close touch with the Belgrade government, constantly laboring for the creation of a Greater Serbia. The conciliating attitude shown toward the Monarchy by Prince Milan Obrenovic and his son, King Alexander, murdered in 1903 by extreme Serbian nationalists, was but an episode in the policy of this Balkan country. The Serbs steadfastly prepared for an opportunity when, aided by Russia, they could swing into action against Turkey or against the Monarchy. Serbia schemed for the possession of Croatia and Bosnia-Herzegovina as well, something which was possible only through the breaking up of the Monarchy. It is beyond doubt that Serbia, instigated by Russia, was the active party in this antagonism, and the Magyars could not have eliminated this, no matter what privileges they might have granted their Serbian minorities. The so-called "pig war" of 1908 gave an excellent opportunity for propaganda against the Monarchy. Under pressure of German protective customs regulations, Austria-Hungary in her turn introduced protective customs duties and lowered its quota of hog imports from Serbia in order to maintain domestic prices. The affair was fully exploited in Belgrade, where a huge packing establishment was soon erected with English capital.

Just preceding the First World War, ultra-nationalist secret societies, like the *Narodna Obrana* and *Crna Ruka* (Black Hand), were organized in Serbia. Their fanatic members committed sabotage and a great number of terroristic acts, the last one against Francis Ferdinand, heir to the Austro-Hungarian throne, whose assassination led to the conflict which resulted in World War I.

Hungarian public opinion recognized the ultimate dangers of the Rumanian question. The platform that called for the creation of a Greater Rumania aimed at the annexation of Transylvania, together with its Rumanian and non-Rumanian population, and the establishment in Transylvania of a Rumanian national regime. This caused already the failure of negotiations by Kossuth's émigré group with the Rumanian prince. The Rumanian problem also exhibited conditions analogous to those of other nationality questions. The conciliatory trend of Babes and Mocsonyi was paralyzed by the party of the younger set, who enjoyed complete solidarity with Bucharest, from whence they expected instructions. Their hopes found expression in Slavici's newspaper *Tribuna,* founded in 1884. Here, too, one finds connections with the plans of Francis Ferdinand which aimed at the overthrow of dualism. Aurel Popovici, one of the followers of the heir to the throne, drafted an elaborate plan for federation, to the detriment of the Magyars. Complaints of the Rumanians were summed up in a memorandum of 1892, which they attempted to present to Francis Joseph direct in Vienna. The suit launched against them by the Hungarian government availed only to enable foreign propaganda to denounce the action. The *Liga Culturala,* founded in Bucharest in 1891, assisted in the organization and fostering of the Rumanian irredentists. As a matter of fact, the Rumanians of Transylvania, instead of being persecuted, became continually stronger, both socially and economically, groups of a self-confident intelligentsia gradually emerging from their midst. Assisted by their numerous financial institutes, and by capital flowing across the boundary from Rumania, they purchased farm properties from Magyars in large tracts. The young Stephen Bethlen warned the government in vain about the weakening of the Magyars in Transylvania. There, too, the minority, the Rumanian element, or rather the government of Bucharest, played the active rôle. When, in 1905, Premier Tisza conferred with the fourteen Rumanian members of the Hungarian parliament from Transylvania, it became evident that they had territorial aims, and that in every important question they depended on instructions from Bucharest.

One of the great drawbacks of the dualistic system was that the Magyars lost their direct contact with the public opinion of Western Europe, since they neglected to follow Kossuth's example in attempting to make their views and difficulties understood. After 1871, French scholars visited the countries east of Germany, making research into the life and circumstances of those peoples whom they might some day count on as allies. Since the Magyars were a leading people in the Monarchy and thus within the system of the German alliance, the French gradually turned to the anti-Magyar factors, favoring Slavic and later Rumanian endeavors. Rumanian and other propaganda shrewdly exploited the vague sympathy shown in Western countries for the smaller and weaker peoples. It publicized and repeated complaints, real and fictitious, of the minorities, denounced Magyar laws and regulations, presenting their case as if it were that of Innocence against Wickedness. In fact, the struggle was not for minority rights but, naturally, for national aspirations, for the establishment of a new and intolerant nationalistic regime. Those influential English and French political writers and historians, like R. W. Seton-Watson, who turned against the Magyars, were originally for equal justice, but finally they came to see the errors of one side only, having simplified the whole problem as a mythical struggle between Good and Evil. They did not realize that nationalism fought nationalism and that the younger, more greedy nationalism utilized ready-made minority complaints to its own advantage, with the cool intent of carrying out its own sacred and selfish national aspirations.

Several minority leaders were in close touch with Archduke Francis Ferdinand, heir to the Austro-Hungarian throne, whose wife, Sophie Chotek, was a Czech countess. He was widely known as an avowed enemy of the dualistic system as well as of the predominance of Hungary in the Monarchy's affairs. It seems probable that Francis Ferdinand wished to assure the future of the dynasty through radical plans which would have completely transformed the Monarchy. These plans underwent several changes. He was planning to overthrow the Dualism and to establish a Trialism, the third state being, according to the first conception, Bohemia, and, in the later versions, a Catholic Southern Slav state. But, at the same time, while emphasizing that he did not wish to have himself crowned king of Hungary, which would have meant adherence to the constitution and parliamentary forms of government, Francis Ferdinand simultaneously stated his intention of returning to the idea of *Gesamtmonarchie,* to the old absolutist idea of a unified Empire. He endeavored to place a unified, non-national army at the disposal of the dynasty. Suffering from an inferiority complex, he spoke of Hungary with unrestricted hatred, and wished that "another Haynau" would terrorize the country. Plans were made for the military occupation of Hungary as early as 1905. The Archduke openly sympathized with political leaders of the minorities, prompted by the naïve expectation that they would renounce their own national dreams and support his plans for the establishment of an autocratic Trialism. In reality, their only common tie was hatred of the dualistic system; and the fanatical partisans of Southern Slav unity saw in Francis Ferdinand one of their outstanding enemies.

The openly avowed anti-Magyar attitude of influential Austrian quarters greatly magnified domestic
political dissension in Hungary. Temporarily, however,
the overthrow of the Liberal Party in 1905 provoked
general enthusiasm. After a struggle of several decades,
the Party of Independence, with Francis Kossuth, son
of the former governor, at its head, had acquired
leadership with 159 members in the House. However,
Francis Kossuth did not inherit his father's intransigent
nature, being peaceful and prone to accept com-
promises. He disliked filibustering and rowdiness in
parliament and did not like an attitude of unmitigated
obstruction. The Independence Party, Andrássy's
group, and the People's Party, in the meantime concluded a so-called Coalition. Temporarily, the king
appointed a cabinet consisting of officials headed by
Géza Fejérváry, former war minister, who conducted
negotiations with the political leaders. Faithful to its
program and to the expectations of the public, the
Coalition refused to take over government without
securing national concessions for the Magyars in army
matters, whereupon the king dissolved parliament.
When, as a consequence, the Coalition parties began
to organize opposition in the counties against the
government, Minister of the Interior Kristóffy decided to send royal commissioners to the counties and
at the same time put forth the question of universal
suffrage with secret ballot. In the end, the Coalition
could do nothing but undertake to form a government
without any concessions and agree to prepare an elec-

toral reform bill. That is to say, no matter how radically they adhered to the program of 1848, they were compelled, on shouldering government responsibilities, to accept 1867 and unwillingly continue the policies of the Liberal Party so vehemently attacked by them not long before.

The political rule of the Coalition was unquestionably disappointing. During four years, under the premiership of Alexander Wekerle (1906–1910), they could not apply the teachings of their great model, Louis Kossuth, either in foreign policy or in the nationality question. It was in this period that Apponyi had the educational law of 1907 passed. Julius Andrássy, Jr. submitted his electoral reform bill in 1908, in which he suggested a plurality system, which was to give two or three votes to more highly educated men. His system was to be a golden mean between the previous franchise and universal suffrage, from which the followers of Francis Ferdinand so hopefully expected the strengthening of the influence of the minorities. It became evident during the debate over the bill that the very parties of which the Coalition consisted did not represent a homogeneous unit. The democratic faction of the Independence Party under Julius Justh refused to endorse the government's electoral bill and declared, besides, that a separate Hungarian national bank had to be established. This declaration set Francis Kossuth against his own party. Wekerle resigned, whereupon the king appointed first Khun-Hédervary and then László Lukács to head a new government.

The elections of 1910 demonstrated that public opinion had lost faith in the Coalition. The parties of Kossuth, Justh and Andrássy elected 55, 41 and 21 members respectively, whereas the Party of National Labor, organized by Stephen Tisza on an 1867 program, gained a majority of 237. Actually this meant the restoration of the old balance, which, however, due to the social problems and the detrimental international situation, had to face extremely difficult tests.

Even now, the leading groups in society remained more or less Conservative, and only a few realized the necessity of far-reaching social reforms. Some smaller intellectual groups on the other hand, leaned toward extreme radicalism, represented since 1905 by Oscar Jászi and the circle formed around the magazine *Twentieth Century*. Jászi's criticism aroused great resentment, mainly because it betrayed more belittling sarcasm than sincere constructive intentions and also because his group was rapidly augmented by too-recently assimilated Jewish intellectuals. No people likes being criticized by newcomers in its own country. The radicals were supported also by Justh's party. But the most significant support was given it by the writings of Andrew Ady, the greatest Hungarian poet of the age, though a man without political experience. Ady brought his enthusiasm for freedom and democracy from Paris and saw the hope of the future in the Magyar peasantry rather than in the aristocratic tradition. For a long time, the leading elements could not understand him on account of his radically novel literary views, and disliked him, though he represented proud Magyar feeling and many genuine old traditions.

Also traceable to the faults of the Era of Dualism was the fact Magyars lost active interest in international questions. Their attentions were concentrated on their relations with Austria. The influence of Magyars upon the conduct of foreign affairs of the Monarchy steadily diminished, in contrast to Andrássy's age, who in his time had formed an up-to-date alliance system. But Vienna was equally unable to produce new diplomatic trends; it clung steadfastly to the old system even when the anti-German coalition began to take shape and England, abandoning her pro-Austrian policy, supported the Russian view even in Balkan affairs. In 1908, the isolation of the Central Powers became quite evident when Aehrenthal, the joint minister of foreign affairs, in spite of the opposition of the Magyars, put into effect the annexation of Bosnia. Now events that weakened the position of the Monarchy quickly followed each other in accordance with Russian plans. In 1912–1913, Serbia, Greece, Bulgaria and Montenegro jointly attacked Turkey already weakened by the Italian war, and in the First Balkan War occupied a great part of her European territory. However, during the division of the spoils, the victors fell out amongst themselves, and in the Second Balkan War Serbia, Greece and Rumania surprised and defeated Bulgaria, the only Balkan state maintaining good relations with the Monarchy. Thus the Balkan wars strengthened the position of Rumania and Serbia; and the latter, always supported by Russia, had never given up her designs against the Monarchy. Hungarian public opinion realized very little the change in the balance of forces, hardly seeing that Germany was face to face with England, France and Russia, though under such circumstances it could hardly be expected that Italy, let alone the two Balkan nations, would side with the Central Powers.

In 1913, Count Stephen Tisza became premier of Hungary. He was one of those statesmen who have had to face the most bitter criticism just because he had great moral courage and unparalleled will power, and was ready, if necessary, to face unpopularity. He too shared the common fault of the Magyar leaders of the age; his conservative Liberalism made it impossible for him to become the advocate of reforms. He disapproved of changes in the electoral system as well as in the system of land-holding, though his admiration for the virtues of the Magyar peasant was well known. Tisza, however, achieved a great task when he undertook to restore order in the embittered and almost chaotic political antagonisms of Parliament. He broke the endless "obstruction", the filibustering of the parliamentary opposition, and thereby secured the acceptance of the Defense Bill which increased the military strength of the Monarchy. Hungary indeed was in great need of a strong leader. On June 28, 1914, the heir to the throne was murdered in Sarajevo. This assassination opened a new and tragic chapter in the history of Europe.

# XII

## HUNGARY IN THE WORLD WAR

*Bolshevism and Its Downfall*
*(1914–1919)*

The assassination at Sarajevo produced a shock in the capitals of Western Europe also. It found an echo comparable to that of the murder of the pro-Austrian king of Serbia and his consort in 1903. There was no doubt that both atrocities were prompted by identical political interests. The leaders of the Monarchy saw in the assassination, prepared, as the evidence showed, in Serbia, another proof of the hostile activities long going on against the integrity and very existence of Austria-Hungary.

Austrian leaders, and especially Count Berchtold, joint minister for foreign affairs, who was influenced by Chief-of-Staff Conrad, wished to take advantage of the murder to bring Serbia finally to account. Conrad had considered the clash inevitable for some time. He feared that later the conflict would be general and that Russia, Serbia, Italy and Rumania would all be on the enemy

348

side. Therefore he wanted to get rid of the enemies successively, one by one, by a preventive war. He regarded the Balkan crises of 1908 and 1912 as good opportunities lost for a Serbian campaign. In 1914, he was of the opinion that a war with Serbia was not only inevitable but that a decision might quickly be reached. Serbia, this small, but warlike country, encouraged by its fresh Balkan victories, seemed to be the advance stronghold of Russian influence which schemed for the dissolution of the Monarchy.

The Hungarian premier, Stephen Tisza, immediately protested against the Vienna plans for war.[1] He expected the immediate intervention of Russia and perhaps Rumania, while Germany, ally of the Monarchy, would be tied down with France. Indeed, the two systems of alliances facing each other were by this time clearly defined. In 1908, Russia, weakened by the disaster of the war with Japan and by revolutionary troubles, had yielded when the Kaiser took sides with his ally. But after that, Russian military strength gradually revived. Germany faced France, England and Russia; the Monarchy faced Russia and its protégé Serbia. Italy and Rumania could no longer be considered as allies.

As early as July 1st, Tisza despatched to the King a memorandum protesting against the idea of immediate settling of accounts, which he considered a "fatal error".

[1] The documents revealing Tisza's attitude are published in *Österreich-Ungarns Aussenpolitik n.d. bosnischen Krise, 1908, bis zum Kriegsausbruch 1914. Dipl. Aktenstücke des Öst.—Ung. Ministerium des äusseren.* Selected by L. Bittner, A. F. Pribram, H. Srbik, H. Uebersberger, Wien 1930. Vol. III.

He requested the King to calm the indignation of Kaiser Wilhelm II. Tisza explained that the position of the Monarchy was to be consolidated in the Balkans through longer diplomatic action and the gaining of Bulgaria's coöperation. His bold frankness surprised Berchtold who counted on the usual passivity of the Hungarian governments in foreign affairs. They were always occupied with domestic problems, and generally accepted later the ways and means proposed by the common ministers of foreign affairs. On the other hand, Austrian statesmen kept their eye primarily on the Balkans and Russia, steadfastly following in other matters the German policy that had succeeded in bringing about a coalition against itself. Berchtold wished to employ the highest influence to overcome Tisza's compunctions and persuaded the aged Francis Joseph to write a personal letter to the Kaiser, stating that it was impossible to bridge the differences between the Monarchy and Serbia. As soon as Tisza had knowledge of this he urged the changing of the text of the letter by telegraph, but it was too late, for the latter had already been sent in its original form.

Germany having given Austria a free hand, Count Berchtold stated at the Vienna cabinet council of July 7 that Serbia was to be rendered harmless and should be asked to accede to unacceptable terms. Tisza was adamant, emphasizing that a diplomatic victory by means of a reasonable note would be sufficient, and he advised resorting to an ultimatum only in case the former would be turned down. He also made it clear that in no case should the annihilation of Serbia be planned, and that he, as head of Hungary's responsible government, would protest against the occupation of any portion of that country. He also explained that the Monarchy was in a position to achieve success through a proper Balkan policy. On July 8, Tisza sent the King another urgent memorandum in the same vein. The Hungarian cabinet council, held on the following day, subscribed to the premier's actions to the last iota. Tisza delivered a conciliatory address also in the Hungarian parliament.

Berchtold who, as the German ambassador wrote, saw a "retarding element" in the Hungarian premier's policy,[1] complained to the King that only the head of the Budapest government stood in his way. In this struggle, naturally, neither diplomacy nor the army was in Tisza's hands. In many respects Berchtold was able to countermand his endeavors with a series of *faits accomplis*. Tisza was in a position to apply the brakes so to speak, determining certain conditions and facing the blame that he was acting against the political and military interests of the Monarchy, in spite of his desire to serve them.

It was a significant phenomenon that the Serbian government, against all expectations, was unwilling to conduct an investigation. Instead, the Belgrade press launched a vehement attack on the Monarchy. The official note of Berchtold stated the responsibility of the

[1]*Die Deutschen Dokumente zum Kriegsausbruch 1914,* Berlin 1927, Vol. I, pp. 35–6.

Serbian government. Berchtold was, at the same time, of the opinion that Germany would consider the Monarchy's possibly reasonable attitude towards Serbia as a "sign of weakness which would unquestionably influence Germany's position in the Tripartite Alliance and her future policy towards the Monarchy".[1]

Influenced by additional information, Tisza finally consented on July 14 that a short term note be sent to Belgrade. However, at the cabinet session of July 19, which approved this note, Tisza urged a unanimous decision to the effect that the Monarchy had no thought of annexation in mind. "No part of Serbia"—he said. Berchtold made the contents of the decision known to the Great Powers, among them the especially interested Italy and Russia, only a full week later. Thus valuable time had been lost because such a statement, made known at the psychological moment, would undoubtedly have softened the impression created by the ultimatum.

The 48-hour ultimatum delivered to Serbia demanded immediate cessation of subversive agitation against the Monarchy, dissolution of the secret terror-organizations and, finally, that the Monarchy's officials be allowed to take part in the investigation of the assassination and movements aiming at the destruction of Austria-Hungary. Serbia refused to comply, whereupon Ambassador Giesl, according to instructions received from Berchtold, left Belgrade. Tisza had not been in-

[1]G. Gratz, *A Dualizmus Kora,* Budapest 1934, Vol. II, p. 296.

formed of this either. He did not regard further diplomatic negotiations impossible even after the ultimatum.

There was no longer a chance to stop the fast-moving events. Russia, which considered Serbia an advanced base for its imperialistic plans, mobilized. One fateful step led to the next. The First World War broke out. There have been numberless arguments about the responsibility for the war; and the problem is too complex to be sufficiently explained on the basis of single factors and by the attitude of single personages. It can be definitely established, however, that, in the light of available documents, it is impossible to brand Hungary's prime minister, who opposed to the limit every step that could lead to a general conflict, as "one of the great fomenters of the Great War."[1] This charge was, perhaps, credible during the World War, for Tisza did not resign in the crucial hour, did not leave his post and did not defend his actions. When the war that he did not want broke out, he courageously undertook also the new difficulties and responsibilities. "In my heart, every war means misery, devastation, and the suffering of innocent women and children", he wrote to one of his relatives. "It embitters my life that I have tasks in the management of such a monstrous conflict. . . . My conscience is clear, however. Already the noose, with which they would have strangled us at a favorable moment, unless we cut it now, had been thrown around our neck. We could not do otherwise. But it agonized me that we had to do as we did".

[1] R. W. Seton-Watson in the *Contemporary Review*, March 1918.

In the era of European imperialism, when "every foreign office cherished dreams that might be realized in war,"[1] Russia wanted Constantinople, and Serbia and Rumania schemed to gain huge slices of the Monarchy. Hungary alone did not want to enlarge its territory. She felt that she could only loose in a war she did not want and for which she was not at all prepared. Even the plans of her allies did not necessarily coincide with hers in every respect. Austria's designs, for instance, as regards possible Balkan annexations, were directly against the interests of Hungary, threatening the balance assured by the Dualistic system. The Hungarians considered the war solely as a means of defending the homeland, the historic boundaries against Serbia and, especially, against Russia, the old enemy who in 1849 had trampled down the War of Independence.

In this grave moment, feuds in domestic politics subsided, all parties declaring a "Truce of God". The greater part of the Hungarian armies originally dispatched against Serbia were almost immediately switched north against the overwhelming Russian forces overrunning Galicia. These were to be stopped, while Germany's military machine was concentrated on the west. Hungarian troops fought chiefly on the Russian and Serbian fronts, and later on the Italian front, where, owing to the relentless wasting tactics of Conrad and his generals, the fine first-line troops of the Monarchy had already been used up in bloody battles in the first year.

[1] H. A. L. Fisher, *A History of Europe*, London, 1938, p. 1119.

Hungary had no separate army, the country's manpower being embodied in the joint army and the meagerly equipped Honvéd defense forces. The Monarchy's troops at the beginning of the World War numbered 1,400,000, but one third of this was only a badly-equipped second line force. An unprepared army, the reorganization of which was delayed partly also by long discussions in the Hungarian parliament, was all that was at the disposal of the pugnacious Conrad. In Galicia, where certain divisions suffered in casualties as much as 70 per cent, the Magyar hussars, like their forefathers in 1849, attacked on horseback Russian positions fortified with barbed wire and defended with machine guns. During the World War, no less than 3,800,000 men were enlisted in Hungary, among whom casualties totalled 56 per cent, with 17 per cent (661,000) dead, 20 per cent (743,000) wounded and 19 per cent (734,-000) taken prisoner.

Unquestionably, the many-tongued "mosaic" army held its ground very well, only the Czechs deserting in large numbers, for political reasons. The Monarchy, which was considered by many as an obsolete organization ready to crumble at the first touch, experienced catastrophe only after four years of exertion and severe privation. Military leadership was entrusted to the Austrian High Command at the city of Teschen, in Silesia. Later direction of the military operations of the Central Powers was mostly taken over by the Germans. The German generals, appearing on critical points of the fronts, commanded respect by their brilliant strategy, as well as by the discipline and excellent equipment of the German army itself.

The first danger arose with the attack by Russia, whose northern armies were stopped by Hindenburg in East Prussia. On the south, the Russian "steamroller" was halted in December 1914, at Limanova and finally settled on the natural barriers of the Carpathians, defended by the masses of nameless Magyar peasants. In the meantime the fortress of Przemysl, in the evacuated Austrian province of Galicia, manned by 100,000 men, mostly Hungarians, finally had to surrender to the Russians after a long siege that exhausted all supplies. Early in May 1915, the armies of the Central Powers under General von Mackensen launched a successful offensive and broke through the Russian line at Gorlice, thus relieving the Hungarian frontier from Russian pressure. Warsaw, capital of Russian Poland was captured, an event which prompted the suggestion of Andrássy, on behalf of Hungary, that an independent Poland be created which could join the Monarchy as a third state. Tisza, a devotee of Dualism, did not consider the plan feasible in this form and, anyway, the Germans had their own plans for the occupied territory.

On the southern front, the first attacks in 1914, led by the Czech general Potiorek and the Austrian Frank, known for their useless sacrifice of troops, were complete failures. In the fall of 1915, Bulgaria, too, joined the Central Powers with the stipulation that an energetic offensive against the Serbs be begun. The large-scale Austro-Hungarian campaign under General von

Mackensen now met with success. Besides occupying Serbia, Montenegro and Albania, it succeeded, despite the Allied expeditionary force in Salonika, in making connections with Turkey, which in October had also joined the Central Powers.

In May, 1915, on the other hand, Italy, once a member of the Triple Alliance, gave up her erstwhile neutrality. At first, she demanded territorial compensation from the Monarchy; then, having received on April 26 guarantees in a secret pact signed in London for the future possession of the port of Trieste, the South Tyrol, and Dalmatia, she entered the war on May 23 on the side of the Ententé Powers. At first, only a few Austro-Hungarian divisions were on the Italian front, to be augmented later by predominantly Hungarian troops. Under the generalship of Archduke Joseph, of the dynasty's Hungarian branch, divisions from the Hungarian Lowlands withstood Italy's furious offensives in the Valley of the Isonzo River and the rocky Doberdo Plateau.

The attitude of Rumania was branded doubtful by Tisza as early as the beginning of the war. The Russians attempted to lure her into hostilities by promising Rumania the whole of Transylvania, but while King Carol I was alive, Russophile tendencies could not gain sufficient foothold. Tisza realized that fortunes of war would finally decide to which side Rumania would swing. He was ready to make concessions to the Rumanian minority in Transylvania, independently of his refusal to the territorial transfer of Transylvania, which

Rumania proper tried to attain through direct intervention to Germany. In Tisza's own statement, "Rumania did not turn from Hungary because the lot of Rumanians in Transylvania was unsatisfactory, but because she coveted the possession of Transylvania." As may be presumed, no offer could match that made by Russia, which promised not only Transylvania, but a large slice of the Hungarian Lowlands as far as the Tisza River. For a while Rumania was cautious, especially after the Russian disaster at Gorlice. But in the following year, the offensive of the Russian general Brussilov, who captured 300,000 prisoners during a successful initial drive, helped Rumania to make up her mind. In the pact of August 17, 1916, "the Allies were able to buy her over at a perfectly scandalous price".[1] This comprised Transylvania, the South Hungarian province of Banat, and a goodly portion of the central Hungarian Lowlands. Ten days later, on August 27, Sunday night, simultaneously with the handing over of a declaration of war, the Rumanian army crossed the practically undefended frontier of Transylvania.

The assault on Transylvania and the pitiful position of the fleeing civilian population gave an opportunity to the parliamentary opposition to launch an attack on Premier Tisza, who, in turn, did not give away the secret that he had previously done all he could to induce the High Command to undertake the defense of Transylvania. The Hungarian parliament was in session dur-

[1] C. A. Macartney, *Hungary and Her Successors, 1919–37,* Oxford University Press, 1937, p. 275.

ing the war (unlike the Austrian legislature, which was suspended by virtue of Section 14, leaving Austria governed without a parliament). The critical attitude toward the Government became increasingly stronger, and the political truce was slowly disappearing. The moderate opposition, headed by Andrássy and Apponyi, was deserted in the summer of 1916 by Count Michael Károlyi, leader of the extreme wing of the Independence Party. This wealthy young aristocrat, originally a Conservative, was touring America at the outbreak of the war, collecting funds for his party. Returning, he too accepted the political Truce of God, but later he and his followers began to agitate for peace and the secret ballot, and against the alliance with Germany. No doubt there was truly a need in Hungary for reforms, and everyone desired peace; but that kind of subversive propaganda did not help in bringing the war to a successful close and making a peaceful evolution possible. The Rumanian army that had invaded Transylvania was expelled in the autumn with the aid of German troops and the bold stroke of von Mackensen. Remnants of the Rumanian forces were crushed in a huge pincer movement, one arm of which advanced from Transylvania, the other through Bulgaria. On December 6, Bucharest, capital of Rumania, fell.

During the first two years of the war, Austria-Hungary was able to defend its own territory against different attacks, its troops standing, in some cases, deep in enemy territory. Yet the aged emperor-king, Francis Joseph, died on November 21, 1916, convinced that the

Monarchy was urgently in need of peace. The sixty-eight years of Francis Joseph's reign comprised the era from the Hungarian revolution of 1848 to the second year of the World War. The aged ruler acquired great experience during this long time. After 1867, he steadfastly adhered to the Compromise he signed with Deák and to the Dualistic System. He performed his duties with punctuality and a sense of duty until his last day. His successor, the young, inexperienced, but well-intentioned Charles IV, was known for his desire for peace and for his endeavor to settle difficulties with concessions rather than with firm resolution.

Hungary fought in the war primarily for the defense of her territory and the repulse of attacks, thus not seeing any need for the continuation of the exhausting struggle. Not even in the midst of the war did she plan any future annexation of alien territory. "Our adversaries thrust upon us to dismember us", wrote Tisza in the spring of 1916, "but there was nothing further from us than to reciprocate such desires; we only cherished our own security".[1] Serious economic conditions within the Monarchy also made an early peace very desirable. The blockade shut off the food and raw material supplies of the Central Powers. As far as industries were concerned, Austria's position was somewhat better, though even she could not fill her own needs in various products. Owing to a shortage in textiles, a general shabbiness resulted. On the other hand, industrial centers and cities suffered mainly from hunger, Hun-

[1]Stephen Tisza, *Complete Works,* Vol. IV, 5, Budapest 1933, p. 202.

gary's "profusion" in foodstuffs being spoken of in other countries of the Central Powers with envy. Yet, in fact, there was no abundance in Hungary either, because she furnished most of the foodstuffs for the Central armies as well. In addition, production continually decreased, owing to a shortage of manpower and machinery. By 1918, the harvest yielded only 58 per cent of the pre-War average. The administration was obliged to introduce measures with which to regulate economic life: central agencies directed the flow of goods, establishing an early form of rigid and planned economy. From 1915 on, food was rationed and the arbitrary setting of maximum prices led to a hoarding of essentials. As in other countries during the war, speculation went hand in hand with misery. On top of this, inflation threatened. Joint expenditures, chiefly financing the war effort, rose to 71 million crowns, part of which was covered by federal loans. The savings of rich and poor alike, the capital of foundations and orphanages went up in smoke with the tragic ending of the war.

The peace offer of the Central Powers, the idea of which was warmly supported by Charles IV himself, was handed over to the Entente Powers by the respective American ambassadors on December 18, 1916. As regards the evacuation of the occupied territories, Tisza's standpoint against any annexation was offered as a basis. The Entente's refusal was delivered on January 12, 1917, demanding the liberation of Italians, Southern Slavs, Rumanians and Czecho-Slovaks from what it called "foreign domination". This stipulation was included upon the urging of Edward Beneš and the Czech émigrés.[1] This was the "first concrete result of their labors" and, simultaneously, "the endorsement of Czecho-Slovak aspirations". Naturally, this was "only possible as the result of the dismemberment of Austria-Hungary." Premier Tisza, trusting the king's desire for peace, contacted American ambassador Penfield at Vienna on January 25, 1917.[2] In his letter he explained that the conditions outlined in the reply of the Entente Powers "are equivalent to a war of destruction." He referred to his statement to the Hungarian Parliament on the previous day, in which he endeavored to harmonize the principles laid down by President Wilson ("every people must have guarantees of free existence"), with the existence of the Monarchy. Enlarging on the subject, Tisza went on to say that the "ideal of the free development of all nations in states having their national character cannot be realized in countries with a mixed population, especially in the south-east of Europe, where no other solution would approach this ideal so nearly as the political system of the Dual Monarchy."

Based on Tisza's approach, Secretary of State Lansing proposed to the British government the establishment of national autonomies instead of the dismemberment of the Monarchy. Premier Lloyd George replied, however, that though they had "no policy of sheer dismemberment", the demands of Rumanian, Slav and

[1] H. Temperley, *A History of the Paris Peace Conference*, London 1921, Vol. IV, p. 254.

[2] *Papers relating to the Foreign Relations of the United States*, Washington 1931, Supplement I, pp. 31–66.

Italian allies would have to be satisfied. Lansing advised Penfield that "the Allied Governments have no desire or purpose to disrupt the Austro-Hungarian Empire," provided the continuance of the war does not alter the conditions. He also instructed the ambassador to continue his negotiations. But when Penfield turned to the new Austrian minister for foreign affairs, Count Ottokar Czernin, once confidant of the murdered Francis Ferdinand, he was told that "a separate peace is out of the question". In the spring of 1917, the young King, through his brother-in-law, Prince Sixtus of Bourbon-Parma, attempted to negotiate with the Western Powers, acknowledging France's desires as regards to Alsace-Lorraine. The Prince's mission was frustrated chiefly by the Italians, who had territorial demands on Austria and were against a separate peace with the Monarchy.

In April 1917, the United States entered the war and the results of this action were of decisive influence as to the outcome of the struggle. At the cabinet council of January 22, Tisza had protested against unrestricted submarine warfare, deeming it unnecessary and unsuccessful. He knew that it would bring forth the intervention of the United States, something which he held of far greater importance than most other statesmen.

In the meantime, domestic political difficulties, too, arose in Hungary. In February, the new Austro-Hungarian economic agreement was signed. On account of the war, Austria wished to have the time limit set at thirty years instead of the usual ten. Finally the Hungarian government acquiesced, despite the protests of the Independents, in a period of twenty years and the raising of its quota by 2 per cent. In reality, the old principle of "parity" was gradually thrust into the background by preparations for a planned "new order" of economy, embracing the whole territory of the Central Powers. In the same year, intensive negotiations were under way to establish a complete customs alliance between the Monarchy and Germany. These plans were parallel with the economic organization by the Germans of the Russian and Rumanian territories occupied.

One of the most controversial issues in internal politics lay in the question of electoral rights. The advisers of the young King, recruited from among former adherents of the late Francis Ferdinand, had, as their chief aim, the curtailing of the long-envied position of Hungary in the Monarchy's affairs. This was their reason for forcing at this crucial time the question of a general secret ballot. As has been pointed out, in this matter Tisza did not represent an up-to-date conception and this problem, together with many others, was timely before the war broke out. It was most unfortunate that war came before social and nationality questions were successfully solved. During the war, everyone realized that veterans would have to be given not only the right to vote, but opportunities for livelihood through generous land reform. But whether a life-and-death struggle was a right time or not for debating these measures is another matter. Without the strong personality of Tisza and the majority party behind him, it hardly seemed probable that internal order and stability could be maintained. At the end of April, 1917, the king instructed Tisza to make a generous extension of electoral rights; but the Premier, unwilling to undertake such a momentous change, handed in his resignation on May 22nd, leaving immediately for the battlefront as a colonel of the Hussar reserve. His departure from the post in which he first protested against the war, and then, when it started, against unrestricted methods of butchery, while doing his best for the organization of national defense,—could not pass without consequence.

Tisza's successor, the young Morris Esterházy, could stand the terrible strain of the Premier's duties only for a short time, though his efforts were unhampered by the majority party of Tisza. As early as the spring of 1917, a so-called "Democratic Bloc for Electoral Rights" was formed from several groups of the opposition. In it were the group of William Vázsonyi, the peace-favoring radicals of Oscar Jászi and the Independence Party of Count Michael Károlyi. Jászi and his friends believed that the Rumanian and other aspirations could be appeased by minority concessions and by the formation of an "Eastern Switzerland". Károlyi's followers, on the other hand, advocated gradual separation from Austria, personal union as against Dualism, and took seriously the idea that with the accentuation of democratic principles, the political sympathies of the Allied Powers might be gained.

Esterházy was followed, without any change in platform, by the aged Wekerle. The latter, like most of his contemporaries, was unable to recognize the grave dangers threatening Hungary and the serious consequences of the war situation. They could not conceive the significance either of the nationality problem or of the South Slav movement. As minister of justice, Vázsonyi presented his Bill of Electoral Rights on December 21, 1917, raising the number of voters more than three-fold. The debate on this Bill lasted for months, amid growing nervousness on the part of the public. The grave economic situation and the long and exhausting war began to make their effects felt. To the American ambassador, Penfield, it seemed already in February 1917 that "the economic life in Austria-Hungary is paralyzed. . . ." with "destitution visible everywhere".[1] Socialists organized strikes and street demonstrations. Radical changes in Russia echoed among the tired peoples of the Monarchy. In March 1917, revolution broke out.in Russia, to be followed in the autumn by Bolshevism, built upon the ruins of the Tsarist Empire. The Germans, holding the central mechanism of the Central Powers within their hands, were still determined to fight for a victorious peace; but the Monarchy itself had arrived at the uttermost limits of its performing capacity.

During the negotiations carried out by President Wilson of the United States, prompted by a desire to prepare a peace based on new and righteous foundations, the wish to "emancipate" Austria from German domination was in the limelight. Colonel House, confidant of the President, in the spring of 1917 proposed to Lord

[1] *Op. cit.* p. 39.

Balfour, British Foreign Secretary, that "Great Britain
and the United States should stand together for a just
peace—a peace fair to all, to the small as well as to the
large nations of the world. Great Britain and America,
I thought, were great enough to rise above party considerations".[1] House's opinion was that "on a basis of
the *status quo ante* the Entente could aid Austria in
emancipating herself from Prussia", and likewise he was
just as much against the dismemberment of the Monarchy as the American committee sent to Europe to
study conditions. "President Wilson", stated Col. House,
"had two alternative policies before him. He might
proclaim war to death upon the Habsburg Monarchy
. . . He would thus bear assistance to a revolution that
might end in the Balkanization of the Danube regions,
but which would, in the meantime, go far to undermine
the strength of the Central Powers. Or he might proclaim the right to 'autonomy' of the subject nationalities . . . The peril of splitting up territories economically interdependent, would thus be avoided at the same
time that the self-government of the nationalities was assured.—The second alternative was chosen by the President. In common with the leading statesmen of Western Europe, he believed that the political union of the
Austro-Hungarian peoples was a necessity, and he seems
to have felt that once freed from German domination,
the Habsburg Monarchy would prove a beneficial
force". As a matter of fact the President said in his ad-

[1] *The Intimate Papers of Colonel House,* London 1928, Vol. III, p. 41.
Other passages are quoted from Vol. I, p. 157, Vol. III, pp. 344–345.

dress to the American Congress on December 4, 1917: "We do not wish in any way to impair or rearrange the Austro-Hungarian Empire . . . We only desire to see that their affairs are left in their own hands in all matters, great or small". Premier Lloyd George of Great Britain stated in the House of Commons on January 5, 1918, that the break-up of Austria-Hungary was no part of their war aim, yet peace may be insured only through "a genuine self-government on true democratic principles". Of President Wilson's Fourteen Points, dated January 8, 1918, Number 10 is explicit in its statement that "the peoples of Austria-Hungary, whose place among the nations we wish to see safeguarded and assured, should be accorded the freest opportunity of autonomous development".

Contrary to this general principle were the nationalist aspirations which the Czechs, Serbs and Rumanians tried to formulate in such a manner that they could be included among the objectives of the war. These plans were worked on since the beginning of the war. At first the Czechs endeavored to establish, under a Russian dynasty, a Bohemian Kingdom, including the northern territories of Hungary. This Czech state would have bordered on Tsarist Russia. According to one of the memoranda submitted to the Allied and Associated Powers, "Russia's wishes and plans" were going to be of "determining influence".[1]

Later, when Russia's luck faded on the battlefields

[1] *The Slavonic Review,* London, 1925, pp. 619–20.—R. W. Seton-Watson, President Masaryk, *Contemporary Review,* 1930, p. 286.

and the execution of the Russophile plan did not appear feasible, the leading Czech émigrés, Masaryk and Beneš, went over to what was considered popular among the Western democracies and, having dropped the idea of a Monarchy, they contrived to prepare the way for the establishment of a Czechoslovak republic. They formed a National Committee and through their friends, the "experts" on the problems of the Monarchy, they were successful in making an impression on the public opinion and governments of the Allied Powers. This was evident from the reply of January 12, 1917, made to the peace offer of the Central Powers. Since even the highest circles had hardly any definite knowledge about conditions in East-Central Europe, the émigrés furnished the most convenient and even the exclusive source for the necessary historical and political information.

These nationalist aspirations, the nature and development of which in East-Central Europe have been touched upon in previous chapters, had to be presented in a form which seemed to suit the political interests and way of thinking of the Western powers. This was served, primarily, by the argument that only through the fulfilment of these very aspirations could democracy be established in Carpathian Europe. Simplified, this sounds rather naïve now, i.e., while the nationalisms of certain peoples are, *a priori*, in their very nature, "democratic", another nationalism, that of the Hungarians, for instance, was, *a priori*, "feudal". But those English experts who for a number of years had looked upon the social problems of Carpathian Europe from a certain angle, were of the opinion that their task was an easy one, namely, that of choosing between Good and Evil. On the other hand, they were favorably impressed by the conceptions of Masaryk, who presented his doctrines in a way which appealed to their interest.

Another widespread argument tried to prove that only the fulfilment of Czech and other Slav desires could stand in the way of Germanic penetration toward the east, the *Drang nach Osten*. As Ernest Denis wrote, the French intended to "build a Slavic wall from the Baltic to the Adriatic, that will place an invincible barrier against the Germanic thrust". This, he continued, necessitated the formation of a single state by the Czechs and Slovaks, to be joined to the new South Slav state by a corridor through Hungarian territory.[1] The same writer viewed Rumania from a different point of view for the simple reason that said country at the time had not yet joined the Allies. He stated that Transylvania was geographically, too, a part of Hungary and its transfer to Rumania would be merely "changing from one oppressor to another".

Beneš's work demanded the destruction of Austria-Hungary, similarly suggesting the future Czechoslovakia, in alliance with Russian and Greater Serbia as a barrier against German expansion.[2] According to Beneš, such an arrangement "would complete the encirclement of Germany", though the Western powers steadfastly

[1] E. Denis, *La Guerre*, Paris, 1915.
[2] E. Beneš, *Détruisez l'Autriche-Hongrie!* Paris, 1916. [English ed. London, 1917.]

repudiated any charge of encirclement laid against them.

No one checked up, of course, as to whether any of these arguments, based on war psychology, were really true principles, on which a lasting, stable and just order was to be built in this part of Europe. All these plans involved Slavs in general, avoiding the mention of deep antagonisms between certain Slavic peoples, like the Russians and Poles, for instance. Since the Monarchy stood in the way of these young nationalistic schemes, they tried hard to convince all concerned that there was no more need for the Monarchy, since they would be able to take its place and fulfil just as well all the rôle played by her in the European Balance of Power. One of the often applied arguments presumed that without destruction of the Monarchy, Germany could not be defeated. The English historian, Seton-Watson, one of the influential experts on the subject, realized that in case the Monarchy disintegrated, Austria would, unavoidably, join Germany. Yet he, too, was of the opinion that "Germany can only be defeated, if we are prepared to back the Slavs".[1]

Against the Habsburg Monarchy, the "living anachronism", it was not difficult to find arguments. This had already been done by Kossuth with unparalleled conviction and logic a generation before, in England and America as well. Whatever rightful criticism could be used, from a modern point of view, against this state

[1] R. W. Seton-Watson, *German, Slav and Magyar,* London, 1916, pp. 174 and 177.

organism, appears even today much more vivid in Kossuth's original words, than in all the later propaganda
pamphleteering taken together, which, with a few ex-
ceptions, is monotonous repetition. It was not given to
Kossuth to place his talents as a statesman and his plans
as an émigré at the disposal of a reorganization that follows a world conflict. In Kossuth's time, the Western
powers were unswerving in their decision to uphold
Austria as an important factor in the European balance,
despite the most bitter protests of Hungarians. "Austria" said Lord Palmerston in the Lower House on July
21, 1849, "is a most important element in the balance
of European power . . . The political independence
and liberties of Europe are bound up, in my opinion,
with the maintenance and integrity of Austria as a great
European power; and therefore anything which tends
by direct or even remote contingency to weaken and to
cripple Austria, but still more to reduce her from the
position of a first-rate power to that of a secondary state,
must be a great calamity to Europe and one which every
Englishman ought to deprecate and try to prevent".
Thus the Hungarians were forced to accept the inevitable, and, in view of the possibilities, to make a Compromise with Austria in 1867. But not so Kossuth, who never
accepted the Compromise and wished to establish a
Danubian Federation. Twenty years after the great
émigré's death, the First World War broke out, at the
end of which the Allied Powers, having forgotten their
own arguments of old, and Palmerston's words, consented to the dismemberment of the Monarchy, of

which Hungary was an important member against her original will.

Czech émigrés and their fellow travelers were clever enough to hold continually in the limelight those Western interests which, according to them, were dependent on the fulfilment of their nationalist aspirations. Then, referring to their important tasks and future services, they demanded large slices of territory from "untrustworthy" Hungary. They based their claims for these territories now on ethnic grounds, now on economic grounds, and again on strategical reasons, and so forth, one often contradicting another. Hungary had no Kossuth in the Western countries during the World War, who could have defended his nation for its own and Carpathian Europe's sake by referring to the moral supplied by history and showing a balance sheet of the different viewpoints. The émigré Kossuth believed and supported the idea of the freedom and autonomous development of every smaller people. He, too, desired a new order in Carpathian Europe, but without disturbing the natural unity of the Carpathian Basin. Kossuth's original plan for a Danubian Confederation against Austria could not be carried out. But whatever plans Kossuth would have been able to submit to suit new requirements, for the sake of the future security of Carpathian Europe, he would surely have allotted a leading position to that nation which for long centuries really played an important, central rôle there. He would not have built his plans on a state newly created by artificially uniting two distinct peoples, the Czechs and Slovaks, who had lived as separate historical units for ten centuries.

Against Number 10 of Wilson's Fourteen Points, those émigrés and "experts" who made an all-out effort to have the Monarchy dissected, lost no time in taking action, in close collaboration with the British Department of Propaganda in Enemy Countries, headed by Lord Northcliffe. Under their influence, Lord Balfour, too, accepted the plan of dismemberment. And, despite United States Secretary of State Lansing's view that America was not bound by any secret agreement, it became evident that the interested peoples would present their bills to the Entente Powers at the end of the war. They were able to sidetrack President Wilson from his original principles with the ruse that the proposed changes were desired by all the peoples involved, by the right of self-determination. One of the documents purporting to prove this was the decision of the Pittsburgh Pact, dated May 30, 1918, signed by Masaryk himself in conjunction with leaders of the Czechs and Slovaks in the United States. In this document, the Slovaks consented to have Northern Hungary joined to the Czechs in a single state, with the proviso, however, that Slovakia was to be granted a separate parliament of its own, an independent administration and independent courts of Justice, and that Slovak should be the official language of education and public life in Slovakia. Slovak nationalists, however, afterwards vainly referred to the Pact as a fundamental agreement between two distinct parties. According to Masaryk, the Pittsburgh

Pact was "but a local understanding" between American Czechs and Slovaks, "concluded in order to appease a small Slovak faction which was dreaming of God knows what sort of independence for Slovakia".[1] Accordingly, those who in one instance accepted the Pittsburgh Pact as a genuine expression of the political desires of the Slovaks living amid the far-away Carpathians, in the same breath denounced it as insignificant and incompetent, when the obligations therein contained had to be fulfilled. President Wilson who had understood the foundation of future peace to be the free acceptance of every settlement by the people concerned, was, through personal contact with Masaryk, won over to the Czech aspirations. The Allied Powers recognized the émigré Czech government in the summer of 1918.

The year 1917 had not brought a decision on any of the battle fronts. In October the Italian army, exhausted by a long series of offensives, was thrown back at Caporetto and was obliged to retire as far as the Piave River, where French and British troops helped it to hold a new line. Early in 1918, peace with Russia was signed at Brest-Litovsk, to be followed on March 5 by the separate peace of Rumania signed at Bucharest. Even then, Hungary maintained her original attitude against the annexation of anyone else's territory, effecting minor border adjustments against possible encroachments only on the uninhabited mountainous Carpathians.

The outcome of the war was not settled by Luden-

[1] Masaryk's words quoted by Macartney, *op. cit.*, p. 97.

dorff's large-scale offensive in March 1918 on the western front either, nor by an unsuccessful Austro-Hungarian thrust at the Piave. The Entente armies launched a counter-offensive on both these fronts. The Bulgarian front was crumbling by the 15th of September. In this fateful hour, Austro-Hungarian Foreign Minister Burian approached President Wilson with reference to the Fourteen Points, but by that time the chief executive of the United States had already accepted the war aims of the Allied Powers as proposed by the Czechs and others.

Austria was perceptibly in gradual dissolution, Charles IV declaring in his Manifesto, in the middle of October, the federalization of the Monarchy, though leaving Hungary's integrity intact. On October 16, 1918, Premier Wekerle of Hungary announced in Parliament that the Dualistic system with Austria was terminated, only personal union being upheld. Hungarian public opinion did not yet recognize the threatening danger, for the boundaries of the country were intact. The Independence Party led by Károlyi cherished the illusion that Hungary, detached from Austria, emphasizing its anti-Austrian attitude, and professing pacifist aims, might yet merit the good-will of the victors. One of Károlyi's followers, Martin Lovászy, stated in Parliament, "we are friends of the Entente". The public awoke to the tragedy on the following day, when even Tisza admitted that "this war we have lost". On October 18, Alexander Vajda-Voevod, leader of the Transylvanian-Rumanian deputies in the Hungarian

Parliament, declared that they wished to be represented at the peace conference by a separate delegation. A few days later, the new minister of foreign affairs, Count Julius Andrássy the younger, who took over his father's former cabinet post, severed all connections with Germany in the hope that this might make possible a separate peace.

The Austro-Hungarian Supreme Command successfully conducted an Armistice in Padua on November 3, with Italian General Diaz as representative of the Entente Powers. Terms of this armistice defined a line of occupation only on the west, leaving the existing political frontiers of the country untouched in any other part. Wekerle resigned and while the King hesitated as to whom to designate to form a new Cabinet, Count Károlyi and his radicals set up, on October 23, a National Council on the Czech and South Slav pattern, which, together with the so-called Soldiers' Council, continued revolutionary agitation with ever-growing intensity. Resistance to subversive propaganda was made awkward by the lack of political organization in the bulk of the social classes, and also by the shrewdly exploited false belief that a lost war is necessarily and inevitably followed by revolution. During the night of October 21, the National Council, aided by socialists and deserted soldiers hiding in the capital, "took over executive powers". Following this day, known as the "aster revolution", this flower being worn by those taking part in it, the King accepted Károlyi as premier. At the same time, Tisza was the victim of assassination.

The position of the Károlyi government was difficult indeed. Hungary was on the side of the vanquished and, consequently, the attitude of the nationalities, comprising 45.5 per cent of the population, became uncertain. The public at first saw the last desperate opportunity in Károlyi's policy, especially so under the influence of the wishful statements of the new government's adherents. According to the latter, the Entente fought "feudal" Hungary only, and would not consider a pacifist Hungary, democratized with revolutionary speed, as an enemy. They contended that it was even possible to switch over in the last minute to the Allied Powers, furthermore, that through the creation of an "Eastern Switzerland" excessive Rumanian and other nationalistic aspirations might be shelved.

Several of the revolutionary leaders really believed in their own suppositions. "We had confidence", wrote Minister for National Minorities Jászi, "in the democratic and pacifist quality of public opinion in the Entente States and especially in the policy of President Wilson. We were convinced that the conquering Allies would show the utmost good-will to her (Hungary's) pacifist and anti-militarist government".[1] First of all they endeavored to get rid of Austria and the Habsburg dynasty. On the day following his taking the oath of office, Károlyi requested King Charles IV to free him of the oath, and he swore a new allegiance to the National Council. In his declaration at Eckartsau, dated Novem-

[1] O. Jászi, *Revolution and Counter-Revolution in Hungary*. London, 1924, pp. 30, 40, 56.

ber 13, the King withdrew from handling state affairs. On November 16, 1918, the Hungarian Republic was declared. Though this moment evoked rejoicing, because with it Hungary regained her long-sought total independence, this was soon to be followed by bitter and complete disillusionment.

The Károlyi government, in order to obtain leniency and good-will, acted, so to speak, according to the wishes and interests of the victorious enemy. Though the Entente Powers had no secret pacts relative to Hungary (the one with Italy touched only Austria, while the one with Rumania became void with that country's separate peace), nevertheless it was evident that the Allied Powers accepted Czech and other aspirations in general. The reply to the Monarchy's offer, received on October 18, 1918, from President Wilson, asserted the acknowledgment of the Czechoslovak National Council by the United States a *de facto* belligerent government, and it likewise asserted the righteousness of South Slav "nationalistic aspirations". It further stated that these movements "shall be the judges of what action on the part of the Austro-Hungarian government will satisfy their aspirations".[1]

Under such circumstances, it would have been the most important duty and interest of Hungary to have her borders, until final settlement, safeguarded with those intact troops she was able to recall from the frontiers in accordance with the Armistice signed at Padua. The interests of the Czechs, Serbs and Rumanians, on

[1]H. Temperley, *op. cit.,* Vol. 1, pp. 452–3.

the contrary, demanded that they hurriedly occupy as large a territory as possible in order to bring about a *fait accompli,* the acceptance of which would be easy with the Council of the Big Four. It was quite clear that these new imperialistic ambitions were not bound by principles of self-determination of nationalities, and were openly aimed also at large territories inhabited by other peoples. At this time, unfortunately, not principles but bayonets decided the issues. The Czechs and Rumanians, fully realizing their golden opportunity, were busily creating armies of their own. The naïve Hungarian pacifists and ideologues, on the contrary, were anxious to disarm and to disperse the troops arriving in perfect order from the battle zones. The explanation for this may be chiefly found in their fear of a possible counter-revolutionary movement among these regiments. Moreover, the revolutionary leaders wished to demonstrate to the Western Powers their sincerely pacifist desires.

Making a stand with the returning troops, whose rushing home was prompted by the very desire to have their country defended, was a real possibility. Following the disarmament of von Mackensen's German army in the Balkans, the Entente would not have dispatched another Expeditionary Force, especially not for an arbitrary realization of commonly acknowledged violations through the loss of English, French or American lives. Probably a conflict arising out of the defense of the Hungarian frontiers would have demonstrated to the leaders of the Peace Conference, buried in several other problems, that panaceas for Carpathian Europe's ailments are not quite so easy to find as they had been told. But Károlyi's defense minister, Béla Linder, was toying with his concept that "there is no more need for an army. Never again do I want to see another soldier". With this he robbed the country of its last resort of self-defense, which could at least have guarded the predominantly Hungarian territories.

Dismal failure of the pacifist platform was once more demonstrated when Károlyi sought to replace the favorable terms of the Padua Armistice with new ones. He thought that he was going to assure a better armistice for the new, pro-Allied Hungary, so he went, probably following Czech advice, to Belgrade, to receive what he thought more generous terms from General Franchet d'Espérey, commanding the French Expeditionary Force in the Balkans. Nothing is better proof of his naïveté than his belief that the French general would receive the representatives of radical pacifists and other extreme left-wing councils with open arms. Their humiliation, indeed, was complete. General d'Espérey had not a single word of consolation for them, and even expressed his sympathy for King Charles, deserted by his subjects. When a socialist member of the delegation was introduced to the French commander, the latter exclaimed, "Êtes-vous tombés si bas? (Have you sunk to such depths?)"

According to terms received at Belgrade, Entente forces, but in practice mostly Serb and Rumanian troops, occupied the southern and south-eastern part of

Hungary, including the city of Szabadka and the line of the River Maros. Hungarian civilian administration was to be continued, but in fact it was soon to be abandoned. Though the Belgrade Convention did not touch upon the northern boundaries, the Czechs began the occupation of Northern Hungary, against which the protests of the Hungarian government were futile. Beneš, moreover, and the South Slavs and Rumanians, were able to wrest ever new concessions and new territories from the peacemakers of Paris. The successive instructions of the Entente Supreme Council were handed over by Lieutenant-Colonel Vyx to the Károlyi government, the protests of which, faced by military force, were of no avail. Thus foreign troops settled in the north and south as well as in Transylvania, attempting to create an anti-Magyar feeling even where there was never a desire for secession.

Such an outside interference was, naturally, of great influence on the attitude of nationalities, contributing to the failure of Jászi's policies. Minister of Nationalities in Károlyi's Cabinet, he was primarily theoretical and a believer in abstract ideologies. He tried to win the nationalist leaders of Rumania in a conference in Arad, November 12, for the establishment of an "Eastern Switzerland". With such a naïve conception the Rumanians could not be bothered, and in their counter-demands outlined their plans for the establishment of an exclusively Rumanian national régime, without consideration for other peoples, in Transylvania and in the eastern portion of the Hungarian Lowlands. Against this intolerant and greedy nationalism, Jászi referred in vain to the large number of Hungarians and Saxons inhabiting Transylvania, who, according to President Wilson's principles, were also entitled to the rights of self-determination. The Rumanians were ready to negotiate only in order to gain time, until, with troops entering Transylvania from Rumania, they were able to establish their nationalist régime by force. Jászi was willing to give autonomy, based on the solution of 1868, to the Slovaks and Ruthenes, who would have been satisfied with such concessions if Czech troops had not entered the territory in question. Jászi himself bitterly admitted later on, "We were doomed by the very internationalism which was the basis of our whole policy . . . The bright promise of President Wilson's League of Nations and the right of self-determination and of plebiscites, in which the Hungarian people had placed their trust, burst like soap bubbles".

The encouragements of Károlyi were followed by a tragic awakening of the public. From the edges of the country, occupied by the troops of the neighbours, thousands of Hungarian refugees arrived. The government was still headed by Károlyi, but not so the control of affairs. Asked by Count Hadik a year previously about his policies Károlyi responded, "I do not know, I am being carried on by the waves".[1]

As soon as it became evident that Károlyi's faith in Allied sympathies toward his trend were childish and his dilettante policies were an utter failure, it also be-

[1]Quoted by G. Gratz, *The Era of Revolutions*, Budapest, 1935, p. 22.

came clear that "on the left of the left there is always a left", and that Hungary was being "carried by the waves" towards Bolshevism. Károlyi, like his followers, believed in the coming advent of world revolution and either could not or would not stand in the way of Communist agitation. Jászi too, the disillusioned, told the Rumanians that peace would finally be dictated, not by the generals, but by a Soviet Socialist Republic of Europe.

Members of the old Independence Party hastened, one after the other, to leave Károlyi, who in January 1919 became President of the Republic of Hungary. The new Premier was Denis Berinkey. By this time, the Social Democratic Party was the strongest political factor in the country. Owing to the near famine that existed, white-collar people as well as other office employees flocked in tens of thousands to become members of the unions, for they at least assured a minimum of foodstuffs as privileges. Though the majority of the Social Democratic Party, including a great part of the trades unions, was opposing Communism, yet the leaders of these groups were unwilling to allow any organizing on behalf of the more conservative, "bourgeois" elements, for fear of a counter-revolution. At the same time, however, they were utterly helpless against the methods of Bolshevist agitation.

Returning from Russia together with the repatriated prisoners of war, there were a number of trained Red agitators, with two young Jewish hoodlums among them. One of them, Béla Kun (Kohn), was once an employee of the Workers' Compensation Board at Nagyvárad. Together with Tibor Szamuelly, he began large-scale underground organizing with money they received from Russia. They relied mainly on armed detachments of terrorists, like the "Lenin Boys". The most infamous were the "marines" of one Czerny, a bloody-handed terrorist, himself with a long prison record. Károlyi was simply unable to cope with impostors and criminals who mysteriously gained control everywhere. The struggle was by now between the Social Democrats and Communists, the latter destroying, during a fierce demonstration on February 20, 1919, the printing establishment of the Socialist daily, *Népszava*. The government finally arrested forty-six Communists, yet it could not decide to take any energetic steps, and the resistance of the Social Democrats, especially their leaders, continually weakened.

The fall of the Károlyi Cabinet was fostered by the Czech and Rumanian demands, routed through Paris and presented in Budapest by the French envoy, Lieutenant-Colonel Vyx. Károlyi could not oppose any of these and this embittered the feelings of the masses. The Czechs, of whom there was no word in the Belgrade terms, advanced to the line of the Rivers Danube, Ipoly and Ung. The Rumanians, overstepping the conditions of the terms, declared on January 1 the annexation of Transylvania. The public was alarmed when it scented that the line of "temporary" occupation might coincide with the new boundaries. The Rumanians were to advance even further toward the Hungarian Lowlands, when three divisions of Hungarian troops, composed mostly of Transylvanian Székelys, stopped them. At this point Premier Bratianu was able to have Paris demand a "neutral belt" between the Hungarian and Rumanian forces, which turned out to be just another farce, for it permitted a further advance by the invaders.

The American delegation to the Supreme Council was of the opinion that a plebiscite was the proper procedure in Transylvania. But when Lloyd George asked Bratianu about the genuine desires of the population and the fate of the Hungarians in Transylvania, the Rumanian premier's plain answer was that "Rumania fought in order to impose her national will on the Hungarian minority in Transylvania". The Czechs and Rumanians, supported by their influential friends, operated with such information and arguments as disregarded the real situation and were used as sheer excuses to assure the carrying out of their nationalistic dreams.

Such new steps meant, beyond doubt, as was expressed in the Memoranda of General Tasker Bliss of the United States army to President Wilson on March 27, 1919, the breaking of both the Padua and the Belgrade Armistices. General Bliss pointed out that according to official reports the Hungarians had carried out conditions of the Armistice, but that the Rumanians had not and that the advance of their troops "subject the Associated Powers to a charge of breach of faith" which "cannot be justified morally before the people of the United States". General Bliss further branded the decision of the Supreme Council which facilitated the advance of Rumanian troops as "absolutely unjust" and deemed its revocation desirable. He also wanted the Supreme Council to assure the Hungarian people that it was the desire of the Allies to sign a peace with Hungary on the basis of President Wilson's declaration.[1]

When Lt.-Colonel Vyx presented still further demands on March 19, the government of Count Michael Károlyi resigned and the Social Democratic leaders, despite opposition by a few of them, soon came to terms with the Bolsheviks. In a statement, Károlyi unintentionally exercised the severest criticism of his policies, admitting that his faith placed in President Wilson's principles and in his own Entente sympathies had been doomed to failure. Károlyi then suggested that the good will of the Workers' International was to be secured. "I turn to the proletariat of the world for justice and assistance," he exclaimed. The scant four months of what was known as "Octobrism" came to a sad end, handing over its place to the Bolshevik terror that had been allowed to grow freely under Károlyi's régime.

With this, the dictatorship of the proletariat began. This was, in fact, the terror of a small but well organized group, which for four months tried to consolidate its rule with every conceivable method of coercion and

[1] David Hunter Miller, *My Diary at the Peace Conference.* Vol. 16, p. 495, also Vol. 17, p. 261.

Baker, *Woodrow Wilson and the World Settlement,* New York 1927, Vol. 111, pp. 238–245.

torture. The Social Democrats were unable to compete with Communist leaders who employed tactics learned from Lenin. The President of the Revolutionary Government Council was one Alexander Garbay, a stonemason, but its real chief was none other than Béla Kun, commissar of foreign relations and representative of Russian Bolshevik dogmatics, who instituted, together with his fellow travelers, a complete despotism.

All industry and mining was immediately "socialized"; and as a result of this step, production immediately dropped by from 25 to 75 per cent. Private property was abolished in principle. The large estates, too, were "socialized", but were not divided. On the other hand, they began requisitioning of foodstuffs in earnest all over the country, a step resulting in the complete antagonism of the farmers. The peasants rejected the anti-religious and anti-nationalist trend of the Bolsheviks from the very beginning, and, with their stubborn passive resistance, they contributed in no small measure to the overthrow of Communism. There was no trust in the new "white banknotes" (so called because they were printed on one side only), and during the whole period the privation of both the middle and lower classes steadily increased. Besides, 32 of the 45 "people's commissars" were Jews, and these most sanguinary among them, like the sadist Szamuelly. In other high positions, their proportion was just as great, a fact which made anti-Semitism very strong and general. A great part of the assimilated Jewry however preserved its loyalty to the country, some of them falling

victims to the Terror. The dictatorship of the proletariat in Hungary might more aptly be called the
revolt of a mob composed of unassimilated, foreign,
chiefly Galician elements.

The leaders of the system knew that they could rely
only on a small minority, the *Lumpenproletariat,* as
against the middle class and the peasantry. Early in
1919, there were hardly a few thousand Communists
active in Hungary. The power of Bolshevism, however,
rested on its methods and not in the number of followers.
In Hungary, the Red régime was maintained chiefly
through the exercise of terrorism, openly approved by
the heads of the Communist government. Instruments
of this terror were the revolutionary forces, without
legal procedure based on constituted codes, but with
immediate carrying out of sentences by the Lenin Boys
and other terror detachments. Whenever there showed
signs of dissatisfaction in the country, the bloodthirsty
Szamuelly was soon on the spot with his armored "train
of death" and pitilessly smothered in blood every
movement, whether real or imaginary. There were
several tragedies which can not even be called mere
executions, but murders executed amidst brutal tortures,
invented by criminals and morbid fanatics. It was probably the darkest chapter of Hungary's history when this
"horrible slum of the revolution", as a Social Democratic
leader called Bolshevism, had in its hands power as
well as the fate of suffering millions.

Dissatisfaction was indeed general. Yet attempts at
the overthrow of the Red rule, isolated and badly

equipped, were doomed from the beginning because the organized and armed minority ruled a people deprived of its remaining means of defense by the Octobrists' inveterate dread of a counter-revolution. The June 24, 1919, attempt was a heroic and desperate one, in which several Danube gunboats and cadets of the Budapest Military Academy took part. Only Italian Colonel Romanelly's energetic intervention on behalf of the Entente Powers prevented a bloody revenge by the Bolsheviks.

Béla Kun proclaimed an alliance with Soviet Russia in the first days after he took over the government. He also invoked the assistance of the world proletariat against the capitalist Entente armies. Yet his aim was not the preservation of Hungary, but the preparation of a revolution involving all Central Europe. He subsidized the Vienna revolutionary movement substantially. In Hungary proper, he began to organize a Red army. Some of the nationalist officers of the disbanded old army, too, joined up; for they were ready to fight for the country's integrity with every desperate implement. In the meantime, the Supreme Council dispatched General Smuts to Hungary, who brought word that the line of military occupation by Little Entente troops did not necessarily indicate the final boundary line. The Bolsheviks, though they did not accept General Smuts' conditions, supported his mission as a diplomatic victory. The Rumanians, simultaneously, advanced as far as the Tisza, under the pretext that the Hungarians were about to attack them. Foreign Commissar Kun, to stabilize his position, ordered the Red army against the Czechs who, until now, had advanced deep into northern Hungary without opposition. The successful offensive of the little-disciplined Red army again proved that Hungary would have been able to defend its ancient frontiers had Count Károlyi's government not dissolved the old army. Kun finally stopped the pursuing of the Czechs on orders from Clemenceau. Then he was to order his army against the Rumanians in Hungary, but the officers discovered by this time that the Bolsheviks do not care about the integrity of the country, and for their "system" they were unwilling to fight. The disintegrating Red army did not offer any serious resistance to the following offensive of the Rumanians. The position of the Bolsheviks was shaken, the farmers by now having all but starved out the Reds' stronghold, Budapest. Having realized that the game was up, Béla Kun handed over the reins to the Socialists on July 31, 1919, and fled the country for Vienna.

There were attempts made at the reorganization of Hungary by some of the Hungarian statesmen who had fled abroad, e.g. Julius Andrássy to Switzerland, and Paul Teleki and Stephen Bethlen to Vienna, where a "White Emigration" was formed endeavoring to obtain the assistance of the Western Powers against Bolshevism. Another group in the meantime was active in southern Hungary, then under French occupation. In the city of Arad, and later in Szeged, a counter-revolutionary cabinet was formed under the premiership of Julius Károlyi. The Minister of Defence in the Szeged Cabinet, recognized by the Hungarian statesmen in Vienna, too, Admiral Nicholas Horthy, energetically began the organization, despite numerous handicaps, of a new national army. Horthy was of old Hungarian Protestant stock, and had once been an adjutant of Francis Joseph. During the World War, he led his cruiser *Novara* through a series of successes with daring and skill. At the end of the World War, he was the last Admiral of the Austro-Hungarian fleet. Horthy's talents and manly character predestined him to become the hope and leader of the nation.

In Budapest, where on August 3 the Rumanians followed the Reds, counter-revolutionaries, headed by Stephen Friedrich, a former adherent of Károlyi, had the Socialist government of Charles Peidl resign. The interests of Hungary's neighbours, who influenced the Entente's action, would have been best served by a radical left-wing "Octobrist" government, unable to exert any strong national opposition. To this end, Julius Károlyi was replaced by Dezső Ábrahám, who was more of a radical. Horthy, heading his disciplined new National Army, left Szeged for Transdanubia, and thence turned towards the centre of the country.

The Entente Powers were represented in Budapest by an Inter-Allied Military Mission, dispatched by the Supreme Council to induce the Rumanians to an urgent withdrawal. The American member of this mission, straightforward General Harry Hill Bandholtz, U.S.A., gives in his *Diary* an indignant account of the lootings of defenceless Hungarian cities and open towns by the occupying Rumanians.[1] General Bandholtz was obliged to wire to Paris on August 16 that, contrary to the wishes of the Inter-Allied Military Mission, "the Rumanians were doing their utmost to delay matters in order to complete the loot of Hungary". He relates that the Rumanians carted away locomotives, railroad cars and other rolling stock, every sort of machine-tool equipment, etc. "Then they proceeded also," writes General Bandholtz, "to clean the country out of private automobiles, farm implements, cattle, horses, clothing, sugar, coal, salt and, in fact, everything of value". Only the personal intervention of the gallant American prevented the Rumanians from trucking away even the permanent exhibits of the Hungarian National Museum. General Bandholtz became convinced through personal investigation that "not a single Hungarian complaint has been exaggerated", and that for instance, the Rumanians cleared out the patients from military hospitals and they were "absolutely gutting" the Central Sanitary Depot and dismantled telephones even in private residences. Within a single month they transferred 17,318 locomotives and cars to Rumania, according to U.S. Major Burrow, in his report to the Inter-Allied Military Mission. The total amount of rolling stock taken by them from the Hungarian State Railways was 1,302 locomotives and 34,160 railroad cars. The Rumanian occupation caused damage, as it was officially estimated, of almost three billions of gold crowns

[1] H. H. Bandholtz, *An Undiplomatic Diary*. Edited by Fritz Konrad Krüger, New York, 1933, pp. 11, 15, 42–43, 151–153, 226.

without counting indirect losses due to Rumanian encroachments.

General Bandholtz had no reason to be biassed and to lean toward an "enemy" country as against a state which was the ally of the Entente. This sharp-eyed, honest American officer saw on the spot the tragic situation of, and had no illusions about, those who, taking advantage of their domination by force, did not hesitate "to pillage and loot like a band of robbers". In his telegram on October 13, addressed to the Supreme Council, General Bandholtz asserted that the Rumanians will have to be coerced by all means to withdraw, for, although they "have sent misleading reports to Paris", they have caused misery and indignation. The telegram quotes the report of the committee of British Food Commission as well as the representatives of the American Red Cross, according to which "in all towns occupied by Rumanians we found an oppression so great as to make life unbearable. Murder is common; youths and women are flogged, imprisoned without trial, and arrested without reason, theft of personal property under the name of requisition. A state of affairs prevails difficult for a Western European to realize who has not seen and heard the evidence . . ."

The unfortunate country needed peace, the restoration of law and order as well as stable government. The Friedrich Cabinet was not accepted by the Entente Powers, for it was inducted into office by Archduke Joseph, upon the latter's authority received in 1918 from Charles IV. According to the Supreme Council,

Friedrich could not represent the will of the people and a Habsburg could not again assume any leading position. Slowly new political parties formed, however, such as the party of National Unity and the Agrarians' Party, the second strongest.

The only pivotal point was the person of Commander-in-Chief Horthy. At the helm of the National Army, he endeavored to reorganize the country and, at the same time, to stem the tide of revenge against Bolsheviks and outbursts of anti-Semitic or, to be more exact, anti-Galician feeling. Colonel Horowitz, U.S.A., member of the American Committee on Army Organization, himself Jewish, visited Western Hungary in person and attested that Horthy's forces "had done everything within reason to prevent any such persecutions", and that "as to there being a real White Terror, there was nothing of the kind".[1] In human life, cruelty generally evokes vengeance. That in Hungary's case, except in a few, isolated and individual incidents, this was not the case in general, was due to the discipline of the National Army.

At the end of October, the Supreme Council dispatched to Hungary Sir George Clark, a British diplomat, to facilitate the formation of such a cabinet as the Entente Powers would acknowledge. As a result, a coalition was brought about by November 24, 1919, under the leadership of Charles Huszár, a former public school teacher and a leading figure in the Catholic People's Party. On November 14, at the behest of the

[1]Bandholtz, op. cit., p. 120.

Supreme Council, the Rumanian army finally withdrew and, two days later, the National Army, headed by Nicholas Horthy, entered the Hungarian capital. It was under his leadership that, after trying years, the rebuilding of Hungary on the ruins began.

# XIII

## THE LAST TWENTY YEARS

### (*1919–1940*)

The era of the Treaty of Trianon, following the World War, was, perhaps, the most critical in all Hungarian history. There were endless arguments about the new order which was radically to transform political as well as economic conditions in Carpathian Europe. Those who had desired and prepared for this hotly defended, until the end, the new solution which was, with human pride and naïveté, thought to be eternal, though it dissected historic units. The reasoning of the Hungarians, on the other hand, often became subjective, because of their bitter feelings, though they protested against an unjust situation and were thus in a favorable moral position.

An era may be viewed in its completeness when its achievements and errors have already branched out. Major consequences of the settlement which followed the World War are by now easily recognizable. Many mistakes of the Treaty of Trianon were brought to light, many illusions disappeared. The following pages, however, propose to relate only in short, concise form the outstanding events of the past twenty years. They have to examine what were the characteristics of the Treaty and what were the results this "new order" brought about, as it affected the development not only of Hungary, but of all Carpathian Europe.

The fixing of the peace terms, as well as the final decision, rested, formally at least, with the Allied Powers. In reality, however, their decisions in the matter were strongly influenced beforehand by the propaganda waged, without competition, by Czech and other leaders and their friends, the "experts". The Allies had by then accepted the idea of the Monarchy's dissection, though some of their leading statesmen were worried about the consequences of the elimination of this major power which had kept the balance between east and west. This propaganda had an easy task against a Hungary which was in the worst imaginable situation. Hungary was in the camp of the vanquished enemy, as the ally of Germany. Her enemies accused her, without any foundation, with responsibility for the Great War. The revolutionary chaos, into which the nation was driven, as a matter of fact, by despair, turned, for a while, the enemies of Bolshevism against Hungary, too. The liquidation of the reign of terror and the restoration of law and order was, on the other hand, represented by anti-Hungarian propaganda as mere reaction and vengeance. Some of those who helped to usher in the

Bolshevik terror, or actually served it, fled, after its collapse, to the West and to America, and, disguised as honest liberals, began to abuse new-born Hungary, allegedly in the name of democracy, with which they had never anything to do, except that they were actually destroying it. The isolated, weakened nation, surrounded by enemies, was unable to defend herself in this respect either.

Members of the Supreme Council considered the Hungarian question of minor importance beside the German one, and besides, had a very meagre knowledge of the political, economic and nationality problems of the region, as may be ascertained from the historic sources at hand. Thus, in most cases, they rather accepted, after little or no resistance, those "solutions" proposed by the Czechs, Rumanians and Serbs, and the ever-popular "experts" supporting their case. These latter were, apparently fully convinced that they were doing the right thing by backing exclusively the interests of their old friends, the nationalistic leaders. All agreed on one thing, the destruction of Hungary. It is humanly conceivable that the statesmen of the Allied Powers believed, amidst a war psychology and after the continual haranguing of anti-Hungarian charges, that the enfeeblement of Hungary was to the interest of all humanity and democracy, and that through a spurious coincidence, these ideals were represented exactly by those whose imperialistic ambitions were directed against Hungary.

The leading statesmen, despite the anxieties of a

Lansing and a Lloyd George, generally agreed to and accepted the solutions as vouched for by these experts. These must have relied on the promises of their friends that they were preparing an era of democracy and liberty in Carpathian Europe. Consequently they were for as great a power to be allotted to the "oppressed" as possible, since they would certainly be absolutely fair and would take good care of other peoples under their domination. It was also presumed that for the sake of the great and general interest one had to overlook certain obvious injustices, such as the placing of millions of "feudal" Hungarians under foreign and hostile rule. Of course the three neighbours of Hungary were out to build up their own exclusive national régimes, but were smart enough to present their aims in such a form, and equipped with such arguments and promises, to the Allied Powers that the latter saw in them the victory and the very incarnation of their own ideals.

The three neighbours, even if there were conflicting interests between them (Rumania and Yugoslavia could not agree for a long time about the distribution of the spoils), always found a common platform against Hungary and employed more or less similar methods. One of these implements was the presenting of "resolutions" of different meetings as the sincere and unequivocal expression of the wish of the whole population of the territory in question. A good example of this was the already mentioned, controversial Pittsburgh Conven-tion, then the decisions of the meeting at Turciansky Sväty Martin (end of October, 1918), held without the participation of those Slovaks who were sympathetic toward Hungary, or of the Hungarian and German inhabitants. The original text, which somehow was lost, is supposed to have contained (according to Slovak nationalists), not only Slovakia's (i.e. Upper Hungary's) rights to autonomy within the future Czechoslovak state, but also its right to decide at the expiration of ten years, whether it wished to remain in union with the Czech state at all. This question had an important bearing in the 1928 trial of Professor Béla Tuka, who was sentenced to fifteen years' imprisonment for demanding the fulfilment of this agreement.

In Sub-carpathian Ruthenia, the acquisition of which did not occur even to the Czechs for some time, the Ungvár (Uzhorod) meeting in November 1918 swore loyalty to the Hungarian government, which granted the province autonomy in the following month. In the meantime, however, Masaryk reached an agreement with the Ruthenes of the United States and, when 67 per cent of these voted for the Czech proposition, this also was presented as a uniform decision of the actual inhabitants of Sub-carpathian Ruthenia. Zatkovic, leader of America's Ruthenes, later on became provisional governor of the province; but when he discovered that the Czechs had no intention of fulfilling their obligations as regards autonomy, he returned to the United States.

In the southeastern part of Hungary, demanded by Rumania, the nationalist Rumanian political leaders passed a resolution on December 1st, 1918, at Gyulafehérvár (Alba Julia), in which they declared the unification of all Rumanians in a single state. That part of the resolution which promised "complete national liberty for all the peoples that inhabit Transylvania," remained an empty phrase.

Croatia, though ties of 800 years bound it to Hungary, was always an autonomous country and the decision of the Croatian *Sabor* (Diet) declaring a union with Serbia, was accepted by the Hungarians. But the new Yugoslavia demanded also certain southern portions of Hungary proper where, in the so-called Voivodina, the different South Slav elements did not amount to more than 33 per cent of the population.

The sincere wish of the population in question could have been best determined through plebiscite, to be held under fair conditions in the different districts affected. This was what the Hungarians, confident in the victory of their cause, really wanted. Receiving the peace draft, Count Albert Apponyi, Hungary's delegate, requested in a memorable address, *"Interrogez les populations intéressées"*, asking the Allies to consult those about whom they are to decide as to their genuine desires. He also announced that Hungary was ready to comply with the verdict of any plebiscite held under just conditions. This most natural solution, however, was not consented to by the new conquerors. The explanation to this may be found in the fact that "national feeling was not nearly so advanced among the minorities of Hungary as the peace conference was made to believe".[1] Great numbers of non-Hungarians were unwilling to break with Hungary and would have been perfectly satisfied with a long-due modern version of Deák's Nationality Bill, more radical changes being propagated only by a minor, yet loud group.

The general plebiscite was prevented also by the *fait accompli* brought about by the military occupation of the territories in question, by the hastily reorganized Czech, Rumanian and Serbian armies. Lacking effective means, the Peace Conference was in no position to remake all that had happened, even had it so desired. Already at the beginning of the Peace Conference, President Wilson protested against the occupation by armed forces of such territories, "the rightful claim to which a Peace Conference is to be asked to determine". He declared furthermore that "it will create a presumption that those who employ force doubt the justice and validity of their claims". All three neighbours were, in fact, already before the Peace Treaty, in military control of the territories which they wished to acquire for themselves.

No Hungarian was allowed to take part in the negotiations preparatory to the peace. Hungary was invited in only after a decision was reached, following the hearing of the Czech, Rumanian and South Slav aspirations and then only for the purpose of accepting the ready-made conditions. The peace was not a negotiated, but a dictated, one. There was no willingness to listen to the Hungarian delegation's arguments. As proved by diaries

[1]Macartney, *op. cit.* Conclusions.

and documents, published since, no one thought of checking to any serious extent the correctness of data supplied by those who wished to document their claims against Hungary. It would be easy to produce a long list of characteristic episodes of such a.nature.

The head of the French sub-committee, fixing the new Rumanian boundaries, admitted that some 600,000 Hungarians (in reality about 1,700,000) were transferred with Transylvania to Rumania, but, as he pointed out, when United States Foreign Secretary Lansing expressed uneasiness, nothing could be done about this. By then, everyone believed the story of the Czechs and Slovaks being but two parts of one and the same nation. But Eduard Beneš had to top this with reference to historic rights, according to which "Slovakia had at one time formed parts of a Czecho-Slovak state", i.e., as against the fact that the territory in question had formed an integral part of Hungary, he revived the legend of Svatopluk's Moravian Empire, which was already non-existent by the end of the ninth century A.D. At every instant Beneš gave out a different figure about the number of Hungarians to be incorporated into the new Czecho-Slovak state along with the parts of the country he coveted. At last he spoke of 650,000, though there were over one million involved. The annexation of the Northern Carpathians of Slovakia was demanded on nationality principles, while, in open contradiction to this, the southern, purely Hungarian districts, were to be acquired on economic grounds, on the basis that since the mountains alone would not be

self-sufficient, the lowlands would have to be annexed
as far as the Danube,—irrespective of the wishes of
their inhabitants. Thus the question automatically
arises, whether these two contradictory arguments
would not result in the maintenance of the old unity.

On March 25, 1919, Lloyd George warned the Allies
in vain that "there will be no peace in south-eastern
Europe if every little state now coming into being, is
to have a large Magyar irredenta within its borders".[1]

In general and theoretically, the nationality principle
was put through, but in practice this was often seriously
modified by economic or strategic aspects, always to
the detriment of the Hungarians. From the detailed
diary of the American, David Hunter Miller, who was
present at the Paris negotiations, the biassed and per-
functory procedure was evident. As a similar eye-
witness, Harold Nicolson, stated in his work, Hungary
was "indolently and irresponsibly partitioned".[2] The
reader and historian must arrive at the painful conclusion that the good will and idealistic efforts of
primarily American statesmen who, like President
Wilson, sincerely wished that the peace should be
concluded on the basis of "the guiding principle of
justice to all peoples and nationalities", failed dismally.[3]

The Hungarian delegation, which arrived in Paris
on January 7, 1920, was billeted at a suburban hotel

[1]Temperley, *op. cit.*, vol. I, p. 548.

[2]Harold Nicolson, *Peacemaking 1919*, London 1933.

[3]The United States never ratified the Treaty of Trianon, but on August
29, 1921, a separate Peace was signed at Budapest by representatives of
the two countries.

and was denied an opportunity to present the maps and memoranda prepared by their experts, among them by the young geographer Count Paul Teleki, and to submit their views to the conference. Apponyi, in his proposal to plebiscite referred to above, also warned the Great Powers not to build the new order on coercion. Yet the Hungarian delegation, in spite of all solemn protests, was forced to sign the settlement, in the Grand Trianon Palace, Versailles, on June 4, 1920, without being given a hearing or a chance to debate it. The only break in the clouds, and one to which Hungarians attached over-zealous hopes for a time, was the letter of Premier Millerand of France, dated May 5, 1920, in which he, speaking for the Peace Conference, declared that if the Delimitations Commissions found that the Treaty anywhere "created an injustice which it would be to the general interest to remove", they might report to the Council of the League, which would offer its services for an amicable rectification. However, no serious result of this letter ever materialized. Similarly great hopes were attached by the Hungarians to Article 19 of the League Covenant stating that the Assembly may recommend the revision of certain treaties. In practice, however, the application in Carpathian Europe of Article 19, which would have met, in case of Hungary, determined opposition on the part of the three Succession States, has never been attempted.

As far as the Treaty of Trianon and its consequences are concerned, the reader is referred to the English historian C. A. Macartney's *Hungary and Her Suc-*

*cessors* (Oxford 1937), a detailed work, considered to be fundamental on this topic in English. The author is one of the few who have made on the spot a thorough study of conditions among the nationalities in Carpathian Europe. He does not shut his eyes to the faults of either party, neither does he follow the illusions of some English historians of the preceding decades, illusions about "good" and "bad" peoples in East-Central Europe.[1]

The Treaty of Trianon was, beyond doubt, the most severe of all post-War treaties. Historic Hungary, including Croatia, had a territory of 125,600 square miles, of which she lost 89,700 square miles, i.e., 71.4 per cent. Of her population of 20,886,487, 63.5 per cent was detached. Hungary was deprived of 61.4 per cent of her arable land, 88 per cent of her timber, 62.1 per cent of her railroads, 64.5 per cent of her hard-surfaced roads, 83.1 per cent of her pig-iron output, 55.7 per cent of her industrial plants, 67 per cent of her credit and banking institutions and her entire gold, silver, copper and salt deposits.

If one discounts Croatia, which stood only in a federal relation, though in one of eight hundred years duration, with other lands of the Holy Crown, Hungary proper was reduced to one-third (32.9 per cent) of her pre-War area, with a little over two-fifths (41.7 per cent) of her population. The inhabitants of dismembered Hungary numbered 7,614,000 on a territory of

[1]Quotations to be found on the following pages with reference to this subject are from Macartney's *op. cit.*

35,900 square miles. Rumania alone received 39,800 square miles, or more,—though a less densely populated territory—than what was left to Hungary. Czecho-Slovakia was presented with 23,800 square miles and Yugoslavia with a similar slice, including Croatia. Of Western Hungary, 1,500 square miles were allotted to Austria, constituting a unique case, when out of the territory of one vanquished state another was compensated. During the period of Dualism, the question of changing these boundaries between the two countries never arose.

These losses were proportionately far greater than those inflicted on Germany or Bulgaria. The new Austria was, true enough, an even smaller fraction of the old, yet, as Macartney states, "the Austria of the Habsburgs had not been a unitary state, but only a federation of kingdoms, duchies and provinces, the hereditary estates of a non-national dynasty, the composition of which was seldom the same for two successive generations". Not counting the loss suffered by the German-Austrian provinces in the South Tyrol (not to be compared with the enormous losses of Hungary), the Treaty of St. Germain simply divided this federation into its constituent elements. "The Hungarian state, on the other hand, existed for a thousand years within frontiers which, if not entirely unchanged, had shown a very remarkable degree of stability. The political state enclosed within those boundaries had been unitary long before most of the states of today. Moreover, its geographical structure

had imposed upon it also a very close economic co-
herence, obviously beneficial to almost all of its inhabitants. The unity of Hungary was thus something of an
entirely different order from that of the Austrian or
of the Ottoman Empire; it was even far more firmly
established than that of Germany or Bulgaria".

In the act of dismemberment, the nationality principle was generally invoked. The south-eastern parts of
the country were transferred to Rumania, the southern
sections to Yugoslavia, a small portion in the west to
Austria, Slovakia to the Czech state; the Ruthenes,
at best very distant relatives, if any, to the Czechs, were
likewise joined to that state. Serious difficulties had had
to be faced, even in case attempts to draw the new
frontiers on ethnic considerations would have been
unbiassed, because these ethnic boundaries seldom
follow clear-cut lines, owing to the centuries-long co-
existence and intermingling of different peoples and to
more recent colonization. Thus the marking of a perfect
ethnic boundary was practically impossible.

But the Peace Treaty, prompted by one-sided economic, strategic and other motives, such as, for instance,
the argument that the dissected territory alone was
"non-viable", pushed the boundary over to include
purely Hungarian districts. As a result of this, according to the last census preceding the Treaty, the number
of Slovaks in Slovakia constituted only 60 per cent
of the total of the population, Ruthenes only 56 per
cent in Ruthenia, Rumanians 55 per cent in the territory annexed by them, and the Serbians only 28 per

cent (all South Slavs 33 per cent) in Voivodina, also known as Bácska and Banate.

Magyars formed about one-third of the population in each territory detached. More than one million of them were transferred to Czechoslovakia, 1,700,000 were placed under Rumanian domination, about half a million were shifted to Yugoslavia and 24,000 to Austria. The number of Magyars detached from the mother country was almost one-third of the whole Magyar people. This proportion made the above figures even more pronounced. As a comparison, we may note here that in pre-War historic Hungary the 1910 census showed out of 18,264,533 inhabitants (Croatia and Slavonia excluded) 54 per cent Magyars, 16.1 per cent Rumanians, 10.7 Slovaks, 10.4 Germans, 3.6 South Slavs, 2.5 Ruthenes and 2.2 others, based on their mother-tongue. It is to be stated that from the viewpoint of the proportion of nationalities no substantial improvement was achieved through the change.

In the place of one state, containing different nationalities, the Peace Treaty created three new, artificial nationality states. For the sake of this, it ruined the economic unity of the Carpathian Basin. Not even mentioning here the usual Hungarian arguments, as that the nationalities were comparatively recent immigrants, the question nevertheless crops up unintentionally as to what purpose was served by such a catastrophic upheaval.

Creators of the Treaty were led by the unspoken belief that the Hungarians were "born oppressors", who always mistreated the nationalities, while the Czechs, Rumanians and Serbs would represent humanity and democracy, an idealistic and decent rule. They believed that the Czechs intended "to make of the Czecho-Slovak republic a sort of Switzerland" to use the catching phrase of Beneš, and that the former "oppressed", in running the show, would in their turn heartily respect the rights of others. It was assumed by the Allied Powers that so far as possible all non-Magyar peoples should be "freed" from Magyar rule. The suggestion that the nationalities to be transferred may be partly pro-Hungarian was never seriously entertained. "It was supposed that the neutral or third-party minorities"—such as the Zipser-Germans in the north, the Saxons in Transylvania and the Shwabians in Southern Hungary—should also be reckoned in the non-Hungarian camp. "Thus in the Voivodina, for example, the Germans were added to the Serbs and it was found that the Magyars were in the minority, whereas if the Germans had been added to the Magyars, it would have been the Serbs whose claims might have appeared thin". The Allies were misled into believing that Hungarian administration was "bad" in its very nature from the beginning, while the future rule of the Succession States would, naturally, be "good". It was certainly regarded as good also because the Allied Powers obliged the Succession States to sign agreements for the "protection of minority rights".

However, those acquainted with the nature and development of nationalistic movements, as related to in previous Chapters, could foresee that such a belief was bound to turn out a naïve illusion. In Carpathian Europe, nationalism faced nationalism, each aiming to realize, to secure and to develop its own aspirations. But the Magyars possessed political experience in promoting the co-operation of other ethnic groups for centuries reaching back to the Middle Ages, and had begun to pass the wishful thinking phase of their nationalism, something which the best brains of the country never considered a happy phenomenon. The younger nationalisms of the neighboring smaller peoples, however, who had never had any experience in dealing with minorities, had just reached the peak of the most feverish and intolerant days of their nationalistic development. Now these nationalisms, once in power, began anew, but with greedy, realistic measures instead of rhetorical phrases, the policy for a weak experiment in which the Hungarians were formerly so vehemently denounced. The change thus did not bring progress, but, to the contrary, it signified a marked retrogression. They considered themselves national states and pursued their own exclusive interests, whatever the costs to other nationalities. The Rumanians did not take into consideration that they were no longer living alone in their smallish Balkan kingdom, but that there were other peoples in their midst in large numbers. The longer they dreamt vainly about the carrying out of their nationalistic aspirations, the more hastily and impatiently they tried to establish their exclusive and complete rule in a "unitarian national Rumanian state".

The minority agreement they had signed did not constitute any serious obstacle. As Macartney stated: "It is useless blinking the fact that no minority protection has prevented any of the Succession States from doing with its minorities precisely as it wished. The only real check hitherto has been such intrinsic strength as some individual minorities may have possessed".

Owing to the nationalistic policy pursued by the Succession States, the position of the Hungarian minorities turned out to be precarious, and indeed critical. The universal acceptance of the principle of Minority Protection brought a substantial change, nevertheless, and accordingly infringement of these rights in the after-War period was to be taken far more seriously than before. Up to the 18th century, it seemed more or less natural that there was a privileged class of nobles and another, without rights to speak of, viz., the serfs. Following the achievement of human rights, such a state of affairs was branded backward and immoral. Similarly, one is bound to view the treatment of nationalities after the War, when the idea of their protection was universally accepted, from a different angle than in earlier periods when there was no trace of such concepts.

This book has no design to elaborate here on the oppression suffered by Hungarian minorities in the Succession States, for such a lot is self-evident from the very nature of the whole process. There was a marked difference, however, in the methods applied by the three states involved, even if the ultimate goal was substantially identical. "Czecho-Slovakia's policy, like that of her Allies, is one of national imperialism," states Macartney, "which is even more successful than the more violent methods fashionable elsewhere, because its direction and subtlety disguise the pertinacious and implacable nature of its pressure". Characteristic of Czech administration were centralization and bureaucracy, on the old Austrian pattern, and cancellation of their own promises of Slovak (and Ruthenian) autonomy. The dissatisfaction of the Slovaks, who felt the pinch economically as well, assumed increasing proportions and was openly manifest at the time of Czechoslovakia's fall. Czechoslovakia, however, only about one-half of whose population was of the ruling Czech race, and, apart even from the Slovaks, with more than five million of its about 14.5 million population composed of minorities, considered itself a national state.

So did Yugoslavia, too, but the latter pursued different methods and treated the minorities with open brutality. Especially after the establishment of dictatorial rule, even the elementary rights of meeting and organization were denied.

As against this rough but frank treatment and the clever methods of the Czechs, in Rumania force was coupled with hypocrisy and corruption. Their problem, as Julio Maniu put it in a speech soon after the Armistice, was to "Rumanize" Transylvania, that is, to secure for the Rumanian element a position of unquestioned superiority. Here, too, the chief enemy, to be weakened at all costs, was the Hungarian.

One of the methods of this procedure was the expulsion of Hungarians, especially of those who were not anxious to swear fealty to the intruders before the final signing of the Treaty. Some 350,000 such refugees from the occupied part of Hungary, mostly of the middle class, including petty officials, lived for a long time under great privation in freight cars, and presented a serious economic problem to a Hungary deprived of its natural resources. In Carpathian Europe, the most active element of national movements was everywhere the middle class. Therefore the new régimes endeavored, first of all, to crush the Hungarian intellectual class, both spiritually and materially, in order to undermine Hungarian culture. In place of the latter, they then attempted to force their foreign culture on the isolated, and with new and artificial foreign settlements to weaken the Hungarian population in order to assimilate the more easily. Among other measures aiming at the destruction of the Hungarian middle class was their evidently tendentious carrying out of the land reform, the termination of employment of Hungarian intellectuals, the complete overhauling of the school system, and in Rumania, where the state religion was Greek Orthodox, the threatening of Catholic and Protestant church property. Rumania created, with great haste, an artificial, young intellectual class, which outdid all its predecessors in intolerance and hatred towards minorities, especially of Hungarians and Jews, and reached almost unparalleled heights. Following the occupation of Transylvania, "a marked decline in the general standards of both technical efficiency and honesty in the administration" was evident, corruption being so general that it provided a certain means of defense for the minorities against the oppression of official machinery. Those attempts which aimed at the eradication of this proverbial corruption, were generally concurrent with the strengthening of national fanaticism and, consequently, of the feeling against the minorities. This state of affairs grew worse year by year "due to the appearance on the scene of the young Rumanian, so-called intellectual class, something which hardly existed before the War and now was turned out by the thousands from high school". This, "nurtured on intellectual pap which consisted largely of national self-gratification and then thrust on the world without an insured future", threw itself with unexampled hatred against the minorities. It was possible, in the Fall of 1936, openly to threaten, in the Rumanian press, the Hungarian minority with complete extermination through a mass murder, a bloody St. Bartholomew's Eve.[1] There is no time here to go into details of oppressive measures like the "Numerus Wallachicus", which meant in practice that Rumanians were to be employed in minority regions and by minority enterprises according to their percentage in the whole country. Another typical measure was the "analysis" of names, according to which any Hungarian child could be declared officially Rumanian upon the spelling of

[1] J. P. Thomas, *Les Roumains nos Alliés?*, Paris 1939. The French author occupied a university position during fifteen recent years in Transylvania. This work gives a vivid description of the Rumanian rule.

his name and forced to attend Rumanian schools.[1] Through certain blood-testing methods ( ! ) the Székely-Magyars were declared falsely to be of Rumanian origin, thus providing an excuse for adopting every possible method of forced "Rumanization". Looking from a distance, the far-away reader in a New World probably cannot see why such active violence should happen in part of another Continent. Nor can he fully grasp the importance and the sentimental background of such animosities and atrocities. Yet they have to be mentioned since they form an essential part of the history of the post-War era. The desperate situation of the Hungarian minorities, the fact that the new boundaries cut through solidly Hungarian territory at a number of points, together with the grave economic consequences of the destruction of the Carpathian unity, made firm in every Hungarian social stratum the conviction that a new deal, or, as it was called, Peace Revision, was inevitable.

Hungary herself at the time of the peace-making was from every respect in a very serious crisis. The task of the new leaders was first of all to help strengthen and reorganize the country. In the political field, the ruins left behind by the Revolution had to be cleared away and order and public law restored, preventing, at the same time, any desperate individual act of vengeance.

[1]In 1913, under Hungarian rule, there were 5,032 elementary schools in Transylvania, among them 2,482 Hungarian, 2,230 Rumanian, 282 Saxon and 58 other schools. In 1931, under Rumanian domination, there were only 4,295 schools, among them 248 ( ! ) Hungarian, 3,978 Rumanian, 67 German and 2 others. The figures speak for themselves.

Sixty-eight of the Bolshevik leaders were executed, not more than in Paris after the collapse of the Commune of 1871. The economic crisis, owing to the losses incurred during the War, the dismemberment of the country and the large-scale inflation, became very serious and literally ruined the bulk of the intellectual class, especially the officials and teachers of fixed salary. This was paralleled by a moral crisis. Many turned away from the old ideals of Western Europe which, they felt, were unreasonable with a nation demonstrating its solidarity with Europe so often. Disillusionment with principles of Democracy was general, for it was in the name of these that Hungary was dissected and almost a third of the Magyars subjugated. As a reaction to Bolshevism, anti-Semitism was strong, yet with only one tangible result, the "Numerus Clausus", according to which Jews were allowed to enroll in universities only in their proportion to the population.

To the picture of the first few years belongs the desperate and romantic form of the irredentist movement, sometimes blossoming out in fantastic plans. Credit is due to the leading statesmen for having transposed it into a peaceful plea, backed by the determination of a united people and referring to European interests involved in the remedying of injustices done to Hungary. It is a proof of the Hungarian people's vitality that it was able to rise from the depths in a comparatively short period. Even if during the past difficult twenty years it could not completely solve every great problem, it emerged from the crisis with renewed strength, regained its confidence, and was able to reach a number of important and promising results as far as the country's economic, social and political reorganization was concerned.

The new National Assembly, elected by general ballot, abolished, as representative of national sovereignty, the 1867 legislation, and declared the end of the revolutionary period. Hungary remained a kingdom, but the National Assembly elected as the head of the state a Regent, who until further arrangement would exercise the sovereign rights within certain limits. The latter, as an expression of gratitude to the present head of the state, were later partially extended. On March 1, 1920, Nicholas Horthy of Nagybánya was elected Regent. He was not only the Commander-in-Chief of the new National Army, but also the acknowledged leader of the whole nation. His office was held in the 15th century by John Hunyadi and, later, in 1849, by Louis Kossuth. Thus Horthy, one of the most solid figures in the Continental flux of post-War history, became the third Regent of Hungary. In the following difficult period, he was able not only to assure national unity and security, but also to rebuild in essential parts his dismembered country.

The government of Charles Huszár was followed in the Spring of 1920 by that of Alexander Simonyi-Semadam, then in the Summer of 1920 by that of Count Paul Teleki. In the Spring of 1921 Count Stephen Bethlen took over the administration and it was during his long premiership that the country's political and

A HISTORY OF HUNGARY

economic consolidation was carried through. Two strong political parties emerged from the 1920 election, the Christian National Party with 77 mandates and the Small Landowners' Party, representing the higher strata of farmers, with 71 mandates. Owing to the extraordinarily hard times, there was need for a strong majority party, which Bethlen was able to forge through the unification of the above two. The necessary balance and stability in political life was rendered possible by this new Party of Unity in the ensuing years. Based on the new Electoral Law, which made the exercise of the franchise dependent on 24 years of age and on graduation from fourth grade Public School, etc., with secret ballot in the cities and towns, the 1922 election brought a majority of 144 for the Party of Unity. Thus the Government was in a position to muster, together with smaller groups, a total of 169 as against 76 of all the Opposition. A similar majority was maintained at the next election. In 1926, the Upper House was again re-instated, with representatives of the municipalities, scientific and economic bodies, etc., among its new members.

In the meantime, the problem of Habsburg restoration twice became timely. The Council of Ambassadors, but especially the Succession States, protested against the restoration, which Beneš declared a *casus belli*. The Succession States were afraid of the magnetic force which the return of the King might exercise upon the provinces torn from the Holy Crown. Beneš preferred to a Habsburg restoration even the Anschluss of Austria to Germany, which later indeed became a reality. In respect to the restoration, Hungary was divided into two parties, the Legitimists, who remained loyal to the king, and the anti-Habsburgs, also known as the party of free election of a national dynasty. The leader of the latter movement was Captain Julius Gömbös, one of the prominent figures of the national movements in the post-revolutionary period. King Charles IV, who lived in Switzerland, anxious to put his restoration in effect, quite unexpectedly arrived in Budapest in the Spring of 1921, but when the Regent informed him that Hungary, with her army reduced by the Peace Treaty to 35,000, would be unable to resist the threatening military invasion of the Succession States, the King left the country again. Charles IV probably received encouragement from French political circles. In October 1921, he returned for a second time, and, while the Succession States were about to carry out mobilization measures, parts of the Hungarian garrisons stationed on the western border of Transdanubia, started a march on Budapest, with the King at their head. Charles IV, arriving with his troops at the vicinity of Budapest and finding stiff resistance, organized mainly by Gömbös, retreated, to avoid bloodshed. He was interned by the government at Tihany and taken by the British gunboat *Glowworm* to the island of Madeira, where the tragic life of the exiled young king soon ended. The National Assembly deprived the Habsburgs of their right to the Hungarian throne, although the "Legitimist" groups clung to the idea that the

Hungarian throne belonged to the young Archduke Otto, eldest son of the late king Charles IV. Nevertheless, in Hungarian political life, as a natural consequence, Gömbös' movement acquired great influence.

In the economic reorganization of the country, the first step was the land reform, prepared by the leader of the small landowners, Stephen Szabó from Nagyatád, himself a practical peasant farmer, and Minister of Agriculture. As a result of this reform, 1,785,000 acres were requisitioned from great landowners, of which 259,000 sites for family dwellings were distributed and 987,600 acres were given for the establishment of small holdings. This land reform was not radical, yet it had great significance and gave the initiative for future gradual reform. The government restored the balance of finances by abolition of all inflationary measures. The value of the Hungarian monetary unit, the "korona" (crown), had gradually diminished to a fantastically small fraction, which at that time was only 1/17,500 of its original gold standard. In consequence the government turned to the League of Nations and through the intercession of this international body, it received a loan amounting to 250,000,000 gold crowns (about $50,000,000). This loan, though received with divided approbation, since many feared the reduction of the country's financial independence, succeeded nevertheless in putting the country's budget in equilibrium and making possible the reorganization of national finances. While this financial reorganization was carried out, the League of Nations sent Jeremiah Smith, a distinguished Boston lawyer, to Hungary as its representative, and he exercised his authority with great understanding and excellent results.[1] The new monetary unit, the *pengő*, was made equivalent to 12,500 crowns. The following gradual economic improvement increased the standards of the impoverished intelligentsia, and, at the same time, it made possible the imposing cultural and educational program of Minister Kuno Klebelsberg. He made a point of building a great number of new schools, particularly on the Great Plains formerly so neglected in this respect, and simultaneously of founding international fellowships and of subsidizing Hungarian universities so as to promote higher education. All his plans were based on the idea that the militarily disarmed Hungary needed moral rearmament to show her talents and to assure her cultural leading rôle in East-Central Europe.

The regeneration of spiritual life was parallel with invoking Christian European principles as well as genuine Hungarian traditions. The last generation was greatly influenced by Andrew Ady, in whose poetry Protestant Hungarian traditions combined with Western Democratic thought, and also by Dezső Szabó,

[1]For two years he has served as Commissioner General of Hungary and he has done the job to the satisfaction of all concerned. His character was well illustrated by his refusal to accept the $100,000 which represented his two years' salary and which the Hungarian Government has devoted to the establishment of a scholarship fund to enable two Hungarian technical students each year to study in America. "The only compensation I desire for my work—Jeremiah Smith said—is the appreciation and friendship of the Hungarian people." And this he has in large measure.—T. J. C. Martyn in the New York *Times Magazine,* July 11, 1926.

whose outstanding novel, *The Destroyed Village,* proposed to see the nation's future in the Hungarian peasantry. The life of the Hungarian farmer has been described with vivid realization in the novels of Sigismund Móricz. On the other hand, high intellectual viewpoints and the finest humanism found their expression in the poetry of Michael Babits.

Parallel with this movement, a new scientific group decided to eradicate false illusions and to return to genuine national traditions. Similarly, Béla Bartók, Zoltán Kodály, to mention only the most eminent, collected the rich and original folk melodies of the Hungarian people and set them to modern harmonies without harming their quaint simplicity. The national past was interpreted with up-to-date scholarly methods and without bias by Julius Szekfü, heading a young group of historians. Very wide influence was exerted by his outstanding critical work, *Three Generations,* published at the beginning of the new period, which pointed out the mistakes and political illusions of previous generations with a frankness and self-criticism so often asked for, a century previously, by Széchenyi. All this was highly instrumental in preparing a young generation endowed with a larger horizon and a strong sense for social reforms. As proof of this, one may point to the number of new sociological works published in the last decade, and to the reform programs advocated by a large number of young publicists and authors.

Perhaps the most difficult problem was that of the international situation. Hungary had to be freed from the iron ring of her enemies and from her isolated position. The three Succession States, Czechoslovakia, Rumania and Yugoslavia, stimulated also by the fear of a possible Habsburg restoration, decided as far back as the beginning of the new epoch, to establish the system of alliances known as the Little Entente. The latter fundamentally desired to secure and perpetuate the situation created by the Peace Treaties and openly avowed to have as its supreme goal the control of Hungary. After a few initial negotiations it became completely clear that Hungary could, under no circumstances, join in an alliance which primarily was directed against herself. It is true that there were plans sponsored by Western statesmen, like Tardieu, for instance, who thought to remedy the ills arising from the breaking up of the great economic unit of the Austro-Hungarian Monarchy by proposing the mutual economic co-operation of the East-Central European peoples. The common mistake of all these plans was the erroneous assumption that it was possible to bring about economic co-operation without solving the acute political antagonisms. In reality, economic co-operation can be created only parallel with political reorganization, of which the former, particularly in our days, forms an integral part. The only possibility left for Hungary was, therefore, to seek the friendship of one or more Great Powers outside of the system of her opponents and to prepare for the time when the dissolution of the Little Entente, predicted by the Hungarian leaders, would take place. While the Western Powers supported the Little Entente,

Hungary found this friendly power first of all in Italy. In the spring of 1927, Count Bethlen concluded the Italo-Hungarian Agreement of Friendship, which since has become the foundation of the constantly improving Italo-Hungarian co-operation.

The world depression brought about new difficulties which reached their height in Hungary in 1930. Under the pressure of circumstances, Premier Bethlen, though his party was in the majority, realized the decline of his popularity and tendered his resignation. After the comparatively short-lived government of Count Julius Károlyi, General Julius Gömbös became Prime Minister in the Fall of 1932, proposing an extensive reform program. During the 1935 elections, he filled the ranks of the government party with new members. His plans concerning further land reform created sympathies among a large part of the younger generation. His efforts resulted in the Entail Reform and the Settlement Act of 1936. The latter made it possible to utilize, down to September 1939, 88,000 yokes for the purpose of allotting land to 21,000 families, mostly owners of "dwarf" holdings. As regards foreign policy, General Gömbös continued the Italian orientation and, at the same time, he favored Austrian connections which resulted in the Pact of 1934 concluded between these two countries. Simultaneously, Gömbös was influenced by the political successes of the Third Reich and favored friendship with the new Germany. After the sudden death of Gömbös and during the premiership of Kálmán Darányi (Oct. 1936 to May 1938) the new "Arrow

Cross" parties gained strength as a result of the spread of national-socialistic political ideas. Their program was radical economic reform, anti-Semitism and, as to foreign policy, co-operation with Germany. The Darányi government introduced a new electoral law giving the secret ballot to the villages. In May 1938, it proposed a Bill limiting the participation of the Jews in industrial and commercial life and in certain intellectual professions, hitherto undoubtedly out of proportion, to 20 per cent, or much more than their percentage in the total population. This was followed by a second law during the premiership of Béla Imrédy, formerly president of the National Bank and one of the best economic experts of the country (May 1938–February 1939). In March 1938, Austria was joined to Germany and thereby the Third Reich became a direct neighbour of Hungary.

In the Fall of this year, the Munich Four Power Pact, settling the German-Czech issue, acknowledged the necessity of frontier revision between Czecho-Slovakia and Hungary. Without resorting to force, Hungary regained by the virtue of the consequent Vienna award, declared by Germany and Italy, ethnically Magyar territories north of the Trianon frontier, of about 4,600 square miles with a population of more than one million. In February 1939, Prime Minister Imrédy was followed in the premiership by Count Paul Teleki, who at the spring elections, despite the gain of the extreme right parties, received a strong majority at the expense of the conservative groups.

Teleki was a geographer of international reputation. In 1922 he was lecturing in the United States at Williamstown. Studying correlations between geographic and human factors, he saw the characteristic feature of Europe in its diversity. "A nation"—he said— "can be useful to the European community by endeavoring to forward and to cultivate her good qualities according to her individuality". On June 12, 1939, after the elections, he gave the following short summary of his program: "Preservation and protection of and adherence to our Constitution by all conceivable means . . . this was our greatest strength in the past and is our strength in the present, at a time when under very difficult circumstances this small nation is bravely holding its own ground, and will be our strength in the future. Another item of our program . . . is that the Hungarian nation stands on its own feet". Teleki saw the future of Europe closely connected with the co-operation of the different regional units. He emphasised the importance of the natural unity of the Carpathian Basin and was convinced that historical and economic factors would bring about, sooner or later, its modern reconstruction. "Twenty years"—he said—"cannot change what a thousand years could not alter". According to him, "every region that forms a geographical unit has its own special form of life and its own community", and the community of the Carpathian Basin must be guided by the "idea of Saint Stephen", the first Christian king of Hungary. This idea "stood for peace, not for war, for co-operation and not for separation

. . . it could bring different peoples into the same fold".

According to this traditional principle, which widely influenced Hungarian public opinion, the natural harmony of the different essential parts of the Carpathian Basin, completing each other, could be disturbed only temporarily, by arbitrary interference, at the expense of its inhabitants. Hungarians saw the justification of this principle in the return of the northern part of their country in 1938, and, similarly, in the re-incorporation of Subcarpathian Ruthenia in the Spring of 1939, when Slovakia was proclaimed an independent state. Thus Hungary again held her historic north-eastern frontier on the ridge of the Carpathians. With Ruthenia, a territory of about 4,600 square miles returned, together with more than 600,000 population, Hungarians saw the renewed assertion of their principle in the return of Northern Transylvania, including the Székely-Magyar districts. This part, together with the Eastern Carpathians was re-incorporated through the second Vienna award on August 30, 1940. Out of 39,800 square miles annexed by Rumania in the Trianon treaty, about 16,-500 returned to the mother country with a population of 2.5 millions. Thus at the end of 1940, Hungary had a territory of roughly 61,000 square miles with a population of 13.5 millions.

During the last twenty years, despite hard times, gradual reform and reconstruction has been going on in Hungary. In this respect the different governments succeeding each other under the Regency of Nicholas

Horthy followed an identical line. Significant results were attained in the matter of the sick benefit and unemployment insurance of the agricultural population, as well as concerning the regulation of working hours and wages. In September 1939, the government submitted to the Parliament a new Land Reform Bill proposing primarily to provide that the area of land to be acquired or leased shall not be less than 100,000 yokes a year. Significant strides were made in intensifying agricultural production and in raising its quality. All these have a special importance since the proportion of people living by agriculture is, as compared with the available area of land under cultivation, much higher than, for instance, in the United States. The number of inhabitants of a typical agricultural county, like Csongrád or Jász-Nagykun-Szolnok, for instance, exceeds 220 per square mile, while, according to 1930 data, there were only 23 per square mile in Kansas, where the rural population reaches 62 per cent. The agricultural population of Trianon Hungary was 52 per cent of all her inhabitants. Of her territory, 60.1 per cent was arable area, 17.9 per cent pasture and meadow, 11.8 per cent forests.

The Hungarian army was also reorganized during recent years to stand on guard on the Carpathians in difficult times. In the field of education, under the ministry of Bálint Hóman, popular education was widely extended, elementary schools were raised to eight grades, high schools were reformed and economic-commercial, industrial and agricultural high schools established.

The aim of this book has been to expound the past, to approach it as closely as a historian, himself subject to human error, may hope to do with historical criticism and a sincere attempt at truth. Having arrived at the present day, the historian would turn his back on this set aim if he were to launch into political argument—even if disguised as current history. Of the newest developments, the appraisal of which has to be based on documentation not yet available, one cannot write at length within the scope of this book. The task of the historian ends here.

# CONCLUSIONS

This volume has attempted to give an account of Hungary's history, not from the exclusive viewpoints of a single nation—a justifiable but more or less selfish method—but referring from time to time to what this history has stood for in the development of all Carpathian Europe.

Some of the underlying issues which, resulting from historical development, influence the position of the Carpathian Region, may probably be approached through the following general aspects:

(i) Carpathian Europe is a sub-type of and a regional unit in the European evolution, with characteristics of its own. Any idea, social, spiritual or political, naturally, has to be brought into harmony with the special conditions prevailing there. Without this, even good intentions were bound to fail as impracticable.

(ii) Political and social problems in a country like Hungary, for instance, are correlated with the natural and inevitable consequences resulting from these historical and geographical conditions. No fact or problem can be properly understood without the close examination of these conditions.

(iii) Nationalism of the small peoples of this region might pass its phase of *Sturm und Drang* if they are given, according to their individual destinies, opportunity to materialize what is realistic and essential in their national endeavors. They would even be able to co-operate as members of an eventual general plan which they would not be in a position to essentially alter. Ethnic fragments, on the other hand, destined to live in a natural unit inhabited by others, need not renounce their individual culture, since their preservation, like that of religions, might be separated from the territorial principle.

(iv) Should the evolution of Europe lead, in one form or another, to a certain sort of chiefly economic integration of the different regional units, this would even more necessitate the maintenance of economic harmony within these units themselves. This again throws light on the significance of the Carpathian Basin.

The vertical belt that stretches from the Baltic as far as the Balkan peninsula in the south, was the frontier zone of Europe, facing the East. It was divided into several sections both geographically and politically. In the wide-open lowland of the north the Poles, in the Bohemian Basin protruding into German Central Europe the Czechs, and in the northern Balkans the Rumanians, Serbs, etc., endeavored to solve their individual problems. In the middle of this belt, between the northern lowland and the Balkans, lies the Carpathian Basin, forming a clearly defined geographic and economic unit. Here the Hungarians organized a strong state, showing remarkable solidarity and cohesion for many a century. It was this system that has contributed most to the equilibrium of the Carpathian region since the Middle Ages. This balance was upset only by the Ottoman onslaught, against which the Hungarians, accepting their part in the defense of Christian Europe, struggled for three long centuries, with grave sacrifices. More than half of this time falls in the period following the defeat of Mohács (1526) which broke the old power of mediaeval Hungary. This could not pass without having an effect on the evolution of all Carpathian Europe.

The Hungarian throne was acquired by the Austrian House of Habsburg, against whose attempts at introducing an absolutist régime the Hungarians bore arms on several occasions. After the expulsion of the Osman (end of 17th century) and the insurrection of Rákóczi (early 18th) a certain balance was created, making possible a peaceful evolution and new life amid the ruins of Turkish times.

When the 19th century arrived, the whole of East Central Europe was under the influence of different Great Powers. The Habsburg Monarchy acted as a composite Empire organizing the Danubian and Carpathian regions. As such, its rôle was deemed important by other Great Powers from the point of view of a European "Balance of Power".

The new ideas of the century, however,—liberty and nationality—were of great importance to the small peoples living in this part of Europe. For Hungary, the first half of the century was of outstanding importance as an era of reforms, the chief figure in which was Stephen Széchenyi. The desire for ancient national independence and for democratic reforms burst forth with mighty force in the Revolution and War of Independence of 1848–49. Organized by its great leader, Louis Kossuth, the nation was crushed by the combined military machines of two of Europe's then greatest powers. After a long attempt at oppression by Austria, the dynasty and Hungary, the latter led by Deák, arrived at a Compromise in 1867.

Following the end of the First World War, a new arrangement was prepared. The Allies invoked the nationality principle, with self-determination as a basic idea. This seemed to justify the dismemberment of historic units, though it was again partly abandoned, to the detriment of the Hungarians, owing to concessions to the nationalistic aspirations of certain other peoples. The Carpathian Basin was dismembered and Hungary with it. She was allowed to hold only the central Lowland, while the remaining territories were distributed chiefly among the three Succession States: the newly created Czechoslovakia, the greatly increased Rumania, and Yugoslavia, composed by Serbs, Croats and Slovenes. These states, including a numerous Hungarian minority, entered upon an alliance for the sake of securing permanent possession. Czechoslovakia was regarded as the cornerstone of this system, a state of fragile structure which, as the French historian J. Bainville wrote, did not represent either an ethnographical, or a geographical, or an economic unit.

As it was pointed out by an English specialist on the problems of the post-War period, "it was in the Danubian Basin that the political earthquake had produced its most complex and spectacular results . . . The economic dislocation produced by such a cataclysm beggars description . . . As the name itself implies, Czecho-Slovakia was made up of two distinct, if kindred peoples, differing in culture, speech, historical traditions, and economic outlook, and geographically divided by a range of mountains from which all the natural communications on the Slovak side let southward into Hungary". According to the same author, Yugoslavia was also a precarious unity, "an ideal conceived by literary men and visionaries and precipitately adopted in the abnormal conditions of war", Croat and Serb being an "ill-mated couple with fundamental differences in mentality".[1]

This new system, in which France had thought to find eastern allies necessary for her national security, failed to recognize the political and economic significance of the unity of the Carpathian Basin. Not taking into consideration the conditions brought about by the historical evolution of Carpathian Europe, it divided

[1] G. M. Gathorne-Hardy, *A Short History of International Affairs 1920–1938*. London, Royal Institute of International Affairs, 1939.

the forces of the region instead of preparing the way for co-operation.

This was the standpoint of the Hungarian leaders who pointed out that their country's fate was closely connected with that of other European nations and, consequently, national interests must be brought into harmony with those of the European community. They pointed out that if fate and history resulted in the fact that different ethnic elements should live side by side in the Carpathian Basin, then it was necessary to solve the consequent problem with sincere human under- standing and with cognizance of the individual conditions of the regions concerned. They pointed out that genuine Magyar traditions aimed at the peaceful co-operation of every people or fragment of people living there, and that Magyars, though not lacking determination, had never been fanatical or violent. The Renaissance in Hungary was the era of the "just" king instead of that of political assassinations. When religious wars were being fought in Europe, various religions lived side by side in comparative peace in Hungary. In the Spring of 1848, democratic achievements were secured by a bloodless revolution.

Those who try to define the character of the Magyar people, point out that it is still "young" in the sense that it has not at all exhausted its energies and that its talents enable it, if well organized, to attain to significant achievements in the future. From an Anglo-Saxon point of view, all the East Central European peoples seem to be more or less emotional. The Magyars, however, have outgrown the uncertainties and exaggerations of many other adolescent small people. During long centuries of statesmanship, the Magyars showed firmness and endurance in the violent storms which were frequent in those parts of Europe. According to some writers, such passive stoicism has preserved this ethnically isolated people, the inner life of which is reflected in an original literature.

This equilibrium could temporarily be disturbed only by great crises, when the genuine traditions of the Magyar people could not assert themselves; and when the crisis began to ebb, the inherent forces came to life in a new generation which had learned from the past, looked the present tasks in the face, and worked for the future.

However, nations, like individuals, need critical appraisal. It was exactly from the best of the nation that "national faults" and mistakes were, with scathing criticism, hurled in their own face, as when, for instance, Széchenyi ridiculed, a hundred years ago, the love of the Magyars for beautiful oratory and their discussing problems from an exclusively legal, instead of a practical, point of view. Positive and negative sides both necessarily belong to a sober and sincere estimate. Those who teach illusions and close their eyes to human error sin against their own people. Sincerity, especially towards ourselves, self-criticism and self-control are rather difficult to practice, yet they are indispensable to individuals and communities alike, in the interest of their own future and of human solidarity.

# BIBLIOGRAPHY

## GENERAL WORKS

APPONYI, COUNT ALEXANDER, *Hungarica* [Works about Hungary printed in Western countries. 16th–18th century]. 4 vols. 1900.

BALANYI, GEORGE, *The History of Hungary* [a short summary]. Budapest, 1930.

BARÁTH, TIBOR, *L'Histoire en Hongrie, 1867–1935.* Revue Historique, Paris, 1936.

BARTONIEK, EMMA, *Magyar történeti forráskiadványok* [List of published historical sources]. Budapest, 1929.

DOMANOVSZKY, ALEXANDER, *Die Geschichte Ungarns.* Munich, 1923.

ECKHART, FRANCIS, *A Short History of the Hungarian People.* London, 1931.

GRAGGER, ROBERT, *Bibliographia Hungariae.* Vol. I. Historica. Berlin, 1923. [A list of works on Hungary published between 1861–1921].

HÓMAN, BÁLINT, ed., *A Magyar történetirás uj utjai* [New Ways of Hungarian Historiography]. Budapest, 1931.

―――――, AND SZEKFÜ, JULIUS, *Magyar Történet* [History of Hungary]. 5 vols. 3rd edit. Budapest, 1935–36. A modern synthesis of the highest standard, the most outstanding historical work published in Hungary in recent times.

KONT, IGNACE, *Bibliographie française de la Hongrie*, 1521–1910. Paris, 1913.

KORNIS, JULIUS, *Hungary and European Civilization.* Budapest, 1938.

LUKINICH, IMRE, *A History of Hungary* [Biographical Sketches]. Budapest, 1937.

————, *L'Académie hongroise et les sciences historiques en Hongrie*, REH. Paris, 1926.

————, *Les Editions des sources de l'histoire hongroise,* 1851–1930. Budapest, 1931.

MACARTNEY, C. A., *Hungary.* London, 1934.

RIEDL, FREDERICK, *A History of Hungarian Literature.* London, 1906.

SAYOUS, EDOUARD, *Histoire générale des Hongrois.* 2 vols. Paris, 1876.

SZEKFÜ, JULIUS, *Der Staat Ungarn.* Berlin, 1918.

————, See also Hóman, B.–Szekfü, J.

SZILÁGYI, ALEXANDER, ed., *A Magyar Nemzet Története* [History of the Hungarian Nation]. 10 vols. Budapest, 1895–98.

TELEKI, COUNT PAUL, *The Evolution of Hungary and Its Place in European History.* New York, 1923.

## PERIODICALS

*Archivum Europae Centro-Orientalis* [Ed. by Imre Lukinich, Budapest, 1936, et seq. Its special series of publications is the *Etudes sur l'Europe Centro-Orientale*].—*Hungarian Quarterly,* [Budapest, 1936 et seq].—*Magyar Szemle* [Hungarian Review ed. by Julius Szekfü, 1927 et seq., since the last year by Alexander Eckhardt].—*Nouvelle Revue de Hongrie* [Budapest, 1927 et seq]. —*Revue des Etudes Hongroises* [abbreviated in the Bibliography as REH], ed. by L. Muller-Molnos, Paris, 1923 et seq.—*Századok* [Centuries], Review of the Hungarian Historical Society, published since 1867.—*Ungarische Jahrbücher,* founded in 1923 by Robert Gragger, ed. by Julius Farkas, Berlin. Its special series of publications is the *Ungarische Bibliothek.*

## CHAPTER I

GOMBOCZ, ZOLTÁN, *Die bulgarisch-türkische Lehnwörter in der ungarischen Sprache*. Helsinki, 1912.

HALPHEN, *Les Barbares*. Paris, 1926.

HÓMAN, BÁLINT, *A magyarok honfoglalása és elhelyezkedése* [Settlement of the Hungarians]. Budapest, 1923.

LUTTICH, R., *Ungarzüge in Europa im Zehnten Jahrhundert*. 1910.

MACARTNEY, C. A., *The Magyars in the Ninth Century*. Cambridge, 1930.

MELICH, JOHN, *A honfoglaláskori Magyarország* [Hungary at the Time of the Conquest]. Budapest, 1925.

NÉMETH, JULIUS, *A honfoglaló magyarság kialakulása* [Development of the Hungarian People until the Time of the Conquest]. Budapest, 1930.

PAULER, JULIUS, *A magyar nemzet története Szent Istvánig* [History of the Hungarians until St. Stephen]. Budapest, 1900.

SZINNYEI, JOSEPH, *Die Herkunft der Ungarn*. Berlin, 1921.

TAGÁNYI, CHARLES, *Lebende Rechtsgewohnheiten*. Berlin, 1922.

TAMÁS, LOUIS, *Romains, Romans et Roumains dans l'histoire de la Dacie Traiane*. Budapest, 1936.

ZICHY, COUNT STEPHEN, *A magyarság őstörténete és müveltsége a honfoglalásig* [Early History and Culture of the Magyars]. Budapest, 1923.

## CHAPTER II

BENDEFY, LÁSZLÓ, *Fontes authentici itinera [1235–38] fratris Iuliani illustrantia*. Budapest, 1937.

DEÉR, JOSEPH, *Die Anfänge der ungarisch-croatischen Staatsgemeinschaft*. 1936.

——, *Heidnisches und Christliches in der altungarischen Monarchie*. Szeged, 1934.

——, *Pogány magyarság-keresztény magyarság* [Pagan Magyars-Christian Magyars]. Budapest, 1938.

DOMANOVSZKY, ALEXANDER, ed., *Magyar Müvelődéstörténet*

[History of Hungarian Culture]. Vol. I. Middle Ages. Budapest, n.d.

ECKHARDT, ALEXANDER, L'Enigme du plus ancien historien hongrois. REH. Paris, 1925.

ENDLICHER, Rerum Hungaricarum Monumenta. Sangallen, 1849.

FEST, ALEXANDER, The Sons of Edmund Ironside at the Court of St. Stephen. Budapest, 1938.

GOMBOS, ALBIN F., Saint Etienne dans l'historiographie du Moyen Age. Budapest, 1938.

HÓMAN, BÁLINT, Magyar városok az Árpádok korában [Towns in Hungary under the Árpáds]. Budapest, 1908.

————, Magyar pénztörténet [History of Hungarian Money]. 1000–1325. Budapest, 1916.

————, La première période de l'historiographie hongroise. REH. Paris, 1925.

————, King Stephen the Saint. Budapest, 1938.

KNIEZSA, STEPHEN, Ungarns Völkerschaften im 11-ten Jahrhundert. Budapest, 1938.

MACARTNEY, C. A., Studies on the Early Hungarian Historical Sources. Budapest, 1940.

MÁLYUSZ, ELEMÉR, Das Bürgertum Ungarns. Viertelj. für Soz.- und W. gesch. vol. 20.

————, Turócmegye kialakulása [Development of the County Turócz]. Budapest, 1922.

MATTHIAS, FLORIANUS, Historiae Hung. Fontes Domestici. 4 vols. Pécs, 1881–85.

MORAVCSIK, JULIUS, Les récentes études byzantines en Hongrie. REH. Paris, 1923.

PAIS, DEZSŐ, Les rapports franco-hongrois sous le règne des Árpád. REH. Paris, 1923.

PAULER, JULIUS, A magyar nemzet története az árpádházi királyok alatt [History of Hungary under the Árpád dynasty]. 2 vols. Budapest, 1899.

SCHÜNEMANN, KONRAD, Die Deutschen in Ungarn bis zum 12-ten Jahrhundert. Berlin, 1923.

SCHWANDTNER, MARTIN, Scriptores Rerum Hungaricarum. 3 vols. Vienna, 1746–1748.

BIBLIOGRAPHY

# BIBLIOGRAPHY

SZENT ISTVÁN EMLÉKKÖNYV [Collective work published by the Hung. Academy of Sciences on the 900th anniversary of the death of St. Stephen]. 3 vols. Budapest, 1938.

SZENTPÉTERY, IMRE, *Scriptores Rerum Hungaricarum Saeculi XI–XIII.* Budapest, 1937 et seq.

VÁCZY, PETER, *Die erste Epoche des ungarischen Königtums.* Pécs, 1935.

## CHAPTER III

BENDA, KÁLMÁN, *A magyar nemzeti hivatástudat története a XV–XVII. században* [Development of Hungarian national conscience]. Budapest, 1937.

ELEKES, LOUIS, *A magyar-román viszony a Hunyadiak korában* [Hungarian-Rumanian relations at the time of the Hunyadis]. In the "Mátyás Király Emlékkönyv," ed. Imre Lukinich, Budapest, 1940.

HODINKA, ANTON, *L'Habitat, l'économie et le passé du peuple ruthene.* REH. Paris, 1924.

HÓMAN, BÁLINT, *A magyar királyság pénzügyei és gazdaságpolitikája Károly Róbert korában* [Financial and economic policy of Hungary under Charles Robert]. Budapest, 1921.

————, Hungary 1301–1490. Cambridge Medieval History. 1923.

HORVÁTH, HENRY, *Zsigmond király és kora.* [King Sigismond and his Age]. Budapest, 1938.

HUBER, ALPHONS, *Ludwig I von Ungarn und die ungarischen Vasallenländer.* Vienna, 1884.

KUPELWIESER, *Die Kämpfe Ungarns mit den Osmanen.* Vienna, 1899.

MISKOLCZY, STEPHEN, *Magyarország az Anjouk korában* [Hungary under the Anjous]. Budapest, 1925.

PÓR, ANTON, *Nagy Lajos* [King Louis the Great]. Budapest, 1892.

RÁSONYI, LÁSZLÓ, *Contributions à l'histoire des premières cristallisations d'Etat des Roumains.* Budapest, 1936.

TÓTH-SZABÓ, PAUL, *A cseh-huszita mozgalmak* [The Czech-Hussite Movements]. Budapest, 1917.

# 444    BIBLIOGRAPHY

## CHAPTER IV

BERZEVICZY, ALBERT, *Béatrice d'Aragon*. 2 vols. Paris, 1911–12.
BIBLIOTHECA CORVINA [King Matthias' Library at Buda], publ.
  by the St. Stephen Academy, Budapest, 1927.
CSÁNKY, DEZSŐ, *Magyarország történeti földrajza a Hunyadiak
  korában*. [Historical Geography of H. in the Time of the
  Hunyadis]. 4 vols. Budapest, 1890–1913.
DOMANOVSZKY, ALEXANDER, ed., *Magyar Müvelődéstörténet*
  [History of Hungarian Culture]. Budapest, n.d. vol. 2. Mag-
  yar Renaissance.
FRAKNÓI, WILLIAM, *Magyarország a mohácsi vész előtt a pápai
  követek jelentései alapján* [Hungary before Mohács in the
  Reports of Papal Legates]. Budapest, 1884.
————, *Hunyadi Mátyás*. Budapest, 1890.
————, *Werbőczi István*. Budapest, 1889.
HORVÁTH, JOHN, *A magyar irodalmi müveltség kezdetei* [Begin-
  nings of Hungarian Literary Culture]. Budapest, 1931.
HUSZTI, JOSEPH, *Janus Pannonius*. Pécs, 1931.
LUKINICH, IMRE, ed., *Mohácsi Emlékkönyv* [Commemorative
  work on Mohács]. Budapest, 1926.
MÁLYUSZ, ELEMÉR, *Matthias Corvinus* (*Menschen die Ge-
  schichte machten*, ed. by Rohden-Ostrogorsky, vol. 2.)
MÁRKI, ALEXANDER, *Dózsa György*. Budapest, 1913.
SZABÓ, DEZSŐ, *A magyar országgyülések története II. Lajos korá-
  ban* [History of Hungarian Diets under Louis II]. Buda-
  pest, 1911.
————, *Küzdelmeink a nemzeti királyságért 1505–1526*
  [Struggles for a National Dynasty]. Budapest, 1917.
TELEKI, COUNT JOSEPH, *A Hunyadiak kora* [The Era of the
  Hunyadis]. 5 vols. Budapest, 1853–56.
TÓTH, ZOLTÁN, *Mátyás király idegen zsoldos serege* [The Alien
  Mercenary Army of King Matthias]. Budapest, 1925.

## CHAPTER V

ANGYAL, DAVID, *Gabriel Bethlen*. Revue Historique, 1928.
————, *Thököly Imre*. Budapest, 1889.

BÁTHORY, ETIENNE, *Roi de Pologne, Prince de Transylvanie* [Collective work published by the Polish and Hungarian Academies]. Cracow, 1935.

FELLNER-KRETSCHMAYR, *Die österreichische Zentralverwaltung von Maximilian I bis 1749.* vol. 1. Vienna, 1907.

FRAKNÓI, WILLIAM, AND KÁROLYI, ÁRPÁD, *Magyar Országgyülési Emlékek* [Documents of the Hungarian Diets]. 12 vols. Budapest, 1874–1917.

GOOSS, RODERICH, *Oesterreichische Staatsverträge, Fürstentum Siebenbürgen.* Vienna, 1911.

HARASZTI, EMIL, *Les Hussard Hongrois.* REH. Paris, 1927.

HENGELMÜLLER, LÁSZLÓ, *Hungary's Fight for National Existence 1703–1711.* London–New York, 1913.

HORVÁTH, JOHN, *A magyar irodalmi müveltség megoszlása* [Division of the Hungarian Literary Culture]. Budapest, 1935.

HUBER, ALPHONS, *Die Erwerbung Siebenbürgens durch König Ferdinand I im Jahre 1551.* Vienna, 1889.

HUDITA, J., *Histoire des relations diplomatiques entre la France et la Transylvanie, 1635–1683.* Paris, 1927.

JÁSZAY, PAUL, *A magyar nemzet napjai a mohácsi vész után* [The Hungarian Nation after the Mohács Catastrophe]. Pest, 1846.

KÁROLYI, ÁRPÁD, *Buda és Pest visszavivása 1686–ban* [Reoccupation of B. and P.]. Budapest, 1886, new edition in 1936.

KOSÁRY, DOMINIC, *Gabriel Bethlen.* Slavonic Review, London, 1938.

LUKINICH, IMRE, *Erdély területi változásai* [Territorial Changes of Transylvania]. Budapest, 1918.

————, *A szatmári béke története* [History of the Peace of Szatmár]. Budapest, 1925.

LYBYER, A. HOWE, *The Government of the Ottoman Empire in the Time of Suleiman the Magnificent.* Cambridge, 1913.

MÁRKI, ALEXANDER, *II. Rákóczi Ferenc.* 3 vols. Budapest, 1907–1910.

MARKÓ, ÁRPÁD, *II. Rákóczi Ferenc a hadvezér* [R. the strategist]. Budapest, 1934.

MAYER, THEODOR, *Verwaltungsreform in Ungarn nach der Türkenzeit.* Vienna, 1911.

PAULER, JULIUS, *Wesselényi Ferenc nádor és társainak összees-küvése 1664–1667* [Conspiracy of Palatine Francis W. and his friends]. 2 vols. Budapest, 1876.

PILLIAS, EMILE, *Etudes sur François II Rákóczi.* Paris, 1939.

REDLICH, OSWALD, *Oesterreichs Grossmachtsstellung in der Zeit Leopold I.* Gotha, 1921.

RÉVÉSZ, IMRE. *A magyarországi protestantizmus története* [History of Protestantism in Hungary]. Budapest, 1925.

————, *La Réforme et les Roumains de Transylvanie.* Budapest, 1937.

SALAMON, FRANCIS, *Magyarország a török hódoltság korában* [Hungary in the Era of Turkish Domination]. Budapest, 1864.

SZEKFÜ, JULIUS, *A számüzött Rákóczi* [R. in Exile]. Budapest, 1913.

————, *Bethlen Gábor.* Budapest, 1929.

SZENT-IVÁNYI, DOMINIC, *L'Occupation turque en Hongrie et ses consequences. Revue des sciences politiques.* Paris, 1926.

SZILÁGYI, ALEXANDER, *Erdélyi Országgyülési Emlékek* [Documents of the Transylvanian Diets]. 1540–1699. 21 vols. Budapest, 1875–98.

————, *Bethlen Gábor levelei* [Correspondence of G. B.]. Budapest, 1879–86.

————, *Actes et documents pour servir à l'histoire de l'alliance de Georges Rákóczi aves les Français et les Suédois.* 1874.

————, *II. Rákóczi György.* Budapest, 1890.

URSU, J. *La politique orientale de François Ier.* Paris, 1908.

TAKÁTS, ALEXANDER, *Rajzok a török világból* [Sketches from the Turkish Era]. 3 vols. Budapest, 1915–17.

## CHAPTER VI

ARNETH, A., *Geschichte Maria Theresias.* 9 vols. Vienna, 1863–1879.

BALLAGI, GEORGE, *A politikai irodalom Magyarországon 1825-ig.*

[Political Literature in Hungary up to 1825]. Budapest, 1888.

BIBL, VICTOR, *Der Zerfall Österreichs*. Vienna, 1922.

CSEKEY, STEPHEN, *A magyar trónöröklési jog* [Law of Succession in Hungary]. Budapest, 1917.

DOMANOVSZKY, ALEXANDER, *József nádor iratai* [Papers of Palatine Joseph]. 2 vols. Budapest, 1925.

ECKHARDT, ALEXANDER, *A francia forradalom eszméi Magyarországon* [French Revolutionary Ideas in Hungary]. Budapest, 1925.

ECKHART, FRANCIS, *A bécsi udvar gazdaságpolitikája Magyarországon Mária Terézia korában* [Economic Policy of the Vienna Court in Hungary under Maria Theresa]. Budapest, 1922.

FRAKNÓI, WILLIAM, *Martinovics élete*. [Life of Martinovics] Budapest, 1921.

GÁLDI, LÁSZLÓ, XVIII. *századi humanizmusunk és a románság* [Hung. Humanism in the 18th cent. and the Rumanians]. Budapest, 1940.

GRAGGER, ROBERT, *Preussen, Weimar und die ungarische Königskrone*. Berlin, 1923.

GUGLIA, E., *Maria Theresa, ihr Leben und ihre Regierung*. 2 vols. Munich, 1917.

MÁLYUSZ, ELEMÉR, *Sándor Lipót nádor iratai* [Papers of Palatine Leopold Alex.]. Budapest, 1926.

MARCZALI, HENRY, *Hungary in the 18th Century*. Cambridge, 1910.

MITROFANOV, PAUL, *Joseph II*. 2 vols. Vienna, 1910.

TÓTH, ANDREW, *Az erdélyi román kérdés a 18.században* [The Rumanian Question in Transylvania in the 18th Century]. Budapest, 1938.

TURBA, GUSTAV, *Die Pragmatische Sanktion mit besonderer Rücksicht auf die Länder der Stefanskrone*. Vienna, 1906.

WERTHEIMER, EDOUARD, *Geschichte Oesterreichs und Ungarns im ersten Jahrzent des 19. Jahrhunderts*. Leipzig, 1884.

448                    BIBLIOGRAPHY

## CHAPTER VII

FARKAS, JULIUS, *Magyar Romantika*. Budapest, 1930.
──────, *A fiatal Magyarország kora* [The Era of Young
    Hungary]. Budapest, 1932.
FRIEDRICH, STEPHEN, *Gróf Széchenyi István*. 2 vols. Budapest,
    1915.
HORVÁTH, MICHAEL, *Huszonöt év Magyarország történetéből*
    [Twenty-five Years of Hungary's History]. 3 vols. Budapest,
    1886.
KORNIS, JULIUS, *A magyar müvelődés eszményei* [Ideals of Hun-
    garian Culture]. Budapest, 1927.
MISKOLCZY, JULIUS, *A kamarilla a reformkorszakban*. Budapest,
    1939.
──────, *A horvát kérdés története* [History of the Croat
    Question]. 2 vols. Budapest, 1927.
SCHLITTER, HANS, *Aus Oesterreichs Vormärz*. 3 vols. Vienna,
    1920.
SPOHR, LUDWIG, *Die geistigen Grundlagen des Nationalismus in
    Ungarn*. Berlin, 1936.
COUNT STEPHEN SZÉCHENYI's works, diaries and his controversy
    with Kossuth were published by the Hung. Historical So-
    ciety. Ed. J. Viszota in the series of *Fontes Aevi Recentioris*.
SZEKFÜ, JULIUS, *Három Nemzedék* [Three Generations]. Buda-
    pest, 1935.
──────, *Adatok a magyar államnyelv kérdésének tör-
    ténetéhez* [Data to the History of the Problem of the Magyar
    Official Language]. Budapest, 1926.

## CHAPTER VIII

Correspondence Relative to the Affairs of Hungary. London,
    1850.
GÖRGEY, ARTHUR, *My Life and My Acts in Hungary in 1848–
    1849*. London, 1852.
HELFERT, A., *Der ungarische Winterfeldzug und die oktroyirte
    Verfassung, 1848 bis März 1849*. Prague, 1886.

HORVÁTH, MICHAEL, *Magyarország függetlenségi harcának története* [History of the Hungarian War of Independence]. 3 vols. Budapest, 1871–72.

JANCSÓ, BENEDICT, *A román nemzetiségi törekvések története* [History of the Rumanian Nationalistic Aspirations]. Budapest, 1889.

JÁNOSSY, DENIS, *Die Russische Intervention* [Yearbook of the Hung. Hist. Institute]. Vienna, 1931.

KÁROLYI, ÁRPÁD, *Gróf Széchenyi István döblingi hagyatéka* [The literary legacy of S. Sz.]. Budapest, 1921.

——————, *Gróf Batthyány Lajos főbenjáró pere* [Capital lawsuit against Count L. Batthiany]. 2 vols. Budapest, 1932.

KLAPKA, GEORGE, *Memoirs of*, London, 1850.

KOSÁRY, DOMINIC, *A Görgey-kérdés története* [History of the Görgey Problem]. Budapest, 1936.

COUNT LEININGEN-WESTERBURG, *His Letters and Diary*, ed. by Henry Marczali, 1920.

PAP, DENIS, *Okmánytár Magyarország függetlenségi harca történetéhez* [Documents relating to the Hungarian War of Independence]. 2 vols. Pest, 1868–69.

SPROXTON, CHARLES, *Palmerston and the Hungarian Revolution*. Cambridge, 1929.

STEIER, LOUIS, *A tót nemzetiségi kérdés 1848–49-ben* [The Slovak Nationality Question in 1848–49]. 2 vols. Budapest, 1938.

——————, *Görgey és Kossuth*. Budapest, n.d.

——————, *Az 1849-i trónfosztás* [The Dethronement in 1849]. Budapest, n.d.

——————, *Haynau és Paskievics*. 2 vols. Budapest, n.d. [The three latter works contain a number of documents].

WARD, A. W.–GOOCH, G. P., *The Cambridge History of British Foreign Policy*. Vol. 2. London, 1922.

## CHAPTER IX

BERZEVICZY, ALBERT, *Az abszolutizmus kora Magyarországon* [The Era of Absolutism in Hungary]. 3 vols. Budapest, 1922 et seq.

450      BIBLIOGRAPHY

FRIEDJUNG, HENRY, *Oesterreich von 1848 bis 1860.* 2 vols. Stuttgart, 1908.

HAJNAL, STEPHEN, *A Kossuth-emigráció Törökországban.* [Kossuth emigration in Turkey]. Budapest, 1927.

JÁNOSSY, DENIS, *Great Britain and Kossuth.* Budapest, 1937.

——————, *Die ungarische Emigration und der Krieg im Orient.* Budapest, 1939.

KOSSUTH, LOUIS, *Irataim az emigrációból* [His Papers from the Emigration]. 10 vols. Budapest, 1881–1904.

PULSZKY, FRANCIS, *Életem és Korom* [Memoirs]. 4 vols. Budapest, 1886.

Works relating to Kossuth's visit and to the Hungarian émigrés in America are to be found in the text of the chapter.

## CHAPTER X

ANDRÁSSY, COUNT JULIUS, JR., *A magyar állam fennmaradásának és alkotmányos szabadságának okai* [Causes of the Survival and Constitutional Freedom of Hungary]. 2 vols. Budapest, 1901.

——————, *Bismarck, Andrássy and their Successors,* London, 1927.

APPONYI, COUNT ALBERT, *Die rechtliche Natur der Beziehungen zwischen Österreich und Ungarn.* Vienna, 1910.

BERTHA, A., *La Hongrie moderne de 1849 à 1901.* Paris, 1901.

DEÁK, FRANCIS, *Ein Beitrag zum ungarischen Staatsrecht.* 1865.

EISENMAN, LOUIS, *Le compromis Austro-Hongrois de 1867.* Paris, 1904.

GRATZ, GUSTAV, *A dualizmus kora* [The Era of Dualism, 1867 to 1918]. 2 vols. Budapest, 1934.

HALÁSZ, IMRE, *Egy letünt nemzedék* [A Generation Gone]. Budapest, 1913.

——————, *Bismarck és Andrássy,* Budapest, 1913.

LUSTKANDL, *Das ungarisch-österreichische Staatsrecht.* Vienna, 1863.

MATLEKOVITS, ALEXANDER, *Die Zollpolitik der Öst-ung. Monarchie und des Deutschen Reiches seit 1868.* Leipzig, 1891.

PRIBRAM, ALFRED FRANCIS, *Austrian Foreign Policy, 1908–1918*. London, 1923.
————, *The Secret Treaties of Austria-Hungary*, English ed. by A. Coolidge. Cambridge, 1920–21.
REDLICH, T., *Das österreichische Staats—und Reichsproblem.* 2 vols. Leipzig, 1920–1926.
SOSNOVSKY, TH., *Die Balkanpolitik Österreich-Ungarns seit 1866.* 2 vols. Berlin, 1913.
WERTHEIMER, EDOUARD, *Graf Julius Andrássy.* 3 vols. Stuttgart, 1910–1913.

## CHAPTER XI

APPONYI, COUNT ALBERT, *Emlékiratai* [Memoirs]. Budapest, 1934.
BEKSICS, GUSTAV, *Mátyás király birodalma és Magyarország jövője* [The Empire of King Matthias and the Future of Hungary]. Budapest, 1905.
EÖTVÖS, JOSEPH, *Die Garantien der Macht und Einheit Österreichs.* 1859.
————, *A XIX. század uralkodó eszméi és befolyásuk az álladalomra* [The Reigning Ideas of the 19th Century and Their Influence on the State].
FARKAS, JULIUS, *Az asszimiláció kora a magyar irodalomban* [The Era of Assimilation in the Hungarian Literature]. Budapest, n.d.
FISCHEL, A., *Der Panslavismus bis zum Weltkrieg.* Stuttgart, 1919.
GUMPLOWITZ, L., *Das Recht der Nationalitäten und Sprachen in Österreich-Ungarn.* Innsbruck, 1879.
JANCSÓ, BENEDICT, *A román nemzetiségi törekvések története* [History of the Rumanian Nationalistic Aspirations]. Budapest, 1899.
————, *A román irredentista mozgalmak* [The Rumanian Irredentist Movements]. Budapest, 1920.
JOHANNET, RENÉ, *Le principe des nationalités.* Paris, 1923.
KERÉK, MICHAEL, *A magyar földkérdés* [The Hungarian Land Question]. Budapest, 1939.

KOVÁCS, ALOYS, *The Development of the Population of Hungary since the Cessation of the Turkish Rule.* Budapest, 1920.
——————, *A zsidóság térfoglalása Magyarországon* [Expansion of the Jews in Hungary]. Budapest, 1922.
SCHMITT, B. E., *The Annexation of Bosnia, 1908–9.* Cambridge, 1937.
SETON-WATSON, R. W., *Racial Problems in Hungary.* 1908.
——————, *The Southern Slav Question in the Hapsburg Monarchy.* London, 1911.
SOSNOVSKY, TH., *Franz Ferdinand der Erzherzog Tronfolger.* Munich, 1929.
STEIER, LOUIS, *A tót nemzetiségi mozgalom* [The Slovak Nationalist Movement]. 1912.
STEINACKER, HAROLD, *Die geschichtlichen Vorauszetzungen der österreichischen Nationalitätenproblems und seine Entwicklung bis 1867.* Vienna, 1934.
SZEKFÜ, JULIUS, *Három Nemzedék* [Three Generations]. Budapest, 1935.
Works relating to Hungarians in America may be found referred to in the text of the chapter.

## CHAPTER XII

APPONYI, COUNT ALBERT, *Lectures in the United States on the Peace Problems and on the Constitutional Growth of Hungary.* Budapest, 1921.
BAKER, R. STANNARD, *Woodrow Wilson and the World Settlement,* 3 vols. New York, 1923.
BANDHOLTZ, HARRY HILL, *An Undiplomatic Diary.* New York, 1933.
BURIÁN, COUNT STEPHEN, *Austria in Dissolution.* New York, 1925.
CZERNIN, COUNT OTTOKAR, *Im Weltkriege.* Berlin, 1919.
FAY, SIDNEY BRADSHAW, *Origins of the World War.* New York, 1928. Vol. II.
FRAKNÓI, WILLIAM, *Die ungarische Regierung und die Entstehung des Weltkrieges.* 1921.

GLAISE-HORSTENAU, EDMUND, *The Collapse of the Austro-Hungarian Empire.* London, 1930.

GOOCH, G. P., and H. M. TEMPERLEY, *British Documents on the Origins of the War, 1898–1914.* London 1926, et seq.

GRATZ, GUSTAV, *A forradalmak kora* [The Era of Revolutions]. Budapest, 1936.

HOUSE, EDWARD MANDELL, *The Intimate Papers of Colonel House, arranged as a narrative by Ch. Seymour.* 4 vols. Boston, 1926–28.

'JÁSZI, OSCAR, *Revolution and Counter-Revolution in Hungary.* London, 1924.

————, *The Dissolution of the Habsburg Monarchy.* Chicago, 1929.

KAAS, ALBERT, *Bolshevism in Hungary.* London, 1931.

MÁLYUSZ, ELEMÉR, *The Fugitive Bolsheviks.* London, 1931.

MARCZALI, HENRY, *Papers of Count Stephen Tisza, 1914–1918.* American Historical Review, 1924.

NYIRI, JOSEPH, *Ce que fut la Révolution d'Octobre 1918 en Hongrie.* Paris, 1926.

*Österreich-Ungarns Aussenpolitik von der Bosnischen Krise, 1908, bis zum Kriegsausbruch, 1914.* Edited by L. Bittner, A. F. Pribram, H. Srbik, and H. Uebersberger. 9 vols. Vienna, 1919. English transl. 1920.

THARAUD, JÉROME and JEAN, *When Israel is King.* New York, 1924.

TISZA, COMTE ÉTIENNE, *Lettres de guerre 1914–1916.* Préface de J. et J. Tharaud. Paris, 1930.

TISZA, COUNT STEPHEN, *Összes Munkái* [Complete works, published by the Hungarian Academy of Sciences since 1923].

TORMAY, CECILE, *An Outlaw's Diary.* The Commune. New York, 1924.

*United States, Department of State, Papers Relating to the Foreign Relations of the United States, 1918. Supplement I.* Washington, 1933.

## CHAPTER XIII

BAINVILLE, JACQUES, *Les Conséquences politiques de la paix.* Paris, 1920.

BETHLEN, COUNT STEPHEN, *Hungary in the New Europe.* Foreign Affairs, 1924.

——————, *The Treaty of Trianon and the European Peace.* London, 1934.

BUDAY, LÁSZLÓ, *Dismembered Hungary.* London, 1923.

CZAKÓ, STEPHEN, *How the Hungarian Problem Was Created.* Budapest, 1934.

DEÁK, FRANCIS, *The Hungarian-Rumanian Land Dispute.* New York, 1928.

—————— and D. UJVÁRY, *Papers and Documents Relating to the Foreign Relations of Hungary, vol. I. 1919–1920.* New York, 1939.

GATHORNE-HARDY, G. M., *A Short History of International Affairs, 1920 to 1938.* London, 1939.

*The Hungarian Peace Negotiations.* Published by the R. Hung. Ministry of Foreign Affairs. 3 vols. Budapest, 1920–22.

KORNIS, JULIUS, *Education in Hungary.* New York, 1932.

LLOYD GEORGE, DAVID, *The Truth about the Peace Treaties.* 2 vols. 1938.

LOCKHART, BRUCE, *Seeds of War.* London, 1926.

NICOLSON, HAROLD, *Curzon, Peacemaking, 1919.* Boston, 1933.

MACARTNEY, C. A., *Hungary and Her Successors.* Royal Institute of International Affairs. Oxford, 1937.

MILLER, DAVID HUNTER, *My Diary at the Conference of Paris.* 20 vols. Privately printed, 1928.

RUTTER, OWEN, *Regent of Hungary.* London. n.d.

*Société des Nations, La restauration financière de la Hongrie.* Geneva, 1926.

SZÁSZ, ZSOMBOR, *The Minorities in Rumanian Transylvania.* London, 1927.

SZEKFÜ, JULIUS, *Három Nemzedék* [Three Generations. New edition with a synopsis of the post-war situation]. Budapest, 1935.

SZEKFÜ, JULIUS, Editor, *Mi a Magyar?* [What is Magyar?—A number of articles attempting to define the Magyar character and attitude]. Budapest, 1939.

SZENTKIRÁLYI, JOSEPH, (Education in) *Hungary*. The Phi Delta Kappan, Nov. 1939.

TEMPERLEY, HAROLD WILLIAM V., *A History of the Peace Conference of Paris*. 6 vols. London, 1920–24.

THOMAS, J. P., *Les Roumains nos alliés?* Paris, 1939.

TOYNBEE, ARNOLD JOSEPH, *Survey of International Affairs, 1924*. London, 1926.

TYLER, *Reports, Financial Position of Hungary*. Geneva, 1931–1933.

ULLEIN-REVICZKY, ANTONY, *La nature juridique des clauses territoriales du Traité de Trianon*. Paris, 1936.

# KINGS OF HUNGARY

## The Árpád Dynasty

| | | | |
|---|---|---|---|
| 1000–1038 | Saint Stephen | 1141–1161 | Géza II |
| 1038–1041 | Peter Orseolo | 1161–1173 | Stephen III |
| 1041–1044 | Aba Samuel | 1162 | László II |
| 1044–1046 | Peter Orseolo | 1162–1163 | Stephen IV |
| 1047–1060 | Andrew I | 1173–1196 | Béla III |
| 1060–1063 | Béla I | 1196–1204 | Imre |
| 1063–1074 | Solomon | 1205 | László III |
| 1074–1077 | Géza I | 1205–1235 | Andrew II |
| 1077–1095 | Saint László | 1235–1270 | Béla IV |
| 1095–1116 | Kálmán | 1270–1272 | Stephen V |
| 1116–1131 | Stephen II | 1272–1290 | László IV |
| 1131–1141 | Béla II | 1290–1301 | Andrew III |

## Other Dynasties

| | | | |
|---|---|---|---|
| 1301–1304 | Wenceslas of Bohemia | 1382–1385 | Mary of Anjou |
| 1304–1308 | Otto of Bavaria | 1385–1386 | Charles the Little of Anjou |
| 1308–1342 | Charles Robert of Anjou | 1378–1437 | Sigismund of Luxemburg |
| 1342–1382 | Louis the Great of Anjou | 1437–1439 | Albert of Habsburg |

456

| | |
|---|---|
| 1440–1444 Wladislas I of Jagiello | 1458–1490 Matthias Hunyadi |
| 1440–1457 László V | 1490–1516 Wladislas II of Jagiello |
| 1446–1452 John Hunyadi Regent of Hungary | 1516–1526 Louis II of Jagiello |

## The Habsburg and Habsburg–Lotharingian Dynasty

| | |
|---|---|
| 1526–1564 Ferdinand I | 1790–1792 Leopold II |
| (1526–1540 John Zápolya national king) | 1792–1835 Francis I |
| | 1835–1848 Ferdinand V |
| 1564–1576 Maximilian I | (1849 Louis Kossuth |
| 1576–1608 Rudolph | Governor of |
| 1608–1619 Matthias II | Hungary) |
| 1619–1637 Ferdinand II | (1848–) 1867–1916 Francis |
| 1637–1657 Ferdinand III | Joseph I |
| 1657–1705 Leopold I | 1916–1918 Charles IV |
| 1705–1711 Joseph I | * * |
| 1711–1740 Charles III | 1920– Nicholas Horthy |
| 1740–1780 Maria Theresa | Regent of Hungary |
| 1780–1790 Joseph II | |

# PRINCES OF TRANSYLVANIA

| | |
|---|---|
| 1541–1551 | Isabella |
| (1551–1556 | Transylvania reunited to Hungary) |
| 1556–1559 | Isabella |
| 1559–1571 | John Sigismund of Zápolya |
| 1571–1581 | Stephen Báthory (King of Poland after 1576) |
| 1581–1586 | Christopher Báthory |
| 1586–1598 | Sigismund Báthory |
| 1598–1599 | Andrew Báthory |
| (1599–1603 | King Rudolph of Habsburg) |
| 1603 | Moses Székely |
| (1603–1605 | King Rudolph of Habsburg) |
| 1605–1606 | Stephen Bocskay |
| 1606–1608 | Sigismund Rákóczi |
| 1608–1613 | Gabriel Báthory |
| 1613–1629 | Gabriel Bethlen |
| 1629–1630 | Catherine of Brandenburg (wife of the former) |
| 1630 | Stephen Bethlen |
| 1630–1648 | George Rákóczi I |
| 1648–1660 | George Rákóczi II |
| 1658–1659 | Francis Rhédey |
| 1659–1660 | Ákos Barcsay |
| 1660–1662 | John Kemény |
| 1662–1690 | Michael Apafy |
| 1705–1711 | Francis Rákóczi II |

# PREMIERS OF HUNGARY

| | | |
|---|---|---|
| 1848 | Count Louis Batthyány | (Liberal Reform) |
| 1849 | Bartholomew Szemere | (Republican) |
| (1849–1867 | Absolutism) | |
| 1867–1871 | Count Julius Andrássy | (Deák Party) |
| 1871–1872 | Menyhért Lónyai | |
| 1872–1874 | Joseph Szlávy | |
| 1874–1875 | Stephen Bittó | |
| 1875 | Béla Wenckheim | |
| 1875–1890 | Kálmán Tisza | (Liberal Party of 1867) |
| 1890–1892 | Count Julius Szapáry | |
| 1892–1895 | Alexander Wekerle | |
| 1895–1899 | Dezső Bánffy | |
| 1899–1903 | Kálmán Széll | |
| 1903 | Count Charles Khuen-Héderváry | |
| 1903–1905 | Count Stephen Tisza | |
| 1905–1906 | Géza Fejérváry | |
| 1906–1910 | Alexander Wekerle | (Coalition) |
| 1910–1912 | Count Ch. Khuen-Héderváry | (Party of National Labor) |
| 1912–1913 | László Lukács | |
| 1913–1917 | Count Stephen Tisza | |
| 1917 | Count Morris Esterházy | |
| 1917–1918 | Alexander Wekerle | |

1918–1919    Count Michael Károlyi   (Radical Socialist Coalition)

1919    Denis Berinkey

(March–July 1919   Bolshevik Terror)

1919    National Government of Arad, later transferred to Szeged. Count Julius Károlyi, Dezső Ábrahám.

August 1919 (Budapest) Julius Peidl (Socialist) ; Stephen Friedrich (Counter-revolutionist)

Nov. 1919–1920   Charles Huszár (National Christian Parties)

1920    Alexander Simonyi-Semadam

1920–1921    Count Paul Teleki

1921–1931    Count Stephen Bethlen   (Unity Party)

1931–1932    Count Julius Károlyi

1932–1936    Julius Gömbös (Party of National Unity)

1936–1938    Kálmán Darányi

1938–1939    Béla Imrédy   (Party of Magyar Life)

1939–1941    Count Paul Teleki

1941–    László Bárdossy

# I GENEALOGICAL TABLE OF THE HOUSE OF ÁRPÁDS

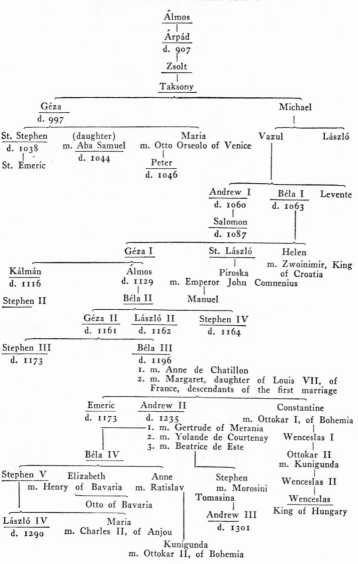

Álmos
|
Árpád
d. 907
|
Zsolt
|
Taksony

Géza
d. 997

Michael

St. Stephen
d. 1038
|
St. Emeric

(daughter)
m. Aba Samuel
d. 1044

Maria
m. Otto Orseolo of Venice
|
Peter
d. 1046

Vazul      László

Andrew I
d. 1060
|
Salomon
d. 1087

Béla I
d. 1063

Levente

Géza I

St. László

Helen

Kálmán
d. 1116

Stephen II

Álmos
d. 1129

Béla II

Piroska
m. Emperor John
|
Manuel

m. Zwoinimir, King
of Croatia
Comnenius

Géza II
d. 1161

László II
d. 1162

Stephen IV
d. 1164

Stephen III
d. 1173

Béla III
d. 1196
1. m. Anne de Chatillon
2. m. Margaret, daughter of Louis VII, of
France, descendants of the first marriage

Emeric
d. 1173

Béla IV

Andrew II
d. 1235
1. m. Gertrude of Merania
2. m. Yolande de Courtenay
3. m. Beatrice de Este

Constantine
m. Ottokar I, of Bohemia
|
Wenceslas I
|
Ottokar II
m. Kunigunda
|
Wenceslas II
|
Wenceslas
King of Hungary

Stephen V
m. Henry of Bavaria

Elizabeth

Anne
m. Ratislav
|
Otto of Bavaria

Stephen
m. Morosini
|
Tomasina
|
Andrew III
d. 1301

László IV
d. 1290

Maria
m. Charles II, of Anjou

Kunigunda
m. Ottokar II, of Bohemia

461

# II GENEALOGICAL TABLE OF THE ANJOU HOUSE

Charles II, King of Sicily
d. 1309
m. Mary, daughter of Stephen V, King of Hungary

Charles Martel | John, Duke of Durazzo

Charles Robert, King of Hungary
1308–1342 | Charles de Durazzo | Louis

Louis the Great, King of Hungary and Poland
1342–1382 | Andrew d. 1345 | Charles The Little King of Hungary and Sicily d. 1386

Maria
m. Sigismund of Luxemburg, King of Hungary who later married Borbala Cillei | Hedwiga m. Wladislav of Jagiello

Elizabeth
m. Albert, King of Hungary d. 1439
d. 1402

Ladislas V
d. 1457

# III GENEALOGICAL TABLE OF THE HOUSE OF JAGIELLO

Wladislav Jagiello
1. m. Hedviga, daughter of Louis the Great
2. m. Borbala, daughter of Count William Cillei

Wladislav I, King of Hungary
1440-1444 | Casimir IV, King of Poland

Wladislav II, King of Hungary
1490–1516 | Albert

Louis II, King of Hungary
1516–1526
m. Marie Habsburg | Anne m. Ferdinand Habsburg, Duke of Austria, later King of Hungary

# IV  GENEALOGICAL TABLE OF THE HABSBURG AND HABSBURG-LOTHARINGIAN HOUSE

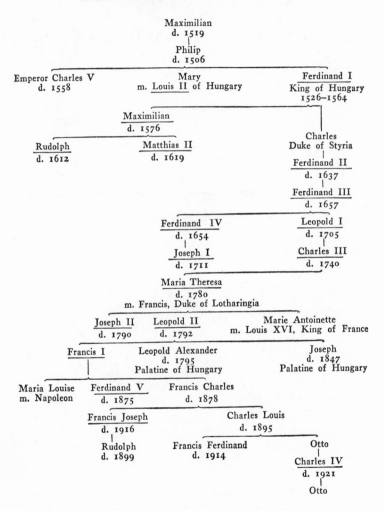

Maximilian
d. 1519

Philip
d. 1506

Emperor Charles V
d. 1558

Mary
m. Louis II of Hungary

Ferdinand I
King of Hungary
1526–1564

Maximilian
d. 1576

Rudolph
d. 1612

Matthias II
d. 1619

Charles
Duke of Styria

Ferdinand II
d. 1637

Ferdinand III
d. 1657

Ferdinand IV
d. 1654

Joseph I
d. 1711

Leopold I
d. 1705

Charles III
d. 1740

Maria Theresa
d. 1780
m. Francis, Duke of Lotharingia

Joseph II
d. 1790

Leopold II
d. 1792

Marie Antoinette
m. Louis XVI, King of France

Francis I

Leopold Alexander
d. 1795
Palatine of Hungary

Joseph
d. 1847
Palatine of Hungary

Maria Louise
m. Napoleon

Ferdinand V
d. 1875

Francis Charles
d. 1878

Francis Joseph
d. 1916

Charles Louis
d. 1895

Rudolph
d. 1899

Francis Ferdinand
d. 1914

Otto

Charles IV
d. 1921

Otto

# STATISTICAL DATA

## I

|  | TERRITORY IN SQUARE MILES | POPULATION IN 1000 |
|---|---|---|
| Hungary in 1914 including Croatia | 125,641 | 20,886 |
| Hungary in 1914 without Croatia | 109,216 | 18,265 |
| Of this territory the Treaty of Trianon ceded to — Austria | 1,552 | 292 |
| Czechoslovakia | 23,797 | 3,518 |
| Italy | 8 | 50 |
| Poland | 227 | 24 |
| Rumania | 39,804 | 5,257 |
| Yugoslavia | 24,360 | 4,131 |
| Total territory ceded | 89,748 | 13,272 |
| Hungary after Trianon | 35,893 | 7,614[1] |
| Hungary in 1938 | 35,893 | 9,129 |
| Part of Northern Hungary returned on Nov. 2, 1938 (1st Vienna Award) | 4,605 | 1,058 |
| Ruthenia, ret. in 1939 | 4,656 | 670 |
| Northern Transylvania returned on Aug. 30, 1940 (2nd Vienna Award) | 16,642 | 2,633 |
| Hungary in Sept. 1940 | 61,796 | 13,490 |

[1]*According to 1910 data. In 1920 Hungary's population, including refugees from the ceded parts, exceeded 7.9 millions.*

II

| AREA[1] | TRIANON HUNGARY | | TERRITORY RE-TURNED IN 1938 | | RUTHENIA RET. IN 1939 | | NORTHERN TRANSYLVANIA RET. IN 1940 | | HUNGARY IN SEPTEMBER 1940 | |
|---|---|---|---|---|---|---|---|---|---|---|
| | | % | | % | | % | | % | | % |
| Arable land | 9,770 | 60.4 | 1,215 | 58.2 | 327 | 15.6 | 2,325 | 31.0 | 13,637 | 49.0 |
| Orchard & Truck Garden | 208 | 1.3 | 36 | 1.7 | 22 | 1.0 | 117 | 1.6 | 382 | 1.4 |
| Meadow | 1,122 | 6.9 | 180 | 8.6 | 293 | 14.0 | 1,080 | 14.4 | 2,677 | 9.6 |
| Vineyard | 362 | 2.2 | 16 | 0.8 | 1 | 0.1 | 27 | 0.4 | 406 | 1.5 |
| Pasture | 1,677 | 10.4 | 175 | 8.4 | 273 | 13.0 | 939 | 12.5 | 3,065 | 11.0 |
| Forest | 1,923 | 11.9 | 348 | 16.7 | 1,128 | 53.8 | 2,735 | 36.5 | 6,134 | 22.0 |
| Others | 1,113 | 6.9 | 117 | 5.6 | 51 | 2.5 | 267 | 3.6 | 1,548 | 5.5 |

[1]In 1000 Cadastral yokes. 1 yoke = 1.412 English acre.

# III

| OCCUPATIONS (ACCORDING TO 1910 DATA) | HUNGARY IN 1914 | TRIANON HUNGARY | TERRITORIES RETURNED IN 1938–39–40 |
|---|---|---|---|
| Agriculture | 64.5% | 56.0% | 59.9% |
| Mining | 1.0 | 1.2 | 1.0 |
| Industry | 16.1 | 20.1 | 18.0 |
| Commerce | 3.5 | 4.6 | 4.2 |
| Transportation | 3.0 | 4.0 | 3.6 |
| Government employees and professionals | 3.3 | 4.0 | 3.8 |
| Laborers | 2.4 | 2.3 | 2.3 |
| Others | 6.2 | 7.8 | 7.2 |

# IV

## PRODUCTION IN TRIANON HUNGARY[1]
### (thousands of metric tons)

| 1. Agricultural | 1930 | 1938 |
|---|---|---|
| Wheat | 2,295 | 2,609 |
| Oats | 411 | 278 |
| Rye | 798 | 781 |
| Barley | 683 | 667 |
| Maize | 1,794 | 2,581 |
| Sugar Beet | 1,607 | 1,053 |

| 2. Mineral | 1930 | 1938 |
|---|---|---|
| Coal | 812 | 855 |
| Lignite | 6,176 | 6,582 |
| Iron Ore | 157 | 248 |
| Bauxite | 108 | 398 |

[1] Cf. South-Eastern Europe. *A Political and Economic Survey. The Royal Institute of International Affairs, London, 1939.*

# V

## FOREIGN TRADE

*(in million Pengős)*

| COMMODITY | YEAR | IMPORT | EXPORT | BOTH | BALANCE | IMPORT % | EXPORT % |
|---|---|---|---|---|---|---|---|
| Raw materials | 1939 | 173.7 | 417.7 | 591.4 | +244.0 | 29.4 | 70.6 |
| | 1940 | 179.8 | 332.3 | 512.0 | +151.5 | 35.1 | 64.9 |
| Semi-manu-factures | 1939 | 146.2 | 50.1 | 196.3 | − 96.1 | 74.5 | 25.5 |
| | 1940 | 182.6 | 49.9 | 232.5 | −133.7 | 78.5 | 21.5 |
| Manu-factures | 1939 | 170.0 | 135.9 | 305.9 | − 34.2 | 55.6 | 44.4 |
| | 1940 | 235.3 | 121.5 | 356.8 | −113.8 | 66.2 | 33.8 |
| *Total* | 1939 | 489.0 | 605.5 | 1094.5 | +116.5 | 44.6 | 55.3 |
| | 1940 | 597.7 | 603.7 | 1201.4 | + 6.0 | 49.8 | 50.2 |
| Total (*for comparison*) | 1913 | 2075.3 | 1904.8 | 3980.1 | −170.5 | 52.1 | 47.9 |

*Percentage of various countries in imports and exports respectively*

| COUNTRY | | 1938 | 1939 | 1940 |
|---|---|---|---|---|
| Germany | Imp. | 41.6 | 48.4 | 52.9 |
| | Exp. | 45.7 | 50.4 | 49.4 |
| Italy | Imp. | 6.3 | 7.1 | 9.3 |
| | Exp. | 8.5 | 15.5 | 15.2 |
| Great Britain | Imp. | 6.3 | 4.9 | 1.0 |
| | Exp. | 8.1 | 5.0 | 2.3 |
| U.S.A. | Imp. | 5.3 | 4.6 | 5.9 |
| | Exp. | 2.4 | 2.5 | 1.0 |
| Rumania | Imp. | 9.8 | 5.9 | 4.0 |
| | Exp. | 4.0 | 2.8 | 2.1 |
| Yugoslavia | Imp. | 4.5 | 4.8 | 5.5 |
| | Exp. | 3.0 | 2.3 | 4.4 |

# INDEX[1]

[1]The Bibliography is not included here.

## The World's Only Corn Palace

They came with knives and sticks—
no one called, no one reminded
the wild man of his right to scream,
to fall sobbing to his knees.
With sticks they came—this pack
so bent on killing all his bones.

Some looked away; others in their throats
began to laugh, not loud, but blue,
a winter blue that followed
mongrels out the door. With knives
those killers carved initials on his heart
till his eyes grew white with wonder.

Thunderbird came heavy on our heads.
Too much of a good thing
can spoil it for poets, you said.
I agreed. Down by the river we sang
sad tunes and O the stars
were bright that melancholy night.

## Trestles by the Blackfoot

Fools by chance, we traveled
cavalier toward death. Fish ran up
to break the black pools
we could not reach. Evening
and the rattle train shook trestles
one quiet inch behind our eyes.

Why not this sentimental stance?
You, me, the shaggy manes
we chose to disappear, inky caps
so spurious we clapped
our hands for calm. You see
the danger in your pose? One foot
between the ties, the other
in your mouth? Inky does

as inky do. It just won't do.
Funky jokes can't separate
this monster from his meal.
Let's be nice, pretend we sail
twelve feet out and down,

perfect cats returning from their night,
sunrise, knives between
their teeth, lies as clean as foam
we leave behind our toes.
Sliced and faded, those fish
will know us by the noise we chose—
black train rattle, steel on steel.

*The Day*
*the Children Took Over*